Building a New China in Cinema

Building a New China in Cinema

The Chinese Left-wing Cinema Movement, 1932-1937

Laikwan Pang

ROWMAN & LITTLEFIELD PUBLISHERS, INC.
Lanham • Boulder • New York • Oxford

ROWMAN & LITTLEFIELD PUBLISHERS, INC.

Published in the United States of America
by Rowman & Littlefield Publishers, Inc.
An Imprint of the Rowman & Littlefield Publishing Group
4720 Boston Way, Lanham, Maryland 20706
www.rowmanlittlefield.com

12 Hid's Copse Road, Cumnor Hill, Oxford OX2 9JJ, England

British Library Cataloguing in Publication Information Available

Library of Congress Cataloging-in-Publication Data

Pang, Laikwan. [DATE]
  Building a new China in cinema : the Chinese left-wing cinema movement, 1932-1937 / Laikwan Pang.
     p. cm.
  Includes bibliographical references and index.
  ISBN 0-7425-0945-1 (alk. paper)—ISBN 0-7425-0946-X (pbk. : alk. paper)   1. Motion pictures—China. I. Title.

PN1993.5. C4 P36 2002
791.43'0951'09043—dc21
                                                                    2002001191
Printed in the United States of America

To my parents and my brother

Contents

List of Illustrations   ix

Translations and Abbreviations   xiii

Acknowledgments   xv

Introduction   1

The History
   1   The Merging of Histories   19
   2   The Left-wing Cinema Movement   ·37

The Filmmakers and the Formation of a Collective Subjectivity
   3   The Role of Authorship in the Age of Nationalism   73
   4   Masculinity and Collectivism: Romancing Politics   91
   5   Women's Stories On-screen versus Off-screen   113

The Spectators and the Film Culture
   6   A Commercial Cinema or a Political Cinema?   141
   7   A Shanghai Cinema or a Chinese Cinema?   165
   8   Engaging Realism   197

Epilogue   231

Appendix I   Chinese Left-wing Movies of the 1930s   241
Appendix II   Popular Chinese Movies, 1932-1937   245

Bibliography and Filmography   249

Index   273

About the Author   279

Illustrations

Front and Back Covers

Front   A production scene from *Sons and Daughters of the Times*.
Back   A public screening of *Street Angel*. The sign hung in front of the theater reads "Full House."

List of Plates (appear after chapter 2)

Plate 1.   *Wild Flowers* (1932). A typical melodrama of a singing girl (right) falling in love with the young master (middle).

Plate 2.   *Spring Silkworms* (1933). Silkworm workers bring their products to sell.

Plate 3.   *Salt Tide* (1933). The salt workers are dwarfed by the ships, which represent the capitalists.

Plate 4.   *Sweetgrass Beauty* (1933). Sweetgrass refers to cigarettes. A film depicting how the Chinese cigarette industry and its workers were oppressed by imperialism, as were innocent girls corrupted by the modern Western entertainment culture. The advertising board in the background is about cigarettes.

Plate 5.   *Three Modern Women* (1932). One of the three modern-woman archetypes created in this film: the infatuated fan who lived on romance alone.

Plate 6.   *To the Northwest* (1934). Mise-en-scène heavily influenced by Hollywood's musicals.

Plate 7.   *City Nights* (1933). The first film of Fei Mu, also starting a cycle of left-wing films equating Shanghai's nighttime with women being trampled or seduced by the corrupt materialist city.

Plate 8.   *Women's Outcry* (1933). The first film of Shen Xiling, another women's liberation film depicting the traumatic experience of a country girl coming to Shanghai.

Plate 9.   *Twenty-Four Hours in Shanghai* (1933). Country people finding themselves alienated and disillusioned in Shanghai.

ix

Plate 10.   *The Sisters* (1933). Spectators were awed by the split screen technique
                 featuring two Hu Dies on the same screen.
Plate 11.   *The Fisherman's Song* (1934). The ending of the film where the
                 protagonists are completely disillusioned. One of the few Chinese
                 movies without a happy ending.
Plate 12.   *New Woman* (1934). The "new woman" worker Li Aying holding up
                 the "old woman" writer Wei Ming.
Plate 13.   *The Goddess* (1934). The headmaster visits his pupil's family and finds
                 himself in sympathy with the prostitute.
Plate 14.   *Queen of Sport* (1934). One of the first Chinese films celebrating
                 athleticism.
Plate 15.   *The Highway* (1935). The famous scene where Moli passionately holds
                 Dingxiang in her arms, revealing her love to all the six male
                 protagonists.
Plate 16.   *A Sea of Fragrant Snow* (1934). In spite of the depiction of poor
                 people's sufferings, this film was not considered progressive because of
                 the Buddhist thinking advocated.
Plate 17.   *The Metamorphosing Girl* (1935). The famous soft-wing film severely
                 criticized by left-wing critics partly because of the lesbian love depicted.
Plate 18.   *Angry Tide in China's Seas* (1933). A scene of workers' insurrection.
Plate 19.   *Sons and Daughters of the Storm* (1935). The poet Xin Baihua
                 passionately looking at his "comrade" Feng putting on her makeup.
Plate 20.   *Spirit of Freedom* (1935). Lan Ping, also Jiang Qing, the late Lady
                 Chairman Mao, as the supporting actress in the film.
Plate 21.   *Soaring Aspirations* (1936). Farmers decided to stand up against the
                 Japanese invasion.
Plate 22.   *Bloodbath on Wolf Mountain* (1936). A representative film of the
                 National Defense Cinema, probably the most political work of Fei Mu.
Plate 23.   *Lost Lambs* (1936). Modeling itself after the Soviet Union's film *Road
                 to Life*, this was one of the first children's films in China.
Plate 24.   *Old and New Shanghai* (1936). The poor versus the rich; the drivers
                 versus the cars.
Plate 25.   *Street Angel* (1937). The most celebrated and well-known film of the
                 left-wing cinema movement.

List of Figures
Figure 3.1   The Headmaster in *Plunder of Peach and Plum* is trapped between a
                 Greek statue and the huge Chinese history cabinet, looking out of the
                 window and pondering China's future.
Figure 3.2   *Sons and Daughters of the Storm*. The romance of Zhao Yuhua and Liu
                 Yuanjie.
Figure 3.3   The comradeship of Zhao Yuhua and Li Tao.
Figure 4.1   The silhouette of Mrs. Shi from the subjective view of Xin and Liang.
Figure 4.2   Cut-back to the two men gazing.
Figure 4.3   A close-up on their representations, the painting of Liang and the poem
                 of Xin, of their gaze.
Figure 4.4   Feng using her mop to protest the water leakage from the upper floor.
Figure 4.5   Cut to Xin and Liang hearing the complaints.
Figure 4.6   Xin going downstairs to apologize.

Figure 4.7   In the party Xin is captivated by Shi's beauty.
Figure 4.8   The reverse shot, but it is slightly off the regular practice as Shi is now looking back directly at the camera instead of paralleling Xin's earlier viewpoint. Here Xin's position is completely overlapped with the viewer's.
Figure 4.9   Xin peeping downstairs again.
Figure 4.10   Cut to his subjective view of Feng and her dying mother. Similar to figures 4.8 and 4.9, this set of shots is not shot/reverse-shot but a direct replication of Xin's subjective view.
Figure 4.11   *Queen of Sport*. One of the many erotic images of Li Lili in Sun Yu's films.
Figure 4.12   *Little Toys* begins with a gracious depiction of Ye Dasao's (played by Ruan Lingyu) happy family.
Figure 4.13   Very soon the film cuts to Ye secretly seeing the handsome Yuan Pu.
Figure 4.14   The bathing scene of the six male protagonists in *The Highway*. It is supposed to be the subjective view of the two girls.
Figure 5.1   The ending scene of *Little Toys*. Ye Dasao is going mad in the center of a crowd.
Figure 5.2   The ending scene of *New Woman*. Wei Ming on her death bed, shouting directly to the camera, "I must live."
Figure 5.3   *New Woman*. On the way to visit her mother whom she has no memory of, the daughter asks her aunt, how does Wei Ming look?
Figure 5.4   She looks out the window of the train trying to catch a glimpse of the possible images of her mother.
Figure 5.5   Cut to her subjective view, seeing two farming women in the field.
Figure 5.6   Not satisfied, she starts gazing upon the women on the train.
Figure 5.7   Cut to her subjective view, seeing an old lady dozing off.
Figure 5.8   Camera slowly pans to the left, replicating the daughter's subjective view, and she sees another old lady.
Figure 5.9   Cutting back to her perplexed look.
Figure 5.10   The daughter continues to beg her aunt to tell her what her mother looks like.
Figure 5.11   The aunt finally takes out a picture of her parents, explaining to her how her father abandoned them.
Figure 5.12   The extensive set of subjective shots ends with the daughter examining Wei Ming's picture.
Figure 5.13   Taotao (played by Ai Xia) in *A Woman of Today* captured in a cell.
Figure 7.1   *The Goddess*. The prostitute (played by Ruan Lingyu) looking out of the window.
Figure 7.2   Cut to her subjective view, seeing an empty sky of the Shanghai night scene.
Figure 7.3   Later, when the rascal looks out the window of his own room . . .
Figure 7.4   . . . what he sees is the same Shanghai night view, but now superimposed with the prostitute's smiling face.
Figure 7.5   The ending scene of *The Goddess*, depicting the prostitute in the prison thinking of her son.
Figure 7.6   *Street Angel*. The elaborate street setting in a studio. The background is particularly lit in order to stress the depth of the scene.
Figure 7.7   Xiao Hong on a plank assisted by Xiao Chen walking to the opposite building where Xiao Chen lives.

Figure 7.8   Xiao Chen's apartment as seen from Xiao Hong's perspective. The
               window curtain serves as a stage drapery.
Figure 7.9   Cut to Xiao Hong sitting on the window frame in her apartment,
               clapping her hands waiting to enjoy Xiao Chen's magic show.
Figure 7.10   Cut back to Xiao Chen's apartment. He now appears on the stage and
               performs his show. He has just created an apple out of nothing.
Figure 7.11   Xiao Chen throws the apple to Xiao Hong. She fails to catch it.
Figure 7.12   The apple flies to the inner room where Xiao Yun is applying her
               makeup. It breaks the two planes of representation and introduces the
               depth of the space.
Figure 7.13   A Ling reluctantly poses for the painters.
Figure 8.1   The dream sequence in *Crossroads* where Zhiying is dressed like a
               Barbie doll and engages in a love affair with the aristocrat-looking Lao
               Zhao in a Western fairy-tale setting.
Figure 8.2   *The Sisters*. The mother looking at Dabao and Taoge.
Figure 8.3   Cut to her subjective view.
Figure 8.4   Slowly dissolves to the childhood of Dabao and Taoge on the same spot.
Figure 8.5   Dissolves back to the current time.
Figure 8.6   Cut back to the smiling mother.
Figure 8.7   The mother sitting by herself looking out of the dark room recollecting
               her past memories.
Figure 8.8   Her subjective view of her seeing the closed door, but it is
               superimposed with the same door opened, introducing us to her memory
               of twenty years ago.
Figure 8.9   Slowly dissolving into the past. We see her husband sneaking out of the
               room. Notice that the position of the camera is now outside the room.
Figure 8.10   She begged her husband to stay, but he refused and finally agreed to
               bring one of their daughters away with him.
Figure 8.11   The carefully orchestrated mise-en-scéne in *Scenes of City Life*.
Figure 8.12   *Street Angel*. Xiao Hong braids her hair refusing to look at her
               customers when singing. Superimposed is the song's script, with a
               function probably similar to today's Karaoke to encourage spectators to
               sing along.
Figure 8.13   Clear light and dark juxtaposed in *Song at Midnight*. The one on the left
               is the defaced Song Danping.

Translations and Abbreviations

For the sake of uniformity, all the English translations of Chinese film titles follow the ones given in *Griffithiana* 54 (October 1995): 7-60. I supply my own English translations only for the films not listed there and when the original translations are inaccurate. For example, the *Griffithiana* translation of *Yecao Xianhua* is *Idle Talk among the Weeds*. Obviously the translator(s) misunderstood the character *hua* as talking. I use the English translation *Wild Flowers* instead. The *Griffithiana* translation of *Zimei hua* is *Sisters' Flowers*. But in the common Chinese usage *zimei hua* really has nothing to do with flowers. The character *hua* (flower) is only a suffix. I translate the film's name simply as *The Sisters*. I use the films' Chinese titles when they first appear in the text, and their English translations are provided within parentheses. For the convenience of non-Chinese readers, these English translations, instead of the original Chinese, are used in all subsequent citations of the films. Readers can consult the filmography at the end of the book to refer the English translations to the original Chinese. This rule also applies to Chinese publications that are mentioned more than once. All the Chinese quotations that appear in the text, unless otherwise indicated, are my own translations.

In the text I use abbreviations to refer to the following publications:

CB   *Chen bao* (Morning daily)
SB   *Shen bao* (Shanghai daily)
SNZDPW *Sanshi niandai zhongguo dianying pinglun wenxuan* (Anthology of Chinese film theories and criticism in the thirties), edited by Guangbo dianying dianshi bu dianying ju dangshi ziliao zhengji gongzuo lingdao xiaozu, zhongguo dianying yishu yanjiu zhongxin (Chinese Film Art Research Center, Leading Group of the Party's Historical Information Collec-

tion, Film Section, the Broadcast, Film and Television Department).

ZDFS   *Zhongguo dianying fazhan shi* (The development of Chinese cinema), by Cheng Jihua, Li Shaobai, and Xing Zuwen.

ZWD   *Zhongguo wusheng dianying* (Chinese silent cinema), edited by Zhongguo dianying ziliao guan (China Film Archive).

ZZDY   *Zhongguo zuoyi dianying yundong* (The Chinese left-wing cinema movement), edited by Guangbo dianying dianshi bu dianying ju dangshi ziliao zhengji gongzuo lingdao xiaozu, zhongguo dianying yishu yanjiu zhongxin (Chinese Film Art Research Center, Leading Group of the Party's Historical Information Collection, Film Section, the Broadcast, Film and Television Department)

ZZXLSJ   *Zhongguo zuoyi xijujia lianmeng shiliao ji* (Historical materials of the Chinese left-wing dramatist association), edited by Wenhua bu dangshi ziliao zhengji gongzuo weiyuan wui (Committee on recollecting Party's historical material, Culture Department)

Acknowledgments

The following analysis of the Chinese left-wing cinema is handicapped by two factors: the almost complete lack of data about Chinese film spectatorship during this period and the few numbers of early Chinese films preserved. Some of the most challenging questions I asked myself in the course of the research are still left unsettled. For example, as there are no surviving reports documenting a more precise demography of the spectators, I am yet able to reconstruct precisely the relationship between cinema and other media in the larger popular culture, and I cannot provide an accurate assessment of to what extent this film movement actually changed viewers' political stance. The lack of available films, as I will repeatedly emphasize below, also hinders my analysis of the stylistic plurality of the filmmaking. In Beijing's China Film Archive, I was allowed to watch only about forty films of this film movement. My presentation of the aesthetic rendering of these films certainly falls prey to my lack of access to the other films I did not, or probably will never be able to, watch and study. Under all these limitations, this project attempts to present a picture of this film movement as complete and as systematic as possible, and this hope would not have been realized without the help of many.

I would like to give my first and most heartfelt thanks to two senior scholars. I am indebted to the encouragement and comments on this work from Professor Arif Dirlik, without whom my work would not be able to be published in the present form. My love, gratefulness, and respect, as always, to Professor Robert Hegel, whose integrity and dignity as a scholar and as a mentor continue to provide me with the guiding principles of research and teaching in the past and in the future. Since this is my first book-length publication, I must thank all those who have encouraged and contributed to my intellectual growth, particularly all my fellow classmates and teachers in the Department of Cinema and the Department of Humanities at San Francisco State University, as well as those in the Department of Asian and Near Eastern Languages and Literatures and the Program of Comparative Literature at Washington University. My colleagues at the General Education Centre at the Hong Kong Polytechnic University have provided me the most congenial and ardent academic environment I needed in the revision of this manuscript while starting my teaching career.

Financially, the project received funding from two sources: the Dean's Dissertation Fellowship of Washington University sponsored the research and writing of my dissertation, and The General Education Centre Research Grant of The Hong Kong Polytechnic University paid for the copyright of the film stills I obtained from the China Film Archive and for other technical supports I needed. I wish to express my gratitude to their generous assistance. But these material supports were negligible when compared to the friendship and encouragement I received during my research. I thank Alfred Wong, La Francis Hui, and Linda Lai for their hospitality when I researched in New York's MOMA. During my research in China, I owe special thanks to the Shanghai Academy of Social Sciences which hosted my stay in Shanghai in 1996, particularly to the researcher Chen Qingsheng and his family who provided me the friendly support I most needed as a foreigner in this polymorphous but also unsettling city. My thanks also to Professor Xu Baogeng, the Chair of the Chinese Department at Qinghua University in Beijing, and to his family for their warm reception in 1996, and to Sheung Yan Lo and Gwenn Lo who hosted my second visit to Shanghai in 1998.

Intellectually, this book owes its existence to many friends and academics whose critical suggestions and corrections fundamentally shaped and reshaped my arguments. All the errors and crude analysis recorded in the following pages are, of course, mine. Although the present form of this book differs greatly from my dissertation, I must first of all express my special thanks to all the seven readers in my dissertation panel whose encouraging and constructive comments to my impetuous and error-ridden drafts are greatly appreciated. Here I would also like to acknowledge those friends and scholars who have generously shared their time and provided their critical and thoughtful comments. I thank Erin Mackie, Stephenie Hemelryk Donald, Chris Berry, Darrell Davis, and Wai-kit Choi for their time and constructive comments for the earlier drafts of my manuscript. The book also owes its existence to those inspiring conversations I had with Leo Ou-fan Lee, Li Shaobai, Zhong Dafeng, Li Yizhong, Dai Jinhua, Huang Wenying, Li Shek, Yeh Yueh-yu, and Stanley Kwan. I am most grateful to Ke Ling and Tong Yuejuan who provided me with invaluable historical information and shared with me their fascinating experiences in the 1930s' Chinese film industry. For editorial and stylistic matters I am also grateful to the professional assistance of Matthew Hammon, Carole Byrd, and Biodun Ignila. I am so lucky that this manuscript went to the hands of the excellent production and editorial crew of Rowman and Littlefield. The last person I want to mention, the one usually not the least but most dear to the thankful heart, is Kwai-cheung Lo; he has accompanied and encouraged me not only in the writing of this project but also in the many journeys in life that enriched and contributed to this work.

Introduction

When I first started my research on this book, which was then already narrowed down within the scope of the intellectual history of modern China, the memoirs and autobiographies of the left-wing filmmakers and critics of the 1930s most deeply engaged and challenged my understanding and affections of this part of China's history. Like many other intellectuals of their age, these film people spent their youth fighting for a utopia, a utopia that they never clearly identified for themselves but that required their most fervent belief and passion to construct. And it was also this utopia, as it came into being, that was to torture their bodies and betray their intellect most brutally. But among other intellectuals who had gone through similar struggles, these filmmakers and critics were the ones who most emphatically and modestly acknowledged the power of the mass, and therefore, they more accurately understood what "politics" pertained. Their films and writings, as a result, readily became sites of negotiation and contestation in spite of their relative simple and straightforward agenda.

My curiosities and interests led me to a further investigation of the relationship between the texts and the authors, examining what these filmmakers and film critics were trying to construct, and how these films represented, or misrepresented, their dreams and anger, their loves and hatreds. The research inevitably developed on a larger scale that concerned not only the filmmakers and their films but also the social and cultural environment with which the movies interacted and engaged in dialogue. The more I learn about the larger cultural-political context of the time, the more I come to understand these filmmakers and critics in their uniqueness. Under the patriarchal binary system, women were forced to represent nature, emotion, and rawness. However, as shown in these films and the related writings, this cinema movement, which was almost completely dominated by male filmmakers and critics, in many ways vividly reflected such "womanly" attributes, although they were clearly "masculine" in outlook and in essence. If the earlier scholarship on left-wing cinema celebrated its heroic and sophisticated achievements, my discovery is precisely the opposite, that the films and the film criticisms were largely raw, emotional, and readily fell prey to the spell of the environment, although they were at the same time patriotic and patriarchal. But it is also this strong emotional inclination manifested in this cinema movement that comes to anchor the following study.

The main objective of this study is twofold: to see this left-wing cinema movement as an illuminating event demonstrating the complexity of Chinese culture, high and low, in the first half of the twentieth century, and to study it as a notable participating member of world cinema illustrating the medium's diversified manifestations particularly in its early phase. I will analyze how the left-wing progressive ideology spread and took root in the 1930s, and I will also discuss how a different approach to filmmaking—its production, reception, and its theorization—was evolved in comparison and contrast to other cinemas. However, I am not interested in canonizing these Chinese films as timeless classics. Instead of treating them as masterpieces transcending their own specific cultural political context, in the following pages I will consider these films as interesting cultural texts, which reveal the diverging discourses and interests of different parties. Such convergence of complexity, in turn, was translated into some cinematic exercises rendering a distinct approach of filmmaking to be developed, which resonated the specificity of both the films and their cultural environment. This cinema movement was a phenomenal event with its own texture, depth, and life that should be studied from more than one perspective.

In the following pages, I will try to develop a coherent theoretical and historical framework to study how these films were regulated in their production and distribution, their understanding and consumption. I will delineate the relationship between the films and China in the 1930s, and how we can relate to these films now when we are seventy years apart from their first screenings. But this study is not a theory of what this cinema movement was; I do not attempt to define and confine these films and the related participants in the following pages. I will treat this Chinese left-wing cinema movement in the 1930s as an open field, to be freely questioned, whose borders can be crossed again and again, both here in this study and later by any subsequent attempts. In fact, one of the greatest fascinations of mine in these films is precisely the filmmakers' honest acknowledgment of their confined horizon and their curiosity and excitement about the practice of cinema and the world at large. As the films did not present themselves as self-sufficient and coherent art that is complete and all-knowing, I am not going to adopt such an autocratic viewpoint to study the film movement, particularly from this historically and academically privileged position.

The Left-wing Ideology

The left-wing cinema movement of the 1930s, due to various political and aesthetic reasons, has been upheld convincingly as the golden age of Chinese cinema, and it was provided an image larger than its life. To oppose and counterbalance these assumptions, most contemporary film scholars explore other sections of China's film history, aiming partly to provide us a more complete picture of Chinese cinema and partly to challenge the valorization of these left-wing films in the 1930s. The few scholars who have continued to study this movement usually turn a critical eye on these films, particularly about their ideological ignorance. I decided to work in this already polemical field not because of a simple urge to celebrate or refute the above two scholarly approaches, but instead, it was this sixty years of divergent hermeneutics, which have constantly been subject to the current political aura, that invited my curiosity. The large volumes of studies and reminiscences about this cinema produced in the mainland, particularly the ones before 1985, might have suffered fatally from ideological bias; but some of the contemporary scholarships, in or outside China, that aim at the correction thereof also show a "reverse" prejudice against the films. Similar to the films themselves, the readings of this cinema movement have also been utilitarian at heart.

In fact, this movement is both a *post facto* reconstruction of later scholars and a real historical event in which the filmmakers and spectators at that time participated consciously. The concept of *zuoyi dianying* (left-wing cinema) first appeared in 1931 in "The Directive of the Most Recent Activities" (*Zuijin xingdong gangling*) of the Chinese Left-wing Dramatists Association (*Zhongguo zuoyi xijujia lianmeng*).[1] The directive suggested launching a "proletarian cinema movement" in the near future; but it did not provide any details about the plan. It only demanded that its members criticize and purge the current Chinese cinema in order to provide a suitable soil for the movement's later development. And interestingly, the term "proletarian cinema movement" was never mentioned again either by the Party or by other left-wing filmmakers and critics. Politically more neutral terms like *Zhongguo dianying wenhua yundong* (Chinese Cinema Culture Movement) or *Zhongguo jinbu dianying* (Progressive Chinese Cinema) were used instead. Ironically, the more ideologically-charged title of this movement appeared only in the writings of their opponents at that time. For example, in Jia Mo's criticism of this cinema movement, he used the term *zuoqing dianying* (pro-left films) to describe the recent films made and promoted by leftist filmmakers and critics.[2]

The exact title of *zuoyi dianying yundong* (left-wing cinema movement) was in fact first "inaugurated" by Cheng Jihua, Li Xiaobai, and Xing Zuwen as an abstraction to define the progressive film culture in the 1930s and the 1940s in their writing of *Zhongguo dianying fazhan shi* (The development of Chinese cinema), the most authoritative piece of history written about pre-1949 Chinese cinema. This was a project supported by the communist government in the late 1950s with the aim of glorifying the political achievement of the left-wing filmmakers and critics in the Nationalist period (1912-1949). Not surprisingly, the hidden political agenda of this project was to legitimate the present government's sovereignty among the people, aiming particularly at intellectuals whose support could not be expected simply from coercive commands, by promoting this historical cooperation between the Party and the left-wing filmmakers. The book for the first time acknowledges the collective identity of a rather loose group of films made in between 1932 and 1937, and it recounts systematically the historical structure of the development of left-wing film circles and the films they produced during this period. The study attributes the leadership of this film movement to the underground Chinese Communist Party (CCP) and dichotomizes the film industry at that time into the revolutionary Left and the reactionary Right. The term "Chinese Left-wing Cinema Movement" and its meanings as described by the three historians gained acceptance by almost all Chinese film scholars thereafter.

Although the term "left-wing film" has been circulating in Chinese film studies for decades now, its definition was always vague, and the demarcations between left-wing movies and right-wing movies were never stated clearly. Only until the late 1980s, when the CCP's Chinese Film Art Research Center determined to publicize once again the historical significance of this film movement, was it defined in a more accurate fashion. Conducting this project became particularly urgent after 1989 when the State desperately sought legitimization. This project presents the films as standing historical documents to endorse the Party's hard-line request of the cordial supports from the intellectuals. The Research Center invited the historian Xing Zuwen, one of the writers of *The Development of Chinese Cinema*, to draft a catalog of the left-wing films and asked Xia Yan, generally known as the leader of this movement, to revise and approve it. An official list of seventy-four left-wing movies is printed in the thousand-page publication *Zhongguo zuoyi dianying yundong* (The Chinese left-wing cinema movement), which includes synopses of these seventy-four films as well as numerous historical and contemporary writings related to this movement. This list has become the official stamp to separate these left-wing films from all others.[3] In the following pages, the Chinese left-wing films in the 1930s I refer to are mostly the ones included in this list, but I use the list also with the critical awareness of its historical limitations.

Recently, more and more contemporary scholars are casting doubts on the entire construct of this film movement precisely because of the Party's obvious involvement in its construction. Many argue that it was fabricated "posthumously" by the government in order to suit their special political intentions. Not long after the publication of this collection, Li Shaobai, one of the authors of *The Development of Chinese Cinema* and one of the most renowned film professors in China today, disputes his earlier research and totally renounces the concept of a "left-wing cinema movement." In an article published in 1994 Li

Shaobai first advocates the titles *Zhongguo dianying wenhua yundong* (Chinese film culture movement) and *Xinxing dianying wenhua yundong* (New film culture movement) to replace "left-wing cinema movement."[4] This title changing is definitely symbolic: the political components of this cinema movement are therefore emptied out, and it now becomes an event whose primary aim was to reform the cinema culture rather than to spread any ideological messages.

In spite of Li Shaobai's effort, we cannot deny that a large-scale cinema movement with a left-wing ideological slant did take place in China between 1932 and 1937, as I will delineate in the next two chapters. I have decided to continue to use "left-wing cinema movement" to describe this group of films not because I agree completely with the historical account provided by *The Development of Chinese Cinema*, but because I have found "left-wing" a notion adequate to describe the intellectual inclination of the progressive film culture in the 1930s. Although historically we tend to use "left-wing" to designate Socialist and Marxist thinking, the term is fluid enough to include many other related social thoughts that are critical of tradition and/or the contemporary. It does not necessarily equate itself to the involvement of a communist party. I use this term here as an umbrella covering, whether completely or partly, for those films that display the filmmakers' strong sense of social mission and ethical commitment to the nation and its people, as well as for the films that contain elements of class consciousness or revolution, and concerns about the poor and the disenfranchised.[5]

Personally, I feel that Li Shaobai is more than justified in using ideologically neutral titles like "Chinese film culture movement" or "new film culture movement" to replace his earlier term. Professor Li is a witness to the large amount of biased readings applied to the films and the filmmakers because of the extreme politicization of the country for half a century. He is right to stop this over-ideologization in order to rescue the films from the political masks applied by earlier theorists. However, the existence of a cinema movement with strong left-wing political assumptions in the 1930s is beyond doubt. Although individual filmmakers were ideologically far from identical to each other, they did share similar moral commitments in a new nation-building project. Most of the filmmakers saw their works as more than sporadic critiques that responded only negatively to the current society; instead there was an ambiguous set of constructive convictions and goals shared by them. Even though it was vaguely expressed, there was a sense of identification among these filmmakers, and most of them understood their works to be efforts belonging to a larger collective project. Other politically neutral terms like "social criticism" are not sufficient enough to describe the close mental and ideological bonds, no matter how unspecified they were, shared among these films and among the filmmakers.

Therefore, it is important to point out that this cinema movement is a construction made up of both historical facts and the hermeneutic imagination of the later generations. Privileging either aspect of this construction would diminish the historical significance of this event. The word "left-wing" becomes particularly important in this regard because the underlying ideology of this term, however vague it has been, is the galvanizing force of not only the participating filmmakers and critics at that time but also most of the later scholars and historians who are interested in the study of this cinema movement. Continuing to adopt the title of "left-wing cinema movement," we are recognizing the many decades of its scholarship, which indeed helps to bring this study into a living tradition.

Propaganda, Art, and Entertainment

The conflicts and dynamics between "politics" and "aesthetics" in art and literature have been axiomatic, and the nuances and complexities are most blatantly reflected in twentieth-century Western thought.[6] Beginning from the Frankfurt School's renunciation of transcendentalism in art, the poststructuralists' theories on "text" and the recent scholarly enthusiasm on "ethics" might all be seen as echoes and spin-offs of the dilemmas caused by the interplay between politics and aesthetics in art and literature.[7] The two notions of arts and politics are constantly intertwined with each other and particularly obvious in the twentieth century when "power" is made more transparent and democratized. Such disputes and perplexities crystallize most quintessentially in the study of cinema, which can be seen as the art par excellence in the twentieth century. The most important scholarly work in this regard is definitely Walter Benjamin's "The Work of Art in the Age of Mechanical Reproduction," in which the author differentiates cinema from other forms of arts in its ability and nature in mechanical reproduction.[8] The distribution or reception of the work can now dissociate itself from the specific context of artistic creation and reproduce its initial mode and form of presentation repeatedly in different circumstances. As a result, certain traditional concepts for art, like genius and metaphysics, are brushed aside, and a new "politics of art" can be formulated through its mechanical reproductivity.

The debate on art versus politics also occupies a substantial position in the intellectual history of modern China, only in radically different social contexts and cultural inference from the West. Because of the historical immediacy of and the catastrophic impacts brought by various political events in this century, the notion of politics is generally understood in China in a narrower scope and concluded with a relatively boorish and unreflexive manner. Liu Zaifu, the famous contemporary Chinese thinker and political dissident who has been residing in the United States and Hong Kong, delineates what he considers to be the ideal relationship between literary art and politics: "The value of literary art resides exactly at its differing position from history. [Literature] must transcend the level of history in order to contemplate on history. There must be a certain distance kept between the two entities to support the freedom [of literature]."[9] This dialectics of art and history is a rendition of the dominant aesthetic theory of contemporary China. After many decades of the over-politicization of Chinese art and literature, contemporary intellectuals overwhelmingly support the split of aesthetics and politics, claiming that only by a separation of the two can art be healthily developed and assigned a role of supervision over the development of history.

Obviously, this claim is itself not deprived of its political anxiety, for a negative definition of art to politics only proves the omnipotent power of the latter. In fact, not only does this "modernist" claim of art dominate contemporary Chinese intellectuals, it was also a common assumption shared by the May Fourth generation in the 1920s.[10] Both generations aspire to liberate art and literature from the control of the political entity in power, as witnessed in Imperial China and the Cultural Revolution in which art was forced to be the mouthpiece and the legitimizing tool of government's sovereignty. Contemporary Chinese intelligentsia indeed share many common attributes with the May Fourth group because of their similar political positions in relation to history. Both are fighting against an authoritative legacy, and both are largely empowered by the Western modernist tradition that asserts the integrity and autonomy of creativity, reason, and freedom. However, while this separation of art and politics is political at heart, the Chinese intellectuals always idealize a transcendental position of art from politics in order to protect the former from the control of the latter. Obviously, with such outright and prominent "political" concerns, these Chinese thinkers are prevented from fathoming the many possible ideas and nuances the two notions "politics" and "aesthetics" may bring along.

My reason for this detour is that I find the leftist cultural heyday in 1930s Shanghai an antithesis to this antipolitics tradition in China. It was during this period that Chinese intellectuals most ardently and unconditionally embraced Socialist Realism, considering it the only cultural aperture to introduce Chinese literature and art to Socialist ideals.[11] It was the organic integration of form and content (i.e., art and politics) that could bring the cultural products to influence the popular mass and help them to understand the social deceptions the dominant class put into force. Between art and politics, it was the latter that, to a larger extent, defined the relationship between the filmmakers and their films. These left-wing filmmakers seldom expressed the artistic excellence of their works, although a discourse of art around cinema did develop around the same time. Almost none claimed a hope of their films being evaluated by people later or of obtaining a place in the transhistorical canonical shrine.

In this sense, the 1930s left-wing cultural environment, more than their Chinese predecessors and descendants, was in closer affiliation with the theories advocated by Benjamin or the Frankfurt School regarding the inherent connections between art and politics, although the Frankfurt School was also critical of it while these left-wing filmmakers were not. In fact, the films produced under the left-wing cinema movement can be seen as enemies of Liu Zaifu's aesthetics because these films presented themselves most unabashedly as "accomplices" of the contemporary political discourse. They vividly witnessed the ideological struggles of the time and felt no shame in being considered "trapped" in the material reality. Therefore, what I am interested in is not the philosophy behind the Chinese films, which was crude most of the time, but precisely those uncurbed ambiguities that these works contain. As shown in the course of this cinema movement, filmmakers and viewers, consciously and unconsciously, were constantly in struggles with the films as art and as political means, trying to define the new form of expression in both aesthetic and ethical terms. It was these debates and reflections that most uniquely characterize the accomplishments as well as the failures of this cinema movement, offering us insights to revisit the affinity and discord between art and politics, and what they might mean to us.

Any simple dichotomization of politics and aesthetics in this cinema movement was further challenged by the mechanism of consumption. Chris Berry is accurate in pointing out the disjunction between Solanas and Getino's "Third Cinema" and this Chinese left-wing cinema in the latter's urban commercial setting. "Film distribution and exhibition was beyond the control of the leftists, and the financial and political restrictions of the time would have prevented them from moving toward an alternative structure."[12] This Chinese left-wing cinema was by and large a commercial one, a successful one indeed, as many of these films set box office records. Its success in ideological terms was necessarily conditioned to the films' popularity among the mass. The filmmakers' political and aesthetic concerns cannot be fully explicated unless the spectators' reception of the films is also taken into consideration. In fact, these 1930s' left-wing films had passed the twilight period of Chinese cinema; an independent set of cinematic experiences and reasoning distinct from other narrative performances were already developed. Most importantly, cinema was becoming a culture industry with its own supporting mechanism and discourse. Films were usually shown in cinemas specifically designed for movie viewing. And the industry also possessed its own star system, with a large commercial device, like the overwhelming number of movie magazines, the specific film sections in most newspapers, and the movie songs that were becoming a genre of themselves, to guarantee its constant regeneration and everlasting glamour. The relationship between the films and their social environment, as well as the one between spectators and filmmakers, was always dynamic. It was neither a top-down ideological didacticism in which the filmmakers retained the sole power to control this movement nor a pure money-making industry determined merely by the tastes or desires of the spectators.

Art and mass culture, like art and ideology, production and consumption, have always been too hastily dichotomized. While the mass culture is oftentimes considered as partaking of profitmaking alone, the aesthetic complexity of true art, as it is claimed by many, is subject to its creativity, its experimentation, and its intellectual challenges which cannot be realized by the techniques producing mass culture. The latter's standardized products are results of the manufacturing of cultural commodities by means of routine, specialized, and fragmented assembly-line forms of production. But the production of true art can never be precalculated and predesigned as such. This cinema movement also problematized this general mass culture/art dichotomization. Many of these left-wing filmmakers openly acknowledged that their films were made to suit the viewing tastes and habits of the spectators. But the artistic achievements of this cinema, as I will argue, were precisely results of these concerns for their viewers. Highlighting the intimate relationship between these films and their surrounding social conditions, this study, therefore, structurally prevents me from canonizing the films in transcendental terms. The text and the context were mutually interwoven, and it is this weaving process that made these films unique.

Between politics and entertainment, this Chinese left-wing cinema produced narrative films only. There was a fierce debate in 1920s' Soviet cinema about how reality should be represented on screen. While filmmaker Sergei Eisenstein argued that the job of the filmmakers was to find the best expressive means and stylistic devices to "represent" reality, Dziga Vertov and his *Kinoks* (Cine-Eye) group, in contrast, opposed any stylistic interventions and upheld documentaries to fictional films: "The film drama shrouds the eyes and brain in a sickly fog. The Cine-Eye opens the eyes, clears the vision."[13] However, there was hardly any voice heard in 1930s' Chinese left-wing cinema circles advocating the use of documentaries, which were produced and watched in China since the 1900s. While documentary was featured in the most progressive cinema all over the world, the Chinese left-wing cinema chose fictional films as their mode of expression. The Chinese filmmakers, unlike their Soviet counterparts, did not excuse themselves from manipulating spectators' emotions. Its deliberate "dramatization" of the left-wing discourse played a key role in rendering this nationalist propaganda less realistic and authentic. Instead, the notion of enjoyment prevailed. It was this romanticized but also fictionalized vision that encouraged and discouraged spectators' identification with the representations. The transmutation between entertainment and politics corrupted each other's controlling power to this cinema movement.

However, I am not arguing the political incompetence of this cinema. Quite the contrary, their commercial success rendered these films more powerful, helping the left-wing nationalist ideology to circulate among Chinese cities during the period. One of the most powerful political attributes of this Chinese cinema was its special status of "national product." Being a Western import, motion pictures had long been condemned in China as a tool for spreading corrupt ideology. But ironically, film production was one of the only two major Chinese industries not yet invaded by foreign capital in the 1930s.[14] Chinese cinema at that time can be seen as a completely national enterprise that escaped controls of foreign political and economic powers. Although individual film-

10

makers and spectators shared dissimilar concerns, the general anti-imperialist anger of the people found an outlet in this Chinese cinema without any foreign intervention.[15] Therefore, the status of cinema in the nationalist project was fortified and its pedagogy legitimated by this relatively independent position of moviemaking. This film movement for the first time produced a local Chinese cinema that could rival imported movies in both quality and quantity. One of the most dazzling and effective advertising tactics of the local film companies during the period was to promote the films' collective identity as "National Cinema" in contrast to the allegedly corrupt Western films.

On the other hand, the imperialist powers exerted their surveillance through other means. The foreign settlements in Shanghai had the exclusive rights to ban any films from showing in their concessions, and many major theaters in the city were located in their controlled area. Due to the concern for revenue, film companies usually rejected those productions that might outrage the foreign powers in Shanghai. In fact, many films shown in Shanghai had to undergo two levels of censorship, one by the *Guomindang* (GMD) government and the other by the foreign settlements in which the films were shown.[16] Interestingly, censorship of this kind made this cinema an even more powerful medium for the left-wing political campaign. Although many left-wing films could not escape the fate of being screened in edited versions, such political surveillance did not restrain but rather promoted the nationalistic urge among spectators and filmmakers alike. Perceiving the impotency of the government, the filmmakers availed themselves of all the anger and moral indignation necessary to raise nationalist passion within the folk culture. And in return the spectators received the films with an equal amount of emotional intensity, which further encouraged the production of films with similar ideological positions. In fact, many of the left-wing films managed to be screened publicly with the political messages relatively intact, once again due to the illusory and dramatic nature of the medium, which often slipped through the policing from the above.

As a mass medium that escaped and resisted both the foreign and domestic "hegemonies," this cinema was placed in a morally advantageous position that helped to solicit support from the mass to legitimate its politics, no matter how vague their ideology was. Michel de Certeau has argued that the contemporary administrative apparatus has more "power" than "authority." They try hard to develop subtle and tightly knit procedures for the control of all social networks that compensate for the gradual loss of their credibility from subjects who no longer commit themselves in believing the "authority."[17] Interestingly, this Chinese left-wing cinema in the 1930s can be read as the exact opposite of this contemporary world de Certeau depicts. Precisely because the political "power" of the filmmakers was severely limited by the censorship machine, the films obtained more "authority" in the market; the spectators' convictions in the films' ideologies were indeed encouraged by the State's open tarnishing of the cinema movement as a whole.

A Brief Summary

The study is divided into three major parts. I start this study in part 1 with the delineation of the cinema movement's history, as the existing versions we have are largely deficient and distorted. The only official and most reliable history of the cinema movement is the one narrated in the aforementioned *The Development of Chinese Cinema*. Because of the Cultural Revolution's destruction of filmic and written materials related to pre-1949 Chinese cinema, this extensive study conducted before the catastrophic event is and will be the most elaborated and comprehensive history of early Chinese cinema written, as admitted by Li Shaobai who is trying hard to revise and supplement his earlier scholarship which he renounced.[18] But the book is notorious for its political bias, overglorifying this film movement as emblematic to the later political triumph of the CCP. Although there have been some efforts in the mainland to redraft the history of this part of Chinese cinema, contemporary research still has to rely on *The Development of Chinese Cinema* substantially.[19] The historical account I offer in chapters 1 and 2 inevitably draws selective information from this book, yet I also provide my own research findings to challenge and elaborate on the standard account. It presents this cinema movement as a product of multiple social, economic, and political discourses, indicating that no one was in control of the event, and it embodies pluralistic voices that include not only the political interests of the two major political camps but also other institutions and structures like the film industry, the Chinese intelligentsia, and the current international environment, etc.[20]

After the first two chapters we will leave behind the archival dimension and embark on the path that connects reconstruction and interpretation. Basically the study is organized around the two major processes of the cinematic event. In part 2 of this book, I will concentrate on the discourses conditioning the films' production and discuss how a male collective subjectivity evolved in this cinema. In part 3, I will demonstrate that this emerging cinematic apparatus was necessarily complicated and challenged by its reception, that this cinema movement was conditioned to both the filmmakers' ideological agenda and the spectators' likes and dislikes. The two parts combined will illustrate how the political, aesthetic, and commercial discourses fought and reinforced each other, which cut through the filmmakers' decisions in productions and crystallized in the cinematic experience in its entirety.

Chapter 3 is devoted to the filmmakers-collective. There was a definite set of left-wing ideologies most of the left-wing filmmakers consciously shared, like anti-feudalism, anti-imperialism, and a unique form of left-wing nationalism. But the actual representations were much more complicated than these self-proclaimed missions of the filmmakers. We will approach the filmmakers both as individual creative agencies and as a collective, and show that their works were merging points of both their personal horizons and social environment. I will examine the filmmakers' underlying assumptions and concerns as displayed in the films and illustrate an "intellectual/revolutionary" model, so frequently observed in this cinema, which reflected the filmmakers' self-fascination. The following two chapters focus on its gender representation, illustrating that the filmmakers' fantasy and anxiety were most intricately revealed in their portrayal of sexuality and women. Chapter 4 concentrates on the opposite sex relationship represented, illustrating how romance and sexuality were essential in this cinema in spite of its highly puritan claim, and its "romantic" urge and youthful spirit were results of the specific sociohistorical position of this cinema. Chapter 5 addresses women's stories and female stardom. My case study of the on-screen and off-screen representations of two famous female actresses, Ai Xia and Ruan Lingyu, who both committed suicide in reality and in the films they performed, reveals how the power of this cinema movement was established by cinematic as well as extra-cinematic strategies of representation. As a whole, in this part, I want to demonstrate that the filmmakers, in spite of their weaknesses and anxieties, were remarkable artists in their own rights as they most readily embraced history and its limitations thereof.

Part 3 concentrates on the analysis of the spectatorship of this cinema movement and examines the culture and location where these films were made. Chapter 6 asks the question if this cinema was as commercial as political, illustrating that the film culture was extremely fluid, embracing the many discursive as well as nondiscursive events and processes taking place between filmmakers and spectators. I will also discuss how Hollywood on the one hand and the Soviet cinema on the other influenced this Chinese cinema. Chapter 7 focuses on the dynamics between Shanghai and China. Almost all of the left-wing films were made and screened in Shanghai. Its urban, cosmopolitan culture was key to defining this cinema, which was never "national" in its comprehensive dimension. It is crucial to analyze the city's culture before we can understand the intricacy of this event in relation to the larger national picture.

After illustrating the many social and cultural dynamics at work in this cinema, the last chapter of this book attempts to define, finally, a cinematic aesthetic produced thereof, which might be the ultimate purpose of this study, but it is also the most reserved part of mine. Chapter 8 presents an "Engaging Realism" by illustrating how the cinema embraces and enriches realism and sentimentalism, the two seemingly contradictory ways of cinematic approaches to representation. The interplay between an objective reflection on the empirical reality and the desire to engage spectators' emotions played a crucial role in the cinema's success as being both political and commercial. I also analyze the role "film songs" play in this cinema, which provided an alternative narrative space to accommodate the spectators' identification with the characters and present the expressionist dimension of art in this otherwise straight political medium. This chapter aims at complicating, instead of defining, the poetics of this cinema, showing that the cinematic form revealed was always more than a conscious concern of art.

Although my study concentrates on only one particular film movement taking place in the 1930s, its ultimate goal is to present the readers with a comprehensive picture of early Chinese moviemaking, acknowledging that the Chinese cinema also had a long and struggling history of experimentation and transformation technically, intellectually, and artistically. Our scholarship of Chinese cinema will never be complete unless we can take its history and development into account, acknowledging that the contemporary Chinese cinema in Taiwan, Hong Kong, and the mainland, which has attracted so much Western enthusiasm lately, does not emerge from a vacuum. I hope that the following pages reconstruct, if only partly, a vigorous and quixotic film culture whose achievements and weaknesses certainly deserve more of our scholarly attention both in the study of cinema and China, and it could highlight some of the more important features, problems, and concerns of Chinese cinema as a continuous tradition.

Notes

1. This directive was first published in *Wenxue daobao* (Directed readings of literature) 1, nos. 6 and 7 (Oct 23, 1931). Rpt. *ZZXLSJ*, 17-19; *ZZDY*, 17-18.

2. *SNZDPW*, 844. For detailed descriptions and discussions of the Soft-cinema versus Hard-cinema debate in which Jia Mo participated, see chapters 2 and 8.

3. I include this list in appendix 1.

4. Li Shaobai, "Jianlun Zhongguo sanxi niandai 'dianying wenhua yundong' de xingqi" (A brief account of the rise of the film culture movement in the 1930s and 1940s), *Dangdai dianying* (Contemporary cinema) 60 (March 1994): 77.

5. I would not, however, characterize these films as fascist, as fascism is characterized by its aestheticization of politics, while most of these Chinese filmmakers were not interested in conceptualizing their works in transcendental terms.

6. The notion of politics, of course, is understood here in its widest sense, corresponding not only to pragmatic human relationships but also to ideas and knowledge of our empirical reality.

7. Theodor Adorno demarcates the committed art from the "autonomous" one (art-for-art's-sake) by the latter's claimed transcendental element, which the former renounces. However, he does not naïvely privilege political knowledge of reality to aesthetic beauty but presents a rather composite and conflicting relationship between the two. To put it in the simplest language, our life-praxis is doomed to be fragmented, distorted, and incomplete. Aesthetic beauty, on the other hand, is achieved only through a synthetic reflection of this material world, be it in form or in content. Because of this inherently negative relationship between art (beauty) and reality (nonbeauty), aesthetic synthesis can only be accomplished by turning against itself and calling its own principle into question. It is the politics of art that dominated Adorno's aesthetic theory. Poststructuralism, particularly the Deconstructionist tradition, can be seen as an alternative to this Frankfurt School's formulation. It insists on studying writing, or any form of cultural production,

within a closed semiotic system in which each term acquires value only through its opposition to the other terms. That is to say, there is nothing outside the text, and the linguistic system is the only place where meanings and values are created, diachronically and synchronically. This claim can be seen as an effort of these contemporary literary scholars to dematerialize language in order to prevent an ideological domination by the political world over the production of values. Therefore, the Poststructuralist enterprise and its likes are often accused of political indifference and capriciousness. However, at the core of their scholarship most of these theorists aim not at privileging text over context, but rather to erode the distinction between the two. Entering the 1990s, the notions of ethics and politics, be they in relation to reading, writing, criticism, or teaching, once again enjoys the academic highlight in the literary studies in the West. Now merged with the issues of identity politics, it is the solidarity of one's gender, sexual, ethnic, and even individual identity against the hegemony of any cultural coercion that is most called for. The political aspects are once again highlighted. Questions regarding the use of aesthetics as a vehicle for political projects and those related to the relationship between art and its social conditions have been popular topics in literary and cultural studies of the twentieth century and attracted a considerable amount of academic enthusiasm.

8. Walter Benjamin, "The Work of Art in the Age of Mechanical Reproduction," in *Illuminations* (New York: Schocken Books, 1968), 217-51.

9. Li Zehou and Liu Zaifu, *Gaobie geming: Huiwang ershi shiji Zhongguo* (Farewell revolution: Looking back at the Twentieth Century China) (Hong Kong: Tiandi, 1997), 248.

10. I call this linkage between the May Fourth and the contemporary Chinese intellectuals a "modernist" tradition because it corresponds closely to the two opposing features of modernity in the West. On the one hand, this Chinese definition of art is oriented towards a pragmatism and a humanism which celebrate the doctrine of progress around which the European bourgeois idea of modernity is to a large extent developed. On the other hand, it also promotes autonomy of art and its antagonistic position to politics—a European modernist aesthetic in view of Baudelaire's work. See Matei Calinescu's *Five Faces of Modernity, Modernism, Avant-Garde, Decadence, Kitsch, Postmodernism* (Durham, N.C.: Duke University Press, 1987), 41-46.

11. Although Socialist Realism also towered above any other methodologies in Chinese literary and artistic production and reception between 1949 and 1979, after the Liberation this became basically a master plan of the State advanced to the people instead of a spontaneous movement sprouted from the ground as we saw in the 1930s.

12. Chris Berry, "Chinese Left Cinema in the 1930s: Poisonous Weeds or National Treasures," *Jump Cut* 34 (1989): 94.

13. Dziga Vertov, "Fiction Film Drama and the Cine-Eye. A Speech." Rpt., *The Film Factory*, ed. Richard Taylor and Ian Christie (London: Routledge, 1994), 116.

14. *SB*, Nov. 27, 1934. There were some initial attempts of Westerners to enter the Chinese film industry in the beginning of the century. For example, in 1909 the American Russian Benjamin Brasky set up the Asia Film Company in Shanghai and made some short films. The British and American Tobacco Company also made a number of shorts to help promote their products. Although for unknown reasons these Westerners withdrew from China in the teens, and distribution was still controlled by foreign capital. This situation was to be changed in the late 1920s when most theaters were taken back by Chinese businessmen.

15. But the lack of international investment also implied a restricted development of

the enterprise under the scanty local resources; it became a detrimental factor preventing any rapid growth of the industry, particularly in terms of its production and screening technology. The restricted technological advancement nonetheless became another factor shaping the unique development of this cinema movement.

16. Eugene Irving Way, *Motion Pictures in China*, Trade Information Bulletin 722 (Washington, D.C., Bureau of Foreign and Domestic Commerce, U.S. Department of Commerce, 1930).

17. Michel de Certeau, *The Practice of Everyday Life* (Berkeley: University of California Press, 1984), 179.

18. Li Shaobai, interview by author, Beijing, China, December 4, 1996.

19. Comprehensive histories of Chinese cinema published recently in mainland China include Zhou Xiaoming, *Zhongguo xiandai dianying wenxue shi* (Literary history of modern Chinese cinema), 2 vols. (Beijing: Gaodeng jiaoyu, 1987); Wang Yunman, *Zhongguo dianying yishu shilüe* (A brief history of Chinese film art) (Beijing: Zhongguo guoji guangbo, 1989); Xu Daoming and Sha Sipeng, *Zhongguo dianying jianshi* (A concise history of Chinese cinema) (Beijing: Zhongguo qingnian, 1990); Feng Min, ed., *Zhongguo dianying yishu shigang* (The structural history of Chinese film art) (Tianjin: Nankai daxue, 1992); Hu Xingliang and Zhang Ruilin eds., *Zhongguo dianying shi* (Chinese film history) (Beijing, Zhongyang guangbo dianshi daxue, 1995); Li Suyuan and Hu Jubin, *Zhongguo wusheng dianying shi* (History of Chinese silent cinema) (Beijing: Zhongguo dianying, 1996); and Ding Yeping, *Yingxiang Zhongguo: Zhongguo dianying yishu 1945-1949* (Imagining China: Chinese cinema 1945-1949) (Beijing: Wenhua yishu, 1998). The last two works incorporate some new perspectives to look at the parts of Chinese cinema they deal with. However, the left-wing cinema in the 1930s is not yet revised by any such efforts in mainland China.

20. Part 1 also serves as an introduction to provide background materials for readers unfamiliarized with the events and figures involved in the early Chinese cinema, as there are few related materials available in Western languages. The only comprehensive history of early Chinese cinema available in English is Jay Leyda's *Dianying: An Account of Films and the Film Audience in China* (Cambridge, Mass.: MIT Press, 1972), which remains largely impressionistic and lacks historical support. But early Chinese cinema is attracting more and more scholarly attention in the West, which begins to piece together a more complete picture of the cinema's early history. See, for example, Zhang Yingjin's anthology *Cinema and Urban Culture in Shanghai 1922-43* (Stanford, Calif.: Stanford University Press, 1999) and chapter 3 of Leo Lee's *Shanghai Modern* (Cambridge, Mass.: Harvard University Press, 1999).

I

The History

1

The Merging of Histories

Like all other historical events, the Chinese left-wing cinema movement was not an independent phenomenon but a converging point of many social and cultural, local and international discourses. This cinema movement found itself at the crossroads of numerous complementing and contradictory interests; this historical event is particularly fascinating as it also integrated high culture and popular culture, but certainly not in any fantasized egalitarian fashion. A fair reading of this cinema movement cannot be obtained without taking these many social conditions together.[1] Before recounting the details of the cinema movement between 1932 and 1937, this first chapter offers a general background of Chinese society in the late 1920s and early 1930s and discusses how the involvement of the three major groups, namely the intelligentsia, the CCP, and the film industry, contributed to the rise of the movement.

Intellectuals versus Filmmakers

To most historians, Chinese intellectuals in the 1920s were defined by the May Fourth demonstrations in 1919 and the accompanying New Culture Movement. The movement was initiated by a group of students and young intellectuals protesting against the military threats from Japan and the imperialistic invasion from the Western powers, showing their anger toward foreign meddling in Chinese affairs. But soon it was transformed into an intellectual reform of colossal scale, embracing almost the entire range of concerns the Chinese intellectuals were confronting, particularly in terms of the reconciliation/scission of China from the past to the future. The general mentality of the intelligentsia then was rather complicated, and it contained many self-contradictory elements. A major

19

knot connecting the many vigorous debates was the relationship between China and the West. While a small group of conservatives (represented by the National Essence Movement and the New Life Movement) upheld traditional Chinese values and ways of living, most of the leading scholars were iconoclasts who were influenced by Western ideas, although to different degrees. One might summarize the general mentality among these intellectuals in this way: to learn from the West in order to combat the West. However, this nationalistic strategy was not necessarily self-empowering. There has always been a strong inferiority complex, if only an unconscious one, in the Chinese intelligentsia during the last two hundred years, and many of them deep in their hearts sincerely believed that things Western were superior to things Chinese. Therefore, an all-encompassing Westernization quickly swept through the entire Chinese cultural world in the twenties. It was also during this craze for the West that Marxism was introduced to China. The Chinese Communist Party was founded in 1921 as one of the many historic responses to the May Fourth event.[2]

The May Fourth also witnessed for the first time in Chinese history the destruction of the scholar-official marriage, as the new Republic government was now composed of a new group of political bureaucrats instead of the Confucian scholars recruited through the Imperialist examination system. Intellectuals had to search for their own independent positions in society. As a result, this movement nurtured not only famous individual cultural figures but also a large number of literary associations and schools of thought in which individuals could join and be defined. Almost all intellectuals were associated with one or more of these groups, and these collectives usually had very clear and strong ideological positions. Although one element of the initiating agenda of the New Culture Movement was to fortify the political transcendence of the new Chinese arts and literature, most of these literary groups became heavily politicized in the late 1920s. There were three major parties in the literary world at the time. "The first group was made up of members of the Creation (*Chuangzaoshe*) and Sun Societies (*Taiyanshe*), the second was headed by Lu Xun and Mao Dun, representatives of the Thread-of-talk group (*Yusipai*) and the Literary Research Association (*Wenxue yanjiuhui*), and the last group was mainly the Crescentists (*Xinyuepai*), with Liang Shiqiu as the key theoretician."[3]

While the first two groups affiliated with leftist ideologies were becoming the leading voices in literary circles beginning in the late 1920s, the last group with a more neutral political standpoint was gradually submerged into the background. Although debates between Lu Xun and the younger figures in Creation Society and Sun Society were constantly heard, their political orientations were more similar than divergent, and their continuing consolidation helped a widespread diffusion of left-wing ideologies among the younger generation intellectuals, no matter how confusing and distorted these left-wing ideologies had become.[4] The establishment of the Chinese League of Left-wing Writers (*Zhongguo zuoyi zuojia lianmeng*) in Shanghai in March 1930 represented the promising opening phase of the left-wing intellectual milieu in the coming decade.

In spite of this dominating leftist atmosphere in the Shanghai cultural world, the relationship between the intelligentsia and the Party was certainly not as direct and concrete as many have claimed. Although the Chinese Communist Party was established in Shanghai in 1921 by Li Dazhao and Chen Duxiu, two city bourgeois intellectuals with no experience with politics and hands-on class struggles, the Party was forced to leave the cities and enter the rural area after the failure of the first United Front with the GMD. The United Front was initiated by Sun Yat-sen [a.k.a. Sun Zhongshan] in 1924 in order to unite all forces to fight the warlords; however, it ended brutally three years after. On April 11, 1927, a five-day GMD massacre took place in Shanghai and gradually spread to the entire country killing thousands of CCP members. The young and angry CCP leaders decided to fight back, but Zhou Enlai failed in his insurrection in Jiangxi as did Mao Zedong in Hunan. The GMD killings spread all over China, and they would continue for the next four years. The disintegrating Party was forced to give up the city bases and to re-station themselves in the most remote areas in China.[5]

Although this massacre performed by the GMD was one of the major reasons leading the city intellectuals to turn away from the Republic government and to align with the leftists, this disastrous failure of the CCP introduced a great distance between the Party and the intellectual activities in Shanghai. On the one hand, communication between the Party and the cities was seriously hampered; on the other, many of the Party's leaders now preferred to devote their energies in reinforcing the support from the peasantry rather than fighting for interests directly with the GMD in the cities. Only a handful of Party leaders, like Qu Qiubai, continued to keep a close relation with Shanghai's cultural circles.[6]

The intellectuals' support of the CCP was therefore mostly spontaneous, largely fuelled by the immediacy of war: China in the 1930s was overwhelmed by war scares. Although the Sino-Japanese war did not officially begin until 1937, Japan had occupied the three provinces in the northeastern part of China in 1931 and had bombarded Shanghai in 1932. While the anti-Japanese mentality quickly spread through the whole country, the Chinese Nationalist government was also under severe criticism for its impotence in standing up against the Japanese invasion. The government prohibited all anti-Japanese activities from taking place and thus indirectly helped the CCP, which was then the major political voice against the Japanese, to gain broad support from the Chinese intelligentsia. Many established intellectual figures were either affiliated with or sympathetic to left-wing ideologies; antigovernment ideologies were particularly popular among the younger generation. Marxism was believed by many to be the foreign means that could redeem the rotten Chinese tradition and help them to fight against the foreign evils, the Japanese troops and Western capitalism alike.

Shanghai's film industry in the 1920s, however, was quite independent from these fervent events in the intellectual world and the political arena; its situation was more intimately connected to the current economic and social reality in Shanghai. After some initial experimentation of the intellectuals and education organizations like Li Minwei, Zheng Zhengqiu, and the Commercial Press (*Shangwu yinshu guan*), cinema was soon taken over by capitalists. The First World War in Europe brought direct benefits to the Chinese economy in the early 1920s. Owing to the increasing residue capital stored up in China, film companies of different sizes sprang up in a surge. By the mid-1920s there were more than 180 film companies established, and they were interested in the cinema industry because they all believed that movie making could bring them quick capital returns.[7] Many of the smaller companies failed in the game, and the three largest studios, Mingxing, Dazhonghua Baihe, and Tianyi, soon took control of the market and made a large number of commercial films tailored for the tastes of the general mass. The late 1920s witnessed the utter commercialism of the industry where period films and swordsman films were produced in high quantity but low quality.[8] According to the commentaries of the time and the available synopses of these films, the local productions must have attracted a large number of spectators who were untiringly fascinated by the convoluted but formulaic plots as well as the visual excitement caused by special effects, violence, and pornography. However, many educated bourgeois abhorred these movies and simply refused to enter the theaters which showed Chinese films; they preferred the films imported from the West, particularly from Hollywood.

According to *The Development of Chinese Cinema*, Chinese cinema in the 1920s was dominated by commercial movies with licentious, criminal, or other morally questionable themes.[9] This depiction of the movie industry corresponds closely to the development of many other national cinemas: very soon after its invention, film was chosen, among many possible directions, to move to the domain of entertainment. The motion picture was seen by many entrepreneurs as an attractive medium to gain quick financial profits. In fact, in hindsight, the motion picture might not have survived if it had not become mass entertainment, as this industry requires a great amount of investment in film stock, advanced equipment, theaters, and large number of personnel. Unlike literature and other forms of high art, film has been closely linked to the masses since its very beginning. Only after the commercial movie industry had become stable and had succeeded in attracting a larger number of spectators did other interested parties discover the power of cinema and begin to experiment with the medium. In Europe and the Soviet Union, this change in the course of cinema history took place in the 1910s and 1920s, and many artists and intellectuals began to participate in the making of and the theorization about cinema; in China, the left-wing progressive cinematic movement did not take place until the 1930s.

Ke Ling, a left-wing scriptwriter and critic in the 1930s and the 1940s, has recently claimed that the film industry in the 1920s was the only cultural form at that time unaffected by the New Culture Movement.[10] Paul Pickowicz also raises a similar assertion about this phenomenon. "It is clear that when the New Culture and May Fourth movements were fundamentally reshaping the world of letters in the teens and twenties, they had almost no direct impact on the film-making circles."[11] This is an accurate depiction to a large extent; but there were always individual intellectual efforts trying to influence the film industry. In fact, much before Lenin commented that: "Of all the arts, for us the most important is cinema,"[12] Chinese filmmakers in the early 1910s had already used film to illustrate their ideological beliefs and to educate their spectators. The first two Chinese narrative films were made in 1913, Li Minwei's *Zhuangzi shiqi* (Zhuangzi Tests His Wife) and Zheng Zhengqiu's *Nanfu nanqi* (Suffering Husband and Wife); the former is a film condemning women's infidelity, and the latter criticizes the traditional marriage system. With the gender prejudices inherent in their messages, the two films were outspoken in their bold and unyielding ethical calls. From its very beginning Chinese films had been associated with pedagogy.

Although the film market in the 1910s and the 1920s was basically a money-making machine, a few important filmmakers managed to find their ways to cinema's pedagogy. Hou Yao, Hong Shen, and Ouyang Yuqian were among the more famous filmmakers who were also actively participating in the New Culture Movement, and their strong ideological concerns are visible in many of their films. In the case of Hong Shen, a Harvard graduate and a well-respected drama director in the early 1920s, for example, he determined to enter the film industry in 1925 in spite of the pressure around him.[13] The general social attitude towards drama and film was different.[14] Being a director and a playwright of western dramas, Hong Shen was considered an artist-intellectual of high esteem. His adaptation of Oscar Wilde's *Lady Windermere's Fan* was considered the first classic of Chinese "spoken drama,"[15] and Hong Shen was well respected by most intellectuals. However, he disappointed many of his supporters by choosing to work in Mingxing as a movie scriptwriter. To most Chinese intellectuals at that time, movies could not be anything more than a form of low-brow mass entertainment. But Hong Shen decided to resist the mainstream as he was convinced of the potential ideological sway of the new media, and history proved him right. Another famous literary figure in the 1920s who was also affiliated with cinema was Tian Han. *Dao minjian qu* (Going to the People) was an independent film project of Nanguo Cinema Society (*Nanguo dianying she*), a branch of Tian Han's famous drama group Nanguo Society (*Nanguo she*), in 1926. As its name suggests, *Going to the People* was a film encouraging intellectuals to leave their ivory towers and go among the mass. But this project was not completed because of lack of funds.[16] As a whole, there were enough spaces in the vigorous commercial movie industry to allow different voices to be heard, no matter how feeble they were.

However, we have to admit that the connection between the world of cinema and the left-wing intellectuals in the 1920s was indeed weak. The initiating factors of the left-wing cinema movement were certainly not as simple as many have claimed—specifically, that it was solely the result of the Party's decision to enter the film industry. History is always full of possibilities and randomness; the CCP in fact had played a minor role in starting and shaping this cinema movement beginning in 1932. The following are some immediate factors preparing for and contributing to the emerging cinema movement.

The Rising of Lianhua Film Company

As I have pointed out, the film industry indeed had little connection with the intellectuals and the revolutionaries in the 1920s. The very first crucial step connecting the two camps was made by Luo Mingyou. The son of a rich businessman and a student of Law at Peking University, Luo Mingyou was instead interested in the movie industry. In 1918 by the age of eighteen, he was already running a theater, the Zhenguang Movie House (*Zhengguang dianying yuan*), in Beijing and began to expand his theater chain. In 1927 Luo Mingyou established the Huabei Film Company, a film distribution company. By 1930 he already owned more than twenty movie theaters in northern China.[17] In the late 1920s he foresaw the change in Hollywood and understood that his theaters would soon have a shortage of American silent films. Statistics show that in 1930 67 percent of the Hollywood films imported to China were sound movies. By 1931 the figure rose to 89 percent.[18] Most of his theaters were not equipped with sound film projectors and speakers; bringing in so much new equipment would have been a large capital investment. This business concern became the reason, or the excuse, for him to enter the film production industry; he decided to establish a big film studio making silent films which would supply films to his own theaters.[19] For the first time in China's film history, a complete studio system was established that controlled all aspects of the production, distribution, and exhibition of its films, which also indirectly delayed Chinese cinema's transition to the sound age.

On the other hand, Li Minwei's Minxin Film Company was established in Hong Kong in 1923. But when the all-city strike against Western imperialism in 1925 tore down the economy of the colony, Minxin was forced to move to Shanghai the same year.[20] Li Minwei invested all he had in the company, but his filmmaking did not suit the popular taste at that time.[21] By 1928 Minxin was in serious financial trouble. As Sun Yu recounted:

> In the autumn of 1929, when Manager Li Minwei of Minxin was deeply troubled by the company's economic difficulties, his old hometown friend Luo Mingyou from Huabei Film Company visited him from Beijing. Luo Mingyou also brought with him the story line of the film *Gudu chuanmeng* (Spring dream in the old capital). After some discussion the two men decided to produce the film and asked me to be the director.[22]

Spring Dream in the Old Capital became a coproduction of the two companies; Huabei was responsible for two-thirds of its production costs and Minxin the other third.[23] Through the course of the film's production, Luo Mingyou and Li Minwei made the agreement to establish a new company and used this film as the company's debut. Before the release of this film, their second film *Yecao xianhua* (Wild Flowers), also directed by Sun Yu, had begun production (plate 1). In the meantime Lo Minyou and Li Minwei continued to raise funds for their new company in different parts of China. The family backgrounds of the two men as well as their personal connections in Hong Kong and Beijing had helped them to gain tremendous financial and political support from the richest millionaires in the British colony and the most powerful politicians in the GMD.[24]

This background support allowed Lianhua to become the biggest film studio in China in a short period. Lianhua Film Production and Processing Company Limited (*Lianhua yingye zhipian yinshua gongsi*) officially became a registered company in March of 1930, and by then Luo Mingyou had already successfully co-opted four existing film studios, including Minxin, Dazhonghua Baihe, Shanghai Yingxi, and Xianggong Yingye, into his "kingdom."[25] These film companies became the four branch studios of Lianhua. With the existing theater-chain owned by Huabei, Lianhua became a completely self-sufficient film company and had all the resources and potential to change the face of the film industry in Shanghai entering the 1930s.

Both the *Spring Dream in the Old Capital* and *Wild Flowers* were box office successes in 1930, which combined with the company's strong political and financial background became a powerful support for Luo Mingyou to raise and carry out the glaring slogan "Reviving the National Cinema" (*Fuxing guopian*) unwaveringly.[26] As a young and ambitious intellectual/entrepreneur, Luo Mingyou was an open-minded reformer who had a wide degree of tolerance for different artistic orientations. But being a devoted Christian, he would not show violence and/or pornography in any of his productions. This marked the clean and vigorous production strategy of the film company. The four already existing studios being assimilated provided a number of talented filmmakers to the new Lianhua, and the new boss continued to attract newcomers to fortify his movie empire.

The film company continued to make box office successes in 1930 and 1931. These films strengthened the financial base of the new Lianhua and for the first time attracted educated Chinese to the local productions. Movie going had already become a highly popular activity among Shanghai citizens earlier in the decade. In a study done in 1930, among the eighty-six college students being interviewed, thirty-nine of them attended movies at least once a week, another sixteen of them at least once every two weeks. However, almost all of them preferred foreign movies.[27] In the large number of film magazines and newspapers in the 1920s, news and pictures were always about Hollywood films and their stars. But *Spring Dream in the Old Capital* and *Wild Flowers* wrote a new page of China's film history, attracting a group of new spectators who had never attended Chinese movies. Lianhua was the first film company that successfully brought educated Chinese to watch local productions; and it helped to pave the way for the introduction of the left-wing cinema.

After the box office success of Sun Yu's *Spring Dream in the Old Capital* and *Wild Flowers* in 1930, Luo Mingyou was convinced that he had chosen the correct strategy for Lianhua. He continued to encourage his filmmakers to make movies of contemporary settings and healthy themes. In 1931 ten films were produced in Lianhua; among the most successful ones were *Lian'ai yu yiwu*

(Love and Duty), *Yijian Mei* (A Spray of Plum Blossoms), and *Taohua qi xue ji* (Peach Blossom Weeps Tears of Blood)—all of them were directed by Bu Wancang.

A Spray of Plum Blossoms was adapted from Shakespeare's play *Two Gentlemen of Verona*, and the entire film was characterized by its Westernized look, almost in a ridiculous way. Because the major part of the story took place in the far south of China, Bu Wancang had all the excuses to create a new environment surreal to Shanghai. In the film we see some Chinese aristocrats living in stylized modern estates with high modernist decor. There is a Robin Hood-like hero-bandit robbing the rich to help the poor, and many women soldiers with loose and long hair in the film ride on horses forming an army themselves. Almost nothing portrayed in the film resembled the reality of Chinese society at that time; instead it was a Shanghai fantasy of the Western world through the mediation of Hollywood movies. Lianhua's early films were titled bilingually (Chinese and English). As there were almost no Westerners who attended Chinese films in Shanghai, these English titles were there more to provide a Westernized aura than to serve any real function.

The next film directed by Bu Wancang, *Peach Blossom Weeps Tears of Blood*, had a very different orientation. A rich boy from the city has been in love with a poor girl from the village since childhood. After growing up they secretly get married, and she becomes pregnant. But the mother of the young man refuses to accept a daughter-in-law of such low social status; she prohibits her son from seeing her again and terminates the employment of the girl's father. Under severe hardships she gives birth to a daughter and dies. After her death, the rich lady finally wakes up from her feudalist bias and accepts the love of her son. At the end of the film we are shown the corpse of the village girl buried in the land of the well-off, which is witnessed by the two families. Another happy ending.

It is important to notice Bu Wancang's transition from *A Spray of Plum Blossoms* to *Peach Blossom Weeps Tears of Blood*. Neither of the movies could be considered as left-wing films because of their reactionary endings: at the end of *A Spray of Plum Blossoms* the bandits are taken over by the warlord and become part of his army, and *Peach Blossom Weeps Tears of Blood* portrays the poor reconciled with the rich. But the later film had a clear consciousness of class difference which was completely absent in the first one (the bandit himself also came from a rich family). In fact, Bu Wancang admitted in an interview: "*Spray of Plum Blossoms* was a box office hit at that time. It was particularly popular among female spectators. However, intellectuals and students criticized the film severely."[28] It is obvious that the director oriented his new film *Peach Blossom Weeps Tears of Blood* from a completely different ideological perspective. The rich and the poor were from the very beginning polarized in the film, and this opposition was paired with other dichotomies, like city and village, man and woman, corruption and purity, in order to illustrate a clear division between the powerful and the powerless. However, this class boundary was not sustained all the way through. In the beginning of the film when the children-protagonists were shown playing together, a title was inserted: "Class distinction doesn't exist among children." The burial at the end also suggested a reconciliation of class differences. The film promoted pure and sincere human relationships, like childhood friendship and romantic love, which could emancipate human beings from the segregation of class society. Although the later left-wing critics would not approve such reactionary readings of current Chinese society, the early consciousness of class difference in cinema prior to the 1932 movement as shown in this film should be noted.

Lianhua was highly affected by the 1932 Japanese barrage of Shanghai, an event I will illustrate in the next section. Its Studio 4 was completely destroyed, and the entire Lianhua faced immediate financial difficulties. Fortunately, Lianhua was able to maintain itself and continued to produce films of high quality in 1932. Sun Yu's *Ye meigui* (Wild Rose) and *Huoshan qingxue* (Loving Blood of the Volcano), Cai Chusheng's *Fenhongse de meng* (Pink Dream), Shi Dongshan's *Fendou* (The Struggle), and Bu Wancang's *Rendao* (Humanity) all achieved good box office results. Among them *Humanity* was the most successful one. In Shanghai the film's first-round screening in Beijing Theater lasted for eleven consecutive days (October 5-15). It broke the record of the first-round screening periods of all films, Chinese or imported, in the city,[29] as most films then stayed first-round for only several days and quickly moved to their second-round screenings with lower ticket prices. Newspaper advertisements of the film also claimed that it broke all box office records in northern China. Because no copy of this film is available now, we are not able to examine the film and explain the reasons for its popularity. According to the synopsis provided in *The Development of Chinese Cinema*, the film tells a story about the son of a farmer being sent from the village to the city to study. There he marries a rich girl and is corrupted by the cosmopolitan life. He is later deserted by his wife and is forced to go home, but his entire family has already died in a famine. The film ends with the son kneeling down on the ground and begging for forgiveness from Heaven.[30]

Although *Humanity* was not a left-wing movie, the film helped the growth of left-wing film criticism as a collective force because it solicited so many negative criticisms from critics. Chen Wu's article "*Rendao* de yiyi" (The significance of *Humanity*) was an excellent piece of newspaper criticism that analyzed the film's ideology acutely yet in a brief and lucid manner. He criticized that the film chose to stay on the level of individuals and families and, as a result, failed to discover the real socio-economic cause of the famine. He also compared the film's dismal ending with the promising one in Ding Ling's novel *Shui* (Water), another narrative work that deals with natural disaster.[31] Chen Wu argued that the novel was much more politically progressive as its ending portrayed the masses bravely confronting the raging flood while the protagonist in *Humanity* was left alone in desperation under darkness. This type of film analysis was new to ordinary newspaper readers at that time; more and more cinemagoers would be affected by this type of ideological reading as more film analysis took this direction. However, this type of analysis would also soon begin to re-produce itself perpetually and was applied to every single movie more or less as a trendy act.

The Japanese Invasion

Although China did not officially declare war on the Japanese until July 1937, the dawn of the Sino-Japanese war should indeed be dated back to September 18, 1931, a date well known to most Chinese. The Japanese army began their military invasion of China on this day and occupied the three provinces in the Northeast, the area also known as Manchuria.[32] Although unaffected physically by the war, the Shanghai film industry was under severe economic threat because most spectators were no longer interested in cinema. The director Hu Peng mentions in his autobiography that: "after the 'September 18 Incident,' the entire Shanghai was involved in endless anti-Japanese protests. The business of cinema suffered from serious recessions."[33]

Because of the Japanese new Manchurian territory, the Soviet Union also began to face the Japanese military threat along its southern border; the Moscow leaders were happy to see a war taking place between China and Japan, releasing the military tension between the Soviet army and the Japanese. On the other hand, a second United Front between the CCP and the GMD was inevitable if China declared war. Either one of these consequences, Soviet Union's easing of war threat or a new United Front with the communists, might cause an immediate revival of the CCP which would threaten the sovereignty of the Nationalist government. After all, China had no confidence that they could defeat the Japanese army. GMD decided to adopt diplomatic efforts rather than military actions to reclaim the land. On May 5, 1932, the Chinese government made an agreement for a cessation of hostilities with the Japanese and ordered both the army and all Chinese people not to respond with anger and hatred to the Japanese. Instead, the spearhead was pointed at the Communists directly. The slogan "*Xian annei, hou rangwai*" (Internal pacification before resistance to the external attack) was raised to legitimate the government in prioritizing the annihilation of CCP in the national agenda.[34]

As I have mentioned, this act provoked another surge of anger from the Chinese intellectuals against the ruling power. The economic difficulties of the country caused great discontent among the people, particularly among the younger citizens who had the most exalted ideals regarding the future of both their lives and the country. The 1927 massacre had already thrown the intellectuals' confidence in the Nationalist government into question; the government's timid response to the Japanese invasion further reinforced this antipathy. This general atmosphere of hostility among the younger intellectuals provided a fertile soil for leftist ideology to take hold and grow.

If the "September 18 Incident" aroused patriotism among the Shanghai intellectuals, the "January 28 Event" simply threw the entire city into utter anger and despair. Four months after its invasion to the Northeast, the Japanese Air Force bombarded Shanghai beginning on the 28th of January the next year, and this barrage lasted for more than a month. Eight film studios and seven movie theaters in the city were destroyed—a complete devastation to the film industry.[35] The film companies, which chose to maintain their fragile business after the barrage, had to look for new strategies and production plans to help them regain the income lost on account of the destruction. Their continuing survival depended on their ability to draw spectators back into cinemas.

The Urge for a New Cinema

As I have mentioned, the Chinese cinema in the late 1920s was dominated by period films. According to incomplete statistics, there were more than seventy-five period films made in the two years 1927 and 1928 alone.[36] However, the Chinese spectators were soon exhausted by this flood of period films with similar plots and images. The genre that replaced them was also a branch of period film; this new trend of swordsman film (*wuxia pian*) simply added some Chinese martial arts and special visual effects into the repeating stories. Pornography and violence were also put into the films relentlessly and irresponsibly. As one may well expect, the spectators' excitement could not be maintained for long. As the appeal of these movies waned, the Japanese invasions in 1931 further splashed water onto the dying flame. The spectators had lost their appetite for martial arts in cinema while violence was all too real and too close for them.

The death sentence on the swordsman films was indeed officially announced by the Nationalist government. The increasing violence and pornography shown in these films had aroused public condemnation since the beginning of this trend. The government for the first time was forced to issue a Film Inspection Law (*Dianying jiancha fa*) in November 1930. The most important section in this law is Article 2. It reads:

II. Films of the following categories cannot be shown:
1. Films that impugn the dignity of the Chinese race;
2. films that violate the "Three Principles of the People" (*Sanmin zhuyi*);[37]
3. films that damage the culture of virtue (*shanliang fengsu*) and public order; and
4. films that advocate superstitions.[38]

The Cinematographic Yearbook of China in 1934 listed the names of sixty films which were banned from public screening between 1931 and 1934.[39] Fifty-two of them (more than 86 percent) violated enactment 2.3; that is to say, the Inspection Committee considered these films as harmful to the traditional Chinese culture and public order. This was indeed an extremely broad and subjective classification, and films of many different kinds could fit into this category. But according to newspaper and journal reports at that time, while some Hollywood films like *The Ten Commandments* and *Ben-Hur* were not allowed to be screened in the name of anti-superstition, most of the films being banned were swordsman films.[40] If the gradual distaste for period movies among the general public was the general driving force urging the industry to abandon their established ways of making films, this censorship policy demanded for the movie industry to break new grounds at once.

There were other reasons for spectators to stay away from cinema in 1931 and 1932. For the people in Shanghai, losing the three provinces in the Northeast was more than a sentimental issue. These areas had been a big market for Chinese products, and their purchasing power had supported a large number of businesses in Shanghai. The Japanese occupation cut off most of the economic tides between this new colony of Japan and the mainland. The establishment of *Manchuguo* under Japan's colonization was a big shock to the already fragile Chinese economy. The impending war between China and Japan as well as the increasing threat from the communists also forced the Nationalist government to spend a larger amount of money on military preparedness. Global economic recession and the severe corruption among officials in the government further deflated the economy. The number of spectators attending movies as a result dropped significantly in the period 1931-1932.

However, the city Shanghai would not tolerate this situation for too long. Shanghai's popular culture soon began another surge of development. Traditional Peking Opera, Western spoken drama, Broadway musicals, and other kinds of variety shows began to flourish once again after the barrage. The radio culture burgeoned, and hundreds of periodicals, serious or popular, were published in the city weekly, which in turn shaped and were shaped by the flourishing advertising culture.[41] New commodities were introduced to the market on a daily basis, which however were never enough to satisfy the ever-expanding consumption desire of the middle class of the city population. Both the intellectual and the popular culture came back vehemently right after the 1931 bombing. As a quintessential form of western and modern entertainment, cinema inevitably was included in this prosperous cultural landscape. After the great depression of the movie industry in the beginning of the 1930s, a new cinema culture was obviously developing out of the crisis. Many new theaters were constructed in the beginning of the decade to satisfy the great demand from the public in movies.[42] The one who could successfully grasp this opportunity to introduce new ideas to the cinema market was likely to be the one to dominate the continual development of the sprouting new cinema culture.

The First Left-Wing Intellectuals' Attention to Cinema

As I have discussed, the relationship between the movie industry and the Chinese intelligentsia in the 1920s was one of mutual apathy, if not aversion. While most of the filmmakers had no interest in listening to the intellectual debates inside the ivory tower, almost all educated people disliked the "corrupt" film industry. The first left-wing intellectual who took notice of cinema was probably Zheng Boqi.[43] In 1928 he used the pen name He Dabai to publish an article "Geming wenxue de zhanye" (The battlefield of revolutionary literature) in a literary publication.[44] A small section of the article was devoted to a brief discussion of some current Western films shown in China. He argued that the hidden corrupt ideology of these films can only be detected by a new form of "Revolutionary literary criticism" in which imperialism, fascism, and class struggles were taken into consideration. This aversion to Western cinema climaxed in 1930 when Lu Xun translated a chapter of Iwasaki Akira's *Film and Capitalism* in the journal *Mengya* (Sprouting).[45] And in the "Translator's Words" Lu Xun severely attacked Hollywood films as a tool of American imperialism to gain control of China's culture and economy.[46]

Although a left-wing cultural movement had been launched full-fledged in Shanghai during the late 1920s, none of the CCP leaders took notice of the Chinese film industry at that time. Qu Qiubai was the first Party leader to remark directly on the local cinema in China. In his article "Pulo dazhong wenyi de xianshi wenti" (Some real problems in popular culture) he briefly touched on the Chinese cinema at that time and described the popular swordsman films as "full of corrupt feudalist devils and the ethics of small grocery markets—the capitalist no-money-no-food ideology."[47] To Qu Qiubai, the current Chinese cultural world was in a chaotic and sinister situation; cinema could be seen as a reflection of this bafflement.

Neither did Zheng Boqi nor Lu Xun nor Qu Qiubai comment on the production of left-wing Chinese films, but their criticisms of American and Chinese films in the late 1920s and early 1930s revealed their general attitude toward cinema as a whole—it was a greenhouse for feudalist and capitalist ideologies. In order to expose the corrupt ideas inherent in these films, intellectuals needed to adopt a critical methodology in which concepts of class struggle and other Marxist theories were utilized. The three writers set their own writings as examples for later critics to follow, who should continue to reveal the negative effects of cinema. They believed that while these criticisms would lessen the films' harm to society, these writings could also help to educate their readers about the hidden logic of capitalist culture.

Although a number of film journals printed in the 1920s, almost all of them were designed as leisure reading. Serious articles about cinematic art could also be found occasionally, but most of them were about techniques of movie making or the relationship between cinema and society; there were hardly any writings devoted to the systematic evaluation and criticism of individual films. The above writings can be seen as forerunners of left-wing intellectuals' participation in cinema; the writers all took a role similar to what we today call film critics, although this term did not yet exist in China at that time. The writings successfully modeled themselves as effective forces of interrogation and intervention to the established cinematic discourse. Similar to many prominent left-wing cinema movements in many other parts of the world, this Chinese progressive cinema began in the form of theory and criticism, which developed vehemently in the beginning of the 1930s.

Diansheng ribao (Diansheng Daily) witnessed the first attempts of film criticism in a Chinese newspaper.[48] The popularity of these criticisms in *Diansheng* was observed by other editors, and film sections soon were added to their newspapers in order to promote sales. In addition to this economic factor, the left-wing dramatists also took notice of cinema and planned to engage in this industry through collective action. Before they could actually produce their films, the first step they chose was to criticize the existing ones. Many of the dramatist-intellectuals took up columns in the newspaper's film sections and organized themselves into powerful critical voices. No matter how brief and subjective these writings were, many readers took them as the authorized reference to guide their film-going activities.[49] Beginning in the early 1930s, critics commented on almost every single film being shown, particularly on the local productions, and many of them were criticized in a derogatory manner. No film companies or filmmakers could ignore this growing power of newspaper film criticism which was mostly dominated by left-wing intellectuals.

The most influential left-wing critics in the 1930s included Ling He (Shi Linghe), Chen Wu (Wang Chenwu), Lu Si, Shu Yan, and Tang Na. Although they were all affiliated with the Party, many times they disagreed with each others' writings and created a liberal and relatively open atmosphere for criticism. They used their different pen names to publish essays in different newspapers and journals, including those newspapers directly controlled by the GMD like *Chen bao* (Morning Daily), *Min bao* (People's Daily), and *Zhonghua ribao* (China's Daily).[50] In addition to *Shen bao 's* (Shanghai Daily) "*Dianyi congkan*" (The Film Page) and *Morning Daily*'s "*Meiri dianying*" (Films of Everyday), other important newspaper pages and columns for film criticism in the 1930s included, "*Dianying shibao*" (Film Daily) in *Shi bao* (Times), "*Hei yanjing*" (Black Eyes) in *Xinye bao* (New Evening Daily), "*Xin Shanghai*" (New Shanghai) in *Shishi xin bao* (New News Daily), "*Ying tan*" (Film Talks) in *Min bao* (People's Daily), and "*Yihai*" (Sea of Art) in *Xinwen bao* (News Daily). There were also numerous journals and magazines publishing film criticisms and essays related to cinema and its social role. Most of these writings were done in an imprecise and subjective way, as almost all newspaper writings are, but a number of them were intelligent and theoretically sound. Although most of these criticisms remained impressionistic and nonscholarly, the criticism in vogue created an encouraging atmosphere to elevate the social status of cinema and prepared a fertile soil for the actual production of left-wing cinema.

Notes

1. In order to accommodate the many different events and debates into the limited space of these two chapters, some details must be sacrificed. I apologize for any simplification of history, but some of the seemingly factual delineation I address in these two chapters will be further discussed and complicated in the other parts of the book.

2. For a general introduction of the May Fourth Movement, see Liu Yu-sheng's *The Crisis of Chinese Consciousness: Radical Anti-Traditionalism in the May Fourth Era* (Madison: University of Wisconsin Press, 1979).

3. Wang-chi Wong, *Politics and Literature in Shanghai: The Chinese League of Left-Wing Writers, 1930-36* (Manchester: Manchester University Press, 1991), 9.

4. For a detailed history of the left-wing cultural movement in the 1930s, read Wang-chi Wong's book.

5. For details about the struggle of CCP after the purge, read Jerome Ch'en, "The Communist Movement 1927-1937," in *The Cambridge History of China, vol. 13, Republic China 1912-1949, Part 2*, ed. John K. Fairbank and Albert Feuerwerker (Cambridge: Cambridge University Press, 1986), 168-203. For a general and comprehensive history of CCP, see *History of the Chinese Communist Party: A Chronology of Events (1919-1990)*, compiled by the Party History Research Centre of the Central Committee of the Chinese Communist Party (Beijing: Foreign Language Press, 1991).

6. Although Qu Qiubai was appointed as the Chief Secretary of the Party replacing Chen Duxiu after the 1927 event, Qu considered himself more a literary person than a political leader. For his self-purgation, see his passionate essay "Duoyu de hua" (Excessive words) in *Qu Qiubai Wenji*, vol. 7 (Beijing: Renmin, 1991), 693-723.

7. Li Suyuan and Hu Jubin, *Zhongguo wusheng dianying shi* (History of Chinese Silent Cinema) (Beijing: Zhongguo dianying, 1996), 81.

8. This is an established view about the current film industry in the 1920s that could not be completely verified, because only very few films made during that time are available now. But there are more recent academic efforts devoted to reconstruct the 1920s' film culture. See Zhang Zhen's articles: "Teahouse, Shadowplay, Bricolage: *Laborer's Love* and the Question of Early Chinese Cinema," in *Cinema and Urban Culture in Shanghai, 1922-1943*, ed. Yingjin Zhang (Stanford: Stanford University Press, 1999), 27-50, "Bodies in the Air: Magic of Science and the Fate of the Early 'Martial Arts' Film in China" *Post Script* 20, nos. 2 and 3 (Winter/Spring 2001): 43-60, "An Amorous History of the Silver Screen: The Actress as Vernacular Embodiment in Early Chinese Film Culture" *Camera Obscura* 16, no. 3 (2001): 229-63. For a Chinese reference, see Dong Xinyu's *Kan yu beikan zhijian: dui Zhongguo wusheng dianying de wenhua yanjiu* (Between looking and being looked at: Cultural studies of Chinese silent cinema) (Beijing: Shifan, 2000).

9. *ZDFS*, vol. 1, 53-57.

10. Ke Ling, *Ke Ling dianying wencun* (Beijing: Zhongguo dianying, 1992), 286-302. Rpt., *ZZDY*, 902-13.

11. Paul Pickowicz, "Melodramatic Representation and the 'May Fourth' Tradition of Chinese Cinema," in *From May Fourth to June Fourth: Fiction and Film in Twentieth-Century China*, ed. Wang David Derwei and Ellen Widmer (Cambridge, Mass.: Harvard University Press, 1993), 296.

12. This statement has been so frequently quoted that it has become a cliché. The original can be found in *Samoe vazhnoe iz vsekh iskusstv. Lenin o kino* (Moscow: Iskusstvo, 1963), 124.

13. An acquaintance of his called this decision a "prostitution of art." See *Hong Shen wenji* (Writings of Hong Shen), vol. 4 (Beijing: Zhongguo xiju, 1957), 514.

14. However, the social status of "spoken drama" (*hua ju*) and "civilized play" (*wenming xi*) varied tremendously in the 1930s. Although both were developed from the same root, spoken drama was considered a form of entertainment of the lowbrow popular culture while the former was considered an elitist art. And most people at that time considered cinema as a branch of civilized play instead of spoken drama. Readers interested in the contemporary drama scene can consult Constantine Tung and Colin Mackerras, eds. *Drama in the People's Republic of China* (New York: SUNY Press, 1987), Chen Xiaomei, *Acting the Right Part: Political Theater and Popular Drama in Contemporary China, 1966-1996* (Honolulu: University of Hawaii, 2002), and Ge Yihong, ed., *Zhongguo huaju tongshi* (History of Chinese dialogue drama) (Beijing: Wenhua yishu, 1990).

15. The Chinese name of the play is *Shaonainai de shanzi* (The fan of young Madame). A copy of the script is printed in *Hong Shen wenji*, vol. 1, 103-80.

16. For details about the production process of this film, please read Tian Han's *Yingshi zhuihuai lu* (Memories about the events in cinema) (Beijing: Zhongguo dianying, 1981) and Gu Menghe's "Yi Tianhan tongzhi zai Nanguo she de dianying chuangzuo" (Memory of comrade Tian Han's film production in Nanguo Society) *Dianying yishu* (Film art) 93 (April 1980): 56-57.

17. Li Suyuan and Hu Jubin, *Zhongguo wusheng dianying shi*, 198.

18. *SB*, Dec. 9, 1932

19. Zhu Jian, *Hu Die* (Lanzhou: Lanzhou Daxue, 1996), 74.

20. Yu Muyun, *Xianggong dianying shihua* (History of Hong Kong Cinema), vol. 1 (Hong Kong: Ciwenhua tang, 1996), 159-62.

21. Li Shek, the son of Li Minwei, interview by author, Hong Kong, Jan. 16, 1997.

22. Sun Yu, *Dalu zhi ge* (Song of the big road) (Taipei: Yuanliu, 1990), 87.

23. Li Minwei's unpublished diary, provided by his son Li Shek.

24. The investors of Lianhua included, among others, He Dong, the allegedly richest man in Hong Kong at that time, Xiong Xiling, the former chair of the GMD government's Executive Council, Huang Yicuo, a famous businessman in the printing industry and later supported the different publications of the film company, and Luo Xuefu, father of Luo Mingyou and also the owner of a large trading company. See "Lianhua yingpian gongsi si nian jing lishi" in *The Cinematographic Yearbook of China*, ed. Zhongguo jiaoyu dianying xiehui (Association of Chinese cinema for education) (Nanjing: Zhongguo jiaoyu dianying xiehui, 1934), n. p.

25. Xianggong Yingye was a Hong Kong company. It was later assimilated by Lianhua and became its branch based in Hong Kong.

26. See his article "Wei guopian fuxing wenti jinggao tongye shu" (An open letter to the filmmaking industry fellows regarding "Reviving the National Cinema") *Yingxi zazhi* (Film magazine) 1, no. 9 (1930). Rpt., *ZWD*, 768-69.

27. Ji Bing, "Daxuesheng yu dianying" (University students and film) *Dianying* (Movie monthly) 5 (Dec. 20, 1930): 69-71.

28. *SB*, Sept. 23, 1933.

29. Because of the lack of box office records, the popularity of a film can only be proved by the length of its screening periods. For details, please see appendix 2.

30. *ZDFS*, vol. 1, 190-91.

31. The short story is anthologized in *Ding Ling wenji* (The writings of Ding Ling), vol. 2 (Changsha: Hunan renmin, 1982), 369-406.

32. For a detailed account of the Manchurian Incident, see Barbara Brooks, *Japan's Imperial Diplomacy: Consuls, Treaty Ports, and War in China, 1985-1938* (Honolulu: University of Hawaii Press, 2000), 117-59, and Akira Iriye, "Japanese Aggression and China's International Position, 1931-1949" in *The Cambridge History of China, vol. 13, Republic China 1912-1949, Part 2*, ed. John K. Fairbank and Albert Feuerwerker (Cambridge: Cambridge University Press, 1986), 492-504.

33. Hu Peng, *Wo yu Huang Feihong* (Me and Huang Feihong) (Hong Kong: Sanhe maoyi, 1995), 56.

34. For a general historical account of GMD's policy to the Japanese and the CCP, read Keiji Furuya, ed., *Chiang Kaishek: His Life and Times*, abridged and translated by Chun-ming Chang (New York: St. John's University Press, 1981).

35. The eight studios are Shanghai, Guxing, Youlian, Changming, Fudan, Huaju, Haifeng, and Lianhua Studio 4; the seven movie theaters are Xin'ailun huodung yingxi yuan, Shanghai daxiyuan, Audi'an daxiyuan, Shije yingxi yuan, Zhabei yingxi yuan, Zhongxing daxiyuan, and Baoxing yingxi yuan. See Li Suyuan and Hu Jubin, *Zhongguo wusheng dianying shi* (History of Chinese silent cinema) (Beijing: Zhongguo dianying, 1996), 284-85.

36. Li and Hu, *Zhongguo wusheng dianying shi*, 210.

37. It is the Party doctrine of the GMD written by Sun Yat-sen. Its English translation: *San Min Chu I: The Three Principles of The People*, trans. Frank W. Price, ed. L.T. Chen (New York: Da Capo Press, 1975); originally published by Shanghai's Commercial Press, 1928.

38. *ZZDY*, 1089-90.

39. "*Dianying jiancha weiyuan hui jiancha yingpian qingxing*" (The censorship of the film censoring committee) in Zhongguo jiaoyu dianying xiehui (Association of Chinese cinema for education) ed. *The Cinematographic Yearbook of China*, n. p. This yearbook was published in 1934 only and had no subsequent issues.

40. For example, see Jin Gaipu, "Shenguai pian chajin hou—jinhou de dianying jie xiang nali zou?" (After the censorship of the films of spirits and uncanny—where should our cinema go?) *Yingxi shenghou* (Life in cinema) 1, no. 32 (1931). Rpt., *ZWD*, 666-67.

41. For a more complete and detailed description of the Shanghai print culture, see Leo Ou-fan Lee, *Shanghai Modern: The Flowering of a New Urban Culture in China, 1930-1945* (Cambridge, Mass.: Harvard University Press, 1999), 120-50. For Shanghai's advertising culture, see Sherman Cochran's acute analysis in "Marketing Medicine and Advertising Dreams in China 1900-1950," in *Becoming Chinese: Passages to Modernity and Beyond*, ed. Wen-Hsin Yeh (Berkeley: University of California Press, 2000), 62-97.

42. Lee, *Shanghai Modern*, 84.

43. There were also a few literary figures, like Tian Han and Yu Dafu, who had written on cinema in the twenties. For example, in 1924 Yu Dafu had already written the article "Ruhe de jiudu Zhongguo de dianying" (How to save Chinese cinema) discussing the importance of nationalizing the Chinese cinema. *Yinxing* (Silver Star) 13 (1927). Rpt., *ZWD*, 715-16.

44. *Jixing* (Odd shape), (June 15, 1928).

45. Lu Xun only translated a part of the original book and had it titled "Xiandai dianying yu youchan jieji" (Modern cinema and the property class). The article and his notes was first published in *Mengya* (Sprouting) 1, no. 3 (March 1930) with a pseudonym

"L." Rpt., *Lu Xun quanji* (Complete writings of Lu Xun), vol. 4 (Beijing: Renmin wenxue, 1989), 383-413.

46. However, Lu Xun's diary showed that among the 149 movies he attended between 1916 to 1936, 127 of them were Hollywood films. See *Lu Xun yu dianying* (Lu Xun and Cinema), ed. Liu Siping and Xing Zuwen (Beijing: Zhongguo dianying, 1981), 221-30.

47. *Qu Qiubai wenji* (Writings of Qu Qiubai), vol. 3 (Beijing: Renmin, 1991), 856.

48. See Li Li (Chen Wu), "Shanghai dianying kanwu de jiantao" (A review of Shanghai film publications), *Minbao* (People's daily), May 1934. Rpt., *ZZDY*, 127.

49. Ke Ling, interview by author, Shanghai, China, Nov. 6, 1996.

50. See Shu Yan, "Yi jiu you" (Memories on an old friend), in *Lun Xia Yan* (Discussion on Xia Yan), ed. Zhongguo dianying yishu yanjiu zhongxin (Chinese film art research center) (Beijing: Zhongguo dianying, 1989), 380.

2

The Left-wing Cinema Movement

The opening page of the official history of the left-wing cinema movement should start with "The Directive of the Most Recent Activities" of the Chinese Left-wing Dramatists Association (*Zhongguo zuoyi xiju jia lianmeng*).[1] This Association was established in January 1931 as a branch organization of the left-wing cultural movement. In September of the same year they published this document announcing the major goals they planned to achieve. Among the six tasks listed in the document, the last three were partly related to film; these suggestions witnessed the first left-wing collective strategic involvement in cinema.

4. In addition to drama, this association should also play an active part in cinema. Besides writing film scripts for and sending our members to different film companies, we should also prepare funding to produce our own films. At the moment, in order to escape government censorship, our scripts should continue to reveal [rather than directly criticize] social problems. There are many existing subjective and objective difficulties; we can only use "small-scale cinema" (*xiaoxin dianying*) to record the situations of factory workers and peasantry.

5. Our Association should actively organize lectures in dramatic art in order to elevate the intellectual level and technical knowledge of the members and to prepare a firm foundation for the left-wing theater. We should also organize a Film Research Group, bringing in progressive performers and technicians in order to establish a solid ground to prepare for the forthcoming Chinese left-wing cinema movement.

6. In order to promote proletarian class struggle through the teaching of theater theory, our Association should establish a set of instructive principles for our members to follow. Because of the pressing demands, we will create and translate different

revolutionary scripts. Meanwhile, we shall also look into the present stage of the Chinese cinema movement in a critical way in order to prepare the upcoming "Proletarian Cinema Movement" for class struggle against the bourgeoisie and feudalism.[2]

This document indicated the left-wing intellectuals' sincere enthusiasm to use films to attain political ends. They planned to take control of the existing film companies first by writing screenplays for the companies and by sending their members to work in film studios. Ultimately they wanted to produce their own films and launch a "Proletarian Cinema Movement," although the directive did not at all explain the term. The directive only hinted that Chinese society at that time was not ready to start this movement. To prepare for a solid foundation, they should first concentrate on training and scriptwriting. An extensive and accurate revision of the ideological components in the current movie industry was also essential. For the actual production of films, the directive only indicated that they should adopt a less elaborate format of filmmaking in order to promote cinema among factory workers and peasantry, encouraging them to be both the spectators and the subject matter. This "small scale cinema" may very well refer to the 16mm productions.

In fact, before this directive, the dramatist Shen Xiling, later an important left-wing film director, had already written about left-wing filmmaking. Using the name Ye Chen, he wrote an article "Guanyu dianying de jige yijian" (Several views on film) in *Shalun* (Siren), a journal edited by Xia Yan. In this article Shen Xiling was rather precise in explaining his understanding of a left-wing cinema movement, and he used the term "small-scale cinema" to illustrate his ideal:

> The implementation of the "small-scale cinema"—this is one of the most urgent plans we have to execute. This idea might not have yet been introduced to Chinese people. . . . The film was only with a width of 16mm [instead of 35mm]. . . . This filmmaking suits our current material resources and deserves our actions.
> a.   Cheap. Its camera costs only about two hundred *yuan*. Its film is about three times cheaper than the regular ones.
> b.   The length of the films is about two and a half times shorter than the regular ones.
> c.   All equipment is smaller and easier to carry.
> d.   The distance between the screen and the projector is shorter; the films can be shown in most indoor spaces.
> This "small-scale cinema" can expeditiously attack the present film industry, and it can also easily be promoted in factories and villages.
> . . . I hope that after this piece of writing, we will soon have some more concrete and practical plans about the implementation of this cinema.[3]

Unfortunately, the 1931 Dramatists' Directive, in its brief and imprecise manner, was the only immediate follow-up on this original suggestion of Shen Xiling. In 1933 Party member Chen Wu also advocated the production of documentaries and shorts in order to reach a bigger audience; but this suggestion remained only a suggestion.[4] The film movement simply failed to grow into a proletarian cinema as wished by the CCP. In fact, the ideas of Chen Wu and Shen Xiling were doomed to be impracticable because the CCP was too poor to support any expensive cultural activities of this sort. Xia Yan recounted in the 1950s that: "The Communist Party [in the 1930s] was a poor-off organization without even a spare penny to spend. It was impossible for the Party to invest in the film industry as it has today."[5] Without any support from the Party, the young filmmakers themselves were not able to raise funds to do any independent filmmaking; Tian Han's failure in his production of *Going to the People* was a good example. But this early writing of Shen Xiling deserves our attention because it had provided an alternative, although only conceptually, to the later left-wing cinema movement. What if 16mm film had been used? What if films were shot among and screened for the proletariat? We might never have had this left-wing cinema but something closer to the Italian Neo-Realism in the 1950s or the French New Wave in the 1960s. Documentaries might have been developed on a much larger scale, and Chinese audiences might have been able to accept a wider range of styles in narrative films. Aesthetically, it might have freed up the stability of many cinematic techniques designed for narrative films and allowed more experimentation. Politically, this film movement might have been more intimately controlled by the Party and able to present a strong revolutionary ideology more forcefully. In fact, a real extensive proletarian film movement might have been realized for the first time anywhere in history. But none of these events happened, and the left-wing cinema movement continued its own historical trajectory.[6]

The Film Critics Group and the Film Group

Although the left-wing film production would never be realized as Shen Xiling and the Dramatists' Directive had suggested, left-wing film criticism bloomed in Shanghai as promised. In accordance with the Party directives, the Film Critics Group (*yingpingren xiaozu*; some used the name *yingping xiaozu*) was established within the Dramatists Association in mid-1932,[7] an organization which can be seen as a direct response to the Dramatists' Directive. Many have confused this group with another film organization established directly by the Party in 1933. For example, *The Development of Chinese Cinema* inaccurately notes that "the underground CCP established the Party's film group in 1932."[8] The film group established in 1932 was not a CCP organization but was the Film Critics Group I mentioned above. According to Xia Yan, this Film Critics Group was a loose association with no fixed members; it organized informal gatherings for film critics and other people who were interested in film criticism. They held irregular tea-meetings and forums, and participants discussed issues related to film criticism. This group would last till the 1940s. Xia Yan commented that the Film Critics Group deserved much historical attention because "this team helped [us] to pave a clear road to progressive cinema. It also showed the public that left-wing cultural activities were not closed-door businesses that rejected co-operation with people from other parts of society."[9]

The Party's film group that was mentioned in *The Development of Chinese Cinema* was in fact the Film Group (*Dianying xiaozu*) established by CCP's Cultural Committee (*Wenhua weiyuanhui*) in March 1933. Because the group was an underground political organization, its structure was different from the open-membered Critics Group, and it was comprised of only five members: Xia Yan (himself also a member of the Cultural Committee), Ling He, Chen Wu, Situ Huimin, and Qian Xingcun (a.k.a. A Ying). They were all Party members actively involved in the film industry: Chen Wu and Ling He were famous film critics; Xia Yan and Qian Xingcun were scriptwriters; Situ Huimin was a set designer and later became a sound recordist and director. Tian Han and Yang Hansheng, although both were Party members involved in the film industry, were not invited to this group because they had other responsibilities in the Party.[10] The group kept a close connection with Qu Qiubai and Yan Hansheng (Secretary of the Cultural Committee); consequently their decisions and actions were seen as representing the Party's policy. Unlike the Critics Group, which would continue for a much longer period, the Film Group basically dissolved when the CCP was besieged by the government in 1935.

It is important for us to differentiate the different functions and historical positions of the two groups, for they helped in clarifying the two major parties participating in this movement. Both groups were core organizations of the cinema movement, but they were established according to completely different agendas. The Film Critics Group was a public cultural gathering, and it wel-comed all interested people to join discussions about film and film criticism. But the Film Group was a strictly Party organization with a concrete political agenda that corresponded closely to other decisions of the CCP. Many film scholars equate the left-wing cinema movement with the 1933 Film Group and consider the movement a direct product of the Party's guidance.[11] However, CCP's Film Group was in fact established in March 1933, at a time when the left-wing in-tellectuals had already gained a strong foothold in the film industry and the new Chinese cinema had already attracted a large audience and social attention. Alt-hough the group had its own historical significance, particularly in conceptual-izing a concrete film policy for the Party and establishing the theoretical direc-tions for left-wing film critics, the Film Group did not alter the development of the film movement to any significant degree. In fact, the 1933 Film Group was more a reaction to, or a product of, this film movement than it was its cause. Instead, the 1932 Film Critics Group had a more important historical role in shaping the movement because it helped in creating a genial and enthusiastic environment for film critics from different backgrounds to gather together and to promote a sense of urgency in introducing new directions for the current cinema. After all, there would never be any one single force powerful enough to direct a historical event of such scale.

Two other major tasks the two groups achieved were the introduction of the Soviet progressive cinema to Chinese readers and the translation of film theories into Chinese. These writings helped to prepare a stronger theoretical ground for China's own film productions. The most famous translated work was Vsvolod Pudovkin's *Film Techniques and Film Acting*. Xia Yan and Zheng Boqi translated parts of this work into *Dianying daoyan lun* (Film directing) and *Dianying jiaoben lun* (Film writing). They were first published in the newspaper *Morning Daily* beginning in July 1932. The two works were collected into one volume and published in 1933.[12] Xia Yan also recounted that in 1933 in *Morning Daily* alone there were more than fifty-five articles introducing and discussing the Soviet film industry.[13] There were also a large number of articles printed in other periodicals regarding all aspects of filmmaking. These writings certainly helped to elevate the cultural status of filmmaking in Chinese society.

Xia Yan basically headed both the film groups, and he himself became the bridge between the Party and the film industry. By the end of the 1920s, Xia Yan had become an active member in the CCP Cultural Committee and one of the leaders in the Chinese League of Left-wing Writers, the leading organization of the entire left-wing cultural movement in the 1930s. Xia Yan studied engineering in Japan and joined the CCP after coming back to China in 1927. He was not, strictly speaking, a writer at that time and had published no major creative writings until 1935, but he was chosen by the Party to work in literary circles because he had been working closely with the members of Sun Society, a major left-wing literary association, and he himself was interested in literature. But most would agree that the major reason for the Party to assign the young Xia Yan to such a crucial position was that he was on good terms with almost everybody, a very rare figure in the Chinese cultural world at a time when factionalism was rampant. After taking up the responsibilities of the Film Group, Xia Yan resigned from the Writer's League and concentrated his energy on cinema. His amiable and tolerant personality helped him to make many noteworthy friendships in the film industry; this encouraged the expansion and diversification of a film movement which otherwise might have been much narrower and less influential.[14]

Mingxing's Recruitment

In fact, both the Film Critics Group and the Film Group were established after one important event: the recruitment of Xia Yan, Qian Xingchun, and Zheng Boqi into the Mingxing Film Company. According to Xia Yan, in May 1932, Zhou Jianyun, one of the directing managers of Mingxing, contacted Qian Xingchun, Zhou Jianyun's hometown friend, and asked him to recruit three writers of the New Culture Movement to be Mingxing's script consultants. Qian Xingchun went to discuss this invitation from Mingxing with Xia Yan and Zheng Boqi. Although they found this offer unexpected, it was tempting, and the three went to seek advice from the Cultural Committee. This led to a debate among the Party's members: Tian Han was the first to express assent to this suggestion, but many members responded negatively because they found the film industry too corrupt for Party members to enter. Qu Qiubai finally approved this action after some serious thought, and he forewarned the three Party members "to be particularly cautious."[15] Huang Zibu, Zhang Fengwu, and Xi Naifang, the pseudonyms of Xia Yan, Qian Xingchun, and Zheng Boqi respectively, officially became members of the Mingxing Film Script Consulting Committee in the summer of 1932. In this committee the three, with several other filmmakers, began to create and rewrite many film scripts of Mingxing in the coming five years.

As literary writers who had never written any film scripts, the three Party members were ignorant about filmmaking. Without any formal training or experience, they began as cinema illiterates. As recounted by Xia Yan, there were not any detailed film scripts available at that time. The notes for performers and other technicians only provided very brief descriptions about the scenes in simple wording like "meeting" or "separation." Books on film writings were also lacking. They could only train themselves in the logic of filmmaking through watching as many films as possible.[16] Situ Huimin also recounted that the Party members began to befriend a number of young filmmakers in Mingxing and Lianhua, like Cai Chusheng, Shi Dongshan, Sun Yu, and Cheng Bugao, in order to, on the one hand, learn the techniques of filmmaking and, on the other, introduce them into left-wing thoughts.[17] History shows that their efforts were fruitful: the Party's members were able to both master the technique of filmmaking and transform the mentality of many of these young filmmakers, although we are not sure whether these were results of their friendships or simply the trends of intellectual circles.

This unexpected recruitment of Mingxing can be seen as the first step toward left-wing film production. As I have pointed out earlier, the entire film industry experienced severe financial difficulties in 1932 as spectators chose to stay away from cinema for various reasons. Mingxing's situation was the worst because of its earlier investment in upgrading its equipment to make sound movies and the unexpected box office failure of its major production, the six-part *Tixiao yinyuan* (Marriage in tears and laughter) in 1932. The company's financial difficulty is clearly shown in *The Cinematographic Yearbook of China* in 1934. The annual balance of the company from 1926-33 was listed in an article written by the company for the yearbook. The company had earned a profit constantly since 1928. But the profits fell suddenly from 19,969 *yuan* in 1931 to a negative 47,321 *yuan* in 1932.[18] This deep financial problem forced Mingxing to look for new ways to attract spectators immediately. Hong Shen was then working in Mingxing and on good terms with many members of the CCP. He therefore suggested the recruitment of progressive literary writers to help Mingxing to develop new screenplays; Hong Shen argued that new blood would attract new spectators.[19] Also, the box office success of Lianhua's films further persuaded the three bosses of Mingxing—Zhou Jianyun, Zheng Zhengqiu, and Zhang Shichuan—of the need of a new form of filmmaking, and they accepted this suggestion from Hong Shen and invited the assistance of left-wing intellectuals.

Ironically, without the capitalists' support, this alleged anti-capitalist cinema movement was inconceivable. But the collaboration between left-wing intellectuals and film companies also sharpened the sensitivities of the filmmakers to the tastes and values of the masses. The contract between Mingxing and the three Party members was based on nothing but profits; they could continue making films as long as their films were making money. This unspoken agreement was valid not only in Mingxing but in other film companies. The filmmakers had to be on the heels of the spectators to understand their values and psychology; attending the cinema to observe spectators' responses directly was one of the very few available ways for filmmakers to understand their clients. Sun Yu, Cai Chusheng, Cheng Bugao, and Xia Yan have all expressed their respect for the "taste" of general spectators. Thus this film movement belonged not only to the intelligentsia but also to a much broader base of the urban mass, a point I will repeatedly emphasize and investigate in the rest of the study.

The Explosion of Left-wing Cinema

The year 1933 was officially designated as the Year of Chinese Products (*Guohuo nian*). This was a government response to China's financial crisis in 1931 and 1932. Chinese people were encouraged to buy products made in China in order to reduce the outflow of Chinese capital and to regenerate the growth of the different national enterprises; a similar movement also began in the film industry to encourage spectators to attend Chinese movies. In fact, many people also called 1933 the "Year of Chinese Cinema" because a large number of local productions of high quality and new content appeared in the market. And as I have mentioned, many of the spectators who attended only Western movies began to pay attention to Chinese films mostly due to the success of Lianhua's new productions. The Association of Chinese Cinema Culture (*Zhongguo dianying wenhua xiehui*), the first film-art society in China, was also established in February of 1933. This was an organization with wide support from different film companies and filmmakers. Although the Association did not accomplish anything significant, the establishment of such a widely-supported organization in the commercial film industry was an enthusiastic symbolic gesture that indicated the filmmakers' collective dedication to create a new cinema. Thus 1933 can be seen as one of the most promising years in the history of Chinese cinema.

44

Chapter 2

On January 1, 1933, Mingxing put up a big advertisement in *Shanghai Daily* entitled "Mingxing yingpian gongsi yijiusansan nian de liangda jihua" (The two major plans of Mingxing Film Company for 1933). The first plan listed in the advertisement was to make a film which would summarize the five-thousand-year history of China; the other one was to make a series of narrative films promoting China's major industries, including silk, tea, coal, salt, etc. Readers of today and at that time might both speculate accurately that the first plan was simply too ambitious to be realized. However, regarding the second plan, three films were successfully produced: *Chuncan* (Spring Silkworms) (plate 2), *Yanchao* (Salt Tide) (plate 3), and *Xiangcao meiren* (Sweetgrass Beauty) (plate 4) for the silk, salt, and cigarette industries respectively. Mingxing, following Lianhua's success, was dedicated to changing the image of the company by emphasizing the social values and functions of cinema; entertaining elements were not mentioned at all in the entire half-page advertisement.

The first left-wing movie listed in *The Chinese Left-wing Cinema Movement* was in fact produced by Lianhua. *Sange modeng de nüxing* (Three Modern Women) (plate 5) was released in December of 1932 and became a highly popular film along with *Humanity* in 1932. This film was also directed by Bu Wancang, and Tian Han, using the pseudonym Chen Yu, wrote the script. Unlike Bu Wancang's earlier film *Humanity*, this new film attracted not only audience support but also accolades from left-wing critics. The newspaper advertisement of the film also quoted critics' compliments in order to attract readers' attention.[20] The film tells a story about the love affairs between a movie actor and three women who represent the three archetypes of contemporary Chinese womanhood: Yu Yu, a woman who frequents parties and balls; Chen Ruoying, a young infatuated fan who kills herself to express her unfulfilled love; and Zhou Shuzhen, the heroine, who successfully transforms herself from a petit bourgeois to a proletarian. Being recognized as the ground-breaking film of this movement, this film successfully portrayed the first revolutionary character Zhou Shuzhen in Chinese cinema who became an ideological model for later left-wing films to follow. The film was symbolic not only from the perspective of this film movement, but it was also one of the major works of Tian Han separating his two creative/ideological phases: from a May Fourth romantic artist to a committed socialist.

The films written and supervised by the three Party members in Mingxing were released in 1933 consecutively. The first was *Kuangliu* (Torrent), directed by Cheng Bugao and written by Xia Yan. Similar to *Humanity*, the film was structured around a real natural disaster: a flood of the Yangzi River in 1931. Cheng Bugao wished to produce a film using the documentary footage of the calamity he recorded in Hankou. After discussing the story with the new Mingxing Script Committee, Xia Yan decided to rewrite it and added elements of class struggle and social criticism into the story.[21] The film recounts the hero, a primary school teacher, leading the entire village to fight the flood while the rich father of his lover uses the name of charity to extort a large amount of money from the public. Although the film is no longer available, Xia Yan's original script is preserved, and in the text we see a carefully written film script with detailed camera positions and editing techniques.[22] In addition to new ideology, Xia Yan also introduced to the Mingxing company a new concept of scriptwriting. As expected, the film was warmly welcomed by the left-wing critics. Wu Cun called the film "the first one in our film history to successfully grasp reality, and it is accurate in detail as well as its progressive ideology."[23] In addition to this overwhelming critical success, the film also enjoyed strong box office receipts. There might be many reasons behind the success of the film: while Xia Yan certainly produced a film script of high quality, one should not overlook the spectators' interests in the flood footage which vividly documented the disaster. As the first attempt of the Party's members in the film industry, *Torrent* passed the entry test with distinction. The collaboration between Xia Yan and Mingxing was to continue gracefully until 1937. Cheng Bugao, a known director since the late 1920s, also started to "turn left" after this film and made some overt left-wing films, like *Qiancheng* (The future), *Tongchou* (Shared hate), and *Dao Xibei qu* (To the Northwest) (plate 6), which were all written by the three party members, in the two years.

Lianhua's *Chengshi zhi ye* (City Nights) (plate 7), the directing debut of Fei Mu, was also shown in March, just when *Torrent* was being screened. Both are listed as left-wing movies in *The Chinese Left-wing Cinema Movement*, although *Torrent* has been considered as a much more important left-wing film, and the box office records and critical acclaims received by *City Nights* outshone *Torrent*. Many critics and spectators were truly astonished by the talents of this young director: Fei Mu was only 27 years old then. The film was shown first-round in the Beijing Theater and Guanghua Theater together for twenty-two days, a record it kept for almost a year.[24]

Similar to *Torrent*, this film portrays a strong contrast between the rich and the poor. A capitalist intends to redevelop a ghetto into a dog-racing club. And the story is about how a man and his daughter living there suffer from this operation. The severe illness of the father and their dire financial situation force the daughter to sell herself to the son of the capitalist. At the end of the film both the son and the residents are forced to leave the city and together they go to a village to start a new life. In spite of the clear message of class struggle in the film, left-wing film historians were particularly annoyed by its ending. *The Development of Chinese Cinema* called this ending a "faked" ideological commitment because "it would only lead the mass to the illusion of the harmony of different classes," referring to the poor and the son of the capitalist living together cordially.[25] Unfortunately, neither the film nor the script of *City Nights* is available for us to study, and we cannot judge fairly how "left-wing" this film was. Judging from the unenthusiastic response from left-wing critics, Fei Mu likely produced this film independent of the influence of the Party's members in Mingxing. Although the film was not a CCP product and might not be passed as a thoroughly "politically correct" work, it clearly reflected the general dissatisfaction with class differences and other social injustices shared among intellectuals at that time.

Another major production of Mingxing in 1933 was *Spring Silkworms*. Xia Yan adapted this story from Mao Dun's short story of the same name.[26] Mao Dun was one of the leading writers at that time, and he was known particularly for his progressive socialist outlook. The story relates the downfall of a family of silkworm growers in order to describe the bankruptcy of the entire silk industry in China under the current foreign economic imperialism. According to the director Cheng Bugao, Mingxing invested a large amount of money in its production.[27] Both the film company and Xia Yan had high expectations for this film: Mingxing anticipated another box office success after *Torrent*; Xia Yan and his comrades wanted to associate left-wing cinema with left-wing literature in order to elevate the former's social status. Unfortunately, the film failed both of these expectations.

The film was shown in Xinguang Theater beginning on October 8, a day when two other Chinese films also debuted: Lianhua's *Xiao wan'er* (Little Toys) at Ka'erdeng Theater and Tianyi's *Zhengzha* (Struggling) at Beijing Theater. All three films were considered left-wing movies. *Spring Silkworms* closed on October 12, the earliest among the three. Considering the short screening period, the film must have failed at the box office, although it attracted a full house on the very first day of its screening.[28] On October 9, a half-page combined criticism of this film by five critics was published in the newspaper *Shanghai Daily*; Ling He, a member in the Party's Film Group, was among them.[29] They severely criticized the film's failure to present a clear message to the spectators. Their comments included: "There was not a single climax in the film; the spectators were not instructed to pay special attention to any parts of the story." "After watching the entire film we still could not figure out its central message." "The spectators could not be provoked by the film to act accordingly in reality." "The plot and the images were too boring and disorganized to present the severity of the real social situation." Not only did these comments reflect the feelings of the general spectators at that time, but they also revealed the critics' ideological frustration: the film just failed as a political tool. Although other left-wing critics immediately launched a pro-*Spring Silkworms* campaign the following day in other newspapers—and Ling He had to reevaluate the film and praise its positive elements the day after in *Shanghai Daily*[30]—the film certainly could not be considered a political success. However, many would agree that *Spring Silkworms* is a masterpiece from today's perspective. Artistically, its poetic ambience and the calm yet passionate depiction of the family should place the film into the highest class of silent movies. But the unenthusiastic response of critics and spectators instructed the emerging left-wing cinema to cast aside artistic ambitions and concentrate on cinema's clarity and emotional engagement.

The failure of this film also had a more important historical consequence: it heralded an apparent segregation between serious literature and cinema in this movement after this initial attempt of Xia Yan to bridge the two. In fact, Xia Yan himself admitted that in producing this film, "Cheng Bugao [, the director,] was too faithful to my script, and I was too faithful to the novel. As a result, this film might be 'too literature-like.' "[31] This comment suggested Xia Yan's belief in the separation between the two media; to him a film being "too literature-like" was derogatory. However, cinema was closely connected to popular literature in the 1920s. The "Mandarin Duck and Butterflies" (*yuanyang hudie pai*) writers were the first group of novelists to enter film industry; they successfully created many popular romances based on their pulp fictions.[32] Entering the late 1920s, most of the period films were adapted from traditional folk stories or the new swordsman novels. Many of these films were highly popular, to the point of even creating a new film genre.[33] However, as Ke Ling accurately pointed out, in the 1920s there had barely been any connection between writers-intellectuals and filmmakers, and no serious literature had been adapted into movies, a situation uncommon in other early cinemas. *Spring Silkworms* can be seen as the very first attempt to bridge the two fields. The film's failure only suggested the disconnection between Chinese cinema and serious literature in the 1930s but not a gap between films and popular writings. One of the possible explanations for this separation might be the failure of highbrow literature to reach the mass audience, a task commercial cinema had to fulfill. This failure once again indicated that this left-wing cinema was less an intellectual than a mass movement.

Mingxing produced twenty-seven films in 1933, thirteen of which are considered left-wing movies, including *Nüxing de nahan* (Women's Outcry) (plate 8), *Tieban honglei lu* (Iron plate and red tears), and *Shanghai ershishi xiaoshi* (Twenty-Four Hours in Shanghai) (plate 9). Lianhua also produced some remarkable films with left-wing ideology after *Three Modern Women*. Sun Yu continued to develop his "Poetic Cinema" in *Tianming* (Daybreak) and *Little Toys*.[34] While most of the young directors at that time were still searching for their individual approaches to filmmaking and shifting from one style to another, by 1933 Sun Yu had already developed a cinema with his own distinctive style; he could be considered as the first "auteur" filmmaker in Chinese film history. The collaboration between Bu Wancang and Tian Han also continued after *Three Modern Women*. Their *Muxing zhi guang* (Maternal radiance) in 1933 was another box office hit. According to Bu Wancang, his progression from *Humanity* to *Three Modern Women* and *Maternal Radiance* was an improvement of his filmmaking both in ideological and commercial terms. In an interview right after the screening of *Maternal Radiance*, the director commented:

> Starting from *Humanity*, I was getting really serious about my filmmaking. The result was a good box office. The company considered it a wonderful work. But after my sincere analysis of the critics' comments, I have found many failures in *Humanity*. In spite of its commercial success, it did not attract any new spectators [to watch Chinese films]. I changed my approach of filmmaking completely only when I made *Three Modern Women*. This helped to add thirty thousand head counts to set the box office record. There were another thirty thousand more who attended *Maternal Radiance*. This proves that we have to produce new types of films to attract new spectators.[35]

Although he was only thirty-four at that time, Bu Wancang was already one of the most respected film directors in the industry. His successful shift to left-wing cinema could be seen as a strong indicator of the new taste of film spectators. However, the active role played by certain individuals in the making of this cinema movement should also be noted. Although Tian Han only wrote two films for Lianhua, his efforts in changing Lianhua's political profile were significant.

Left-wing movies began to attract new spectators to Chinese films in 1933; by 1934 the two major film companies, Mingxing and Lianhua, were tasting real profits. Zheng Zhengqiu's *Zimei hua* (The Sisters) (plate 10) was released in February 1934 and set a record of sixty consecutive days in its first-round screening in Shanghai. This result was beyond the imaginations of the entire film industry at that time. This amazement was further amplified five months later when Cai Chusheng's *Yuguang qu* (The Fishermen's Song) (plate 11) set a new record of an eighty-four-day screening period. This record was to be maintained for a decade until Cai Chusheng himself broke it again with his *Yijiang chunshui xiang dong liu* (A Spring River Running to the East) in 1947, which is still considered by many as the single most popular Chinese film ever made.

Although neither of the two popular films was written or directed by any Party members, both *The Sisters* and *The Fishermen's Song* were considered left-wing productions because of their depictions of class oppression. *The Sisters* was an adaptation of Zheng Zhengqiu's civilized play *Guiren yu fanren* (The VIP and the Criminal). Zheng Zhengqiu was among the first in China making feature films and has been considered the Father of Chinese Cinema. Other than a committed artist, he was a typical Chinese intellectual who carried strong social responsibilities. Just before his death, he summed up his directing career: "As a film director, I always consider pedagogy essential in my films. . . . I never changed this principle throughout my filmmaking career."[36] But he was a reformer, not a revolutionary. Although Zheng Zhengqiu was famous for his films' liberal messages, like promoting women's liberation and criticizing social injustice toward the poor, he was not considered a leftist. The endings of his films were always reconciliation instead of confrontation—the poor pacified by the rich, or the suffering woman assimilated into the established gender structure, with *The Sisters* as a clear example. The film depicts the different fates of a pair of twin sisters: the older one grew up in the village with her mother under economic hardship and is later accused of homicide; the younger one grew up with her corrupted father in the city and is indulged in material comfort. They are antagonized when they meet again because of the different classes they belong to. At the end of the film the older sister steps into the younger sister's car which hints at the reconciliation between the two classes; but a strong voice condemning the oppression of the poor by the rich is obvious throughout the film. *The Sisters* certainly reveals Zheng Zhengqiu's apparent ideological leap when compared to his earlier films. The film was released shortly after his article "Ruhe zoushang qianjin zhi lu?" (How to step on the progressive road?), in which he proclaimed his transformation from a liberal in the 1920s to a left-wing intellectual in the 1930s.[37] He argued that Chinese cinema must take leave of Hollywood practices and learn from the experience of the Soviet Union. *The Sisters* can be seen as the work marking Zheng Zhengqiu's dedication to move to the left, if only conditionally.

Cai Chusheng also had a similar history of an ideological shift in his directing career. His 1932 production *Pink Dream* was heavily criticized by left-wing critics.[38] The political orientation of his following film, *Early Morning in the Metropolis*, changed dramatically. Similar to *The Sisters*, the film depicted two brothers growing up in two different environments: the elder brother was raised as a foster son by a poor rickshaw man and grew up to be an honest and upright character; the younger one stayed in the rich family and became a good-for-nothing scoundrel. This story reflects Marxist environmental determinism and attempts to prove that class status decides a person's attitudes and behavior. Cai Chusheng's next movie, *The Fishermen's Song*, was even more overt in advocating class struggle. The film shows the ordeals of a fishing family under the financial oppression of the capitalists. Not only did the film appeal to spectators and critics in China, it was also the first Chinese movie to win an international film award. It was awarded an "Outstanding Film" in the First International Film Festival in Moscow in 1935. *Xin nüxing* (New Woman) (plate 12) which Cai made in 1934, was arguably the most politically committed one among his films made before the war, as he created a new factory-woman type figure who was incredibly strong and machine-like. Another remarkable left-wing film of 1934 was *Shennü* (The Goddess) (plate 13). Although it was the first film directed by the set designer Wu Yonggang, the film was widely applauded by spectators and critics alike. Sun Yu and Fei Mu also continued to produce remarkable films for Lianhua in 1934 and 1935, including *Tiyu huanghou* (Queen of Sport) (plate 14), *Dalu* (The Highway) (plate 15), and *Xiangxue hai* (A Sea of Fragrant Snow) (plate 16). Although neither one of the above directors was directly related to the CCP, the many outstanding films they produced became some of the best representatives of the left-wing cinema movement, and the directors themselves were to become some of the most important filmmakers in Chinese film history.

The Continuing Development of Film Criticism

As left-wing film production bloomed in the market, film criticism also continued to develop. *The Development of Chinese Cinema* mistakenly records that the article "Women de chensu: jinhou de pipan shi 'jianshe de' " (Our declaration: criticisms from now on will be 'constructive') was written in June 1932. In fact, it was published in June 1933.[39] This was an article co-signed by sixteen left-wing critics declaring the future direction of their film criticism. The authors of *The Development of Chinese Cinema* claimed that this article was part of the agenda of the Party's Film Group in film criticism.[40] However, according to the account of Xia Yan, this article was produced in response to an invitation of the editor of the "Films of Everyday" section in *Morning Daily* as a celebration of the anniversary of this page.[41] According to an interview with Ke Ling, who was also one of the critics drafting this declaration, he and other non-Party members did not even know who the Party members among them were, even though they were aware of the subtle relation between their works and the CCP.[42] Once again, it is important not to overemphasize the Party's involvement in this film movement, although some individual Party members did play an active role.

Despite that this article did not indicate the political decisions of the Party, it was still historically significant because it represented a consensus among sixteen popular film critics of that time about the general direction of their criticism. They listed the four major tasks to accomplish: "1) Criticize the poisonous films; 2) praise the educational films; 3) inform the readers about filmmaking techniques in editing, performing, and other cinematic styles; 4) point out and analyze the films' social signification, production purposes, and other cultural issues."[43] Among these four goals, only the third one was related to the stylistic rendering of the art form; three were associated with the films' ideologies, demonstrating the general direction of film criticism at that time.

The first major theoretical battle the left-wing film critics had to fight began in April 1933 when Liu Na'ou, the famous modernist writer, published his article "Zhongguo dianying miaoxie de shendu wenti" (Questions about the depth of expression in Chinese cinema). In the midst of the public acclaims made to the new cinema, this article was one of the earliest critiques to the developing trend of left-wing movies. Left-wing critics wrote back later, and a surge of articles were produced from the two camps—this became the famous Soft-cinema versus Hard-cinema debate.

Liu Na'ou expressed his discomfort about the current new cinema in a sarcastic tone.

> Looking at contemporary Chinese films, among the many problems I think the most serious one is their overpoliticized contents. I remember that not long ago our national cinema was still accused as shallow. Now we observe this delightful (?) situation where our films chose this correct path to become saturated with messages. This might be a gift bestowed by some critics—particularly the Marxist ones—but before we have found a mature cinematic style, too many messages can be extremely dangerous. . . . Function is only a by-product of art; art is not equivalent to utilitarianism.[44]

Whether we agree with Liu Na'ou's idea of art or not, in hindsight this article was a pertinent and accurate criticism, if only partly, of the left-wing cinema movement. However, this writing did not attract much attention from the public at that time. Half a year later, Jia Mo published two articles in the same journal, further criticizing the current left-wing movies.[45] In his second article he used the terms "Soft-cinema" (*Ruanxing dianying*) and "Hard-cinema" (Yingxing dianying) to refer to the entertainment/artistic cinema and left-wing cinema respectively. He did not point out precisely what Soft-cinema was: he only considered it the genuine form of cinema because, as an allegory, film itself is a soft element. On the other hand, he clearly defined Hard-cinema as the films which contained left-wing ideology, and he argued that the current Chinese society had already had too much of it.

These two essays brought strong reactions from the left-wing critics; a vigorous debate developed between the two groups and was to continue for three years until 1936. Xia Yan, with the pen name Lo Fu, published several short articles in *Morning Daily* criticizing the social irresponsibility of the commercially-oriented Soft-films, although their left-wing films were also by-and-large commercial. Other film critics like Chen Wu and Lu Si (who used both this name and his other pen name Ke Ping) chose to stay on a more theoretical level arguing the importance of ideological messages in cinematic art. Other left-wing critics involved in this debate included Zhao Mingyi (using the pen name Mu Weifang) and Zhu Chongbin (using the pen name Ping Hua). In addition to Liu Na'ou and Jia Mo, another two important critics in the Soft-cinema camp were Jiang Jianxia and Mu Shiying.[46] The debate first began with the discussion of the current Chinese cinema. And very soon the critics shifted to other issues including the role of cinema as an art form and the role of film critics.

When discussing the accomplishments of the current film criticism, the Soft-cinema critics' comments were simple and direct: most of the Chinese film critics at that time were not qualified as professional ones. They did not understand cinema well enough because they only talked about the films' ideological messages and ignored all other cinematic aspects.[47] This criticism was, once again, valid because many left-wing critics were not well trained in cinema appreciation. They knew almost nothing about film criticism and had to start everything from the ground up, yet they were too busy earning a living and lacked the time to learn more about film. In an interview Ling He admitted that frequently he had to watch three films a day. Many times he was holding his child and writing film criticism at the same time.[48] Their analyses were inevitably mediocre and formulaic, criticizing the obvious of the films. Other aspects they might touch on were mostly acting and plot: whether the actor's performance was persuasive, whether there were any contradictions in the story. The major merit of this type of film criticism was that without any theoretical jargons their essays were readily accessible to the general public. But some individual readers might want more.[49] The left-wing critics did not deal with this negative comment in the debate; they seemingly recognized the poverty of their theoretical background when compared to, for example, Liu Na'ou's.

This debate, in fact, was more than a simple theoretical discussion, because the two camps were directly connected to the two rival political parties. Many of the Soft-cinema critics were patronized by the GMD, and their writings were connected to the government's agenda. For example, Jia Mo's article was published right after the government's vandalism of Yihua Film Company (to be discussed in the next section). Since there were many other factors influencing this theoretical debate, it is impossible for us to give a simple conclusion to this battle. The Soft-cinema critics seemed to have gained an upperhand at that time because some of them entered Mingxing and Yihua and replaced the positions of the left-wing filmmakers in 1935 under an arrangement with the government.[50] They produced some popular movies, and among them the most famous one was the two parts of *Huashen guniang* (The Metamorphosing Girl) (plate 17) written by Jia Mo, a light comedy depicting transvestism and lesbian love.[51] But on the other hand, the left-wing critics were supported by a broader base of intellectuals. History, particularly the history controlled by the CCP, has legitimized the ideas of the left-wing critics, and the writings of their enemies have been completely debased. It is interesting to notice that many of the Soft-cinema critics were also novelists of the New Perceptionist School (*Xin ganjue pai*). These writers consciously modeled their works after the Western modernist tradition with high literary techniques, and some of their works were truly remarkable within the current national literature. But most of their creative works, like their film theories, were forced to fade into Chinese literary history's background due less to the works' achievement than to the authors' political stance.[52] This is another incident proving that the cultural sphere of China has always been more dominated by politics, in its narrow sense, than by anything else.[53]

Other Production Sites: Yihua, Diantong, and Xinhua

The film industry in the 1930s was basically dominated by three film companies: Mingxing as the big brother, Lianhua as the new but potent force, and Tianyi which produced mostly commercial entertainment movies. Smaller companies like Tianbei, Xinshidai, and Jixing had also made some commercial films, but their films mostly followed the trend instead of leading it. In addition to Mingxing and Lianhua, there were three new film companies established in the 1930s which also actively participated in the left-wing cinema movement: Yihua, Diantong, and Xinhua.

Yihua Film Company was established in September 1933, an important event not only for the film industry but also for the entire left-wing cultural movement because it once again proved the success of left-wing intellectuals' strategic collaboration with capitalists. According to the recollections of Tian Han, the two famous martial art actors Cha Ruilong and Peng Fei invited him to write them a patriotic film script because the films they had been making were no longer appealing to spectators. They believed that left-wing films were in vogue. This project was to become Yihua's first film, *Minzu shengcun* (National Existence). The film was originally a small project sponsored by Peng Fei's teacher Yan Chuntang, who was a famous Shanghai drug dealer, in order to help in solving Peng Fei's financial problems. But Yan Chuntang found the film industry a profitable business after the small success of this film, and he decided to shift his capitals from opium to movies! By historical coincidence, Tian Han became the major coordinator of this new Yihua company financed by criminals.[54]

Although Yihua belonged to Yan Chuntang, the drug dealer did not have any experience in the film industry, nor was he aware of the subtle political battle taking place there. Because Tian Han had written two extremely popular films, *Three Modern Women* and *Maternal Radiance*, Yan Chuntang was glad to leave the entire business up to Tian Han. Not only did Tian Han write film scripts for the company, but he also introduced other left-wing filmmakers like Yang Hansheng, Xia Yan, and Shi Dongshan to Yihua. Within two years four left-wing films were produced: *National Existence*, *Zhongguohaide nuchao* (Angry Tide in China's Seas) (plate 18), *Roubo* (Hand-to-Hand Fighting), and *Lieyan* (Raging Flames). None of these films were major hits, but their clear left-wing ideology attracted much attention from the GMD government.

On November 12, 1933, seven or eight persons with blue outfits went into the Yihua studio and destroyed everything in the offices. They also went outdoors and destroyed two cars and a film processing machine. Before their departure, they dispersed leaflets on the ground with anticommunist statements, and they were signed by The Association for the Anti-Communist Comrades in the Film Industry (*Zhongguo dianyingjie changong tongzhi hui*).[55] This vandalism was the first instance in the film industry of the white terror, which had already spread throughout other parts of Shanghai society.[56] Another declaration of the same association was published in *Damei Evening News* the following day advising Yihua not to continue producing films written, directed, or performed by leftist intellectuals including Tian Han, Xia Yan, Bu Wancang, Hu Ping, and Jin Yan. Otherwise, violence would be the result.[57] Xia Yan speculates that Yihua was chosen as the first target mostly because it was a film company with no support from big capitalists or famous politicians. While the government could not afford to lose connections with Mingxing and Lianhua, it was so much easier to threaten a drug smuggler like Yan Chuntang.[58] Interestingly, in spite of this incident, the production policy of Yihua did not immediately alter, and the close tie between Yihua and left-wing filmmakers continued until 1935. Only when the Soft-film critics were recruited to Yihua and those famous Soft-films like *The Metamorphosing Girl* and *Bai bao tu* (100 Treasures Picture) were produced did the left-wing intellectuals retreat from Yihua completely. The final "divorce" between Yihua and the left-wing cinema movement was announced in November 1936 when thirty-two left-wing critics published an open letter to Yihua in different newspapers criticizing severely the production policies of the company and claimed that the recent commercialism of the company completely betrayed its earlier commitment and accomplishments in the new Chinese cinema.[59]

Diantong Film Company was another important base for the left-wing cinema movement. In its short life, from 1934 to 1935, the film company produced only four films, but all were outstanding left-wing movies. Diantong was originally a film equipment company established in 1933 by Situ Yimin, Gong Yuke, and Ma Dejian, who were all graduates from engineering departments of famous American universities.[60] It was a time when the entire film industry was caught in the transition from silent to sound film, but the production of talkies required a complete renewal of equipment, which was too expensive a project for many Chinese film companies. One of the solutions to the problem was to build sound equipment locally, instead of purchasing the expensive machines from abroad. Several Chinese engineers experimented with film sound recorders, and two were successfully produced: *Heming tong* and *Qingxian shi*, but neither could reproduce an acceptable quality of sound.[61] In September 1933 the three American graduates produced their recorder *Sanyou shi*, the first made in China that could record film sound with a quality close to the Western standard. With Situ Huimin, the cousin of Situ Yimin and a CCP member, they established Diantong to provide technical support for other film companies. Both the dialogues of Mingxing's *The Sisters* and the sound effects of Lianhua's *The Fishermen's Song* were recorded by this sound recorder. After these successes they decided to make sound films themselves. Because of Situ Huimin's association with the CCP, and because other film companies were being policed by the GMD too closely, Diantong soon became a major base for the left-wing cinema movement.

As a new company, Diantong had to acquire a crew of its own. Due to the close connection established between Situ Huimin and left-wing drama circles— he had been a set designer in a leftist drama group Shanghai Artistic Drama Association (*Shanghai yishu jushe*)—many dramatists were recruited to the new film company. Situ Huimin recounted that one of the major reasons for the absence of any experienced filmmakers and performers in their film company was the prevailing white terrorism in the film industry at that time—most established figures worried about their future career if they joined the company.[62] All the four films Diantong produced were directed by first-time film directors—Ying Yunwei, Xu Xingzhi, Situ Huimin, and Yuan Muzhi; many leading performers in these films, including Yuan Muzhi, Chen Bo'er, and Tang Na, were also new to the film industry. Party members Xia Yan, Tian Han, and Yang Hansheng also actively participated in the company and wrote film scripts for them. The four films produced by Diantong were *Taoli jie* (Plunder of Peach and Plum), *Fengyun ernü* (Sons and Daughters of the Storm) (plate 19), *Ziyoushen* (Spirit of Freedom) (plate 20), and *Dushi fengguang* (Scenes of City Life). *Plunder of Peach and Plum* was the debut of Diantong, and it received a warm welcome from spectators, particularly from young, educated people. The film was about the disillusion of two graduates after entering society. It was claimed that some young people were incited to join the Communist Party after watching this film.[63] The other three films were all outstanding as propaganda and art works in their own rights.

The Development of Chinese Cinema claims that Diantong closed down its business in the winter of 1935 due to GMD's political pressure.[64] Situ Huimin also recalled that Diantong was forced to shut down its productions because of white terrorism.[65] But this blame on the Nationalist government, therefore a form of self-glorification, revealed only a small part of the reality, as Diantong was also experiencing a lot of financial and personnel difficulties around 1935.[66] Of all the film companies that participated in this film movement, Diantong was the one most intimately connected to the Party. It is easy to glorify its success, but explaining its closure became a difficult task as it would directly affect the image of the Party.

Another major company in the advent of left-wing cinema was Xinhua. Zhang Shankun had been the manager of the famous Shanghai Peking Opera theater "Theater Gong" (*Gong wutai*). He began to show interest in films when he, with the technical support of Diantong, made and screened a filmed section of dance for and in the Peking Opera performance *Hong yang haoxia zhuan* (The tale of the gallant Hong Yang) in Theater Gong, expanding the narrative as well as imaginative space of the piece.[67] It can be seen as the first multimedia concept in the history of Chinese performing arts. In 1935, with the accumulated capital he earned from Theater Gong, Zhang incorporated financially troubled Diantong to establish his own movie kingdom. The first two films Xinhua produced, *The Tale of the Gallant Hong Yang* and *Xin taohua shan* (The new peach blossom fan), were box office hits. Similar to many other left-wing movies at that time, *The New Peach Blossom Fan* also easily bypassed the censorship by replacing the GMD government in the 1930s as the corrupt warlords in the 1920s. The film's commercial success brought its director Ouyang Yuqian, a famous liberalist playwright, to the attention of Zhang, and films with progressive ideologies continued to be produced by Xinhua. Between 1935 and 1937, thirteen films with a wide range of themes and styles were produced: while Shi Dongshan, Wu Yonggang, and Ma Xu Weibang were producing famous left-wing films like *Zhuangzhi lingyun* (Soaring Aspirations) (plate 21), *Yeban gesheng* (Song at Midnight), and *Qingnian jinxinqu* (March of Youth) in Xinhua, commercial entertainment movies like *Taoyuan chunmeng* (Spring Dreams of the Land of Peach Blossoms) were also made. Many of these films were box office successes, and they made Xinhua not only an important company for left-wing movies but also a truly exciting site in the entire film industry. Xinhua was the only film company active before 1937 to continue its business in the orphan island period (1937-41), and after the war it slowly evolved into a movie kingdom surpassing the glamour that Mingxing and Lianghua had achieved in the 1930s.

The Government's Reactions

As the left-wing intellectuals were taking control of the film industry beginning in 1933, the Nationalist government had also started to pay attention to cinema. In fact, the government first saw cinema more as an educational than a political tool. An Italian expert named Sardi was invited to China by "The League of

Nations for the Reform of Education in China" to give lectures at the end of
1931 about the use of film as a teaching tool. His idea of using film as pedagogy
was welcome by many film people and the government.[68] As a response to
Sardi's suggestion, the Association of Chinese Educational Cinema (Zhongguo
jiaoyu dianying xiehui) was established in July 1932 in Nanjing. In addition to
the many high government officials involved, some famous intellectuals and
filmmakers like Tian Han, Hong Shen, Ouyang Yuqian, Zheng Zhengqiu, and
Sun Yu were also invited to be members.[69] The Association listed five major
tasks to be achieved through cinema: (1) to promote the spirit of the [Chinese]
race; (2) to encourage film productions; (3) to teach scientific knowledge; (4) to
spread the government's ideology; and (5) to raise the moral standard of the
people.[70] The Association was set up at a time when the cultural world was
shifting left, and the government urged it to take back the control of its people
and society. Among the five goals of the Association, only the third one about
the teaching of scientific knowledge was ideologically neutral; all the others can
be seen as related to the reinforcement of GMD's control. Li Shaobai might be
right to argue that the hidden agenda of this association was to repress the revolutionary voices of the communists,[71] but GMD's major spearhead was not
likely to be pointed at the film industry because there was no apparent leftist
influence in cinema circles then. The Association was only a political mouthpiece for the government to maintain its dominant voice in society. As a historical
coincidence, both the left and the right discovered the potential ideological power of cinema and decided to take its control in the beginning of the 1930s.

The Central Film Studio (Zhongyang dianying shezhi chang) was the government's own film company. The studio produced only short documentaries in
the beginning; its first feature-length film, Xinfu zhi huan (Ailments Within
Heart and Stomach), was shown in Shanghai in July 1933; the film depicted the
crimes and destruction perpetuated by the CCP in the Jiangxi area. Advertised as
a documentary, the film also included some fictive sections acted out by performers to show the heroic deeds of the government officials in fighting with the
rebels.[72] Although the film was not a box office hit, the studio continued to produce films of various lengths depicting battles between the government and the
communists. The other two features produced by this studio were Zhanshi (Soldier) and Mi dianma (Secret Code) in 1936 and 1937; both were heavily loaded
with GMD ideology, and neither was particularly popular. In addition to their
own studio, the government also patronized other companies to produce movies
for its interests. Lianhua was the ideal site because of the company's large
spectator-base as well as the intimate connection between Luo Mingyou and the
GMD. Along with other left-wing films the company was also producing,
Tieniao (The Iron Bird), Guofeng (National style), and Xiao tianshi (Little Angel) were produced by Lianhua in collaboration with the government and made
good box office records.

As I have pointed out in the earlier chapter, the beginning of film censorship had nothing to do with the left-wing cinema because it was implemented in

1931 at a time when the industry was still untouched by left-wing intellectuals. Most of the censored materials were stigmatized due to ethical problems rather than ideological disputes. The second target of censorship was the anti-Japanese films produced after the "January 28 Event" in 1932. The GMD government had promised the Japanese government to prevent all anti-Japanese sentiments from circulating among Chinese people. Films with racial hatred had to be banned; but anti-Japanese films continued to find their way to be shown—filmmakers and companies simply replaced the words "Japanese" or "the Japanese army" with terms like the enemy or the invaders. Filmmakers also continued to make films about Manchuria; they just had to look for different allegorical ways to express their emotions and present their messages. Foreign films were also being censored, but statistics showed that local films were the major targets.[73]

The GMD censors very soon shifted their attention to left-wing movies when these films began to dominate the film market in 1933. When the first Film Inspection Law was set up in 1930, film censorship was carried out by a special committee composed of four officials from the Education Department and three officials from the Internal Affairs Department.[74] However, in 1934 this committee was replaced by another group directly under the control of the Central Propaganda Committee, the GMD's ideological center, to supervise film censorship.[75] This policy signaled clearly that the criteria and execution of film censorship had shifted from the educational perspective to a political one. Films were also requested to be inspected twice, the earlier one in script form before production and the other as a finished product. It guaranteed the government's total control of the films' messages. For the films intended to be shown in the foreign settlements in Shanghai, they were requested to pass one more stage of inspection from the colonial administrations, forging a triple-level censorship machine.

In fact, film censorship had affected the left-wing cinema since the beginning of this movement. According to Li Shaobai, films of 1933 being edited by the Film Inspection Committee included Mingxing's *Iron Plate and Red Tears*, *Women's Outcry*, *Sweetgrass Beauty*, *Yabi* (Oppression), and Yihua's *National Existence*.[76] *Three Modern Women* also suffered from the choppy cutting so that the flow of the narration was greatly impeded.[77] Shen Xiling's *Twenty-Four Hours in Shanghai* was planned to be released in early-1934.[78] But the censors froze the film for close to a year, and its highly edited version was finally released in Shanghai on Dec. 15, 1934; this caused Mingxing major financial losses.

Self-censorship also took place among filmmakers themselves. In the original film script of *Zhifen shichang* (Cosmetics market), Xia Yan arranged an ending with the heroine walking into the crowd hinting at her decision to abandon her petit bourgeois status and join the proletariat. But Zhang Shichuan, the director of the film and also a boss of Mingxing, felt the danger of such a provocative ending and made a new one: the heroine opens up a small business of her own and leads an independent and happy life. Therefore, the original message of Xia Yan was completely turned around. Xia Yan was not informed about this alteration; he could only voice his complaints by publishing them in a newspaper.[79]

Yihua's *Angry Tide in China's Seas* also suffered fatally from the editing of the Inspection Committee. After watching the film in a theater, the left-wing critic Ling He wrote in March 1934:

> I have watched this film before its public screening. The version we saw that time had already passed the first inspection. But we were still happy about the film: both the narrative structure and the images were fresh and powerful. However, the film shown in this public screening is no longer the one we saw last time. . . . A film can hardly appeal to its spectators if it is cut time after time. There are many instances in the film when sequences cannot be connected together—spectators are completely puzzled. Someone suggested that we should put in blank films to indicate the cut sections. . . . Also someone suggested that this film should change its name from *Angry Tide in China's Seas* to *Nothing Happened in China's Seas*.[80]

According to an unofficial estimation, there were about 600 CCP members arrested by the government in the first six months of 1933.[81] As the war with the Japanese was becoming less pressing, the GMD government refocused their attention on the internal problems. The CCP was gaining popularity in cities as anti-Japanese sentiments developed, and the government could not afford to ignore the possible detrimental effects. The vandalism of Yihua was a clear warning from the government to film companies. The "Films of Everyday" section in *Morning Daily* was under severe pressure, and Chen Wu was forced to step down from his editor position. Xia Yan also recalled that Mingxing was under heavy surveillance by the government, and the contracts with the three Party scriptwriters had to be terminated in 1934—although the three continued to write film scripts for the company in secret.[82] In February 1935, Yang Hansheng and Tian Han were arrested by the GMD, and Xia Yan and Qian Xinchun were fortunate enough to escape, but they had to leave Shanghai immediately. With the prevailing white terrorism and the closing down of Diantong, the entire left-wing cinema movement basically came to a halt in 1935.

But other than political censorship and ideological control, the government did not intervene in the film market, allowing Hollywood films to monopolize the majority of film exhibition. Unlike many countries in which the import of foreign films was heavily controlled in order to protect the survival of the domestic cinema industry, the Chinese Nationalist government in the 1930s allowed, or failed to pay attention to, the jeopardizing share of Hollywood films in the Chinese market. Astonishingly, due to various bureaucratic procedures, Chinese films ended up having to pay a higher tax than most foreign films did, giving the national productions an extremely unfavorable commercial environment.[83] The domination of Hollywood films in the Chinese market was particularly clear in 1935 when the number of local productions dropped significantly. Without the judiciary and administrative support of its own government, the local film industry felt the clear reluctance of Chinese movie-goers to attend China's productions. There was a stronger demand in film circles to promote a national cinema movement in order to compete with the Hollywood blockbusters for the mere reason of survival.

National Defense Cinema

Under increasing pressure from the GMD government and the declining economy of the nation, the film industry faced another recession in 1935. As Shen Xiling wrote:

> At present in 1935, the Chinese film industry is facing a catastrophic depression. Externally, our local productions fail to grasp spectators' interests, and the box office records are decreasing abruptly. Internally, the film companies are busy in layoff, salary reduction, and requesting loans. The situation is chaotic. The entire industry is on the verge of complete collapse.[84]

No film companies were able to escape this severe recession, but show business was not the sole victim—the whole Shanghai city was suffering. Between 1934 and 1936, 238 factories in Shanghai were forced to close down, and another 839 factories had to undergo reorganization: these financially troubled factories comprised a quarter of all the factories in the city.[85] Fortunately, 1936 witnessed a regeneration of the country's economy, and the film industry also benefited from it. Most of the film companies were able to survive the recession, and they were ready to launch new production plans in 1936. One of the most important events taking place in film circles was the widespread promotion of "National Defense Cinema" (*Guofang dianying*).

According to Wang-chi Wong, the slogan "National Defense Literature" (*Guofang wenxue*) was first introduced in China in October 1934 when Zhou Yang, using the pen name Qi, published an article titled "Guofang wenxue" (National Defense Literature).[86] Under this towering banner all schools of thought were to be grouped together. Individual writers or groups should eliminate their personal biases and create literature for the sole purpose of fighting against the Japanese. This idea was later developed into the famous "Two slogan polemic" in 1936 within the left-wing literary group. Under the directions of the central Party, Zhou Yang and his followers advocated this concept of National Defense Literature in order to unite writers not only within the left-wing circles but also those from outside. It presented a friendly gesture toward the GMD for establishing a second United Front. However, Lu Xun and his followers continued to favor their left-wing tradition and rejected co-operation with people other than their own. Therefore, Hu Feng proposed an alternate slogan—"Mass Literature for the National Revolutionary War" (*Minzu geming zhanzheng de dazhong wenxue*)—in order to confine this "National Defense Literature" movement within the boundary of the left.[87]

Similar patriotic concepts and debates also appeared in the film industry at the same time. Movies with anti-Japanese sentiments had been produced in China since the early 1930s. In fact, the slogan "National Defense Cinema" appeared earlier than "National Defense Literature."[88] In a 1934 article Zheng Boqi expressed his discomfort about fighting only against the Japanese and ignoring Chinese traitors. In principle he supported a Chinese cinema with the objective in National Defense, but in reality the left-wing filmmakers' struggles with the right-wing powers could not be sacrificed in the name of national unity.[89] But this suggestion of Zheng Boqi represented only a feeble voice in the left-wing cinema at that time. Because many Party members in the film industry like Tian Han, Xia Yan, and Yang Hansheng were intimately affiliated with Zhou Yang, Zhou Yang's suggestion of a nondiscriminating united front against the Japanese was soon strongly promoted in cinema.

As the critic Meng Gongwei suggested in 1936: "There are certainly many conflicts among the classes in Chinese society. However, in the face of this solemn anti-imperialist national protection movement, all these minor problems should be cast away temporarily."[90] Song Zhide (using his pen name Huai Zhao) also commented that " 'National Defense Cinema' is the slogan that can unite all subject matters."[91] Song Zhide argued in this essay that all current problems China was facing were more or less related to the Japanese invasion. Filmmakers were obliged to point out the hidden correlation between the Japanese invasion and the current Chinese reality at this critical time, and films unrelated to national defense did not have the urgency to be produced immediately. These writings all encouraged a united effort in the film industry to produce films with the sole anti-Japanese objective.

On January 27, 1936, the National Salvation Association of Shanghai Cinema (*Shanghai dianying jie jiuguo hui*) was established. Mingxing's director Zhou Jianyun and left-wing filmmakers including Sun Yu and Cai Chusheng were among the initiators.[92] The association released a statement containing four goals they wanted to achieve:

1. Unite the entire film industry to participate in the National Liberation Movement.
2. Abolish the present film censorship system.
3. Use our own criteria to inspect and ban those local or imported films that might be against people's common interests or harm the National Liberation Movement.
4. Use all our efforts to make films that support the National Liberation Movement.[93]

This assertion both advocated a National Defense cinema and protested against the government's censorship, two emotional issues strongly felt by the entire

film industry then. Under this slogan of "National Defense Cinema," we observed a regeneration of the Chinese cinema in 1936. Fei Mu's *Langshan diexue
ji* (Bloodbath on Wolf Mountain) (plate 22) was one of the best examples. The
story takes place in a village which is constantly under the threat of wolves.
Most of the people there choose to protect their village passively rather than to
take the initiative to kill the wolves. When the number of wolves suddenly in-
creases, not only cattle but people are killed, forcing the entire village to rise up
to fight the wolves. Obviously, the wolves were an allegory for the Japanese
military. The film attempted to encourage Chinese people to assume an active
role in self-defense. In a newspaper article Fei Mu wrote about the film:

> The story [of *Bloodbath on Wolf Mountain*] was so simple that two
> sentences can summarize it. However, after watching the film some
> people suspected that it was in fact a metaphor for another hidden
> story. This is certainly a misunderstanding, and these people might
> have some other intentions. This is a realistic story—hunters hunting
> wolves is definitely ordinary. But because of certain technical limita-
> tions I cannot use realism completely. About this shortcoming, I
> greatly felt my impotency and stupidity.[94]

This was obviously double talk. This writing in fact revealed, more than concealed, the allegorical approach of this film. As hunters should hunt wolves,
Chinese should also fight against the invaders. Fei Mu had to deny the anti-
Japanese elements so bluntly because the Chinese government was still bound
by their agreement with the Japanese to prohibit any incidents and actions that
might destroy the "friendship" between the two peoples. Ke Ling recounted that
many National Defense movies were censored by the government under the Japanese pressure. They included Mingxing's *Rexue zhonghun* (Ardent, Loyal
Souls), Yueming's *E lin* (Evil Neighbor), and Xiao Shanghai's *Huan wo shanhe*
(Return Our Mountains and Rivers).[95] Fortunately, *Bloodbath on Wolf Mountain*
did not have a similar fate. It was screened in November 1936 and was wholeheartedly accepted by both critics and spectators. Cai Chusheng's *Wang laowu*
(Fifth Brother Wang) and Fei Mu's short film "Chungui mengduan" (Broken
Dream in the Women's Apartment), part of *Lianhua jiaoxiangqu* (Lianhua sym-
phony), also had a strong anti-Japanese undertone.[96]

Mingxing in fact openly declared their support for "National Defense Cinema." As I have shown, Zhou Jianyun, one of the Heads of Mingxing, was
among the initiators of The National Salvation Association of Shanghai Cinema
Circles. One of the plans listed in Mingxing's Declaration for Improvement in
1936 was to produce National Defense films.[97] The statement also asserted that
the first national defense film of Mingxing, *Yuewumu jinzhong baoguo* (The
Martial and Mighty Yue [Fei] Loyally Fights for His Country), was soon to be
produced; but the film was never made. Xinhua produced some of the most important National Defense Films in 1936 and 1937 to become the leading company in the event. They included Wu Yonggang's *Soaring Aspirations*, Ma Xu

Weibang's *Song at Midnight*, and Shi Dongshan's *Qingnian jinxinqu* (*March of youth*). This sub-movement was highly symbolic to the progressive cinema because patriotism was right at the heart of the ideology of this cinema movement, whose continual development was therefore fuelled instead of prohibited by the increasing Japanese war threat.

The End of Left-wing Cinema

After a glamorous five-year reign as the King of the new Chinese cinema, Luo Mingyou found himself in serious financial difficulties in 1936. Although Lianhua had attracted strong economic support in the beginning, the long production period and high budgets of its films gave the company a huge overhead. While Mingxing produced twenty-seven movies in the year of 1933, the four studios of Lianhua combined made only twelve altogether.[98] As the leading directors in Mingxing, Cheng Bugao directed four movies and Zhang Shichuan directed five that year. But the situation was drastically different in Lianhua: only Sun Yu and Bu Wangcan were able to produce two movies in 1933, and all the others directed only one. The box office success of individual films was not able to cover the high production costs.

Luo Mingyou experienced his first financial difficulties at the end of 1931. Many theaters of his were located in the parts of northern China occupied by the Japanese after 1931.[99] Lianhua Studio 4 was also destroyed in the war in January 1932. He went to Southeast Asia to raise funds to meet the immediate financial needs,[100] but what he obtained were only oral promises.[101] Although he had managed to hold up the debts, the company's financial situation did not improve. In May 1934 he borrowed thirty thousand dollars from a man named Yu Kangmin and used the prints of *Baoyu lihua* (Pear Blossom in the Storm), *Gurou zhi en* (Flesh and Blood Kindness), and *A Sea of Fragrant Snow* as collateral.[102] In the beginning of 1936, Luo Mingyou went to Nanjing to raise funds once again but was rejected.[103] Lianhua had no choice but to look for new investors. Although still carrying the title of the company's managing director, Luo Mingyou retreated from its administration completely in 1936. Lianhua was now controlled by the new bosses Tao Boxun and Wu Bangfan.[104] Its Studio 1, directed by Li Minwei, became independent and resumed the name of Minxin Film Company in May 1936. A new Hua'an Company was also established to manage the production and distribution of the films of Lianhua. Although the name of Lianhua was still retained, the administration was completely different. Fortunately, this structural transformation of Lianhua did not affect the quality of the company's productions. Sun Yu, Fei Mu, and Cai Chusheng continued to produce left-wing films of high quality, like the first children's left-wing movie, *Mitu de gaoyang* (Lost Lambs) (plate 23) made by Cai. Another important director, Zhu Shilin, also directed two of his early classics *Cimu qu* (Song of a

Loving Mother) and *Renhai yi zhu* (Lost Pearl in the Crowd) in Lianhua in 1937. As the latest participant in the production of sound films in the Chinese film industry, Lianhua released their first sound films in 1936; they included *Bloodbath on Wolf Mountain* and Sun Yu's *Dao ziren qu* (Back to Nature). In spite of the new administrative structure, the two years 1936-1937 provided a promising opening for a new age of Lianhua.

In Mingxing's Declaration for Improvement in 1936, another task listed there was to found a new Mingxing Studio 2, and it was established in July 1936. Many of the ex-Diantong employees were recruited into this new studio, and there they produced some of the best films in the early Chinese cinema. These classics included *Xinjiu Shanghai* (Old and New Shanghai) (plate 24), *Shengsi tongxin* (Unchanged Heart in Life and Death), *Yasuiqian* (The New Year's Gift), *Shizi jietou* (Crossroads), and *Malu tianshi* (Street Angel) (plate 25). Together with Lianhua's *Bloodbath on Wolf Mountain, Lianhua Symphony, Fifth Brother Wang*, and Xinhua's *Song at Midnight*, these outstanding films of 1936 and 1937 represented not only the climax of the left-wing cinema movement but also a golden two-year period in Chinese film history. Several different film genres were becoming mature: Yuan Muzhi and Cai Chusheng showed us that light comedy could carry heavy social messages, and Ma Xu Weibang proved himself as a master of the thrillers.[105] We witness the rapid maturation of these new filmmakers who maneuvered the medium so much better when compared to their earlier works. In the last phase of the movement some filmmakers successfully got rid of the formulaic plots and structures embedded in their earlier works and began to acquire their own unique cinematic styles. From *Scenes of City Life* to *Street Angels*, Yuan Muzhi became a master in depicting the metropolitan culture of Shanghai through cinema. In *Fifth Brother Wang* Cai Chusheng also showed us the lives of the Chinese proletariat most intimately and passionately. Although Fei Mu's talent would not be completely revealed until a decade later, *Bloodbath on Wolf Mountain* and *Broken Dream in the Women's Apartment* had already proved his unique sensibility in film art. Shen Xiling and Ying Yunwei also affirmed their outstanding directing skills and creativity in *Unchanged Heart in Life and Death* and *Crossroads*.

The entire nation, on the other hand, also experienced a new sense of optimism and national unity beginning in the autumn of 1936. According to Lloyd E. Eastman, this new national mood was reinforced by three factors. GMD finally suppressed the revolts in Guangdong and Guangxi, the two provinces which had blatantly proclaimed their opposition to the Nanjing rule. Also, as the Head of the Party, Jiang Jieshi appeared to have aligned himself with prevailing anti-Japanese sentiment: the distance between the people and government seemed shortened. And most enthusiastically, the government launched a relatively successful currency reform which gave hope for a recovery of the national economy.[106] Considering this general optimism in both the film industry and society at large, I am obliged to ask a question: What if the Japanese hadn't come?

But the Japanese army did come; it officially "entered" China on July 7, 1937. On that day some Japanese soldiers gunned down several Chinese soldiers in a Beijing suburb, and the Chinese government was forced to declare war on Japan. Although the foreign settlements of Shanghai stayed untouched by the war for another four years until the outbreak of the Pacific War, and many left-wing films made before the incident continued to be shown, a big part of the Shanghai film industry was dissolved in the later half of 1937, and so was the left-wing cinema movement.

Beginning on August 7, a large number of left-wing film people participated in the performance of the patriotic drama *Baowei Lugou Qiao* (Protecting the Marco Polo Bridge), a play Tian Han wrote in three days.[107] However, this popular performance was forced to an end on August 13 because of the Japanese invasion of Shanghai. This invasion also caused the biggest damage to the film industry after the bombardment in January 1932. Mingxing's studio was damaged extensively, and Lianhua also suffered from greatly delayed productions.[108] In November 1937, the unleased area of Shanghai was occupied by the Japanese, and the two foreign concessions were to become the famous orphan island for another four years.[109] Most of the participants in the left-wing cinema movement, directors, performers, and critics alike, partook of the overwhelming patriotic aura and organized themselves into the famous thirteen Rescue Drama Groups (*jiuwang yingju tuan*) and went to different parts of China to perform patriotic dramas.[110] Some, like Cai Chusheng and Xia Yan, went south to Hong Kong trying to establish another new cinematic base for filmmaking. The development of the left-wing cinema movement in China came to an extended "time-out" in the coming eight years of wartime. Right after the war, these people were to gather back in Shanghai and begin another new surge of intellectual filmmaking.[111]

Notes

1. There is not yet any major scholarly work about this association published in English. For a good Chinese reference, see *ZZXLSJ*.

2. *ZZXLSJ*, 17-19; *ZZDY*, 17-18.

3. *Shalun* (Siren) 1, no.1 (June 16, 1930): 45-50.

4. Chen Wu, "Zhongguo dianying zhi lu" (The road of Chinese cinema) *Mingxing banyue kan* (Mingxing bi-monthly) 1, no. 1 and 2 (May/June, 1933). Rpt., *SNZDPW*, 601-13.

5. *Dianying lunwen ji* (Writing on films) (Beijing: Zhongguo dianying, 1985), 83.

6. Some 16mm documentaries and noncommercial left-wing films were actually produced in the "Liberated Areas" during and after the Sino-Japanese war. But their distribution was so limited and investment so meager that they did not make any big impact on either the current film market or the latter development of Chinese cinema. See *ZDFS*, vol. 2, 337-416

7. A minor point: Xia Yan wrote that this group was established in July 1932, *ZZDY*, 782. But Yao Shixiao recounts that the group was established in June 1932, *ZZXLSJ*, 483.

8. *ZDFS*, vol. 1, 183.

9. *ZZDY*, 782.

10. *ZZDY*, 787.

11. Many recent mainland film scholars continue to hold onto the rhetoric of *ZDFS*. See, for one example among many, Yao Guohua and Zhou Bin, "Wengu zhixin, jiwang kailai—jinian zuoyi dianying yundong liushi zhounina" (Revising the old and understanding the new; continuing the tradition and bringing it to the future—The sixtieth anniversary of the left-wing cinema movement), in *Dianying zhongheng* (Cinema horizontal and vertical) (Shanghai: Sanlian, 1993), 6-7.

12. For Pudovkin's original in English, see *Film Techniques and Film Acting/V.I. Pudovkin*, translated by Ivor Montagn, (New York: Grove Press, 1970).

13. Xia Yan, "Zuoyi shinian," (A left-wing decade) in *Lanxun jiumeng lu* (Too lazy to look for old dreams) (Beijing: Sanlian, 1985). Rpt., *ZZDY*, 784. A further analysis of the influence of Soviet filmmaking on the Chinese will be discussed in chapter 6.

14. This character appraisal of Xia Yan came from an interview I had with Huang Wenying, a famous Xia Yan scholar in the mainland. (Shanghai, China), Oct. 25, 1996.

15. Xia Yan, "Zuoyi shinian," 778-79.

16. Xia Yan, *Dianying lunwen ji* (Film writings) (Beijing: Zhongguo dianying), 94-95.

17. Situ Huimin, "Wangshi bu yi hou you lai zhe—san ji zai zuolian de qizhi xia jinbu dianying de feiyue" (The past has gone, the future is coming—scattered records of the advance of the progressive cinema under the flag of the Left League) *Dianying yishu* (Film art) (June 1980). Rpt., *ZZDY*, 878.

18. "The History of the Mingxing Film Company in these twelve years," (Mingxing yingpian gongsi shi'er nian lishi) in Zhongguo jiaoyu dianying xiehui (Association of Chinese cinema for education) ed. *The Cinematographic Yearbook of China* (Nanjing: Zhongguo jiaoyu dianying xiehui, 1934), page number not printed. Rpt., *ZWD*, 43.

19. Xia Yan, "Zuoyi shinian," *ZZDY*, 778.

20. *SB*, January 7, 1933.

21. Xia Yan, "Zuoyi shinian," *ZZDY*, 778-79.

22. The script was first printed with his translation of Pudovkin's writing, *Dianying daoyan lun dianying jiaoben lun* (Film directing and film writing). It has been reprinted in different collections, e.g., in *Xia Yan dianying juzuo ji* (Film writings of Xia Yan) (Beijing: Zhongguo dianying, 1985), 25-53.

23. *CB*, Feb. 25, 27, 1933. Rpt., *SNZDPW*, 244.

24. According to a newspaper article, it also broke the box office record in Tianjin. *SB*, Feb. 19, 1933.

25. *ZDFS*, vol. 1, 257.

26. Mao Dun's short story has been translated into English. "Spring Silkworms" in *Spring Silkworms and Other Stories*, trans. Sidney Shapiro (Peking: Foreign Languages Press, 1956), 9-38.

27. Cheng Bugao, *Yingtang yijiu* (Old memories of the film industry) (Beijing: Zhongguo dianying, 1983), 1-2.

28. *SB*, Oct 9, 1933. The full house on the opening day might have been the result of the big advertising scheme Mingxing had launched for the film.

29. *SB*, Oct 9, 1933.

30. *SB*, Oct 10, 1993.

31. *CB*, Oct 8, 1933. Rpt., *SNZDPW*, 255.

32. A comprehensive study of this "Mandarin Duck and Butterflies" literature can be found in *Yuanyang hudie pai wenxue ziliao* (Information about "Mandarin Duck and

Butterflies" literature) ed. Rui Heshi (Fuzhou: Fuzhou renmin, 1984). The book anthologizes a large number of important novels and critical writings at that time with a comprehensive bibliography. Also see E. Perry Link Jr., *Mandarin Ducks and Butterflies: Popular Fiction in Early Twentieth Century Chinese Cities* (Berkeley: University of California Press, 1981) and Rey Chow's *Woman and Chinese Modernity: The Politics of Reading between West and East* (Minneapolis: University of Minnesota Press, 1991), 34-83. But there is no major study of this genre in cinema published yet, mostly due to the lack of available films.

33. The most famous example was the eighteen parts of *Huoshao Hongliansi* (Burning the Red Lotus Temple). For the history of its adaptation from the book *Jianghu qixia chuan* (The Story of an Extraordinary Knight) to the film, see Li Suyuan and Hu Jubin, *Zhongguo wusheng dianying shi* (History of Chinese Silent Cinema), 225-28.

34. Shen Xiling gave the nickname "the poet of cinema" to Sun Yu. See Sun Yu, *Dalu zhi ge* (Song of the big road) (Beijing: Zhongguo dianying, 1990), 104. I will discuss further the cinematic style of Sun Yu in later chapters.

35. *SB*, Sept 24, 1933.

36. Zheng Zhengqiu, "Zi wo daoyan yilai" (Since I became a director), *Mingxing banyue kan* (Mingxing half-monthly) 1, no. 1 (1935). Rpt., *ZWD*, 397.

37. *Mingxing yuekan* (Mingxing monthly) 1, no. 1 (May 1933). Rpt., *SNZDPW*, 614-17.

38. These criticisms include the three articles written by Zheng Boqi, Su Feng, and Lu Si, which were published in *CB*, Sept. 6, 1933. Rpt., *SNZDPW*, 323-32.

39. *CB*, June 18, 1933. Rpt., *ZZDY*, 25-26; *SNZDPW*, 667-68. The critics who signed this article were: Hong Shen, Shen Xiling, Ke Ling, Ji Naifang, Zhang Changren, Lu Si, Meng Ling, Hei Xing, Cai Chusheng, Zhang Fengwu, Zhu Gongnü, Shu Yan, Chen Liting, Yao Sufeng, and Tong Bai.

40. *ZDFS*, vol. 1, 186-87.

41. Xia Yan, "Zuoyi shinian" (A left-wing decade), in *ZZDY*, 786.

42. Ke Ling, interview by author, Shanghai, China, Nov. 6, 1996.

43. *SNZDPW*, 668.

44. *Xiandai dianying* (Modern cinema) 1, no. 3 (April 6, 1933). Rpt., *SNZDPW*, 837-39. The question mark is original.

45. Jia Mo was certainly a less theoretically-oriented writer when compared to Liu Na'ou. The two articles are "Dianying zhi sesu yu dusu" (The color pigment and the poisonous elements of cinema) *Xiandai dianying* (Modern cinema) 1, no. 5 (October 1, 1933). Rpt., *SNZDPW*, 840-842, and "Yingxing dianying yu ruanxing dianying (Hard-cinema and Soft-cinema) *Xiandai dianying* (Modern cinema) 1, no. 6 (Dec. 1, 1933). Rpt., *SNZDPW*, 843-45.

46. Most of the important articles from both sides involved in this debate are anthologized in *SNZDPW*. Interested readers can consult the originals directly.

47. Jiang Jianxia, "Guanyu yingping ren" (About the film critics), *Xiandai yanju* (Modern drama) 1 (Dec. 20, 1934). Rpt., *SNZDPW*, 853-54.

48. Wang Xiangmin, "Shi Linghe" (Shi Linghe), in *Sanshi niandai zhai Shanghai de "zuolian" zuojia* (The Shanghai "left-league" writers in 1930s), ed. Shanghai Academy of Social Science (Shanghai: Shanghai Academy of Social Science, 1988), 360.

49. An example can be seen in Liu Hua'nan's article "Jingzhi dianying pipian jia" (Respectfully to film critics), *SB*, Nov. 16, 1933.

50. *ZDFS*, 310, 494.

51. A brief synopsis of the film can be found in *ZDFS*, 495-496.

52. The Perceptionist School is beginning to attract scholarly attention in recent years. Some recent English studies include: Zhang Yingjin's "The Texture of the Metropolis: Modernist Inscriptions of Shanghai in the 1930s," *Modern Chinese Literature* 9 (1995): 11-30, Yomi Braester's "Shanghai's Economy of the Spectacle: The Shanghai Race Club in Liu Na'ou's and Mu Shiying's Stories," *Modern Chinese Literature* 9 (1995): 39-57, Leo Lee's *Shanghai Modern* (Cambridge, Mass.: Harvard University Press, 1999), 153-231, and Shu-mei Shih's *The Lure of the Modern* (Berkeley: University of California Press, 2001), 276-371.

53. Other aspects of this debate will be discussed in later chapters.

54. The history of Yihua is recorded in Tian Han's *Yingshi juihuai lu* (Memories about the events in cinema) (Beijing: Zhongguo dianying, 1981), 21-25.

55. *Damei wanbao* (Damei Evening News), Nov. 13, 1933. This news was copied down by Lu Xun and printed in his *Zhun fengyue tang* (The allowed talk about wind and moon). Rpt., *Lu Xun quanji*, vol. 6 and *ZZDY*, 40-43.

56. See Dooeum Chung's *Elitist Fascism: Chiang Kaishek's Blueshirts in the 1930s China* (Aldershot: Ashgate, 2000).

57. *ZZDY*, 40-43.

58. Xia Yan, "Zuoyi shinian" (A left-wing decade), in *ZZDY*, 792-93.

59. *SB*, Nov. 23, 1936. Rpt., *ZZDY*, 48-49.

60. According to Cheng, et al., Situ Yimin and Gong Yuke graduated from Harvard, and Ma Dejian was from either Washington University in St. Louis or The University of Washington in Seattle (the Chinese translation was not clear). *ZDFS*, vol. 1, 379.

61. *SB*, July 5, 1934.

62. Situ Huimin, "The past has gone, and the future is coming," in *ZZDY*, 882.

63. According to an unpublished survey conducted by Zhong Dafeng. Zhong Dafeng, interview by author, Beijing, China, Dec 12, 1996.

64. *ZDFS*, vol. 1, 393.

65. Situ Huimin, "The past has gone, and the future is coming," in *ZZDY*, 883.

66. See Li Yi, "Ershisi nian de Zhongguo dianying" (The Chinese Cinema in 1935), *SB*, Jan. 1, 1936. Another report indicated that the employees of Diantong were not receiving their salaries due to the company's financial problems, *Dianying xinwen* (News of cinema) 1, no. 6 (Aug. 11, 1935): 4. Newspaper articles reporting the personnel problems of Diantong can be found on *SB*, Nov. 2, Nov. 9, Dec. 24, 1936 and April 14, 1937.

67. Chen Dieyi, et al., *Zhang Shankun xiansheng chuan* (The biography of Mr. Zhang Shangkun) (Hong Kong: Dahua, 1958), 4-5.

68. Peng Baichun and Zhang Pairong translated Sardi's report into Chinese: Sa Er'di, *Dianying yu Zhongguo* (Film and China) (Nanjing: Association of Chinese Educational Cinema, 1933). The translation did not put down his first name, and it did not specify the clear identity of this Italian.

69. Guo Youshou, "Zhongguo jiaoyu dianying xiehui chengli shi" (The history of the establishment of Association of Chinese Educational Cinema), in Zhongguo jiaoyu dianying xiehui (Association of Chinese cinema for education), *The Cinematographic Yearbook of China* (Nanjing: Zhongguo jiaoyu dianying xiehui, 1934) , n. p.

70. Guo Youshou, "Zhongguo jiaoyu dianying xiehui chengli shi."

71. Li Shaobai, "Liangzhong yishi xingtai de duili" (The antagonism of two ideologies), *Dangdai dianying* (Contemporary cinema) 61 (April 1994): 37.

72. According to the descriptions in the newspaper articles about the film. *SB*, July 18, 19, 20, 1933.

73. In 1932, there were fifty-one films banned from screening: thirty-one of them were Chinese films. However, the Chinese productions comprised only one-tenth of all the films shown in China at that time. Obviously the local productions suffered severely from censorship. *SB*, March 18, 1933.

74. *ZZDY*, 1089.

75. *ZZDY*, 1103-05.

76. Li Shaobai, "Liangzhong yishi xingtai de duili," 36-37.

77. *CB*, Dec. 30, 1932.

78. The advertisement of the film appeared in a number of newspapers in Feb. 1934.

79. *CB*, May 15, 1933. One section of the article was reprinted in *ZDFS*, vol. 1, 230.

80. *SB*, March 1, 1934.

81. Xia Yan, "Zuoyi shinian," 787.

82. Xia Yan, "Zuoyi shinian," 794-95.

83. Wang Chaoguang, "Minguo nianjian Meiguo dianying zai hua shichang yanjiu" (The marketing research of American cinema in Republican China) *Dianying yishu* (Film art) no. 258 (Jan 1998): 57-64.

84. Shen Xiling, "Zhongguo dianying qiye de weiji yu bujiu fangfa" (The calamity of Chinese film industry and its remedies) *Shenbao yuekan* (Shenbao monthly) 4, no. 10 (Sept. 15, 1935): 79-81.

85. Xin Ping, *Cong Shanghai faxian lishi* (Discovering history from Shanghai) (Shanghai: Shanghai renmin, 1996), 316.

86. Wang-chi Wong, *Politics and Literature in Shanghai: The Chinese League of Left-wing Writers, 1930-36* (Manchester: Manchester University Press, 1991), 183. Zhou Yang's article was published in *Dawanbao* (The great evening news) Oct. 1934.

87. This famous "Two slogan polemics" was a complicated historical event. Interested readers can consult Ma Liangchun and Zhang Daming's *Sanshi niandai zuoyi wenyi ziliao xuanbian* (Selected collection of research materials about the left-wing literature in the 1930s) (Chengdu: Sichuan renmin, 1980).

88. I am not yet able to locate when this concept was first advocated in the film industry. It must have been around 1932.

89. Zheng Boqi, "Tan guofang dianying" (A discussion of National Defense Cinema) *Dianying huabao* (Cinema pictorial) 33 (Sept. 1934). Rpt., *ZZDY*, 179-80.

90. Meng Gongwei, "Guofang dianying zhu wanti—guofang dianying lun zhi yi" (Some questions for National Defense Cinema—A discussion on National Defense Cinema, I) *Dawanbao* (The Great Evening News) May 15, 1936. Rpt., *SNZDPW*, 648-51.

91. Huai Zhao, "'Guofang dianying' xiaolun" (A small discussion of National Defence Cinema) *Dawanbao* (The Great Evening News) Aug. 30, 1936. Rpt., *SNZDPW*, 659-62.

92. *ZDFS*, vol. 1, 416.

93. "Shanghai dianying jie jiuguo hui xuanyan" (Declaration of The National Salvation Association of Shanghai Cinema Circles). Rpt., *ZZDY*, 33-34.

94. Fei Mu, "Langshan diexue ji de zhizuo" (The production of *Bloodbath on Wolf Mountain*), *SB*, Nov. 21, 1936. Rpt., *SNZDPW*, 419-20.

95. Ke Ling, "Guofang dianying Mantan" (Talking about National Defense Cinema). Rpt., *ZZDY*, 181.

96. "Broken Dream in the Women's Apartment" was collected in *Lianhua jiaoxiangqu* (*Lianhua Symphony*) with seven other short films.

97. "Mingxing gongsi gexin xuanyan" (Mingxing Company's declaration for improvement), *Mingxing banyue kan* (Mingxing half-monthly) 1 (1936). Rpt., *ZZDY*, 27-29.

98. According to the filmography in *ZDFS*, vol. 1, 519-635.

99. *ZWD*, 293.

100. *SB*, Nov. 28, 1932.

101. *ZWD*, 294.

102. Unpublished diary of Li Minwei, provided by his son Li Shek.

103. Unpublished diary of Li Minwei.

104. *SB*, Feb. 15, 1936.

105. Ma Xu Weibang is among the very few Chinese filmmakers who are devoted to the horror film genre. In fact, his oeuvre reveals an obsession with some specific themes related to the genre, like deformed figures, unconsummated love, and the rite of fire. His masterpiece in this regard is *Qionglou Hen* (A Maid's Bitter Story), which he made in Hong Kong in 1948. For an in-depth discussion of his film *Song at Midnight*, see Yomi Braster, "Revolution and Revulsion: Ideology, Monstrosity, and Phantasmagoria in Ma-Xu Weibang's Film Song at Midnight" *Modern Chinese Literature and Culture* 12, no. 1 (Spring 2000): 81-114.

106. Lloyd E. Eastman, "Nationalist China during the Nanking Decade 1927-1937" in *The Cambridge History of China, vol. 13, Republic China 1912-1949, Part 2,* ed. John K. Fairbank and Albert Feuerwerker (Cambridge: Cambridge University Press, 1986), 116-67.

107. Yu Ling, "1927-1937 de juzuo," *ZZXLSJ*, 404.

108. *ZDFS*, vol. 2, 8-9.

109. The Japanese army did not invade the foreign settlements of Shanghai until the beginning of the Pacific War. And this "peaceful" land was named the "orphan island" because it was completely surrounded by areas of Japanese occupation between 1937 and 1941.

110. In fact, right after the termination of the Dramatists Association in 1936, many film people, who had been dramatists before, participated in different left-wing drama productions and brought dialogue dramas back to big theaters. There were many subtle parallels and conflicts between the left-wing drama movement and the left-wing cinema movement, which certainly deserve more scholarly attention. Unfortunately, the drama movement lies outside the scope of the book.

111. I discuss the later development of this left-wing cinema after the war in the epilogue.

Plate 1. *Wild Flowers* (1932). A typical melodrama of a singing girl (right) falling in love with the young master (middle).

Plate 2. *Spring Silkworms* (1933). Silkworm workers bring their products to sell.

Plate 3. *Salt Tide* (1933). The salt workers are dwarfed by the ships, which represent the capitalists.

Plate 4. *Sweetgrass Beauty* (1933). Sweetgrass refers to cigarettes. A film depicting how the Chinese cigarette industry and its workers were oppressed by imperialism, as were innocent girls corrupted by the modern Western entertainment culture. The advertising board in the background is about cigarettes.

Plate 5. *Three Modern Women* (1932). One of the three modern-woman archetypes created in this film: the infatuated fan who lived on romance alone.

Plate 6. *To the Northwest* (1934). Mise-en-scène heavily influenced by Hollywood's musicals.

Plate 7. *City Nights* (1933). The first film of Fei Mu, also starting a cycle of left-wing films equating Shanghai's nighttime with women being trampled or seduced by the corrupt materialist city.

Plate 8. *Women's Outcry* (1933). The first film of Shen Xiling, another women's liberation film depicting the traumatic experience of a country girl coming to Shanghai.

Plate 9. *Twenty-Four Hours in Shanghai* (1933). Country people finding themselves alienated and disillusioned in Shanghai.

Plate 10. *The Sisters* (1933). Spectators were awed by the split screen technique featuring two Hu Dies on the same screen.

Plate 11. *The Fisherman's Song* (1934). The ending of the film where the protagonists are disillusioned. One of the few Chinese movies without a happy ending.

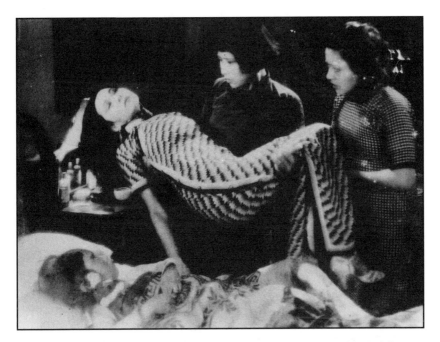

Plate 12. *New Woman* (1934). The "new woman" worker Li Aying holding up the "old woman" writer Wei Ming.

Plate 13. *The Goddess* (1934). The headmaster visits his pupil's family and finds himself in sympathy with the prostitute.

Plate 14. *Queen of Sport* (1934). One of the first Chinese films celebrating athleticism.

Plate 15. *The Highway* (1935). The famous scene where Moli passionately holds Dingxiang in her arms, revealing her love to all the six male protagonists.

Plate 16. *A Sea of Fragrant Snow* (1934). In spite of the depiction of poor people's sufferings, this film was not considered progressive because of the Buddhist thinking advocated.

Plate 17. *The Metamorphosing Girl* (1935). The famous soft-wing film severely criticized by left-wing critics partly because of the lesbian love depicted.

Plate 18. *Angry Tide in China's Seas* (1933). A scene of workers' insurrection.

Plate 19. *Sons and Daughters of the Storm* (1935). The poet Xin Baihua passionately looking at his "comrade" Feng putting on her makeup.

Plate 20. *Spirit of Freedom* (1935). Lan Ping, also Jiang Qing, the late Lady Chairman Mao, as the supporting actress in the film.

Plate 21. *Soaring Aspirations* (1936). Farmers decided to stand up against the Japanese invasion.

Plate 22. *Bloodbath on Wolf Mountain* (1936). A representative film of the National Defense Cinema, probably the most political work of Fei Mu.

Plate 23. *Lost Lambs* (1936). Modeling itself after the Soviet Union's film *Road to Life*, this was one of the first children's films in China.

Plate 24. *Old and New Shanghai* (1936). The poor versus the rich; the drivers versus the cars.

Plate 25. *Street Angel* (1937). The most celebrated and well-known film of the left-wing cinema movement.

II

The Filmmakers and the Formation of a Collective Subjectivity

3

The Role of Authorship in the Age of Nationalism

Since its invention, cinema, due to its tremendous impact on society, has been put to service for different powers, so was the case in 1930s' China. The left-wing films produced then and there also reflected, candidly or through detours, the discursive forces at work in the contemporary sociocultural context. These films combined to form the first coherent identity of Chinese cinema, and for the first time a Chinese national cinema was conceived on a theoretical level. Starting from here we will leave behind the historical reports and investigate the intimate relationship between these films and the vehement Chinese society, hoping to examine the films and the film culture more intimately within its own specific environment.

In the following chapters, I will argue and demonstrate that this left-wing cinema movement addressed and erected a new Chinese identity in the face of a new era, therefore a new collective subject was constructed in and through cinema. In her seminal book Miriam Hansen demonstrates that Hollywood's silent cinema successfully forged a new spectatorship by regulating acts of reception both stylistically and ideologically.[1] I will argue in the following chapters that a similar process also took place in Chinese cinema in the 1930s, which, however, was not solely fashioned by a modern consumer culture as argued by Hansen but also by a unique masculine left-wing political milieu. A coherent and consistent address observed in many of these left-wing films produced a new collective subject, referring both to the filmmakers and the viewers, who in turn made this cinema an eccentric composite of modern commodity and pre-modern ethical instrument. I believe that the filmmakers' and the viewers' shared identity and social commitment to a nation-building project was a key feature distinguishing this left-wing cinema from many other early commercial cinemas. Therefore, this cinematic subjectivity I will explore is collective in two senses: it represented the common identity of the filmmakers, and it also addressed the spectators in a relatively coherent and structured fashion.

Questions we will ask here include: What were the messages, anxieties, and desires the filmmakers conveyed? How were they conveyed? And how did the cinematic discourse manifest itself under and in spite of these maneuvers? As a whole, did a new subjectivity emerge in these left-wing films? And how did it come into being? To adequately answer these questions, we must consider more than just the filmmakers and the films but include the dynamic reception process. We will first tackle the identities, intentions, and anxieties of the filmmakers here in part 2 of this book and leave the issues related to reception and the larger film culture for part 3. In chapters 4 and 5 I will use gender representation as the locus to elucidate how this subjectivity was both filmic and extra-filmic. And in this chapter I will first focus on the filmmakers and discuss how their projects were influenced by their social identities. Through a close study of their lives and works, in this chapter we will explore the filmmakers' own self-perceptions or self-fascinations in this era of turmoil and idealism, with the aim of not only understanding this group of interesting individuals microscopically but also analyzing the cinema in its formation.

Naturally, what I am interested in is less auteur studies, in the sense that certain stylistic presentations or specific themes are identified as trademarks of individual filmmakers, than the running stylistic and thematic features revealed in a large number of these films that demonstrated the common struggles and ideals shared by these filmmakers. This approach must have sacrificed some of the diversity hidden in this cinema, and it might be criticized as predicated on the presumption that this cinema had a coherent identity to start with. But, as revealed in the filmmakers' writings and interviews, most of them, in spite of their different authorial visions, ideological commitments, and aesthetic concerns, saw themselves differently from what contemporary film studies call "auteur." These Chinese filmmakers identified themselves more with the left-wing film movement at large than with their own individual arts. Their films showed their common wish to bring a unity between art and politics, between theory and practice of their nationalist enterprise. They characterized the struggles of a new generation of young Chinese intellectuals in the 1930s, who were trapped between an inescapable spell of impotency and the fantasy of heroism.

The Filmmakers: Individual versus Collective Identity

Before going directly to the film texts, we may need to acquaint ourselves with these Chinese left-wing filmmakers first. This film community was certainly not homogenous. The list of left-wing movies published in *The Chinese Left-wing*

Cinema Movement is rather subjective and arbitrary. The book's editor herself is not able to elucidate clearly the basic criteria behind the selection.[2] Clearly there was not a set of stylistic rules and political tasks these self-proclaimed left-wing filmmakers all assumed, and the ideological standpoints of these filmmakers were difficult to define. For example, Wu Yonggang was one among several others who made films with drastically different political orientations within this period. His first film, *The Goddess,* made in 1934, has been acclaimed as one of the finest works of this left-wing cinema movement with the clear message of revealing the dark side of society; however, his second and third films, *Little Angel* and *Waves Washing the Sand,* made in 1935 and 1936 respectively, were fiercely attacked by left-wing critics as reactionary and as mouthpieces of the ruling GMD to present a harmonious and caring society.[3] His fourth film, *Soaring Aspirations*, made in 1936, once again showed Wu Yonggang's return to his earlier social concerns and his total embrace of the left-wing slogan of "National Defense Cinema."[4] Similar situations can also be observed in the works of other filmmakers like Fei Mu, Sun Yu, and Bu Wancang. The most dramatic case was Yue Feng, whose *Angry Tide in China's Sea* and *Runaway* were among the left-wing films most politically aggressive in propagating anti-Japanese sentiments. But in the period when Japan occupied China, Yue was accused as a traitor because he produced pro-Japanese films in the Japanese funded Huaying Film Company. The ideological variations shown in their films should not be seen as political failures of the filmmakers but as a testament to the extremely transient and volatile cinema culture at that time; a reconstruction of it is bound to be partial. There were many factors influencing the final political renderings of a film; left-wing ideology was only one among many.

On the other hand, there was another group of filmmakers who were more consistent in ideological commitment. CCP members like Xia Yan and Tian Han were the ones most dedicated to the Party's directions. The scripts they wrote were politically more assertive and transparent. These movies, nonetheless, cannot be seen as model products of the political machinery because each of their works was marked with their personal creative touches and many other unique aesthetic and ideological constituents. Some others filmmakers like Zhu Shilin and Zheng Zhengqiu were committed less to revolution than to reform, and their films manifested more empathy with traditional Chinese culture. But progressive and critical ideas can also be found sporadically in some of their films, like Zhu's episode "Gui" (Ghost) in *Lianhua Symphony*, which depicted the rape of a little girl by a man in the neighborhood, was clearly angry in tone and allegorical to contemporary China.

In fact, all filmmakers involved in this movement had their own unique experiences, training, and ideological makeup; they could never be seen as a homogeneous community. There were, as I have illustrated, a group of CCP members who started filming with clear political agendas. But there was another group of filmmakers, like Cheng Bugao, Bu Wancang, and Zheng Zhengqiu, who were directors themselves since the 1920s and turned political only during the maturation of this left-wing cinema movement. Others came from theater, like Ouyang Yuqian, Yuan Muzhi, Ying Yunwei, and Hong Shen, who were drawn to the film industry because of cinema's alluring power and its intellectual spin developed in 1930s' China. Some others were either fresh from foreign film school, like Sun Yu, or had been film critics, like Fei Mu, or artists, like Xu Xingzhi. There were also a group of studio apprentices who acquired their filmmaking techniques through working in various production positions before becoming directors, like Cai Chusheng, Shi Dongshan, and Situ Huimin. Obviously, these filmmakers shared some common ideological concerns and commitments in cinematic art, but their diversity was too obvious to ignore. Also, these filmmakers working for different film companies easily became enemies among themselves commercially, as cinema in 1930s' China was similar to most film industries in its fierce competitiveness. In place of a harmonized monologue, in this film movement there was clearly a polyphony of voices, contradictory and ambiguous, affirming, opposing, or negotiating their views with the left-wing ideology.

However, these individual voices should not be understood as isolated artistic articulations. The common political and ethical concerns as well as the daily reality of the generation discouraged the young filmmakers from separating themselves from the collective and claiming individual creative agency. Films produced in this left-wing film movement, quite different from the case of the Chinese Fifth Generation Cinema in the 1980s for example, were seen less as autonomous individual artworks than interrelated pieces within a larger corpus. Many times the unique features shown in the individual films were not manifestations of independent creative choices but the inevitable products of the larger film community under the similar artistic and ideological influences.

Since François Truffaut first advanced the idea *politique des auteurs*, the term and concept of "auteur" has been widely used in studying prominent film directors, with the assumption that their films bear the signature of the filmmaker's personal style, rather than being the work of some corporate collective. Specifically within the context of Hollywood cinema in the 1950s, Truffaut argued that in spite of its rigid structure, many American directors were able to leave their signatures in their films.[5] Other theorists also asserted that the director's ability to triumph over the limitation of his restrictions and materials marks his/her success as an auteur film artist.[6] However, despite the fact that a rigid studio system and firm marketing mentality had not been developed in Chinese cinema in the 1930s, and that its filmmakers had much freedom in the production process to experiment with and develop their own artistic manners, most of them were interested more in identifying with the progressive film culture than emphasizing their individual political/artistic positions. Other than some exceptional cases, spectators and critics could seldom identify the specific stylistic marks of individual filmmakers, as most of them did not deliberately put their own stamps on their films. This enormously encompassing collective identity came to condition the many commonalities of these films.

There are many studies devoted to the account of the collective ethos of China's intellectual culture that developed in the first half of the twentieth century. Many of these scholarships connect its formation to the growing affinity with nationalism and socialism in China, which were partly results of the contemporary imperialist meddling.[7] But some of these studies also demonstrate that this collective identity was ridden with the intellectuals' individualist urges. Critics of modern Chinese literature have used different literary works as examples to analyze how the authors were torn between the search for one's individual identity and the ethical project of bringing collective good to China. Lydia Liu, for example, discusses the works of Lu Xun and Yu Dafu and illustrates that the quest for the self by modern Chinese intellectuals ended in profound disillusionment in the May Fourth period.[8] In the context of the 1930s' left-wing culture, Kirk Denton also argues that the artistic subject of Hu Feng, a leading leftist critic of the time, is "schizophrenic: drawn with the opposing discourses of romantic individualism and revolutionary collectivism, at once autonomous from history and inseparable from it."[9]

Beyond doubt the left-wing filmmakers also confronted similar ideological dilemmas; they were trapped in a time when "History" was looming so large that no one could escape. Many Chinese at the beginning of the century left their communal lives in villages to become lost and isolated individuals in the city. At the same time they were bombarded with the news of their country being invaded by foreigners. There were many reasons for the Chinese to choose nationalism and socialism; both of them provided a way out of the uncertain individualistic chaos. It was the time when they, like all other Chinese intellectuals, had to choose between the West and China, between the future and the past; the rapid cultural and political changes made their decision-making hasty yet importunate. Most of them were ready to replace two thousand years of tradition wholesale with Western ideas, yet they retreated immediately back without hesitation when they discovered that the West also meant political and economic transgression. As Marxism was a branch of Western thought that seemingly subverted the entire base of the Western civilization, many found in it a solution for their intricate emotional and intellectual dilemma. They found their justification for challenging the imperialistic West legitimated by the intellectual West. It was the national situation of China that brought Marxist ideology, which was one among many other competing Western thoughts available, to the attention of Chinese intellectuals.[10] Similar to its fate in other countries, philosophical Marxism in China was easily transformed into a didactic doctrine less because of the intrinsic deficiencies of the ideology than the complicated political situations and cultural problems inherent in the adopting countries.

However, in addition to these abstract ethical and political calls, there were more practical reasons that bound these young filmmakers physically and emotionally together. Chinese cinema in the 1930s was still a new, emerging industry, immature and disorganized. The film market was relatively small, as only a small part of the nation's population had access to cinema. Politically and economically China was also in a turmoil in the 1930s; most film studios were

struggling to make ends meet instead of benefiting from the emerging modernization. Most filmmakers were not well paid, and they were far away from the
decent lives their Hollywood counterparts were enjoying. Both in theory and in
practice, these left-wing filmmakers belonged more to the lower-middle class
that could not afford individualism. The lack of support on the institutional level
also brought the filmmakers close together. The success of the American studio
system was largely contributed to their producers who, after much marketing
research and institutional planning, make the final decisions from the business
viewpoint; and therefore the producer is usually the one, instead of the director,
who is most crucial in defining the Hollywood film.[11] The careful division of
labor marked the commercial success of the American studio system in the
1930s to the 1950s.[12] However, as Shen Xiling illustrated, there were almost no
producers or scriptwriters in place in the 1930s' Chinese film industry, and the
director had to assume major responsibilities in almost all aspects of pre-
production, production, and post-production. He wrote in 1935:

> There are plenty of directors and talents in today's Chinese film stu-
> dios, but there are almost no real professional producers or script-
> writers in place . . . [Without producers], our film industry is without
> a pivot. The studio, like an anarchy, has no overall business plan in
> film productions. The directors make their films according to their
> individual concerns and wishes without the check and balance of any
> institutional system, and coarse products are inevitable. . . . The di-
> rector also suffers from exhaustion without a healthy system in
> scriptwriting. . . . He has to assume his directing job, at the same time
> he also has to prepare for the next script. Under such circumstances,
> how dare could we expect him to produce good works in a short
> turnout rate?[13]

To many Hollywood directors and critics, the rigid studio system is a major im-
pediment to artistic exploration and achievement. However, in the 1930s' Chinese film industry, the unsystematic structure of the corporation and little input
from other staff and departments were detrimental to the directors' devotion to
their cinematic art and craft. Most of these directors were in their twenties or
thirties without rich life experience, and they were expected to produce several
films a year under stringent budgets. Other than relying on each other and on the
collective creative impulse, there was little they could count on to provide aesthetic or ideological incentives for their works, as they had no extra time and
support to research their subject matter. If we have to criticize these filmmakers
of not executing individual, independent thinking, it was more the environment
of their time than their own conscious choice that should be held responsible.
Politically, economically, and institutionally, they just could not afford to stay
alone. However, one of the most fascinating dimensions of this cinema movement was precisely the ability of this collective ethos to harbor a multitude of
artistic expressions.

James Snead argues that, in constructing a national literary canon, authors such as Homer, Dante, and Shakespeare are often seen as "consummate geniuses" of a given national spirit, but ultimately they are able to attract greater interest due to their alleged embodiment of "universal truths," defacing specific cultural manifestations. These geniuses ultimately dissolve the claim of nation and nationalism, which constructed their canonical status in the first place.[14] Under this definition, I would certainly not call these Chinese left-wing filmmakers "consummate geniuses" as they seldom had the desire or freedom to call spectators' attention to their own individual authorship. They defined themselves less as autonomous artists than as committed members of this artistic/political enterprise. They might not be those "geniuses" as Snead would call Homer and Dante, and they both started and ended as subordinates of the nation, but their works were as respectable and culturally significant as those canonical cultural products, for these filmmakers candidly and unpretentiously confronted themselves and the time. Although they might have failed to come to terms with both art and politics, the films reflected their struggles and commitment to society as well as to themselves, which were, as a result, always ridden with conflicting constituents ranging from confidence to impotency. To illustrate how these anxieties and flights of fancy were translated into cinematic representations, let us go to the text and explore how a collective male subjectivity representing the filmmaker-collective emerged.

The Impotent Intellectual

The Goddess is a passionate mother-son story. A villain offers his protection of a beautiful and kindhearted prostitute from police's arrest yet asks for money and control from her in return. She bravely confronts her misfortunes, as she is willing to sacrifice herself, in body and soul, in order to bring a bright future to her only son. However, her son's school receives complaints from many parents claiming that this hooker family was contaminating the good name of the school. The headmaster then goes to visit the prostitute, and he discovers her noble character and promises to protect her son (see plate 13). But the headmaster's single and feeble voice is ignored, and the son is expelled from school in the name of the institute's collective good. Enraged by this decision, the prostitute decides to leave Shanghai with her son in order to start a new life, but she discovers that her savings have been taken away by the villain. The angry mother goes to ask for the money back and accidentally kills the villain with a glass bottle. At the end of the film the headmaster goes to visit her in jail and promises to raise her son as if he were his own.

Besides the mother and the son, there are two minor figures in the film: the villain and the school principal. As Wu Yonggang wrote: "The role of the rascal who tramples her and robs her money is to bring the dramatic conflicts in focus. The role of the conscientious old headmaster, on the other hand, is there to represent righteousness. I use his mouth to tell the spectators that the film reflects a problem for which our society should be responsible."[15] According to this statement, this school principal is obviously the director's mouthpiece in which Wu Yonggang's personal sentiments are demonstrated and released. As obvious in the film, the headmaster is a lonely intellectual trapped between moral responsibility and mass pressure, as he feels obliged to transform the evil world but is too powerless to accomplish the job. Although he heads the school, under the pressure of the parents and the trustees he cannot even prevent a student from being expelled. This is a frequent and tormenting tragedy in Chinese intellectual history: a man has no control over the responsibilities he assumes. However, the film allows the headmaster to shoulder the final hope: being powerless to change society, he is assigned the task of teaching the next generation to build the new nation. While this generation is doomed to failure, hope is projected onto the next one, calling for linearity under the nationalist project. The preservation of a nationhood is achieved by the hope continually placed on the next generation.

A similar headmaster character can be found in another famous left-wing movie: *Plunder of Peach and Plum* directed by Ying Yunwei. This film, like *Crossroads*, is about the disillusion of two graduates as they leave school and enter the real world. Tao Jianping and Li Lilin are lovers at school and get married right after graduation. The husband fails to find a job to support the family, and the housewife decides to enter the work force and later becomes a secretary in a trading company. Very soon Tao also begins a promising career through the help of a schoolmate. However, he soon finds his schoolmate's corruption intolerable and quits the job; Li is also forced to leave the company because of the sexual aggression on the part of her boss. The two fall into poverty, and Tao becomes a shipyard laborer. After giving birth to their first child, the wife falls ill. The husband has to steal money from the office to pay for her medical expenses. But the money comes too late; she dies, and Tao has no choice but to entrust their child to an orphan's home. He is later charged for theft. During the arrest he resists and kills a policeman; and he is ultimately condemned to capital punishment for murder.

The film begins with the headmaster reading the death sentence of Tao, one of his favorite students, in a newspaper. He goes to visit Tao in jail, and the film retells the above story through Tao's narration of repentance to his former headmaster. At the end of the film the headmaster painfully witnesses his beloved student being taken to execution. The upright and responsible character of the headmaster is evidenced in the love and care he gives to his students. His erudition and devotion to his job are also shown clearly in the scenes of his office where he is always positioned between a big Chinese history cabinet in the background and a Greek statue on the foreground (figure 3.1). His later departure to the West to study education further testifies to his devotion in his career. Despite all these, he is still too powerless to prevent his favorite student from being crushed by society.

Both the beginning and the end of the film show a group of high-spirited graduates singing a graduation song during the commencement, which is in ironic contrast to the film's overall bleak atmosphere. Written by Tian Han, the lyrics of this *Biye ge* (Song of graduation) are:

> Fellow students, let's rise!
> Let's change the world.
> Listen! The groaning of the mass is everywhere.
> Behold! A year and another, we witness our land being transgressed.
> Should we choose fighting or giving in? We should be the master and sacrifice ourselves in the battlefield.
> We don't want to be slaves, but we should rise up to touch the sky.
> Today we are transmitting the fragrance of peach and plum;
> tomorrow we will be the foundation of society.

This song reflects the unyielding belief of Tao Jianping and Li Lilin in their responsibilities as high-school graduates to China's redemption, which was the very lesson they learned from their headmaster. The tragedy of two leading characters, therefore, also implies the failure of the headmaster. However, placing the same song once again at the end of the film shows that the song's ideology is not mocked, as the headmaster continues to lecture the same message to the next generation. In asking his students to choose fighting instead of giving in, he is running the risk of sending the new graduates, too, to death.

The characterization of the two headmaster figures would not strike those familiar with modern Chinese literature as novelty, as they echo a famous archetype male figure of Lu Xun's writing. The well-known anecdote of Lu Xun goes: A group of sleeping people are trapped in an iron house with no windows and doors which would allow their escape. Before long they would all die from suffocation. Should we let them die peacefully? Or should we wake them up and let them confront their inevitable deaths? Lu Xun chose the latter. As he wrote: "Though I was convinced to my own satisfaction that it wouldn't be possible to break out, I still couldn't dismiss hope entirely, for hope belongs to the future."[16] As Leo Ou-fan Lee argues, a running theme in Lu Xun's poetry is the notion of being trapped between hope and desperation.[17] And we can also find many of Lu Xun's male characters in his novels confronting similar struggles. This sense of impotency was shared by Wu Yonggang, the director of *The Goddess*, and he explained his personal grip on the film on a similar ground: "[Through the headmaster figure] I did not solve any problems. The empirical reality allows me only to express some sentimental outcry. I admit that I am feeble; I can only do so little."[18] Both the director and the headmaster figures were put into the same dilemma many Chinese intellectuals were facing.

However, these two headmasters reflected only one facet of the collective male subjectivity developing in this left-wing cinema, as the collective identity of these filmmakers, if we believe that there was one, was more complicated and less organically coherent than that of Lu Xun. Michael Chang has demonstrated in his recent article that there was a clear shift of public attitude to movie actresses from the 1920s to the 1930s, that the degraded and evil image of female stars was replaced with a modernized and Westernized persona in the 1930s.[19] Parallel developments were also observed among the filmmakers behind the screen, which might well be the major reason contributing to the image shift of the movie actresses. As I have mentioned, as a highly respected college professor and stage director in the 1920s, Hong Shen received a tremendous amount of resistance from intellectual circles when he decided to enter the film industry.[20] Shi Dongshan in 1926 also claimed that: "In these years no one would not shake their heads when talking about the film industry."[21] However, the progressive cinema in the 1930s was so successful in upgrading its social position that the public saw the new cinema as a completely fresh start, allowing the filmmakers to assume a brand new identity as intellectuals, which was almost unheard of in the former decade. They did not need to struggle hard to assure themselves and the public that their new identity was legitimized and honorable, as it was all of a sudden taken for granted, marking an abrupt but interesting fracture in the history of Chinese cinema.

With this sudden discursive shift, the young and progressive filmmakers found themselves at the crossroads of an ideological network. They were optimistic, as 1930s' China endowed her young people with a strong sense of political idealism, particularly to these filmmakers who were suddenly notified of their significance to society. But they were also desperate being filmmakers, with Wu Yonggang as the typical example, whose tools were considered inadequate to assume the political task they and society had assigned them. They enjoyed their elitist and intellectual position, yet they could not afford losing the contact with the masses—they had to face a much wider reception when compared to their fellow writers. If Lu Xun has been celebrated as the major Chinese writer in the twentieth century because of his ability to construct a coherent and organic artistic world, our interest in this cinema might be more in its conflicts and varieties than consistent representation tactics.

The Intellectual-Revolutionary Mirroring

Although the collective identity among these young filmmakers was strong, they still envisaged individual heroes who could save the country from foreign and internal humiliation. Other than the impotent intellectual who was too weak to rescue China, this left-wing cinema also created a different form of hero to assume the duty, which can be demonstrated in *Unchanged Heart in Life and Death*. The story took place in the warlord period of the 1920s—a time often employed by the left-wing films to represent their chaotic contemporary political world, with the evil warlords representing the GMD government and the civil wars standing for Japanese invasion. *Unchanged Heart in Life and Death* is about the misidentification of two people, a GMD revolutionary Li Tao and a high school teacher Liu Yuanjie, who look identical. While Li Tao has just escaped from prison, Liu Yuanjie is on his way back home after quitting his teaching position in South East Asia and is mistakenly arrested by the warlord's police as the fugitive Li. Liu shows the court all of his legal documents to prove his innocence, but justice seems not to be in power at that time. He is imprisoned and has to place his hope on his fiancée Zhao Yuhua to make connections with the high officials for his release. Her efforts are futile, but she meets Li, who encourages her to participate in revolutionary actions. Li is later arrested and imprisoned in the same cell where Liu resides. In an attempt to escape prison, the revolutionary succeeds, but the intellectual is arrested. Li later meets Zhao and other revolutionaries, and they decide to attack the prison to release their other comrades. Liu is finally rescued, but the noble Li Tao dies heroically in the action. At the end of the film Liu picks up a gun lying on the ground and marches off with his fiancée as well as Li's resurrecting spirit to join the parading revolutionaries.[22]

The most interesting and crucial element in the narrative is the mirroring character of Li and Liu, who are both performed by Yuan Muzhi, the famous actor-director who had participated in many left-wing dramas and films, like *Scenes of City Life* and *Plunder of Peach and Plum*. In the beginning of the film the director Ying Yunwei brilliantly intercuts the fugitive escaping from the prison to the scene where the high school teacher shaves and combs his hair on a train, creating an illusionary identification between the two. Only when Li secretly enters Liu's house and sees the latter's portrait hanging on the wall do he and the spectators finally realize that they are two different people. It is also in this scene, when Li looks at the picture of Liu, that the film's major motif—the mirroring of the intellectual and the revolutionary—is established. This theme of mirroring image is further reinforced by the parallel relationships between the romance of Liu and Zhao (figure 3.2) and the political collaboration of Li and Zhao (figure 3.3).

Before the major dramatic conflicts are introduced, the film includes an uncommonly long sequence about the romantic relationship between Liu and Zhao, portraying the passion and tenderness Liu shares with his fiancée, which, quite similar to *Sons and Daughters of the Storm* I will discuss in the next chapter, diverts the young teacher's attentions from national issues. This sequence has a more important function structurally than just depicting romance: it is through Zhao that the two mirror images finally reconcile. After knowing the identity of Li, there is another set of sequences depicting Zhao assisting him with his revolutionary activities and assists in putting up propaganda materials on the streets at night. Later the two also collaborate in the freeing of Liu from prison. During a political meeting, Zhao humbly confesses her naïveté in political ideology and praises Li as her teacher who has helped her to understand the real meaning of revolution.

Structurally Zhao's romance to Liu the intellectual is parallel with her comradeship to Li the revolutionary. The major objective of the film is to depict how the intellectual is transformed by his mirror image, the revolutionary, to become the ideal composite figure of intellectual-revolutionary. Zhao is highly symbolic in this unification: the separated mirror images are bridged by their common relationship with her, who, at the end of the film, finally brings together her lover and her teacher marching along the revolutionary path. She is the catalyst to effectuate the otherwise impossible fusion between intellectual and revolutionary, between theory and practice, between individuals and the mass.

The writer of the film, Yang Hansheng, was the only figure in the movie industry in the 1930s who had fought in real political battles. After becoming a member of the CCP in 1925, he participated in the famous August First Insurrection in Nanchang two years later and thereafter became an important figure in the Party. In discussing this film, Yang Hansheng wrote: "The major objective of this film is to create a dignified revolutionary; a revolutionary who has suffered all pains in the world—imprisonment, flight, capture, poverty—but continues to be unyielding; a revolutionary who sacrifices his noble life on the battlefield at the end."[23] But what Yang Hansheng did not mention here is the other side of the story: how about Liu Yuanjie?

The most interesting question about this film is who the real hero is. Although Yang Hansheng proclaimed that the film centered on the revolutionary Li Tao, his death at the end of the film denies altogether our wishes on him to rescue the country. Instead, he can only be seen as an intermediate figure, like John the Baptist, who sanctions the revolutionary ideology of Liu Yuanjie the intellectual. *Unchanged Heart in Life and Death* depicts the theme of initiation not of the revolutionary Li Tao but of the intellectual Liu Yuanjie, showing that it is the school teacher being positioned as the ultimate leader of revolution. The film hints that he is forced to return to China because of his participation in Chinese nationalist activities in South East Asia. But after coming home he begins his romance with Zhao Yuhua and spends all his time enjoying life. It is the imprisonment that widely opens his eyes on the meaning and urgency of revolution. In fact, the real hero, I would argue, is neither Liu Yuanjie nor Li Tao but the summation of the two mirrored figures. The marching of Liu Yuanjie and Li Tao's spirit together on the battlefield signifies the final resolution of the divided intellectual/revolutionary dichotomy. The real hero of the Chinese left-wing cultural enterprise must develop the dual identities of both intellectual and revolutionary. Maybe this figure is only an ideal self-image of the scriptwriter of the film, Yang Hansheng, who himself embodies both identities. But similar arrangements of character pairing can be found in a number of the left-wing films like *March of Youth, Night Run,* and *Sons and Daughters of the Storm* in which the intellectual character in the film is finally transformed into a revolutionary. This new male image combines intelligence and bravery to represent an ideal figure without which China could not be saved.

However, despite this lofty ideology in combining knowledge and action, theory and practice, we have to note that individualism as a form of heroic pursuit is inherent in this representation. To link this heroism back to the political project, the sublimation of Li and Liu is made possible only after they march together toward the masses at the end. Without the embrace of the collective, an individual can never be granted the status of revolutionary. He could not be considered ideal even by embodying the identities of both an intellectual and a revolutionary, but he must also give up this dual identity ultimately and let go of himself within a larger body. Similar depictions of the individual protagonist becoming one with masses can be found in the endings of many other left-wing movies, like the primary school teacher in *Torrent*, the saleslady in *Cosmetics Market*, the female factory worker in *New Woman*, the feeble student in *March of Youth*, the poet in *Sons and Daughters of the Storm*, the jobless youths in *Crossroads*, and the construction workers and their female friends in *The Highway*, etc.

Ban Wang has argued that in Modern China the individual being engulfed by the collective does not necessarily suggest his/her death but a sublimation of this individuality into a transcendental entity.[24] The transcendental entity achieved by the intellectual/revolutionary dissolving into the masses represents the most idealistic aspect of this collective subjectivity, marking an opposite counterpart with the headmaster figures we have just visited. But these two seemingly contradictory male personalities might ultimately represent two sides of the same man, who was trapped between the urge for power and spell of impotency.

Male's Sentimentalism

In spite of the diversified personas, these conflictual representations made this collective "he" more coherent and three-dimensional, referring less to an imagined figure composed of abstract concepts than to the actual struggles and identity constructions these filmmakers actually went through. The male subjectivity we observed in this cinema is impotent and guilty, but he is also pressed with nationalist demands. He embodies both the essence of intellectual/artist and revolutionary, and is therefore trapped between the artistic urge of self-representation and the social responsibility called for from the nation. He is the master between the two genders, yet he must constantly rely on the female other to set off and sanction his heroic deeds. Below the surface of celebrated chivalry and glorification, the male characters are in fact ridden with anxiety. The young men were torn between extreme idealism on the one hand and the inevitable awareness of their limited power on the other. If this cinema reflected the filmmakers' own perception during this period of unrest in China, what the spectator witnessed was their tormenting sway between the image of a hero and that of a loser. The more fanatic the idealism was that dominated the filmmakers, the more distress hidden under their representations. There was clearly a prominent dimension of this cinema movement that was self-referenced, particularly in relation to the male's position in their collective political project.

This self-allegorization of the filmmakers in their films also implied the large dosage of emotion they invested in their male characters, which characterized, partly, the strong sentimentalism we observed in these films. As I will argue in chapter 8, the left-wing films were often accused melodramatic. Many of the emotion features were, not surprisingly, driven by female desire and the processes of spectator identification governed by a female point of view, as many critics have argued for the genre of melodrama. But an equal amount of emotions was also invested in the male characters. Many of these Chinese left-wing melodramas discussed overtly "masculine issues," like the nation and brotherhoods, with high emotional pitch. This male sentimentalism, so obviously observed in this cinema, reflected as much the emotional stamp of male spectators as the strong identification of the filmmakers to their films.[25]

A good example to illustrate this male sentimentalism is Cai Chusheng's *Early Morning in the Metropolis*. It recounts the story of a pair of siblings, Huiling and Qiling, who grew up in two different environments. Qiling, an illegitimate child of Huang Menghua, was abandoned by his father and later picked up by a rickshaw man, Xu Ada. He grows up in this family, with Xu Ada's daughter Lan'er, as an upright and benevolent young man. Huiling, on the other hand, is the second but legitimate son of Menghua and becomes, not surprisingly, a vicious and self-centered loafer. In order to possess Lan'er, whose beauty captivates him, Huiling puts Qiling in prison. When Qiling finally escapes the jail and rushes to Huiling's mansion, Lan'er is already raped. At the same moment the weak father also gets up from his sickbed and staggers to Huiling's room. He announces the relationship between the two brothers and begs the elder son to stay and inherit all he has. The righteous Qiling, as the spectators expect, acts according not to greed but self-dignity, and the film ends at his walking away with his poor sister from the mansion.

Similar to *The Sisters*, a film I will illustrate in detail in chapter 8, *Early Morning in the Metropolis* narrates and discusses the lives of a pair of siblings who grow up in two completely different environments. In *The Sisters*, although Dabao and Erbao are twins, they develop contradictory character traits in the two different social conditions. Similarly, Huiling and Qiling, the half-brothers, are also transformed by their upbringing and develop completely contradictory personalities.[26] However, unlike *The Sisters*, this film is directed completely from male's perspective. There is almost no cinematic or narrative mechanism in the film emphasizing the emotions of the women's characters. Its narrative is developed around the father and his two sons, and the film's emotional knot is tied at the father character: the film condemns yet pities Menghua who has made an irreparable mistake due to his irresponsibility, and this error is transformed into guilt accompanying him his whole life.

Although films concentrated entirely on men were not common in this cinema, the male sentimentalism in *Early Morning in the Metropolis* was typical.

The masculine collective subjectivity evolved in this left-wing cinema was as rational as it was sensational. Not only did men participate in the nation-building project, but they were also obsessed with domestic and familial matters. The patriarchal order remained intact in spite of this highlight of male emotion. For example, the evil in *Early Morning in the Metropolis* is rooted in the father who represents capitalist lust and depravation, but it is not the mother nor the daughter but his son and himself who are responsible for the redemption. It is the father, due to his own selfishness, who separates the siblings and corrupts the one who stays with him. But it is also him who condemns himself and begs for forgiveness. The film does not question the entire construct of "fatherhood" and propose other alternatives. In fact, many left-wing films are critical of fathers, but the condemned ones continued to be the speaking subjects and were endowed with the power to corrupt and repent.

Both the headmasters and the intellectual/revolutionary composite figures we have analyzed are much more sentimental than most other standard hero figures we see in other cinemas. They weep and whine, and close-ups are directed on their faces revealing their internal feelings which are often concealed in other male representations. They are constantly reflecting upon their relationships with the others, and they do not hide their weaknesses to spectators. Many of the left-wing films reflected a primordial male's desire and passions, guilt and pressure. Here we clearly witness not only the intellect but also the emotions of the male filmmakers. They condemned their fathers' impotency in corrupting the nation, and they fancied themselves as national heroes paying their fathers' debt and ultimately replacing their own fathers. In contrast to the male sentimentalism we observed in May Fourth literature, which was usually individualistic and effeminate, the emotions attached to these male characters on screen were more masculine in tone, which could, interestingly, tie to both the family and the nation at the same time. Unlike Lu Xun's male archetype, the emotional male characters in these left-wing films were not discouraged to devote themselves in the masculine collective project. If the above analysis has yet to prove that a collective subjectivity evolved in this cinema, in the following two chapters I will further illustrate it by analyzing how this male subject constructed, and was constructed by, his female counterparts, demonstrating that the female representations and stories were also part of this collective masculine project.

Notes

1. Miriam Hansen, *Babel and Babylon: Spectatorship in American Silent Film* (Cambridge, Mass.: Harvard University Press, 1991).
2. Zhu Tianwei (one of the editors of *ZZDY*), interviewed by author, Beijing, China, Dec. 12, 1996.
3. See *ZDFS*, vol. 1, 351, 459-61.
4. For a reading of Wu Yonggang's ambivalent attitudes towards the West and modernity in his 1930s films, see Zhiwei Xiao's "Wu Yonggang and the Ambivalence in the

888

Chapter 3

Chinese Experience of Modernity: A Study of His Three Films of the Mid-1930s." *Asian Cinema* 9, no. 2 (Spring 1998): 3-15.

5. François Truffaut, "Une certaine tendance du cinéma français," *Cahiers du cinéma* 31 (Jan. 1954). Rpt. "On a Certain Tendency of the French Cinema" in *Movies and Methods I*, ed. Bill Nichols (Berkeley: University of California Press, 1976), 224-237.

6. See, for example, Andrew Sarris' article "Notes on the Author Theory in 1962," *Film Culture* (Winter 1962-63). Rpt. *Film Theory and Criticism: Introductory Readings*, ed. Leo Braudy and Marshall Cohen (Oxford: Oxford University Press, 1999), 515-35.

7. See, for example, Joseph Levenson's *Confucian China and Its Modern Fate*, vol. 1 (London: Routledge & Kegan Paul, 1965); C.T. Hsia's *A History of Modern Chinese Fiction* (New York: Columbia University Press, 1979); Li Zehou's *Zhongguo xiandai sixiang shi lun* (The discussion of modern Chinese intellectual history), rev. ed. (Taipei: Fengyun, 1990); and Lydia Liu's *Translingual Practice: Literature, National Culture, and Translated Modernity—China, 1900-1937* (Stanford, Calif.: Stanford University Press, 1995).

8. Lydia Liu, "Narratives of Modern Selfhood: First-Person Fiction in May Fourth Literature" *Politics, Ideology, and Literary Discourse in Modern China: Theoretical Interventions and Cultural Critique*, ed. Liu Kan and Xiaobin Tang (Durham, N.C.: Duke University Press, 1993), 102-123.

9. Kirk Denton, *The Problematic of Self in Modern Chinese Literature: Hu Feng and Lu Ling* (Stanford, Calif.: Stanford University Press, 1998), 22.

10. This historical situation finds its echo in the 1990s when many scholars are now upholding postmodernism or postcolonialism from the West to reinforce the new surge of Chinese nationalism.

11. Thomas Schatz, "Introduction: The Whole Equation of Pictures," *The Genius of the System* (New York: Henry Holt and Company, 1996), 3-11.

12. See, for example, chapter 9 of Bordwell, Staiger, and Thompson's *The Classical Hollywood Cinema* (New York: Columbia University Press, 1985).

13. Shen Xiling, "Zhongguo dianying qiye de weiji yu fujiu fangfa (The crisis of Chinese film industry and its remedy)" *Shenbao yuekan* (Shenbao monthly) 4, no. 10 (Sept. 15, 1935), 80.

14. James Snead, "European Pedigrees/African Contagions: Nationality, Narrativity, and Communality in Tutuola, Achebe, and Reed," in *Nation and Narration*, ed. Homi K. Bhabha (London & New York: Routledge, 1990), 233.

15. Wu Yonggang, "Shennü wancheng zhihou" (After finishing *The Goddess*) *Lianhua huabao* (Lianghau pictorial) 5, no. 1 (Jan. 1, 1935). Rpt., Wu Yonggang, *Wo de tansuo he zhuiqiu* (My search and pursuit) (Beijing: Zhongguo dianying, 1986), 134.

16. This anecdote was included in the "Preface" of the short story collection *Nahan* (Call to arms/Outcry). For its English translation, see *Diary of a Madman and Other Stories*, trans. William Lyell (Honolulu: University of Hawaii Press, 1990), 21-28.

17. Leo Ou-fan Lee, *Voices from the Iron House: A Study of Lu Xun* (Bloomington: Indiana University Press, 1987), 89-108.

18. Wu Yonggang, "Shennü wancheng zhihou," 134.

19. Michael Chang, "The Good, the Bad, and the Beautiful: Movie Actresses and Public Discourse in Shanghai, 1920s–1930s" in *Cinema and Urban Culture in Shanghai, 1922-1943*, ed. Yingjin Zhang (Stanford, Calif.: Stanford University Press, 1999), 128-59.

20. See *Hong Shen wenji* (Writings of Hong Shen), vol. 4 (Beijing: Zhongguo xiju, 1957), 514.

21. *ZWD*, 371.

22. This ending is similar to that in *The Highway* when Dingxiang and the dead protagonists rise to march toward the collective. For detailed analysis see next chapter.

23. Yang Hansheng, "Guangyu 'Shengshi tongxin' " (Regarding *Unchanged Heart in Life and Death*) *Mingxing banyuekan* (Mingxing half-monthly) 1, no. 4 (1936). Rpt., *ZZDY*, 376.

24. Ban Wang, *The Sublime Figure of History: Aesthetics and Politics in Twentieth-century China* (Stanford, Calif.: Stanford University Press, 1997), 130-31.

25. Perry Link observes that most of the pulp fiction readers in the 1910s and 1920s were male because of the large proportion of illiteracy among women. Therefore, most popular stories of the 1910s invite identification with male much more than with female protagonists. See *Mandarin Ducks and Butterflies: Popular Fiction in Early Twentieth-Century Chinese Cities* (Berkeley: University of California Press, 1981), 195. However, literacy was less a determining factor in cinematic participation as many theaters hired simultaneous narrators to read out the films' titles, in the local dialects of course.

26. Ke Ling has pointed out that the traditional Chinese narrative structure of parallels and contrasts (*duibi*) exerted a great influence on Cai Chusheng, whose films always showed the counterbalance of harmony and contrast. Ke Ling, "Introduction" in Cai Chusheng, *Cai Chusheng xuanji* (Selected writings of Cai Chusheng), 7.

Figure 3.1.
The Headmaster in *Plunder of Peach and Plum* is trapped between a Greek statue and the huge Chinese history cabinet, looking out of the window and pondering China's future.

Figure 3.2.
Sons and Daughters of the Storm. The romance of Zhao Yuhua and Liu Yuanjie.

Figure 3.3.
The comradeship of Zhao Yuhua and Li Tao.

4

Masculinity and Collectivism: Romancing Politics

With the paired sense of crisis posed by the Japanese military invasion on the one hand and the impotency and extreme corruption of the GMD government on the other hand, the leftist cultural whirlwind swept across almost the entire progressive intelligentsia in the span of several years in the 1930s. During such a turbulent period, gender was inevitably constitutive of, as well as constituting, this collective identity. As maintained by Christina Kelley Gilmartin regarding the development of China's feminism in the beginning of this century, "gender issues were at the crux of this explosive effort to create a new nation because they were so central to the redefinitions of the political order, family, morality, and the very meaning of masculinity and femininity."[1] Only by including gender in the picture can we understand more intimately this significant part of modern China, as the reconstruction of gender order was considered by many as the key to modernization.

After illustrating the filmmakers' struggles in coming to terms with their identities in this nationalist project, in these two chapters I will focus on the cinema's gender representation and discuss how it penetrates the surface of the leftwing ideology and reveals a collective subjectivity in its formation. In the previous chapter, I demonstrated that the male images represented in this cinema embodied the filmmakers' struggles in positioning themselves and their films in this tremendously alluring yet impossible project of "building a new China in cinema." In this chapter I will continue to investigate this collective subjectivity characterized by the struggles between an impotency anxiety and a juvenile idealism. But here I carry on this exploration in sexual terms and explore the construction of masculinity in relation to the opposite sex, as this cinema movement

91

was as much about China as about men. In fact, the opposite-sex relationship was so essential in this left-wing cinema, in spite of its loud assertion of the opposite, that this was, I believe, the most "romantic" period of the entire history of Chinese cinema up to date, in the double sense of the word "romantic" referring to both the abounding representation of love affairs and the overall youthful and sentimental aura. While the left-wing ideology accused sexual and romantic relationships as being politically unproductive, the overtly revolutionary films were often heavily underpinned with libido, which defined both its ardor to the nation and to the opposite sex. And since romance and nationalism are complementary forms of the release of narcissistic energies, the romantic love depicted in these films reveal the lack and anxiety less of the object of love than of oneself.

The Evil of Romance

The May Fourth period witnessed the rejuvenation of the representation of human emotions and sexuality in Chinese literature after the centuries long Qing puritanism. Romance and sexuality were once again employed as weapons to challenge the traditional power structure,[2] as shown in Ding Ling's *The Diary of Ms. Sophie* that directly equated sexuality with Westernization and women's liberation.[3] However, revolutionary literature in the 1930s, as I have argued, could no longer tolerate the groaning of individual youths, which were deemed irrelevant to the larger national issues. Romanticism was replaced with socialist realism; sentimental authors like Bing Xin, Zhu Ziqing, and Yu Dafu were rapidly losing their readers to the much more politically engaged Guo Moruo, Mao Dun, and Chen Duxiu, with Lu Xun as one of the few leading literary figures who could continue to hold sway from the idealistic 1920s to the revolutionary 1930s. Le Zehou might be exaggerating that 90 percent of the novels and short stories published in the 1920s were about romantic love,[4] but the rapid disappearance of romance in the 1930s' revolutionary literature was obvious.

This literary phenomenon found a parallel development in cinema. As I have mentioned, the movie industry in the 1920s was basically untouched by intellectuals. Despite the absence of the May Fourth spirit in cinema, movies in the 1920s were, not surprisingly, dominated by films about romance and sex. According to the synopses of all films released in the 1920s, romantic love was one of the favorite themes of Chinese cinema. Sex and romance were inevitable elements even in those whimsical period films and violent swordsman movies.[5] Similar to other commercial cinema markets elsewhere, the relationship between the sexes was the most appealing and powerful box office guarantee, which can easily be fitted into all genres and stories.

Romantic and sexual yearnings in the left-wing cinema of the 1930s, however, were very suppressed when compared to the commercial cinema of the

1920s. None of the seventy-four left-wing films listed in *The Chinese Left-wing Cinema Movement* were devoted to self-avowed romantic subjects. Romantic relationships were either hidden in the background or employed as a means to support the political theme, which complied with other left-wing cultural products in different periods and different parts of the world. Love itself was seen as a meaningless entity in the revolutionary enterprise, contrary to its allegorical function as self-liberation in late Ming or May Fourth literature. For example, in a newspaper article promoting the production of anti-imperialist films, the author exclaimed: "During this critical period in China, all film companies and filmmakers should retreat from making love stories. They should give up all those proposals which aim at entertaining young ladies and rich fellows with romance; instead, they should determinedly take up the important mission of fighting against imperialism."[6] Romantic affairs were seen as obstructive to the great historical task of nationalist struggle not only because they were individualistic at heart but also because they could not escape the evil implication of sexuality.

When comparing *Torrent* with *City Nights*, the two most celebrated left-wing films in 1932, the famous left-wing writer and literary critic Mao Dun honored the former also because of his doubt in romance. He wrote:

> A romantic relationship is portrayed in *Torrent*: the daughter of a landlord falls in love with a primary school teacher who is also the leader of the peasantry. *City Nights* also has a similar romantic story which depicts the love between the son of a capitalist and a female worker. In both films romance is paired with the struggles between fathers and sons. However, there is an essential difference between the two stories. In *Torrent*, the ardent love of the landlord's daughter is generated by her lover's courageous and enlivening character. How about the passion of the capitalist's son in *City Nights*? According to the plot, it is provoked by some shallow sense of humanism or the so-called mystified "Love." . . . [Unlike *Torrent*, *City Night*] fails to expose urban metropolitan's depravity and is not able to reveal the dark side of society.[7]

Love for the sake of love, according to Mao Dun, was shallow and illusory. It satisfied no social missions and had to be cast away due to its opposition to social realism. In contrast, because the romance in *Torrent* served a higher symbolic function, insofar as it brought out the noble personality of the working class hero, Mao Dun praised it as fulfilling a revolutionary pedagogical purpose. Some other critics of *Torrent* were not pleased even at the minor line of romance contained in this progressive movie. Another critic argued that "the film succeeds in depicting the oppression experienced by the peasantry and the evils of the depraved gentlemen. But there is no need for the writer to impose a romantic story into this 'torrent.' On the one hand, it reduces the impact of the film to spectators; on the other hand, this romance forces us to doubt whether this is a realist film."[8] Another critic wrote about *Cosmetic Market*: "*Cosmetic Market* correctly grasps and reveals the realist subject of [the career problems of women]. Although it is an appropriate gesture, we find its social exposition not deep enough, and there is no reason to place a love story in the film to confuse the plot and the spectators' minds."[9] There was no dispute within the left-wing nationalist project that sex and romance were not only socially and politically unproductive but also already obsolete in this new progressive era.

This general hostility toward romance was not only heard among critics and spectators but also clearly seen in many left-wing films, with examples like *Spirit of Freedom*, *New Peach Blossom Fan*, and *March of Youth*, that all ended up cursing the romance established earlier in the narratives. However, a closer examination of the films reveals the complexity behind them—that no matter how hard Chinese leftist movies suppressed romance, romantic relationships remained omnipresent. The representation of romance and sexuality revealed the discursive struggles between cinema's urge for romance and the left-wing ideology which was, in certain ways, hostile to humanity.[10] On the one hand, the representation of romance in this cinema differed greatly from the spectator-oriented commercial Shanghai cinema in the 1920s in its curbing of desire. Yet, on the other hand, no matter how hard the left-wing ideology might have tried to repress sexuality, this cinema's passionate view of life remained less stringent and more placid to romantic love if compared to the later revolutionary films produced in the next decade. In spite of its overt realist and political claims, this was a period of romanticism in Chinese cinema, in the sense that the films fancied revolutions as gestures of love. Although one might consider this cinema politically naïve, its embrace of romance marked not only its ideological inconsistency but also an experimental stage of Chinese cinema, which since then has been struggling with the suppression of sexuality or a critique thereof.

In other words, puritanism tried but failed to take over romance in this left-wing cinema. In spite of the impending political and economic crisis, Shanghai in the 1930s was not yet under direct military threat, and most of the filmmakers were still able to afford their idealism and courage in experimentation. It was the first time that Chinese intellectuals used filmmaking with artistic and political objectives—the possibilities of this medium were far from exhausted. The filmmakers were trying out new ways to understand cinema, fostering a relatively robust and pluralistic film culture. In the following, I will provide close textual analyses of two famous left-wing films, *Sons and Daughters of the Storm* and *The Highways,* to illustrate how romance persisted in this youthful cinema under the disguise of political idealism, gratifying not only patriotism but also sexual desire.

Nation and Romance

Sons and Daughters of the Storm was written and directed by Xu Xingzhi, who studied art in Japan in the 1920s and later became a fervent follower of the left-wing Mass Culture Movement (*Dazhong wenhua yundong*) in the next decade. As a poet, artist, and critic, Xu Xingzhi had published different forms of works, including poetry, paintings, films, and critical writings, to argue for a new proletariat Chinese art.[11] He despised the earlier generation's individualist quests and saw the nation as the most crucial intellectual enterprise.[12] The negative depiction of romance represented in *Sons and Daughters of the Storm* was consistent with his ideological makeup at that time. The film begins with the writer Xin Baihua, famous for his patriotic poems and also known as the "Great-wall Poet," and his friend Liang Zhifu meeting a neighboring girl Feng (meaning phoenix). The two young intellectuals decide to sponsor Feng's education after the death of her mother. Liang is later arrested for his patriotic terrorist activities, and the police also order the arrest of Xin. A rich widow, Shi, who has been admired by Xin, rescues the poet, and the two move to a resort area in Qingdao to escape the police. In this German colony Xin partakes of a licentious life and becomes detached from pressing national issues. Meanwhile Liang Zhifu is bailed out from jail and later joins the army. Before he is killed on the battlefield, Liang writes his last letter to his pal, and it brings the poet to deep shame about his present indulgence in romance and extravagance. At the same time the poet also meets Feng, as she has joined a dancing group which is now touring around Qingdao. Feng is disappointed seeing Xin and Shi together leading a lavish life, and she decides to quit the dancing group and go to Beiping (Beijing) to look for her grandfather. At the end of the film Xin finally decides to leave his romantic life behind and follows the footsteps of his friend by joining the army. On the frontline Feng and the now new intellectual/revolutionary composite figure meet again; the last scene shows their marching together with a mass singing the film's theme song, *March of the Youth*, which would later be chosen as the National Anthem of the People's Republic of China.

One of the key messages of the film is to condemn the romance developed between Xin and Shi, which leads to the self-indulgence of the young intellectual. This theme is obviously spelled out in the last letter Liang writes to the poet: "Please don't give up your responsibility to defend the Great Wall just for the sake of a woman." Liang is clearly referring to the rich Shi here, who is portrayed in the film as an elegant and attractive lady, but her indulgence in romance and lack of concern for national issues cannot be excused. Her frigid appearance and sentimental personality are tremendously alluring to the idealistic poet whose quest for beauty can be seen as the prototype of the May Fourth spirit. Xin's final transformation from a maudlin poet to a courageous soldier echoes the development of the Chinese intellectual history from the romantic 1920s to the revolutionary 1930s. And this transformation is made possible only through the poet's decision to leave the seductive Shi and the individualism represented in this romantic relationship.

Under this avowed condemnation of romantic love, the romance between Xin and Shi seems to be replaced by the political comradeship between Xin and Feng. However, a closer examination of the narrative reveals that romance is being fulfilled instead of being sublimated, as the relationship between the poet and Feng, although depicted as purely asexual, is indeed the major romantic line in the film. In the opening shot of the film, we are already introduced to the relationships among the poet and the two female characters through their spatial locations. The film begins with the melancholic widow playing piano alone and then walking across her apartment to a window. Then the film cuts to the apartment on the opposite side of the street where the two friends Xin and Liang reside. The two men are gazing at the silhouette of Shi behind the curtain of her apartment, and the two are so captivated by her charm that the poet begins to write a poem and his friend draw a sketch in praise of her gracefulness (figures 4.1-4.3). The spectators then hear the singing of Feng, who is living on the floor below the young men's apartment. The two are annoyed by her voice, and Xin bangs on the floor to protest. Later, Feng finds her song scripts on the table soaked with water leaking from upstairs, and she uses the mop to return her complaints. The two men later go down to the lower floor to apologize for their earlier rudeness and the water leakage they have caused; after that, they become good friends (figures 4.4-4.6). The relationship among the three main characters is already clearly established in this opening sequence, and through the physical locations of the characters, the spectators are given hints about the later developments of their relationships. Although the two young men are attracted to the beauty of Shi, she clearly belongs to another world where they will, ultimately, not intrude. However, Feng resides in the same building as the two men; the poet "lowers" himself, symbolically, to the floor beneath to befriend her, which foretells their later relationship.

This triangular relationship among Xin, Feng, and Shi is further reinforced by their regional roots: later in the film we are informed that while both the poet and Feng came from the North, which was then occupied by the Japanese, Shi's hometown is in the southern province of Guangdong. The two northerners have the same roots and therefore are the legitimate pair; the southern Shi cannot succeed in breaking the intrinsic link between them. The bond between the two is also implied in an earlier scene when the poet explains to Feng the message behind the picture hung on his wall depicting the rebirth of a phoenix under fire. Feng is highly excited about the story, and the poet decides to give her the name Xin Feng (new phoenix) to give her a new identity after her mother's death. This allegory becomes an important theme in the film, referring less to Xin Feng than to the poet himself, as the film depicts the process of his metamorphosis into a new man.

Clearly the triangular structure among the three characters dominates the narrative, a structure that is essential in many romance, in which the progression of narrative rests on the excluded subject seeking to substitute one of the original pair and form a new couple. As David R. Shumway argues, "The viewer or reader of a romance is typically sutured into the position of exclusion; like the odd person out in the narrative triangle, the viewer experiences a lack, and the resulting desire motivates and structures his or her attention."[13] In the case of *Sons and Daughters of the Storm*, there was a similar cinematic mechanism at work: the film clearly invites the viewer to identify with the relationship between the poet and Feng instead of his with Shi. But the viewer is sutured into the position of the poet instead of Feng, which can be explained by the fact that, as I have illustrated in the earlier chapter, the new subject constructed in this cinema was a male composite figure of the filmmakers' collective, while the Hollywood screwball comedies Shumway analyzed were clearly targeted to female spectators. Other than this divergence, *Sons and Daughters of the Storm* is similar to Hollywood's screwball comedies in supplying competing romance lines but approving only one of them.

One of the major stylistic marks signaling the entrance of Chinese cinema in the 1930s classical stage was its application of suture.[14] Suture is a psychoanalytic concept referring to a multiple functioning of the discursive organization that forms and defines a subject in the signifying chain. Applying this concept to cinema, film theorists generally refer suture to the use of certain cinematic mechanisms, specifically shot/reverse-shot most of the time, to anchor the viewer to the position of a specific character through the organization of looks. Suture "names the dual process of multiplication and projection, the conjunction of the spectator as subject with the film."[15] In this film, while most of the scenes are shot from a neutral third person position, in the beginning sections the film introduces two specific sets of subjective shots to suture the viewer to the position of the poet. The first one appears in the party when the poet and Shi are first introduced, and a frontal close-up on Shi's beautiful face is shown replicating the poet's subjective view (figures 4.7-4.8). The second one appears in the scene when the two friends hear women's sobbing and groaning from the lower floor. They peep down the hole on the floor, and they hear and see the dying mother saying her last words to Feng worrying about her daughter's situation after her death (figures 4.9-4.10). These two subjective shots serve important narrative functions in securing the spectators' identification with the poet, who is introduced to one woman's beauty and the other's misery at about the same time. And through these two subjective shots the two rivalry relationships are already positioned on two separate grounds, one on lust the other on pity, which should not take most Chinese spectators of the time too much effort to decide which romance is more legitimate.

The suggestion is that Shi is seen as the obstacle to the romance of the poet and Feng is spelled out clearly in Shi's attachment to the depraved side of society. Because of the police order for his arrest, the poet is forced to leave Feng behind, and as a result Shi enters his life and brings him away from Shanghai, the place of patriotism, to Qingdao, the escapist haven. If the arrest represents the opposition to Chinese patriotic acts, Shi is a product of this wretched situation that should be overcome in the same way that the Chinese should not stay idle in the national crisis. When the three finally meet in Qingdao, Shi is extremely jealous and the poet and Feng act very uneasy. The poet's later decision to leave Shi is as much a gesture of recommitment to the nation as to Feng, although the sexual components of this romance are completely repressed, and they are depicted as brother and sister all through the film.

In other words, the relationship between Xin and Shi is cursed, both in the names of revolution and morality, because of the spectators' already established sympathy with Feng. Although the new comradeship carries no sexual undertones, the traditional power difference between the sexes is fully upheld. The female singer is the one being assisted in living and education by the male poet; she is also named by him. What has developed between Feng and Xin since the beginning of the film is not a revolutionary but a romantic relationship, in the most traditional and reactionary sense indeed, and their final reunion only fulfils the earlier obstructed erotic drive. Although the gratification is not "the bliss of the genital" as in the case of most Hollywood films, their unification in the name of the nation is no less suggestive. The two marching along together with the song *March of the Youth* playing in the background at the end of the film finally unites the legitimate romance, and spectators could leave the theater feeling satisfied not only with the bright future of the nation but also with the couple's cheerful, and probably sexual, life afterward. In other words, rather than romance being sublimated by the nation, in this film the latter was only a disguise to fulfill the libidinal drive that was not permitted in this allegedly political cinema. We have no doubt of Xu Xingzhi's sincere convictions and determination in transforming the romantic relationship into a revolutionary one. However, the obvious residual romantic underpinnings only proved a sublimation, as such, unsuccessful. *Sons and Daughters of the Storm* was not a unique case in this left-wing cinema showing such an uneasy representations of love and sexuality. Other similar ambiguous representations of romance can be found in many other left-wing films of the time, like *New Woman, Spirit of Freedom, Spring Silkworms*, etc. The juggling between romantic love and national love may only have shown that the two were indeed two sides of the same coin. This "*lian'ai yu geming*" (Romance and Revolution) formula might ultimately reveal that this male collective subject was far from stable and secure, and that the two elements composing this subjectivity were always in constant battle and conflicts. Let us examine another film, *The Highway*.

Sexing *The Highway*

The theory of sublimation has been frequently used to describe romance or sexuality depicted in Chinese revolutionary films. For example, Ban Wang argues that the romance portrayed in the 1959 Chinese revolutionary film *Nie Er* is, at the end, sublimated to political ends, as Nie Er's lover, Zheng Leidian, "starts as an object of romantic desire but ends as a revolutionary mentor. Nie Er's feeling for her also undergoes a psychic purification in the direction of politics: his private sexual passions are sublimated into a powerful creative energy that allows him to write revolutionary music."[16] Similar arguments can also be found in Chris Berry's reading of *The Highway*, and I believe that we can gain a better picture of the role that romance and sexuality played in this revolutionary cinema with a closer examination of this film through the concept of sublimation. Before we go into the details of the film and Berry's analysis, let us get to know more about the film's director, Sun Yu, first.

Sun Yu was the only Chinese filmmaker of the time who had received formal film training abroad. He received his B.A. at the University of Wisconsin, Madison, in literature, and he continued his graduate studies at New York Institute of Photography and Columbia University in photography and filmmaking.[17] Sun Yu was one of the few Chinese directors then who wrote his own scripts and was able to provide systematic and detailed production plans. Yet it was not the professional knowledge and foreign education that made his name known; he was widely called the "poet director," referring to his cinema's strong passion in humanities. He admitted in an interview: "My ideal world is beautiful, powerful, and glistening, where I can find archetypes of perfect images of women, students, and even workers."[18] He argued that although many people criticized his films as illusionary, he believed his cinema represented the ideal world he wanted to offer to the public. As shown in his films, this ideal world is surprisingly egalitarian, in which we observe his optimism in the world and the human race, sometimes to the point of ignorance. Sun Yu's films were often considered as romantic and unrealistic, that his worldview and values were marginal to the larger left-wing culture which was much more combative and urgent in tone. However, I see Sun Yu's representation of romance and sexuality, although usually much more explicit than the others, as another variation of the same dilemma, or conspiracy, of the left-wing films in coming to terms with the libido on the one hand and the nation on the other.

Judging from the development of his corpus of works, Sun Yu seemed to intentionally hide the romantic lines of his stories when he was beginning to identify with the left-wing cinema movement in 1933; friendship and family love were instead glorified. His later left-wing films prevented any pure and strong emotional attachment between the two sexes from gaining narrative momentum, which might reflect his gradual disbelief in romantic love. As the critic Liu Ying has accurately observed: "In the earlier films of Sun Yu like *Wild Rose*, romantic love occupied an important position in the narrative. But less and less worldly passions could be found in his later films. Even for the rare romance portrayed in these films, he deliberately denied their significance."[19]

However, the development of Sun Yu's left-wing cinema was, I would argue, more complicated than this gradual displacement of romance and sexuality to patriotism, which can be most apparently and contradictorily observed in the "exhibition" of his favorite actress, Li Lili, whose feisty and thigh-flashing image was constant in almost all his films made in the 1930s (figure 4.11), including his left-wing films. His famous 1934 film, *The Highway,* is the most interesting one to illustrate the complex relationship between sex and nation in his cinema. Jin Ge's mother died on the road when the family fled from the countryside to escape their homeland's recent natural disasters. He and his father finally arrived in Shanghai only to find out that city life was no less difficult, and his father soon died from hardship. Jin Ge grew up by himself and survived by being a coolie. He and his five friends find themselves fed up with the city's colonial injustice and decide to go inland to build roads. There they meet two girls, Dingxiang and Moli, who work in a restaurant. Later, the Japanese ordered the supervisor of the construction company to stop building the highway, preventing the Chinese army from transporting their supplies to the front. Jin Ge and his friends are bribed to stop the construction but are soon captured because they refuse to cooperate. Dingxiang and Moli finally save the men by seducing the traitor, and the highway is finished on time. The ending shows the construction site being bombarded by the Japanese airforce; Moli and the six young men are all killed. Watching the massacre nearby, the heart-broken Dingxiang decides to continue the road building, and she takes up the equipment to continue the construction with the risen spirits of the dead.

In one famous scene of the film, Moli admits to Dingxiang about her love for all the six male characters (see plate 15). Romantic love is there transformed into a form of unconditional maternal care that embraced not only the earlier romantic relationship suggested between her and Jin Ge but also the friendship, or some argue lesbian love, between the two girls. Chris Berry has carefully examined the text and suggested a sublimative system at work that transformed the earlier aroused sexual desires of the characters and the spectators to political ends. "Specifically, it attempts to arouse revolutionary ardor in its audience by the arousal of libidinal drives and their redirection towards the object of revolution."[20] However, Berry raises some questions at the end of the article about the last scene of the film:

> After Moli and the road workers have been shot and are lying dying on the ground, Dingxiang and her father help Moli and Jin Ge to positions where they may clasp hands and stare into each other's eyes, close to a kiss, before they finally pass away. There has been no earlier hint of any attachment between Jin Ge and Moli and the complete lack of narrative motivation for this incident is startling. What does it signify? Might it be a figure for a reverse of the sublimative process, a return to sexuality after the work of sublimation has achieved its end? If so, does this indicate that, after all, sublimation is not enough in and of itself? Must there be some compensation, some reward, for a successful sublimation?[21]

To answer Berry's questions, I would argue that such a sublimative system was never securely developed in place in *The Highway,* that romance and politics in many 1930s' left-wing films were not in simple hierarchical order. To Freud, sublimation is a psychological defense mechanism to avoid confronting ungratifiable libidinal desire. It is a technique for fending off suffering, to redirect instinctual desires to other socially approved activities, such as an artist receiving joy in creating, or a scientist in solving problems or discovering truths.[22] However, in Sun Yu's *The Highway*, sexual urges are not avoided but indeed fulfilled through political participation, although the libidinal is ultimately satisfied in a destructive way through death.

Berry is right that the love between Jin Ge and Moli was never clearly stated in the film until the very end when they die together. But their intimacy is hinted at in the restaurant scene when Jin Ge flirted with Moli to sing, and it is subtly suggested in a number of other scenes when the *mise-en-scène* clearly emphasizes the two parallel pairs between Jin Ge/Moli and Xiao Luo/Dingxiang. In fact, I would argue that sexuality and revolution are two discursive lines supplementing each other in *The Highway*, in the sense that the film does not sublimate the former to the latter but insists on the coexistence of the two. However, this idealist objective seems to be too unrealistic, and the narrative ultimately has to rely on death to fulfill men's desires both to women and the nation.

Unselfish love is clearly proposed in one of the restaurant scenes when the six young men are fighting for a cup of tea, which has been sipped by both Moli and Dingxiang. The jolly fight ends up tearing the teacup apart, which is broken into six pieces, each held by one of the young men. The camera then shows a close-up on the six pieces held up in the air being pieced back one after another into a whole. The suggestion that the six men share the two girls sexually is more overtly pronounced in another scene, which will be further analyzed later, when the six guys run up naked from the river to embrace the two gazing women. Together the eight of them break the two watermelons and share the good taste in gaiety. The melon-breaking (*pogua*) is such a common Chinese idiom referring to the loss of a woman's virginity that spectators can hardly miss the sexual undertone there.

Sexuality is indeed celebrated and glorified in the film, but only under the condition of being a collective activity. Other than the Japanese invaders and the national traitors, there is another object of criticism in the film: the men who are disrespectful to women, like Zhang Da in the beginning of the film when he lusts after women on the street, and Supervisor Hong who violates Dingxiang's and Moli's bodies in the restaurant. They are both fiercely punished by Jin Ge and therefore by the film's central ideology represented by him. The film criticizes the sexuality that is directed and performed under men's sole interests. Yet those achieving collective pleasure are glorified, as evidenced in one of the last scenes when Moli uses herself as sexual bait to capture the traitor, Ho, and release the guys under Ho's arrest. No one in the scene cares to find out if Moli has engaged with Ho sexually; they only praise her bravery and shrewdness.

The seemingly mutual respect between sexuality and nationalism revealed in *The Highway* can in fact be found in many other Sun Yu's left-wing films. For example, in *Little Toys*, the extramarital romance between Ye Dasao and her young handsome lover, Yuan Pu, is not subdued and detested under the celebration of Ye's maternal love to her children in this age of national crisis (figures 4.12-4.13). Although Ye does reject the love of Yuan Pu, her reason is not due to her loyalty to her husband, but because she wants Yuan Pu to go to university in order to fulfill his social responsibilities first. Interestingly, combining the May Fourth sexual liberation in the 1920s and the nationalist ideology of the 1930s, the film gives the married, yet young and beautiful, Ye Dasao every right to fall for a handsome and intelligent young man, as freedom of love must be respected. But this romance is conditioned under the even more romantic nationalism that can, however unconvincing and naïve it may seem, bring individual sexual needs and collective patriotic sentiments together.

Collectivism Reconsidered

In this regard, *The Highway* is particularly ambitious in its attempt to reconcile the conflict between the individual and the collective. Beyond a doubt, the film is a celebration of Jin Ge's heroism: it portrays how Jin Ge succeeds as a leader in getting the mass to participate in revolution. When Jin Ge decides to leave Shanghai for road construction inland, not only his five buddies but also the entire neighborhood enthusiastically respond to his call. Later in the film he also proves his personal charisma in persuading the workers not to be panicky of the approaching Japanese invasion but to stay for the road construction in order to bring the Chinese army and resources directly to the frontline. However, as I argued in the earlier chapter, this celebration of Jin Ge's growth and leadership must be inscribed within the collective, and this individual/collective wedding is manifested drastically differently from the heroism portrayed in Hollywood.

In the following, I will compare *The Highway* to two Hollywood productions of the time, *The Big Parade* (King Vidor, 1925) and *All Quiet on the Western Front* (Lewis Milestone, 1930),[23] to illustrate how the Chinese film's representation of heroism was different from the two American ones. As I have mentioned, Sun Yu studied film in the United States during the 1920s and was very honest in admitting his debt to the Hollywood cinema. However, I would not insist *The Highway* to be Sun Yu's conscious effort to reproduce the two American films in a Chinese context, as he never admitted so. I would only like to point out that certain elements in the three films were intricately related to each other, yet *The Highway* chose to interpret and present the rite of passage so differently, showing how consistent and evasive Sun Yu's idealistic world could be.

The theme of initiation is a narrative structure that can be found in literary traditions all over the world. In this left-wing cinema this structure was particularly cardinal, as it helped to highlight the political significance of the film to the personal realities of individual viewers. While the personalities and deeds of most characters remain constant throughout the film, the major leading characters undergo many drastic transformations in the course of the narrative portraying their growth in revolution. This is evidenced in many films, including *Crossroads, Three Modern Women, New Woman,* and *March of Youth*; yet in *The Highway* the theme of initiation most aptly illustrates the complementary instead of opposing relationship between individuality and collectivity through the fulfillment and destruction of the libido.

The Big Parade centers around James, the aimless son of a factory owner, who fights in World War I due to peer pressure and curiosity. In a French village next to the battlefield, he meets a Frenchwoman, Melisande, and very soon they find themselves in love. The continuation of the war compels him to depart from his lover. Later his two army pals, Slim and Bull, die in trench fighting, and James himself is shot in the leg. After coming back to the United States and joining his family, he discovers that his true love still resides in France; he decides to go back to look for Melisande. The ending scene of the film is set in a wide French valley where the two lovers run to embrace. *All Quiet on the Western Front* is also set in the First World War, but the protagonists are not American but German. Paul and his other six teenage classmates join the army after being emotionally compelled by the patriotic agitation of their school teacher. Experiencing the brutality of war, like James in *The Big Parade*, they are soon disillusioned. One after another, the six schoolboys either die or are crippled on the battlefield, and Paul is the only one who could go back to his hometown on a short leave. But he is so disgusted by the blind patriotism of his fellow townsmen that he decides to cut short his vacation to return to the war. At the end of the film, Paul is shot by the enemy while he is attempting to catch a butterfly on the battlefield.

The Highway, made ten years after *The Big Parade* and five years after *All Quiet on the Western Front*, also has a war theme, although the protagonists in this Chinese film are not soldiers but road-construction workers who build highways for the army. Each of the three films has one scene seemingly identical with the others. In *The Big Parade*, there is a scene showing the two American soldiers taking a "hand-made shower" by a stream in the French village, and there Paul first meets Melisande. There is also a similar bathing scene in *All Quiet on the Western Front* in the middle part of the film. The army was taking a rest in a French village. The three boys still surviving are shown taking a bath in a river with an older soldier when they are discovered by three French women. There is also a similar scene in *The Highway*, where the six male protagonists bathing in a river are watched by Dingxiang and Moli (figure 4.14). All of these three scenes show a reverse "peeping Tom" convention in which women are the voyeurs. However, if we take into consideration the general narrative structure of the films, we find the women here represent less female desire and viewing power than the necessary components in men's maturation processes.

The major theme of war notwithstanding, all three films portray the growth of an individual man: James, Paul, and Jin Ge respectively. James and Paul begin in the films as ignorant boys protected by their families and schools. It is their battlefield experience that elevates them into the realm of adulthood. Although the films were considered antiwar statements, the fighting portrayed in the films serves less as an end in itself than a testing ground for the boys' transition from adolescence to adulthood. This experience of manhood includes the confrontation of fraternity, sexuality, combat, and death. Upon their return to their hometowns, both James and Paul are disillusioned with their prewar values and soon find out what is essential to their individual lives, that is, his love for Melisande for James and the butterfly—a symbol of beauty and freedom—for Paul. *The Highway* is similar to the two films, particularly in its portrayal of the growth of Jin Ge from the loss of his parents to his death in a Japanese invasion, documenting his personal growth from an orphan in Shanghai, the semicolonial city, to a patriotic hero dying for the nation hand in hand with his comrades.

If we take this theme of initiation into consideration, it is not difficult to see the importance of the bathing scenes. The gaze of the women invites the men into the realm of sexuality, a crucial step for the boys to reach manhood. Without prior knowledge, the boys' sexual urges have to be initiated by experienced women, as shown by their voluptuous bodies and sensual laughter, in these sexual rites. A river seems to be the ideal place for this important ritual to take place. This is particularly clear in the scene in *The Highway* where the men leave their initial shyness and rush forward to embrace the women. As I have pointed out, at the top of the hill the men break a watermelon brought by the girls and share it with each other, suggesting quite candidly men's penetration and breakage of women's virginity. However, such a direct depiction of women's seduction must be mediated before showing directly to the general film audience; as a result these women were all presented as foreigners. In both the Hollywood films, the sexually aggressive women are all French, complying with the stereotypical, fantasized image of European women in American society, with the most obvious example being Marlene Dietrich at that time. Because these female characters are foreign and therefore not restricted by the "civilized codes," they can trespass the norms of the proper and leave the established gender structure unharmed. This strategy is also obvious in *The Highway*, when, of the two women, it is Moli who gazes and Dingxiang who is embarrassed by the watching scene. Earlier in the film we are told that Moli has been a flower-drum girl, a form of street performer. They were usually wandering entertainers who came from minority groups in the North. Like other wandering minstrel types, Moli is therefore considered marginal to society.[24] By contrast, Dingxiang is the daughter of the restaurant owner, a Chinese girl who has been brought up in accordance with the "proper" gender codes. This juxtaposition of the two women reveals the significant role played by marginal females in all three films, and yet, due to their marginal positions, the superiority of these "untamed" women to the males did not render the sexual themes of these films too rebellious.

The most obvious differences among these three films are to be found in the films' endings. In the two American films, fraternity is only one among other means for James and Paul to reach manhood. Manhood in the American context is ultimately individualistic, and therefore an adult man should be detached from his prior brothers to become independent, which might explain why the wartime pals of James and Paul are all killed in the battlefield (except one being seriously wounded). Jin Ge, however, takes an opposite route that leads to his transformation from an individual to a member of a collective. As a baby he is taken away from his hometown to Shanghai, and he soon becomes an orphan after the death of his father. From Shanghai back to the mainland to build roads, however, he finds himself a new family that is composed of his friends. He finally constructs a new spirit of community through his and his friends' sacrifice for the nation, the ultimate ideal of Chinese collectivity. The two American films were antiwar propaganda; they challenged the national myths of patriotism, and they evoked individuals' rights and freedom. However, Sun Yu could not afford to leave the collective well-being of the nation behind in this age of national crisis. Therefore Jin Ge the leader must join his comrades in the passage from life to death to resurrection.

Another major discrepancy between the Chinese film and the two American films is the death of Moli with the males at the end of *The Highway*, which might offer answers to those questions posed by Berry, which I quoted earlier. At the end of *The Big Parade* although Melisande succeeds in bringing James away from his nation, she continues to remain the sexual object for him. And in the case of *All Quiet on the Western Front*, woman simply disappears at the end, and the object of desire Paul that dies for, the butterfly, signifies an abstract concept of freedom and beauty. Yet in *The Highway* Moli dies with the six men, suggesting her participation in this new collective. And to a lesser degree Dingxiang is also one component in the ideal ending. Sun Yu dreamt a peaceful egalitarian world where sexuality would not be condemned and subdued in the name of the nation. But this dream, transgressing the boundary between and at the same time fulfilling both romantic love and national love, can only be realized in death, nakedly revealing the libido in its kernel. In *Sons and Daughters of the Storm* we are shown the competition and conspiracy between nationalism and romance/romanticism; here in *The Highway* their intricate relationship is even more pronounced, as they are different manifestations of the same narcissistic death drive.

It was after the First World War that the two Hollywood films were made, and the Americans had experienced, although to a far lesser degree than in the Second World War, the trauma of war. But in the 1930s the Chinese had not entered a real warfare with the Japanese, so they could still conjure up the beauty of war/death through a cinematic fantasy. According to Kaja Silverman, the trauma of war represented in the American cinema immediately after the Second World War was linked to the death drive, through which the subject reduces itself to a psychic nothingness.[25] But in *The Highway*, in which war is also equated with death, death brings a coherence of the ego, consolidating the libido with the super ego, also reconciling the individuals with the collective. Unlike the way in which Silverman describes the Hollywood cinema in the mid-to late-forties when cinema followed quick on the heels of the general loss of faith in the dominate fiction, in China the socialist nationalist dominated fiction was being fabricated and becoming more and more powerful. In the case of Sun Yu's cinema, his films were not only politically committed but also original, refreshing, and joyous. This unconfined and lifted spirit marked the uniqueness of this cinema. In spite of the cinema's clear devotion to national issues, its politics was often contaminated by this youthful exploration of the world in which sex and romance were significant components and motivations. It is therefore not surprising to see such youthful gaiety and romantic immaturity completely disappear in the second phase of the Chinese left-wing cinema movement during 1945-49, as the brutality of war would soon shatter such idealism into pieces.[26]

Notes

1. Christina Kelley Gilmartin, *Engendering the Chinese Revolution: Radical Women, Communist Politics, and Mass Movements in the 1920s* (Berkeley: University of California Press, 1995), 119.

2. See Tani Barlow, "Theorizing Woman: *Funü, Guojia, Jiating*," in *Body, Subject and Power in China*, ed. Angela Zito and Tani Barlow (Chicago: The University of Chicago Press, 1994), 253-89.

3. For the English translation of the story, see *Miss Sophie's Diary and Other Stories*, translated by W. J. F. Jenner. (Beijing: Chinese Literature, 1985).

4. Li Zehou, *Zhongguo xiandai sixiang shi lun* (The discussion of modern Chinese intellectual history) (Taipei: Fengyun, 1990), 176.

5. For a complete filmography and synopsis of all Chinese narrative films produced in China before the 1930s, see Zhu Tainwei and Wong Zhenzheng, eds., *Zhongguo yingpian dadian: gushi pian, xiqu pian, 1905-1930* (Encyclopaedia of Chinese films: narrative films and opera films, 1905-1930) (Beijing: Zhongguo dianying, 1996). There are few films of the time still available now, but according to the advertisements and film stills printed in newspapers and magazines, pornography and violence were presented quite boldly in cinema.

6. *SB*, June 29, 1933.

7. The article was written under Mao Dun's pen name "Xuan." *SB*, March 24, 1933. Rpt., *ZZDY*, 413.

8. *SB*, March 7, 1933.

9. *SB*, May 18, 1933.

10. The depiction of romance and sexuality was to a great extent a result of box office concerns—we will discuss it in more detail in chapters 6 and 7.

11. One example is his poem *Xin Shiji* (The new era) in *Wenxue congbao* (The journal of literature) 2 (June 1936): 147. The last stanza reads: "For tomorrow / For the new era / To break old society / into pieces / The new era must be built / from our own hands." The simple language and political rhetorics of this poem were apparently influenced by the Mass Culture Movement.

12. See, for example, his article "Zhongguo meishu yundong de zhanwang" (The

prospect of the Chinese art movement), *Shalun* (Siren) 1, no. 1 (June 16, 1930): 32.

13. David R. Shumway, "Screwball Comedies: Constructing Romance, Mystifying Marriage," in *Film Genre II* , ed. Barry Keith Grant (Austin: University of Texas Press, 1995), 384.

14. I use the term and meanings of "classical cinema" following Bordwell, Staiger, and Thompson's reading of Hollywood between 1917 and 1960, acknowledging also the many criticisms this reading has attracted. For Bordwell, Staiger, and Thompson's reading of classical cinema, see *The Classical Cinema: From Style and Mode of Production to 1960* (New York: Columbia University Press, 1985). For its criticism see, for example, Miriam Hansen's "The Mass Production of Senses: Classical Cinema as Vernacular Modernism" in *Reinventing Film Studies* (London: Arnold, 2000), 332-50. Bordwell's concept is useful in the study of this left-wing cinema as we also discover a process of stylistic standardization conditioning the reception process. But the characteristic of this cinema is, as I have argued and continue to argue, more cultural than stylistic.

15. Stephen Heath, *Questions of Cinema* (Bloomington: Indiana University Press, 1981), 109. For a more concise discussion of suture, see Kaja Silverman's discussion in *The Subject of Semiotics* (Oxford: Oxford University Press, 1983). Rpt., Leo Braudy and Marshall Cohen, eds, *Film Theory and Criticism: Introduction Readings* (New York: Oxford University Press), 137-47

16. Ban Wang, *The Sublime Figure of History: Aesthetics and Politics in Twentieth-century China* (Stanford, Calif.: Stanford University Press, 1997), 141-42.

17. Sun Yu, *Dalu zhige* (Song of the big road) (Taipei: Yuanliu, 1990), 68-70.

18. *SB*, Oct. 19, 1933.

19. Liu Ying, "Lun Sun Yu dianying chuangzuo de yishu tezheng" (A discussion of the artistic characteristics of Sun Yu's films), *Dianying Yishu* (Film art) 120 (Jan 1990): 92.

20. Chris Berry, "The Sublimative Text: Sex and Revolution in Big Road," *East West Film Journal* 2, no. 2 (June 1988): 79.

21. Ibid., 84.

22. Sigmund Freud, *Civilization and Its Discontents* (New York: W.W. Norton & Company, 1961), 29.

23. The film won the 1930 Academy Award of Best Film of the Year.

24. As Chris Berry argues: "Like all other minstrel types, [being a flower-drum girl] would place Moli in a marginal group in traditional society, including also slaves and prostitutes." See Berry, "The Sublimative Text," 68.

25. Kaja Silverman, *Male Subjectivity at the Margins* (New York: Routledge, 1992), 63.

26. I will discuss in more detail the second phase of this left-wing cinema movement in the epilogue.

Figure 4.1.
The silhouette of Mrs. Shi from the subjective view of Xin and Liang.

Figure 4.2.
Cut-back to the two men gazing.

Figure 4.3.
A close-up on their representations, the painting of Liang and the poem of Xin, of their gaze.

Figure 4.4.
Feng using her mop
to protest against the
water leakage from
the upper floor.

Figure 4.5.
Cut to Xin and Liang
hearing the complaints.

Figure 4.6.
Xin going downstairs
to apologize.

Figure 4.7.
In the party Xin is cap-
tivated by Shi's beauty.

Figure 4.8.
The reverse shot, but it
is slightly off the regular
practice as Shi is now
looking back directly at
the camera instead of
paralleling Xin's earlier
viewpoint. Here Xin's
position is completely
overlapped with the
viewer's.

Figure 4.9.
Xin peeping downstairs
again.

Figure 4.10.
Cut to Xin's subjective
view of Feng and her
dying mother. Similar
to figures 4.8 and 4.9,
this set of shots is not
shot/reverse-shot but a
direct replication of
Xin's subjective view.

Figure 4.11.
Queen of Sport. One of
the many erotic images
of Li Lili in Sun Yu's
films.

Figure 4.12.
Little Toys begins with
a gracious depiction of
Ye Dasao's (played by
Ruan Lingyu) happy
family.

Figure 4.13. Very soon the film cuts to Ye secretly seeing the handsome Yuan Pu.

Figure 4.14. The bathing scene of the six male protagonists in *The Highway*. It is supposed to be the subjective view of the two girls.

5

Women's Stories On-screen versus Off-screen

In the previous chapter, we discuss the representation of the relationship of the two genders in this film movement and discover that the cinema was more romantic and sexual than it proclaimed itself to be. Although revolution was considered morally sacred and therefore pertained to celibacy, this young and energetic left-wing cinema either failed to or never tried to suppress sexuality. Through the relationship of the two genders we discover that individual and collective identities were reconciled either through an affirmation of asexual romance, as in the case of Feng and Xin in *Unchanged Heart in Life and Death*, or through an idealistic celebration of collective sexuality, which is clearly observed in *The Highway*. The films reveal that this collective masculine subjectivity formed in this cinema fancied, either directly or indirectly, a simultaneous existence of romance and politics in the way that political participation also fulfilled sexual urge, if only cinematically. However, while this masculinity had to rely on the opposite sex as the legitimizing "other," this "other" in turn also threatened the original ideology.

In fact, a manifestation of this new masculine subjectivity was this cinema's unyielding devotion to women's liberation, giving women a substantial position in this revolutionary project. Zhao Yuhua, Xin Feng, and Moli might not have contributed in direct ways to the building of a new China, but they remain essential, or even all-powerful, in this cinema. In this chapter, I will illustrate how women's stories dominated and defined this film movement, calling our attention to the development of this collective subjectivity that might have overwhelmed itself. We will explore how the left-wing ideology appropriated the representation of women violently to consummate itself, as the male characters' strength can only be actualized by the imaginary presence of this powerlessness, which might ultimately refer to no one but the heroes' own impotency. However, this desire to tell women's stories does not stay only on the level of cinematic

113

representation; I will also go outside the films and illustrate the fervent attempts of the left-wing filmmakers and critics to incorporate the suicides of two women film stars into their ideological structure. Through a comparison between the readings of these suicides performed in "reality" and those represented on screen, I will illustrate a cinematic mechanism that gave the women's characters more autonomy than the actresses in reality had, showing that female representation in this cinema was not controlled solely by the dominant power structure but was also the site of contestation embodying many discourses and desires all at once. In her studies of Shanghai's silent films, Miriam Hansen observes that "what makes the heroines of Shanghai silent films so memorable is that they oscillate among different types and incompatible identities."[1] This is even more obvious in the left-wing films which were often so political in outlook and emotional at heart. The cinema's attempt to incorporate the many different contradictory agenda was clearly revealed in its telling of women's stories.

The Obsession with Women's Stories

Zhang Yingjin argued recently that this left-wing cinema transformed women into "*wo-men*," the Chinese *pinyin* transcription of "we," because the femininity of the female characters was gradually stripped away to become the genderless object of representation in the male filmic discourse.[2] This analysis follows and verifies a granted gender relationship in which the male remains powerful and women disenfranchised. However, a more intimate examination of the movement in entirety demonstrates otherwise: femininity in this left-wing cinema was not removed but in fact emphasized. Instead of dominated by a simple gender representation of containing and policing, this left-wing cinema was obsessed with women's stories, which was brought about by a diverse array of cultural issues and underlying forces.

Chinese cinema in the 1920s can be seen as a typical woman's cinema. Romance and domestic stories dominated. Almost all performers who attained stardom were women: they include Yin Minzhu, Wang Hanlun, Zhang Zhiyu, and Hu Die.[3] And most films, including those swordsman movies, featured the principled female actress and developed the narrative around her. Not until the advent of this left-wing cinema movement did we see an attempt to reverse this representation agenda. *Torrent*, one of the first and most important movies of this film movement, glorifies the heroic deeds of Liu Tiesheng, the ideal left-wing cinema prototype of intellectual/revolutionary (he is both a primary teacher and a leader of peasantry), who leads the mass to revolt against their landlord. So is the case in *The Highway*, the film I analyzed in length in the last chapter.

However, this will of some individual filmmakers was too insignificant to influence the development of this left-wing cinema. Films featuring female leads continued to dominate this new cinema commanded by male filmmakers.[4] Although these films differed from the women's films of the 1920s in their obvious revolutionary ideology, a majority of the left-wing films produced in the 1930s focused on the theme of women's liberation. These films include *Three Modern Women, City Nights, Women's Outcry, Cosmetics Market, The Future, Daybreak, Maternal Radiance, Flying Catkins, Wandering, The Sisters, The Classic for Girls, Country Worries, Little Toys, The Goddess, The Boatman's Daughter, New Woman, Spirit of Freedom, The Crabapple is Red, Little Lingzi,* and *Flower of Society*.[5] Although these films were marked by overt nationalist concerns, women's fates and struggles were the focus. Among the many pressing social issues concerning the filmmakers, gender inequality was singled out as the most captivating theme. Even in those films focused on other sociopolitical issues, the female characters oftentimes occupied the major attention in the overall story. *Torrent* and *The Highway* were two of the very few left-wing movies that placed so much emphasis on the male leads.

I agree with Zhang Yingjin about the policing of women's voices in this cinema, but his claim of de-femininity and the complete domination of left-wing masculinism in fact conceals the complexities involved, as the exploration of femininity was central to this cinema. It was a time when men completely dominated the film industry, left-wing or not. There were almost no women participated in the making of this left-wing cinema other than those occupying roles of performers. But the male filmmakers chose to tell their own stories through women. The obsession with women's stories was particularly apparent in the early phase of the movement, from 1932 to 1934, during which the theme of women's liberation dominated about half of the left-wing films. Many young progressive directors chose women's stories as the focus of their first films, like Shen Xiling's *Women's Outcry*, Fei Mu's *City Nights*, Wu Yonggang's *The Goddess*, and Situ Huimin's *Spirit of Freedom*.[6] The more rounded male roles, like Lao Zhao in *Crossroads*, Xiao Chen in *Street Angel*, and Wang Laowu in *Fifth Brother Wang*, were not created until the latter half of the cinema movement, when the directors were becoming more confident in their art. While some directors, such as Fei Mu, continued to tell women's stories for the rest of their filmmaking careers, other more ideologically committed ones, like Shen Xiling and Situ Huimin, shifted to male stories later in the decade and successfully made overtly masculine movies during and after the war period.[7] Ironically, although women were treated only as mouthpieces of the male filmmakers, the female characters initiated the young men's exploration in their cinematic art and legitimized their ideological agenda. There was a complex discursive structure at work that made woman the surrogate to bear men's anger and dreams at the same time.

First of all, we have a long tradition of Chinese males telling their stories through the experience of women; the description of woman's suffering enjoyed a pivotal position in the male-dominated literature of China. Exceptions notwithstanding, the woman figure in Chinese literature is usually the personification of the tragic spirit; she is made to shoulder all grief and agonies by herself. Although the forced link between woman and victim can be seen in other literary traditions, the Chinese case is unique. There are strong components in Confucian ethics preventing people from interrogating society and encouraging their tolerance towards human suffering. Under such a social system, anger is oppressed and hopefully sublimated into some more positive energy such as kindness and sympathy. Almost the entire Chinese literary history is composed of cases in which the defeating intellectuals had nowhere to go except to literature to express their frustrations in life.[8] Woman, who always occupied the lowest position in society, was the best persona to represent the powerless individuals who wanted but failed to engage reality politically.[9]

The progressive culture in the 1930s struggled hard to invalidate this Confucian tradition. On the one hand, they saw the tragic women stereotypes as evidence of China's backwardness; the male filmmakers in modern China wanted to will women's victory into being. As Tani Barlow demonstrates, many Chinese intellectuals in the first half of this century gained important discursive advantages in self-legitimization by manipulating new gender ideologies appropriated from the West.[10] The left-wing filmmakers also idealized their female characters into Westernized and independent women as a collective symbol for the new China. On the other hand, the practice of using woman's suffering as evidence of general social injustice persisted. As a result, many leading women characters portrayed in this cinema movement, like Lingling in *Daybreak*, Cuifen in *Cosmetic Market*, and Ye Dasao in *Little Toys*, were depicted as both victims and heroes, representing contrasting dramatic personae. They were usually the most mistreated ones under the oppressive social order, but always at the end of the stories they abruptly become masters of their own lives, walking away from the traditional imprisonment of family and marriage to become truly independent new women.

Another major motive for the filmmakers to make woman's films was the large female market developing. Although there is no creditable accounting for early Chinese spectatorship, according to the various contemporary journal and newspaper descriptions, women must have been a large spectator group at that time. For example, a reporter classified the film spectators he observed into three groups: intellectuals, professionals, and petty urbanites. He claimed that women dominated the third spectator group, which was obviously the largest group compared to the first two.[11] If this was purely impressionistic personal judgement, we can still safely infer the high number of women spectators attending these films according to the similarities observed between early American cinema and early Chinese cinema. Melvyn Stokes argues that the large number of female-centered melodramas and romances made in the 1920s and 1930s proved that Hollywood considered women to be its primary market. The films were often written by women scriptwriters, frequently adapting material from popular fiction also written by women mainly for women. They feature female stars, who outnumbered their male equivalents and seemed to spring from an apparently endless pool of talent.[12] Although the Chinese left-wing filmmakers strove to purge from cinema the Mandarin Ducks and Butterflies (popular romances) elements that were extremely popular in the 1920s' cinema, the female components of the 1930s' Shanghai cinema were as prominent as those described by Stokes. Not only were there a large number of films centered on women stories, but female stars also dominated the star system. We also saw the emergence of female scriptwriters, like Ai Xia whom we will discuss in detail. The films' advertisements used as many masculine adjectives, like heroic, historical, and grandiose, as sentimental descriptions, like soul-stirring, tear-driven, mesmerizing, etc. Masculine didacticism carefully incorporated romance and domestic stories in order to not alienate the large number of female spectators. The heroines of this left-wing cinema bore the duties of male self-allegorization, the representation of a new revolutionary archetype, and female identification all at the same time. The male filmmakers relied on the suffering woman to illustrate social oppression, but they also had to put together a strong woman's figure to legitimize their politics. Yet the commercial setting did not allow them to appropriate women impudently, which might alienate the female spectators. Thus a very unique woman's representation resulted. In the following, I will examine three films directed by three young and prominent male left-wing filmmakers from 1933 to 1935 to illustrate how all these macro cultural conditions were translated into cinematic representations. Specifically we examine how the representations facilitated more than one form of identification, and how the heroines, all performed by Ruan Lingyu, were made to embody different voices and desires. And then we will visit the real lives of Ruan Lingyu and Ai Xia, Ruan's uncanny predecessor, and examine how this desire to tell women's stories went beyond the cinematic frame.

Motherhood and Identification

Ruan Lingyu is one of the most well-known actresses in the history of Chinese cinema, and her legacy is intimately connected to the left-wing cinema movement. She started her acting career in 1925 when she was fifteen, but she did not immediately rise to stardom, mostly because her film company, Mingxing, already managed the then most popular actress, Hu Die. In 1929 Ruan Lingyu transferred to the newly established Lianhua Film Company, and her fame skyrocketed in consonance with the development of the progressive cinema. In Lianhua, she participated in the best productions with the best crew, and many of these films became some of the most famous left-wing films: *Three Modern Women, City Nights, Little Toys, The Goddess,* and *New Woman,* etc. High praises for her acting from filmmakers and spectators were so frequently heard that Ruan Lingyu was often considered as the most talented film performer, male or female, of the time.

However, we should not overemphasize her popularity. Ruan Lingyu was certainly not the single most popular actress in Shanghai at that time. Her lofty position towering above all others was rather largely constructed by later historians, who often associated the "progressive" characters she performed with the full-fledged development of the left-wing cinema movement. Some of the characters she portrayed were seen by critics and spectators then as realization of the new womanhood, which otherwise remained imaginary, bringing about her symbolic position representing the film movement. And most importantly, her lower-class background and widely-publicized suicide on International Woman's Day, as I will elaborate in detail, added much drama to the movement, and she served as an excellent real-life example to legitimate the movement's underlying ideology.

Over the entire oeuvre of Ruan's performance, *Little Toys*, *The Goddess*, and *New Woman* were the most famous ones and generally considered as the representative examples of her fine performances. And interestingly, in all of these three films, she performed a mother role. To most moviegoers then, Ruan Lingyu was not only an icon of the left-wing cinema movement, but she also represented an ideal and modern motherhood. This maternal weight defined not only the actress's public image but also left-wing filmmaking as a whole. These mother figures, I would argue, were more than just mouthpieces of the filmmakers but were also invested with a multitude of interests and discourses. They were sources of empowerment and legitimization, as well as anchors of identification for both male and female spectators.

In *Little Toys*, as I have illustrated, Ruan portrayed a radiant, assertive, and loving mother, Ye Dasao. At the end of the film, we see an elaborate street scene portraying the mother going insane, yelling among the passersby that the war is coming (figure 5.1). Ye's heart has been broken because her elder daughter has just been killed in a Japanese bombing. She is struggling hard to pick up her courage to live again and has just started to go back to her normal life in selling toys on the street. But now she is further agitated by seeing her son on the street, who was lost ten years ago in an earlier warfare, who no longer recognizes her. All of a sudden, the sounds of firecrackers celebrating the New Year overwhelm the street, and Ye goes crazy by associating the blasting noise of firecrackers with the Japanese bombing. This final scene made many spectators breathless when the film premiered in the New Year of 1934.

In *The Goddess*, a film I have discussed in chapter 3, Ruan is a suffering prostitute who lives only for the hope of raising her son, and the film also ends with Ruan's consciousness. When she is imprisoned for killing the rascal who has been controlling her life, we see the prostitute smiling alone in a dark cell, her face superimposed with her son's cheerful face, suggesting her contentment with the status of her son who is now kept guardian by the kindhearted school principal (see figure 7.5). The title states that "the prison is the only place in her life that gives her peace and comfort." She can now spend all her time fantasizing about a bright future for her son. The film bitterly suggests that the prostitute finally succeeds in escaping the city by capturing herself in the cell, by sacrificing herself to give a new life to her son.

Ruan also portrayed a passionate and suffering mother in Cai Chusheng's

New Woman. Wei Ming is a divorced teacher and writer who is forced to prostitute herself because she needs the money to save her daughter's life. After much struggling, she chooses to commit suicide as she loses both her daughter and her dignity. This is noticed by a tabloid editor who has failed to win her heart and now decides to take revenge by exposing her prostitute identity and condemning her suicide in the newspaper. At the end, the film insists on bringing her back to temporary consciousness in the hospital after her suicide attempt. She shouts to the camera directly with wishes to survive and to seek revenge. In this silent movie, which cannot allow her determining voice to be heard, the subtitles of "I must live" were printed in larger and larger fonts, revealing her growing reluctance to be killed by the narrative's condemnation (figure 5.2). Intriguingly, this ending shows the tug-of-war between the narrative and the mother's will, revealing a certain uneasiness and ambivalent relationship within the left-wing cinematic discourse that condemns the emotional-therefore-weak mother on the one hand and relies on her strength for legitimization on the other.

The three films all glorified the maternal love of the female characters and condemned society for sacrificing her saneness, freedom, and life. The visualization of her sufferings and the representations of her consciousness dominate these left-wing films and instill them with obvious masculine messages. While the end of *Little Toys* represents the mother's mental disorder by showing her jumping and yelling on the street, *The Goddess* and *New Woman*, through either images or words, also end with the disclosure of her consciousness. Here we see how the representation of motherhood, particularly her subjectivity, serves many different functions. First, she is both the victim and the hero, concurring in the traditional woman-victim stereotypes and the new revolutionary female image, both imposed on the basis of man's fears and desires. This is most obvious in *Little Toys*: the insane mother/prophet is not only victimized by, but also the only one to stand awakened among, the ignorant and pleasure-seeking mass, referring both to the well-dressed passersby and the film spectators themselves. She embodies the conflictual desires of the male director who followed, but at the same time, was anxious to break through, traditional female representation.

Secondly, the constant referral to her subjectivity, particularly in *New Woman* in which most of the important characters and events are introduced from her perspective through shot/reverse shot or superimposition, also actively invites identification of the female spectators.[13] Spectators can engage with, and therefore enjoy, the emotional intensity of the story by suturing into the characters' mental positions. However, in the above-discussed scenes the mother is at the same time the one looking and the one being looked at, and she is also to different degrees objectified. The look at her is structured on multiple planes. While the films encourage spectators to recognize the sufferings of the mothers, they also facilitate their identification with her child, who occupies the symbolic position of both the directors and the spectators. We should notice that in the above three films, the mother's consciousness revealed is all related to her lost child, with whom the directors and the spectators might have identified in terms of the Oedipal love they desire. As Sally Taylor Lieberman carefully documents

in her book, motherhood was one of the most favored themes among male intellectuals in modern Chinese literature, and particularly in the works of Lu Xun
and Yu Dafu, she finds that the writers' sense of political frustration is often
allegorized in the relationship between a powerless son and a strong mother.[14]
The son's failure either to rescue his mother from pain or to punish her tyranni-
cal acts demonstrated the frustrated identity-construction process of modern
Chinese intellectuals in relation to their nation-building wishes.

The child's special position is most obvious in *New Woman*.[15] Wei Ming, a
single parent, left her baby daughter to her sister in their hometown to go to
Shanghai for a living. As their lives are getting more difficult, the aunt brings
the now juvenile girl to visit her mother of whom she has no memory. On the
train, the aunt tells the story of Wei Ming to the girl. There is an elaborate system of subjective shots in this scene, which is not frequently seen in Chinese
cinema during this period, demonstrating the face of the daughter looking at
different women around her, imagining if her own mother looks like anyone of
them. At the end, her aunt takes out a photo of Wei Ming from her baggage, and
the series of subjective shots ends on this picture. After a careful scrutinizing of
the picture, the young daughter concludes that Wei Ming is both a loving mother
and a suffering woman (figures 5.3-5.12). Through this series of subjective shots,
the film carefully facilitates the identification between the spectators and the
daughter in relation to Wei Ming, who are both investigating Wei Ming's personal stories through visual means.

Therefore, the film invites spectators' multiple identifications with the
mother: one can identify with Wei directly, seeing her as surrogate for themselves in bearing and purging suffering. But these spectators, as well as others
who are not emotionally sutured into the mother position, could also at the same
time identify with the daughter, who represented either the strong masculine
agency appropriating her mother's sufferings into the film's overarching left-
wing discourse, or the vulnerable and deprived subject desiring maternal protection. This plural identification, both empathetic and sympathetic, allowed a more
fluid relation to be built between the film and the spectators. While the film arti-
ficially constructed a "new woman" to legitimize its patriarchal agenda, Wei
ended up possessing a life richer than it was designed. She might always remain
an object, but as her objectification was carried out from diversified sources, the
character was given a larger space to assert her meanings in and to the film,
therefore in and to the left-wing ideology. It demonstrates the uniqueness of the
woman's representation in this cinema, as it serves as a site of ideological contestation instead of simply allowing one voice to be heard. This was made possible partly by the filmmakers' ambivalent relationship with their women characters, partly by cinema's own characteristic relation with reality. Occupying the
unique position between fiction and reality, cinema disallowed the left-wing
cinema's control over women's representation to be total and stable.

Ai Xia—The Condemned Woman Warrior

The desire of this cinema to claim women's stories and women's consciousness its own did not stay only on the cinematic level but projected itself to the extra-cinematic dimension, yet this appropriation desire also ultimately failed to stabilize its objects. As shown in its reaction to the suicides of two famous actresses, Ai Xia and Ruan Lingyu, the left-wing discursive machine was anxious to prove its omnipotence not only in fiction but also in reality. However, I will argue that filmic representation, through the protection of the cinematic frame, gave a certain amount of autonomy to its characters not available in reality.

Ai was always seen as a symbol of renegade. She left her own middle class family in Beijing and came to Shanghai to start a new life in show business in the late 1920s.[16] Although as an actress Ai never attained real stardom in her short life span, she was famous for her multifaceted talents. The first woman film scriptwriter in China was Pu Shunqing, the wife of the famous director Hou Yao, who wrote the script for *Aishen de wan'ou* (The Cupid's Doll).[17] The second female film scriptwriter (female directors would appear much later in the history of Chinese cinema) was Ai. As well as being the scriptwriter of *Xiandai yi nüxing* (A Woman of Today), she also played the film's female lead (figure 5.13).[18] The film depicts the romantic affair between Taotao, an employee of a real estate company, and her reporter lover Yu Leng, a father of two children.[19] She is so infatuated with him that she embezzles her company's money in order to support his luxurious lifestyle. Taotao is later arrested for her criminal act, and during her imprisonment, Yu Leng deserts her. In the end she finally wakes up from her romantic dream and decides to lead a new life. The ending title of the film is: "Lying ahead is a bright road. Go—the ocean is wide, the sky is open."[20]

The story can be seen as a typical left-wing cultural product that condemns the earlier May Fourth indulgence in romance and embraces women's liberation in the new era. As Ai admitted, she identified her own filmmaking with the current progressive left-wing cinema.[21] Ideologically, *A Woman of Today* did not deviate from the left-wing films made by most of her male counterparts. Taotao's story was only one rendition out of many under the same formula where the suffering and victimized woman suddenly turns into a triumphant figure transcending gender boundary. But the left-wing critics did not stamp their approval onto this film; the inconsistency of her character trait was particularly pointed out. They found the shift of Taotao from a devoted lover to a devoted revolutionary too abrupt and unconvincing: her indulgence in sensual love was too vividly depicted in the earlier part of the film, but it was not addressed at all in the end.[22] But the real motivations of these attacks were probably not initiated by this characterization, which was recurrently found in many other left-wing films, but the eroticism depicted. Many comments about the film were related to its candid portrayals of sexuality.[23] For example, Ling He, the famous left-wing film critic of that time, disapproved of this film because he considered it to be more pornography than pedagogy.[24]

Ai committed suicide in the Lunar New Year in 1934. Why would she, as a rising movie star and a promising new writer, choose to end her life? There were more than seven special issues in newspapers and magazines devoted to her death right after the incident,[25] and the general conviction was that she ended her life because of her illicit relationship with the director Li Pingqian.[26] In a newspaper article entitled "Memorializing Ai Xia" published right after her suicide, the author Chen Ping wrote that:

> Most female intellectuals are highly aware of the illusion of romance and despise unconditional love. However, in reality they still hold on to the fantasy and see ideal love as the fist of their lives; tragedies are often the results. Ai Xia clearly suffers from the same problem. Although in *Mingxing Monthly* she writes that she does not believe in unconditional love, her incessant search for it clearly states the opposite.[27]

Interestingly, the critic's rationalization of Ai's death can easily be linked to the character Taotao she created and played in *A Woman of Today*. Chen Ping wrote in the same article: "Intellectually, Ai Xia has gained new insights [about social reality]; but she failed to accommodate her emotional sensibilities accordingly. This disharmony is the leading factor to her suicide." Here we can interchange the name Ai Xia with Taotao, and the criticism still remains valid, with the only difference being that Ai suffers the consequences in reality, while Taotao's successful transformation remains in fiction and unconvincing. In a criticism in *Morning Daily* published after Ai Xia's death, the writer wrote:

> We were chatting about *A Woman of Today* one day. All of us respected Ai Xia's courageous and vivid creation and performance of [Taotao], but we also found the abrupt shift [of Taotao] at the end not convincing. One of us asked: "What will be the future of [Taotao]?" Another responded offhand: "How can she have any future? Either she becomes depraved or dies!" Now, the heroine in *A Woman of Today* has transformed herself successfully, but the author of *A Woman of Today* chooses death.[28]

Although Ai had claimed that the story of *A Woman of Today* reflected her own life,[29] the mirroring connection between Ai and Taotao made by critics and viewers was more than a common scholarly practice in relating the life of an author to his/her works. It was also an attempt to conflate the public and private discourses of cinema, connecting cinematic and extra-cinematic reality in order to support an omnipotent left-wing nationalist ideology that governs both. In one year, this ideology found another incident in which to invest and further its power, although the appropriation desire was manifested in a slightly different way.

Ruan Lingyu—The Truly Liberated?

Ai's death was only a prelude to a much bigger social event that happened one year later: the suicide of Ruan Lingyu, and both incidents were somehow related to Cai Chusheng. Rumor was that Cai had an intimate friendship/affair with Ai Xia, and her suicide broke his heart. In order to wage a war against the reporters, whom Cai blamed for Ai's death, he made the film *New Woman*, recounting Ai's tragic life and condemning the paparazzi's aggressions. In an uncanny way, Ruan Lingyu, who played the film's heroine Wei Ming modelled after Ai Xia and who also fell in love with Cai, committed suicide very soon after making the film. And the reason for Ruan's death was very similar to Wei Ming's (therefore Xi Aia's) problems; she was not able to face up to the press and the public about her adultery scandal. Fiction and reality were so complicatedly linked with each other in these two incidents that they demonstrated the very complex relationship between cinema and history. Interestingly enough, this dilemma between fiction and reality was also what the left-wing cinema movement strove to reconcile and conflate.

As I have illustrated in detail, the left-wing cinema needed a new revolutionary-woman image to represent a new China. The life, on-screen and off-screen, of the glamorous superstar can be seen as the epitome of this new politics of female representation. Although Ruan's story had been frequently told and appropriated, the importance of her legacy in this left-wing cinema deserves our effort to read about her life once again.[30] Ruan in real life was the daughter of a maid in a rich household.[31] Similar to the plots of many popular novels and movies, the poor girl fell in love with the master's son, Zhang Damin, but was rejected by the conservative matriarch because of her lower class status. Secretly married to her young lover, Ruan moved out of the household with her mother, taking the financial responsibilities for supporting the new family as a film actress. With the earnings of his now famous wife, Zhang began to indulge himself in his previous promiscuous and extravagant lifestyle, which enraged the actress. Ruan left Zhang for a rich businessman, Tang Jishan, but Zhang continued to harass her through charges of adultery and by spreading rumors about her to the press. Unable to endure such torment, Ruan committed suicide on the International Woman's Day, March 8, of 1935. With the heavy melodramatic and class elements, this real-life story can be seen as a rendition of the typical left-wing movie.

Many famous left-wing intellectuals published articles immediately after Ruan's suicide to condemn society for killing this actress renowned for portraying progressive women. Ruan's suicide was seen as a manifestation of social injustice, in contrast to Ai's suicide that was interpreted as the result of her romantic illusions. It shows that the left-wing culture reacted quite differently to the two suicides in spite of their resemblance. Similar to the case of Ai, Ruan's suicide coincided with the experience of the character Wei Ming, whom she portrayed in the aforementioned *New Woman*, which premiered just one month before her death. In fact, the director Cai was inspired by the death of Ai and created the story of this film based on her life.[32] However, while Ai was directly connected to Taotao, the May Fourth archetypal woman image, the left-wing discourse did not link Ruan's suicide to Wei Ming, who is also a typical rendition of the May Fourth spirit. These different interpretations may be due to the different star images the two represented; Ai represented the wayward individualist, while Ruan, as I have illustrated, often portrayed the strong mother figure whose strength and love the left-wing masculine discourse feared and desired. Therefore, while Ai is responsible for her tragedy as an individualist should be, the personal experiences and weaknesses of Ruan's were glossed over, and her suicide was made into a symbol that represented the collective sufferings of Chinese women. For example, the famous left-wing essayist Nie Gannu argued: "The one who killed Ruan Lingyu was not herself. The murderer was not an individual person like Zhang Damin or Tang Jishan. The killer is the residual feudal morality that still infatuates our minds."[33] Although recognizing Ruan Lingyu's own emotional weakness in committing suicide, the famous film critic Chen Wu similarly blamed society for her death. "The sole cause of Ruan Lingyu's suicide is the remaining feudal power. The representatives of feudalism in this case are the irresponsible reporters, Zhang Damin, Tang Jishan, and Ruan Lingyu's own mentality."[34] Even the respectable Lu Xun wrote an article to criticize the corruption of the newspaper business, which, as he believed, caused the death of Ruan Lingyu.[35]

The left-wing filmmakers were among the most vocal and emotional ones. The famous director Fei Mu exclaimed agitatedly: "It is the feudal residual in our society that killed Ms. Ruan."[36] Li Minwei, the well-respected producer, explained Ruan's death in this way:

> Ms. Ruan had seen all the brutalities of social injustice, particularly those related to the inferiority of women. Women can never elevate their positions in this semi-feudal society, and Ruan Lingyu felt powerless to redeem her and tens of thousands of other suffering women from this injustice. Therefore, on March 8th the International Woman's Day she ended her own life. Protesting with her dead body, she demands justice from us all.[37]

Li Minwei here overlapped Ruan Lingyu's personal encounters with an imaginative public experience. He interpreted her suicide not as her private decision but representing the demand of women in general for gender equality. Luo Mingyou, another film director and the boss of Lianhua Film Company, also righteously proclaimed that "Ms. Ruan did not die of suicide; she sacrificed herself to society and all women."[38] Under the endorsement of these filmmakers, from a victim, Ruan Lingyu was transformed to a heroine who was courageous enough to rage war against the corrupt social structure by sacrificing her life.

According to the last letter Ruan Lingyu wrote just before her death, the major reason leading to her suicide was her refusal to face her ex-husband's adultery charge and the following public condemnation. The trial was to commence the day after her suicide; her choice of March 8 might have little to do with the date's symbolic significance but her own personal considerations. But these details were all ignored; the intellectuals were concerned more about the propaganda of this death to support their own ideological beliefs, although their self-justifying passion and anger can also be understood. The two different, yet similar, reactions of the left-wing intellectual machine showed that the actresses' private emotions and experiences became an access to the investigation of social reality, and both the on-screen and off-screen female stories were organized into a coherent ideological structure. The personal and private components of the suicides were emptied out to be refilled by the collective will and interests of the filmmakers and critics, making the left-wing ideology seemingly all-embracing.

Cinema and Its Frame

The representation politics of this left-wing cinema movement and the public discussions generated by the two suicides combined to illustrate the degree of ferocity and anxiety of the left-wing patriarchy in appropriating women's stories, both in filmic representation and in reality. And this appropriation mechanism was driven not only by the filmmakers' identity-struggling but also by the cinema's aesthetic ideology. It is well recognized that socialist realism was the aesthetic *tour de force* of the global left-wing culture in the early decades of the century. China's left-wing cinema was not an exception, and most of the related filmmakers and critics considered artistic representation valuable to humankind only if it had direct reference to social reality. Gender inequality was so highlighted in this cinema also because it was seen as evidence of China's moral backwardness. And in order to prove the validity of its ideology, this realist cinema associated its cinematic representation to reality by connecting their fictive world to the stars' own private lives. Through such conflation and reinforcement between the private and the public, the actresses' suicides became vivid and powerful manifestations of the old world, which in turn legitimated the consolidation of the progressive culture as a whole. The gender discourse and the national discourse were woven by this realist desire into an interlocking network in which the lives and the film roles of these actresses intersected. It was at this point where realism and nationalism converged; it is also here where we observe how the patriarchy struggled to be omnipresent.[39]

However, the more ardent was this desire, the more anxiety was shown embedded. Being so indulged in persuading themselves and the spectators about the degree of "realism" in the films, the filmmakers and critics might only have displayed their anxiety in the illusionary nature of film, acknowledging that there was a distance between cinema and reality, between women's personal experience and male's ideology. The filmmakers and critics had to rely on the "reality" out there to authenticate and validate their filmmaking and criticism. Only when the narratives set up on screen found direct bearing in the reality off screen could the filmmakers assure the public and themselves that the oppression the women experienced in films was not an imaginative conception; and only upon such equation could the critics find themselves at ease in their cinematic pedagogy. Instead of a simple coercive relationship, this gender relationship showed more about the filmmakers' struggles and distress than their total tyranny.

In fact, cinema played a conflicting role forging this new masculine subjectivity. On the one hand, the left-wing intellectuals made the clever move to drop anchor in cinema because of the medium's substantial market potential and its visual nature. Cinema has the tendency to homogenize a large population, as the capital-intensive nature of film production and distribution requires large potential spectator groups. While films are made with the heavy concerns of their clientele in mind, spectators inevitably are subject to cinema homogenizing effects that mould their emotions, tastes, and values. Cinema's photographic resemblance to reality also makes it the most effective means, among other available ones, to consolidate a new collective subjectivity in the first half of the twentieth century.[40]

However, cinema sometimes also disrupts the overarching ideological structure that mediates our reception. For example, when we compare the suicide of Wei Ming in *New Woman* with Ruan's own, it clearly shows the difference between cinematic representations and the extra-cinematic ones. While Wei Ming's direct protests to the camera rendered both the spectators and filmmakers breathless,[41] Ruan Lingyu herself had no such space of attestation when it came to her own suicide. In the film we observe that although the narrative clearly condemns the May Fourth woman who is doomed to fail history, she is also allowed to tell of her reluctance to comply. However, under the public discourse, Ruan's real voice was completely silenced and appropriated by the left-wing propaganda machine. As argued by Mirian Hansen, "the bourgeois public sphere was gendered from the start—as an arena of virtuous action, and civilized interaction, for the 'public men.' "[42] Attempting to redeem Ai and Ruan from the criminal act of suicide, the male critics in fact victimized them further by making them available for discussion in the public sphere. After all, it was the horror of the overwhelming public condemnation that forced both Ai and Ruan to commit suicide. They might have chosen otherwise if they had recognized that their suicides did not halt but indeed accelerated their helpless falling into the public sphere.[43]

Interestingly, the female characters seem to have retained more power within the cinematic frame than in those unprotected public spaces like newspapers and magazines. Rey Chow and Slavoj Žižek explore this power dynamic in cinema from different perspectives. Analyzing the films made by the famous Chinese Fifth Generation director Zhang Yimou, Chow argues that women are always the objects of cinematic close-ups and slow motions, and they provide the suturing points at which the narratives hang together.[44] Zhang Yimou relies on women characters to display a Chinese culture because the sheer visuality of woman's sexuality made the director's display of "China" accessible and conceivable.[45] But it is also this "force of surface," as argued by Chow, which challenges the deep assumption that reality is at the core waiting for us to reveal it; it forces us to meet head on the exteriors and requires us to recognize and come to terms with cinematic visions which all are comprised of the surfaces alone.

In the analysis of Hitchcock's *Rear Window*, Žižek argues that the desire of James Stewart is produced by what he can see through the window. Grace Kelly finally succeeds in becoming worthy of his desire by literally entering the frame of his fantasy, by crossing the courtyard and appearing "on the other side" where he can see her through the window.[46] This analysis provided by Žižek can be seen as a cinematic rendering of Chow's idea, while Chow's argument also helps us further understand the implication of this Hitchcock scene. Woman is employed in the Fifth Generation Chinese cinema because the new cinematic "ethnography," quoting Chow's word, must be established through the visuality created by the "shallow" display of women's bodies within the cinematic frame. But while the audience is absorbed in this display, the object also exhibits its effect to those who hold the gaze. "Like Fassbinder's, Zhang's cinema is about the affect of exhibitionism rather than that of voyeurism."[47] Grace Kelly in Žižek's example can also be understood in this way. By entering the frame of James Stewart's fantasy, although she becomes the object of his desire, she is also protected by this frame. Chow argues that "the power of surfaces is thus the power of confrontation, which ultimately makes us, the spectators, aware of the sensation of being stared at."[48] Following this argument, entering the male's frame of fantasy and transforming oneself from a three-dimensional "reality" to a flat representation, Grace Kelly, however, resumes the power of confrontation, forcing James Stewart to recognize her presence which has been ignored. Not only is she able to occupy the full attention from her lover, but her action of entering the murderer's apartment also escapes the verbal control of James Stewart. Instead, he is forced to recognize her independent existence, which is nonetheless still inside the frame of his projection.

Following Chow's and Žižek's analyses, we can go back to our earlier analysis of the suicides of Ruan Lingyu on and off the screen. Dialectically, the patriarchy must rely on, therefore is conditioned to, an "other" to define its power and identity. It is true that in any patriarchal discourse woman represents not herself but, by a process of displacement, man's desire and anxiety; but she, in the metonymical chain, will not only end up in but also easily trespass the phallus. As the young male filmmakers in the Chinese left-wing cinema showed so much anxiety in inscribing women's private stories and experiences into their nation-building process, their films, in fact, reflected either their childlike dependence on the "mothers" to authenticate their wills and reasoning, or their eagerness to rebel against the source of empowerment to assert individuality. Both processes seem to be doomed, because the mothers might overpower them any moment.

Cinema is most revealing in illuminating this power dynamic. When the visual and illusionary nature of the medium coincides with the vulnerability of female representation, it becomes most seductive to male's confiscation. But this sheer vulnerability, as discussed in Chow's and Žižek's analyses, can also exert power back to such seizure, ultimately invalidating this appropriation mechanism. Cinema is able to protect its subjects within its frame, particularly in those close-ups or direct frontal views, in the sense that when the objectification of woman is intensified to the degree that little space is left between the characters and the spectators, the latter is made to confront the former directly, bypassing the ideological mediation of the patriarchy. While female representation is invested with various interests of different parties, the direct visual portrayal of hers also facilitates a head-on collision between the viewer and the viewed, allowing her a certain autonomy not available in the public discourse. As the Chinese left-wing cinema was so anxious to seek the endorsement of the woman characters, the anxiety was translated into visual terms that overwhelmed the action itself.

In the case of *New Woman*, for example, the director seemed to be so anxious to portray Wei Ming's image and thoughts in order to express himself, to the extent that his own control threatened to vanish. Instead, the gaze of the spectator was returned directly with the gaze of the character, forcing the spectator to recognize his/her position hitherto defined by the cinematic apparatus. Comparing Wei Ming's suicide to Ruan's own, the actress could not confront the public directly because the overall ideological function of movie stars, as argued by Richard Dyer, is to help preserve the dominant power structure.[49] The star is composed entirely of social mediation, powerless in his/her actual social political autonomy but extremely powerful in reflecting the control of the dominant ideology to the public. While Ruan fell prey to this mechanism, Wei Ming did not. Interestingly, this left-wing cinema was clearly patriarchal in structure, but it also set up a boundary that protected and showcased women's autonomy, no matter how insignificantly it was in view of the all-powerful patriarchy. Under the current academic hyperbole in celebrating borderlessness and trans-bordering, the tangible border of the cinematic frame might be most illuminating in offering us alternative tactics to those de-territorializing mechanisms ruling our world.

The flourishing of women's stories in this cinema movement demonstrated that, in order to make themselves heard, the filmmakers had no other tools more powerful or more handy than speaking for the women. Wishing to start a new page of Chinese history, the filmmakers ended up on a traditional path. And more ironically, only through the representation of the opposite sex did a new masculine subjectivity truly consolidate in Chinese cinema, as the domination of male subjectivity, instead of masculinism, clearly distinguishes the 1930s' left-wing cinema from the previous Chinese cinema. However, in contrast to the general belief that this cinema was single-handedly pushed through by the left-wing discursive machine, this gender politics also demonstrated that this movement was a spontaneous cultural process and was conditioned to many diverging discourses and conflicting interests. The dialectic between victimizing and heroizing woman characters, between their servility to different interests and their autonomous existence, only revealed the process of a discursive formation in its organic way. The accounts equating communist control with the development of this cinema fail to acknowledge the complicated co-web set up among gender and other discourses in any cultural phenomenon, in which no one's interests can completely dictate others'. We might never be able to define and, therefore, confine this subjectivity, but the most equivocal discourse may ultimately be the most powerful one.

Notes

1. Miriam Hansen, "Fallen Women, Rising Stars, New Horizons: Shanghai Silent Film as Vernacular Modernism," *Film Quarterly* 54, no. 1 (2000), 16.

2. Zhang Yingjin, "Engendering Chinese Filmic Discourse of the 1930s: Configurations of Modern Women in Shanghai in Three Silent Films," *positions* 2, no. 3 (Winter 1994): 603-28. A similar version can be found in Zhang's book *The City in Modern Chinese Literature and Film: Configurations of Space, Time, and Gender* (Stanford, Calif.: Stanford University Press, 1996), 185-207, 229-231.

3. There are few biographical materials of Yin Minzhu, Wang Hanlun, and Zhang Zhiyun available. But there are several books published recently recounting the life of Hu Die, which are important documents to our understanding of early Chinese cinema. These writings include her autobiography *Hu Die huiyi lu* (The Reminiscence of Hu Die), ed. Liu Huiqin (Taipei: Lianhe baoshe, 1968) and a better biography of hers written by Zhu Jian, *Dianying huanghou Hu Die* (The Queen of Cinema: Hu Die) (Lanzhou: Lanzhou University, 1996).

4. The only male character whose star status exceeded many famous female performers at that time was Jin Yan. Later in the decade the names of Zhao Dan and Yuan Muzhi were also getting famous. Interestingly, all the three male performers had strong left-wing political ties, and their stardom was to a large extent promoted by this left-wing cinema movement.

5. For the synopses of these films, see *ZZDY*, 229-345.

6. Among the four films, only *Women's Outcry* and *The Goddess* were written by the directors themselves. But Fei Mu and Situ Huimin were also actively involved in the choosing and writing of the scripts.

7. This tradition of women's tragedies continued in the cinema of Hong Kong and Taiwan after 1949. It was not until the 1960s and the 1970s when the economy of the two places soared did the position of male figures in films begin to surpass that of females. And interestingly, the concerns for women's sufferings continued to be central in the mainland cinema until the Fifth Generation cinema. This is a rather complicated phenomenon that involves many cinematic as well as extracinematic issues. A more systematic, theoretical framework must be formulated before jumping to a conclusive statement

130

Chapter 5

about the gender manifestation of Chinese cinema. Unfortunately, this topic lies beyond the scope of this book.

8. Rey Chow argues that the predominant feature of Mandarin Duck and Butterflies fiction was that women's problems served as the hinges of many narratives written by male authors. *Woman and Chinese Modernity: The Politics of Reading between West and East* (Minneapolis: University of Minnesota Press, 1991), 34-83. Joseph Allen also provides some interesting examples to show how the male poets assumed feminine voices to tell their own stories in the *yuefu* poetry. See his *In the Voice of Others: Chinese Music Bureau Poetry* (Ann Arbor: Center for Chinese Studies, University of Michigan, 1992). Lawrence Lipking, from a different perspective, provides a similar conclusion in his analysis of the abandoned women images in the poetry written by Li Bai, Cao Zhi, and Ezra Pound: "They serve both as 'allegories' of masculine frustrations and as a servile other self who reminds the male of his power." *Abandoned Women & Poetic Tradition* (Chicago: The University of Chicago Press, 1988), 134.

9. See, for example, Wang Hongwei's *Mingding yu kangzheng: Zhongguo gudian beiju ji beiju jingshen* (Fate and struggle: Chinese classical tragedies and tragic spirit) (Beijing: Sanlian, 1996), 61-65.

10. Barlow, "Theorizing Woman: Funü, Guojia, Jiating," in *Body, Subject & Power in China*, ed. Angela Zito and Tani Barlow (Chicago: The University of Chicago Press, 1994), 253-89.

11. "Dianying de sanzhong guanzhong" (Three types of Cinema spectorships), *Lianhua huabao* (Lianhua pictorial) 6, no. 3 (Aug. 1, 1935): 18-19.

12. Melvyn Stokes, "Female Audiences of the 1920s and early 1930s," in *Identifying Hollywood's Audiences: Cultural Identity and the Movies*, ed. Melvyn Stokes and Richard Maltby (London: BFI, 1999), 44.

13. Kristine Harris has already elaborated the various subjective shots of Wei Ming in the film, which I do not need to repeat. See "The New Woman Incident: Cinema, Scandal, Spectacle in 1935 Shanghai" in *Transnational Chinese Cinemas: Identity, Nationhood, Gender*, ed. Sheldon Hsiao-Lu (Honolulu: University of Hawaii, 1997), 277-302.

14. Sally Taylor Lieberman, *The Mother and Narrative Politics in Modern China* (Charlottesville: University Press of Virginia, 1998). For her analysis on Lu Xun and Yu Dafu, see chapter 3 of the book.

15. The film depicts a daughter instead of a son for whom the mother sacrifices herself probably because the daughter is ultimately the one to assume the "new woman" identity.

16. Wu Dong, "Ai Xi fulu zisha zhi zhenyin" (The real cause of Ai Xia's killing herself by taking toxic drugs), *Diansheng zhoukan* (Cinema voice weekly) 3.6 (March 1934): 109.

17. Li Suyuan and Hu Jubin, *Zhongguo wusheng dianying shi* (The history of Chinese silent cinema) (Beijing: Zhongguo dianying, 1996), 143.

18. It is believed that the film, like so many other valuable ones at that time, is no longer available; nor has this film, to my knowledge, been analyzed in detail by any later scholars and film historians. But judging from the newspaper reports and criticism at that time, this film must have been one of the most controversial movies in the new 1933 cinema. The following synopsis is reconstructed from related materials published in newspapers and magazines at that time.

19. The names of the lovers were certainly symbolic. The character *tao* means grapes; its erotic evocation is obvious. The family name of the man is *yu*, which means *I* or *me* in

classical Chinese. *Leng* means *cold* or *coldness*. The sexual relationship between the two was likely to be revealed in their names.

20. *SB*, June 26, 1933.

21. *SB*, Jan. 1, 1934. In another magazine article she also proclaimed that a good movie should "reveal how capitalists and landlords exploit the poor." "Gei youzhi dianying de zimei men" (To the sisters who are ambitious in filmmaking), *Dianying huabao* (Cinema pictorial) 5 (Sept. 1933): 12

22. See, for example, the comments of an audience printed in *SB*, June 20, 1934.

23. Some of these comments can be found in *SB*, June, 16, 20, 28, 1933.

24. *SB*, June 16, 1933.

25. For example, one-third of the volume of *Dianying huabao* (Cinema pictorial) 9 (March 1934) was devoted to a eulogy of Ai Xia. *CB* also devoted a special issue on Ai Xia's death on Feb. 17, 1934.

26. See, for example, Gong Jia'nong, *Gong Jia'nong congying huiyi lu* (The memories of Gong Jia'nong regarding the film industry) vol. 2 (Taipei: Chuanqi wenxue, 1980), 255-256, 261, 348. However, I must point out that the three volumes of Gong Jia'nong's writing suffer from many factual mistakes and deliberate misrepresentations of the left-wing filmmakers. We cannot take his words for granted.

27. *SB*, Feb. 17, 1934.

28. Nai Fang, "*Xiandai yi nüxing* de si" (The death of *A Woman of Today*), *CB*, Feb. 21, 1934.

29. This is suggested in an article in *SB*, June 20, 1933.

30. Recent studies on Ruan's life and career can be found in her biography written by Chen Ji, *Yidai yingxing, Ruan Lingyu* (The film star of a generation: Ruan Lingyu) (Xianan: Shanxi renmin, 1985); an anthology and picture collection edited by the historian Cheng Jihua, *Ruan Lingyu* (Beijing: Zhongguo dianying, 1985); and the recent Hong Kong film *Ruan Lingyu* (*The Actress/The Centered Stage*) (Stanley Kwan, 1993).

31. The following description of Ruan Lingyu's life is summarized from Chen Ji's work.

32. See Cai Chusheng's own account in *Cai Chusheng xuanji* (Selected writings of Cai Chusheng) (Beijing: Zhongguo dianying), 468-69. As hinted by the 1993 Stanley Kwan film *The Actress*, Cai Chusheng had affairs with both Ai Xia and Ruan Lingyu. I requested references from Stanley Kwan, and he admitted that these were only hearsay. I could not find any historical evidence to prove the affair of Cai Chusheng and Ai Xia; but Ke Ling, who knew both of them personally at that time, verified the affair of Cai Chusheng and Ruan Lingyu to me in an interview. Interview with Stanley Kwan, Hong Kong, Jan. 14, 1997. Interview with Ke Ling, Shanghai, China, Nov. 6, 1996.

33. Cheng, *Ruan Lingyu*, 20.

34. Cheng, *Ruan Lingyu*, 16.

35. Lu Xun used the pen name Zhao Lingyi in publishing this article. *Lun "Renyan ke wei"* (A discussion of "People's words could be horrifying") *Taibai* (Taibai monthly) 2, no. 5 (May 20, 1935). Rpt. in Cheng's *Ruan Lingyu*, 13-14. "*Renyan ke wei*" is a Chinese idiom meaning that people's gossip is destructive. This idiom was written in Ruan Lingyu's last letter. The letter is reprinted in *Ruan Lingyu*, 12.

36. Letter reprinted in Cheng's *Ruan Lingyu*, 24.

37. "Ruan Lingyu jinian zhuanhao" (The special issue memorializing Ruan Lingyu), *Lianhua huabao* (Lianhua pictorial) 5, no. 7 (April 1, 1935): 23.

38. "Ruan Lingyu jinian zhuanhao," 24.

39. This politics of appropriation is definitely not unique in China. In many other so-

cialist cultural movements gender is also made a component of the larger ideological framework by conditioning females' private experiences to the collective ones. See, for example, Renate Holub's criticism of Antonio Gramsci on his feminist outlook being severely curtailed by his determinist view of progress, which deems feminine sexuality only a function of the larger nationalist interests. *Antonio Gramsci: Beyond Marxism and Postmodernism* (London: Routledge, 1992), 198.

40. Theorists like Christian Metz, Stephen Heath, Laura Mulvey, and Kaja Silverman have provided us a rich array of scholarship demonstrating how the viewing subject, whose identity is always in its construction, inserts itself into and is defined by the symbolic register of the film text. However, there are more and more reservations raised to these "subject-position theories" as totalizing and ignorant to the dynamic reception process. For a detailed response of some contemporary film scholars to this set of "subject-position theories," see David Bordwell, "Contemporary Film Studies and the Vicissitudes of Grand Theory," in *Post-Theory: Reconstructing Film Studies*, ed. David Bordwell and Noël Carroll (Madison: The University of Wisconsin Press, 1996), 6-9.

41. This is splendidly portrayed in Stanley Kwan's *The Actress*. In the scene depicting Wei Ming's death, the crew is so overwhelmed by Ruan's performance that everybody stays motionless watching Ruan's continual crying even after Cai says "cut."

42. Miriam Hansen, *Babel and Babylon: Spectatorship in American Silent Film* (Cambridge, Mass.: Harvard University Press, 1991), 10. Here Hansen is reiterating the discussions of some feminist historians including Joan B. Landes and Jean Bethke Elshtain about the debate on the public sphere.

43. The article of Kristine Harris also analyzes the relation between the suicide of Ruan Lingyu and the film *New Woman*. We arrive at two different conclusions: Harris claims that critics saw the actress' suicide as showing her weakness and powerlessness. But I argue that the left-wing filmmakers heroized, more than dispowered, her. This discrepancy is mainly a result of our diverging focus: Harris' interests are the popular culture while I concentrate on the reactions of the intellectual culture.

44. Rey Chow, *Primitive Passions: Visuality, Sexuality, Ethnography, and Contemporary Chinese Cinema* (New York: Columbia University Press, 1995), 146.

45. Chow, *Primitive Passions*, 147-49.

46. Slavoj Žižek , *The Sublime Object of Ideology* (London: Verso, 1994), 119.

47. Chow, *Primitive Passions*, 169.

48. Chow, *Primitive Passions*, 168.

49. Richard Dyer, *Stars* (London: BFI, 1979).

Figure 5.1.
The ending scene of
Little Toys. Ye Dasao is
going mad in the center
of a crowd.

Figure 5.2.
The ending scene of
New Woman. Wei Ming
on her death bed,
shouting directly to the
camera, "I must live."

Figure 5.3.
New Woman. On the
way to visit her mother
whom she has no mem-
ory of, the daughter
asks her aunt, how does
Wei Ming look?

Figure 5.4.
She looks out the window of the train trying to catch a glimpse of the possible images of her mother.

Figure 5.5.
Cut to her subjective view, seeing two farming women in the field.

Figure 5.6.
Not satisfied, she starts gazing upon the women on the train.

Figure 5.7.
Cut to her subjective
view, seeing an old lady
dozing off.

Figure 5.8.
Camera slowly pans to
the left, replicating the
daughter's subjective
view, and she sees
another old lady.

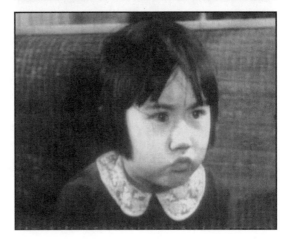

Figure 5.9.
Cutting back to her
perplexed look.

Figure 5.10. The daughter continues to beg her aunt to tell her what her mother looks like.

Figure 5.11. The aunt finally takes out a picture of her parents, explaining to her how her father abandoned them.

Figure 5.12. The extensive set of subjective shots ends with the daughter examining Wei Ming's picture.

Figure 5.13. Taotao (played by Ai Xia) in *A Woman of Today* captured in a cell.

III

The Spectators and the Film Culture

6

A Commercial Cinema or a Political Cinema?

I have demonstrated in the last chapters that certain common features found in many of these left-wing films were results of the filmmakers' shared ideological and emotional structure, but in the following three chapters, I will shift my focus from production to reception, exploring the larger film culture and spectators' collective tastes and interests. The success of this cinema was conditioned as much to the filmmakers' efforts as to the spectators' stamp. In spite of its clear political claim and vision, this cinema was also largely commercial and relied heavily on the identification of spectators to the plot and characters, and the films often evoked emotions without providing epistemological solutions to change the social situation. It might be more adequate to describe the accomplishments of these films in terms of their sentimental appeal than any abstract concept of ideological correctness, particularly in consideration of the official Chinese film history that celebrates the latter as the sole merit and foundation of this movement.

This left-wing cinema, as I will argue in the following pages, relied heavily on sentimentalism and populism. Obviously, Marxists should be critical of such emotional appeals because they encouraged the passive participation of the consumers. However, as a form of mass media, cinema could not afford to lose sight of the market, which is ultimately the most crucial support of its survival. To put it in another way, no popular films can function in purely ideological terms because the spectators would find their way to receive the films according to their everyday life habits and values. In fact, in this cinema movement, socialist ideology and the market often found themselves in an antagonistic yet cooperative relations. There was, on the one hand, an incompatible distance between the filmmakers who aspired to present the films as their ideological statements and the many spectators who saw the movies as nothing but a form of entertainment; on the other hand, however, the spectators' reception of the films was often influenced by and entangled with the filmmakers' struggles and states of mind, and vice versa. In the actual cinematic experience, the filmmakers and the spectators reconciled and competed with each other that the viewing process pivoted on multiple axes.

In this chapter, we will investigate the position of this cinema along the commercial-political spectrum. Illustrating the different impacts of Hollywood and Soviet films on this Chinese left-wing cinema, we will investigate who its spectators were, and how they influenced this cinema on different grounds. This left-wing cinema was most unique in its vast support from the mass, particularly among the petty bourgeoisie. An analysis of the spectatorship will certainly complicate what this film movement was, and it can further explain the reasons behind its popularity. The purpose is to reveal a fluid and complex film culture of the time, privileging neither the filmmakers' subject positions nor the spectators' oppositional readings of the films. As Judith Mayne argues: "one of the problems in spectatorship studies is the desire to categorize texts and readings/responses as either conservative or radical, as celebratory of the dominant order or critical of it."[1] The relationship between the filmmakers and the spectators in this cinema was certainly not a fixed, one-way, top-down model of agent and object; however, the spectators should not be celebrated and idealized on the basis of their autonomies to the filmmakers' intentions. Instead, their positions shifted constantly. It is more important to illuminate the contradictions and tensions inherent in the film culture that existed not as theoretical abstractions but as daily practices.

The Dilemma of Commercialism

Was this cinema a commercial or a political one? The easiest answer is apparently "both"; but the intricacies behind this "both" are perplexing, as the contradictions and conflicts between the logic and structures of cinema are enormous and complicated. This cinema was deeply entangled and trapped between itself as an intellectual movement and a populist movement. It, on the one hand, lacked a vigorous philosophical foundation to back up its intellectual endeavor but, on the other hand, remained generally elitist in its underlying structure and objectives. It was under this theoretical negotiation and hesitancy that the politics of this cinema developed waveringly. At the same time, the committed filmmakers were highly aware that the popular taste could not be sacrificed in the name of artistic and ideological excellency. While this left-wing nationalism was constantly contaminated by the commercial nature of cinema, the market helped to promote and realize the infiltration of the ideology among the mass.

Zheng Zhengqiu, the most prestigious Chinese filmmaker in the early 1930s, in the article "Ruhe zoushang qianjin zhi lu?" (How to enter the progressive path?), proclaimed that the progressive ideology of Chinese cinema should follow the "Sanfan zhuyi" (The three "anti-" principles), a new term circulating among left-wing intellectuals then, which included anti-imperialism, anti-capitalism, and anti-feudalism.[2] He argued that the three ideologies are Chinese cinema's leading principles, as China's future was dependent upon the citizens' adequate grasp of these principles. Zheng's article was only a formal announcement of some commonly held principles shared by other progressive filmmakers, as their films had reflected such directions long before the writing of this article.

However, Chen Wu, a Communist Party member and also a famous film critic, published another long article in the same magazine immediately afterward arguing that the most important task of Chinese cinema at that time was to disseminate the seeds of anti-imperialism and anti-feudalism, but not of anti-capitalism.[3] He argued that the Chinese capitalist class was too impotent either to take up the bourgeoisie revolution or to become a major hegemonic force over the Chinese mass.[4] The immediate enemies Chinese left-wing cinema had to confront were, instead, imperialism and feudalism. This article was a clear demonstration of Chen Wu's insightful analysis of the current situation of Chinese cinema—it was considered the Party's directive to the cinema movement in 1933. But his analysis of the capitalists was comparatively unsound, such that his neglect of their social function in the Chinese film industry of the time was hardly convincing.

A major reason behind this oversight was, I believe, the Party's reliance on the capitalist cinema industry to produce their films. The movie-making business was simply too expensive for any non-capitalists to plunge into. Unlike the Soviet cinema in the 1930s which was funded by the State, the Chinese Communist Party then had no financial backing to support a cultural project as costly as filmmaking. All the left-wing films were produced in established commercial film studios that were interested more in profit-making than ideological correctness. This commercial factor was for sure not formulated in the Socialist doctrine, that the communist think tank, like Chen Wu, had to explain and solve theoretically. This article was hardly convincing in justifying the Party's association with the film companies; instead it only proved that this left-wing movement was operating within the capitalist machine.[5]

It is crucial to notice this superimposition of intellectual cinema and commercial cinema in order to read these Chinese films more vigorously. Despite their highly politically charged messages, many of these films were also extremely popular among spectators at that time. The two films with the longest screening periods in Shanghai during the 1930s, *The Sisters* and *The Fishermen's Song*, were both considered left-wing films.[6] But this complicity between politics and marketability burdened the definition of this film movement. While some left-wing filmmakers were working out a new socially committed cinema with impressive box office results, there were inevitably others, including the left-wing filmmakers themselves, who saw this as a new cinematic trend they had to follow as a business tactic. After all, the social issues that most concerned the left-wing filmmakers (i.e., the social injustice faced by oppressed groups, like women, factory workers, and the peasantry) always contained many highly dramatic elements that also had great entertainment appeal.

In fact, it is extremely difficult to argue whether some of these acknowledged left-wing films were deliberate ideological pedagogy or products aiming at commercial success. Films with similar left-wing social content were simply produced as a trend between 1932 and 1937. One unfortunate consequence was the decreasing creativity observed in some of the later films; an intellectual cinema with active audience participation was partly transformed into a commercial entertainment cinema in which spectators became passive and uncritical. The symbiotic relationship between a political cinema and a commercial cinema implies an inevitable mutual trade-off. And the practical concerns of this film movement can be well elucidated by a 1937 statement made by Shen Xiling, one of the most ideologically committed directors:

> When we have conceived a film story, the first question we need to ask is whether the spectators will accept it. The second is the viability of this film under the poor financial and technological conditions of the present Chinese cinema. And then we need to consider the appropriate performers. The last question is the difficulty of escaping the double gates in the censoring machine [the censorship of the GMD government and that of the foreign concessions].[7]

Among the many stringent limitations, Shen Xiling emphasized that his first concern in making films was the mass spectators. In another instance the director Cheng Bugao, right after making the famous left-wing film *Spring Silkworms*, also admitted that, "film is an art in its making; but it immediately becomes a commodity after its production process."[8] Therefore, the left-wing filmmakers were always concerning about the balance between political effectiveness and spectators' pleasure. Highbrow intellectual artworks would only alienate their spectators, who were both their commercial and ideological targets. However, the political effectiveness of these films could not be curtailed under these concerns. It was also this intervention of commercialism that brought into question the assumed equivalence among the notions of "intellectual cinema," "avant guard cinema," and "left-wing cinema."

Between the Soviet and the Hollywood Models

To further examine how the political film movement evolved under the spell of the popular taste, we can first investigate a specific selective process performed by this cinema before we proceed to the actual interactions that harbored the socio-cultural conditions of the cinema culture. Hollywood and the Soviet cinema were the two most influential models shaping this left-wing cinema, and the Chinese choice between the two cinematic approaches most intricately revealed the latter's particular concerns and decision makings within the unique conditions of its own context.

Between Hollywood and the Soviet cinema, the latter seemed to have enjoyed the overwhelming support and endorsement from the left-wing filmmakers and critics. In addition to filmmakers' oral appraisal of the Russian films, *The Development of Chinese Cinema* counted that there were fifty-five articles about Soviet cinema published in newspapers or journals in the year of 1933 alone.[9] This reverence could be understood more as a political gesture than as a pure artistic disposition. Most of the Chinese left-wing intellectuals knew very little about the new Soviet Union because the Soviet government released little information about their development and political situations to the world at that time. But this did not prevent the Chinese intellectuals from idealizing the new political regime. The supreme position of Soviet cinema helped to convince both the filmmakers themselves and their spectators of the legitimacy of the new left-wing cinema developing in China.

However, the real impact of the Soviet cinema to the Chinese one was restricted to this symbolic level. In fact, Chinese spectators at that time only watched a handful of Soviet productions, far fewer than the Hollywood films. Soviet films were not allowed to be shown in China in the 1920s because the Chinese government refused to acknowledge the Bolshevik revolution and the legitimacy of the new socialist state. The first Soviet film shown in China was *Battleship Potemkin*, which was screened in 1926, just one year after its release in Moscow, yet it was not screened publicly but only in a private gathering organized by Tian Han and his Nanguo Society.[10] Not until China established diplomatic relationship with the Soviet Union in 1932 did the Nationalist government accede to the screening of the "red" cinema in China. The first film shown was *Road to Life*, a film highly acclaimed by Chinese critics and spectators. Other Soviet films were gradually introduced to the Chinese market, including *Mother*, *The Heir to Jenghis-Khan*, *Golden Mountains*, *Chapaev*, and *We Are from Kronstadt*. As Xia Yan recalled: "After 1931, some early Soviet films like *Road to Life*, *Golden Mountains*, and *Chapaev* were gradually introduced to China. Not only did these new films attract a lot of attention from youths and intellectuals in Shanghai, but they also produced good box office receipts."[11] Proved by their lengthy screening periods and positive responses from critics, many of these Soviet films were indeed popular in China. *Road to Life* was particularly influential; so much so that Cai Chusheng decided to produce a film modeled after it: it became the famous left-wing film *Lost Lambs*.[12]

The Soviet silent cinema in the 1920s was one of the most powerful and admired film traditions of all time, and their montage theories are still discussed and studied today. One of the major reasons contributing to its superior position in film history was its success in consolidating ideology and aesthetics, which is now standard textbook material. To summarize briefly, Sergei Eisenstein, Vsevolod I. Pudovkin, Lev V. Kuleshov, Dziga Vertov, Aleksandr Dovzhenko, and other filmmakers contrived and developed a cinema theoretically corresponding to Marxist dialectics. These montage filmmakers and critics argued that spectators would go through a dialectic experience when exposed to juxtaposed images, as a synthesized meaning would be created by the clash of two separate visual units together. In addition to this dialectic system between and among images, another one is also set up between the film and the spectator, in which a synthesis, which is the ideological transformation of the latter, is obtained. The filmmakers' artistic creativity is ultimately not an end in itself but serves a higher ideological mission. The ultimate significance of their films therefore resided in the active intellectual participation of the spectators.[13] Theoretically, form and content do converge in these films, producing a truly political art. However, in terms of practical effects, the Soviet efforts in the 1920s could not be seen as successful because of the simple reason that their obscure manipulation of the images were just too sophisticated for the mass to apprehend, and most of the spectators were more confused than enlightened by the films. Sadly enough, although many films created by the Soviet filmmakers have been considered masterpieces of World Cinema, they failed to achieve their most prioritized political mission.

It is important to notice that most of the Soviet films popular in China were Pudovkin's films and the productions in the 1930s instead of the famous montage films produced in the 1920s. The isolated studies of Eisenstein were restricted to their borrowed acclaim for *Battleship Potemkin* or his more elementary theories on montage editing. Other important filmmakers and theorists of the 1920s like Kuleshov and Vertov were only mentioned by name. The first and only systematic study of any Soviet filmmaker done by Chinese intellectuals was devoted to Pudovkin alone. Xia Yan and Zheng Boqi in 1932 translated his writing from Russian into *Dianying daoyan lun* (Film directing) and *Dianying jiaoben lun* (Film writing). As compared to the other Soviet filmmakers, Pudovkin's films and writings were embraced much more wholeheartedly by Chinese left-wing critics in the 1930s. In fact, his films were also accepted more widely among Russian spectators at that time when compared to other famous montage filmmakers. Eisenstein's famous "montage of attractions" was based on juxtaposing images of opposition or the ones with no necessary relations (i.e., thesis and anti-thesis). However, Pudovkin favored a "montage of associations" that connected rather than contrasted individual shots. To him, the ultimate guideline in cinematic practice resided not in the unique character of the medium, i.e., editing, but in its narrative structure.[14] The reason for the tokenization of Pudovkin, rather than any other director in the golden era of Soviet filmmaking, in the Chinese left-wing cinema was not difficult to understand, as most spectators found Pudovkin's films more approachable.

Other than Pudovkin's, most of the other Soviet films celebrated in China were the ones produced in the 1930s. A "cultural revolution" in cinema took place in the Soviet Union at the end of the 1920s, the beginning of the famous First Five-Year Plan. This cultural revolution was born out of frustration among politicians who saw the current cinema not living up to their expectations: commercial directors cared little about ideology and more about spectators' appeal;

the great masters were, however, alienating the spectators so much that their political efforts became futile. The famous directors were charged with indulging in "formalism," sacrificing the correct ideological messages to aesthetics in its most abstract terms. Critics also participated in this purgation and leveled criticisms of the best directors condemning their failure to use films as propaganda instruments. Eisenstein, for example, did not make any new films for a decade between 1929 and 1938. A new cinema, as a result, evolved under this political atmosphere, although both the quality and quantity of its films could not at all match the productions in the golden era between 1925 and 1929.[15] *Road to Life*, the first Soviet film screened in China publicly, attracted overwhelming support both from Chinese critics and spectators and was a typical product of this movement. The movie deals with a contemporary social problem of juvenile delinquency. Its story is told simply and effectively, and the film contains no highbrow symbolism and was highly popular with spectators in the Soviet Union. In fact, most of the Soviet films celebrated by the Chinese critics and spectators were in this strand of the new Russian cinema.

While modern Chinese literature was marked by the prominent Russian literary influence since the May Fourth period,[16] the left-wing filmmakers' direct appropriations of the Soviet cinema were not as noticeable, although we can still find sporadic examples testifying to the Soviet influence. For example, Ma Ling demonstrates that the opening sequence of *Street Angel* was indebted to the Soviet montage cinema.[17] However, these attempts were usually consciously executed as specific political statements that could hardly be considered as major stylistic trends. Lin Niantong, the famous late Chinese film scholar, has argued that "montage aesthetics was a creative foundation of Chinese cinema beginning in the 1930s. We can almost say that most progressive films at that time employed the idea of conflicts to develop their structures."[18] Lin seems to be confusing form with content. While Chinese spectators most of the time favor those stories full of antagonist struggles on the semantic level of plot, they enjoy continuity and clarity on the syntactic level of form. If Lin is accurate that "conflict" structured many Chinese films beginning in the 1930s, this notion of conflict was definitely more "melodramatic" than "montage," refers more to the content than to the form. That is to say, Chinese films in the 1930s were highly aware of using conflicts, which correspond, however, more to the emotional confrontations within the story than to Soviet montage designed for intellectual enlightenment.[19] It is therefore hardly convincing that the conflictual confrontation we observed in the plots of left-wing films was a Marxist dialectic; rather it was a practice rooted in a traditional aesthetics that valued the balance of oppositional forces into harmony, which would be further discussed in chapter 8.

Although there were many original or translated articles about the Soviet film industry published in China then, most of these studies remained factual reports or general subjective impressions, and none of them analyzed the Soviet films in any detail. Ironically, it was Liu Na'ou, the later "Soft-film" critic and

filmmaker, who first introduced the Soviet montage film theory to Chinese readers in 1930, despite the fact that the study was not done in a systematic way.[20]
Although the filmmakers and critics participating in the left-wing movement
were self-proclaimed Socialists, their understanding of the ideology was often
secondhand and heavily tinged with the current national concerns China was
facing. Their reading of intellectual Marxism was limited: they were concerned
less with the real ideological meaning of historical dialectics than with the possibilities of applying them in the Chinese situation. As a whole, the Soviet
cinema was important to the Chinese left-wing cinema mostly on the political
level; stylistically it was Hollywood that held sway.

According to an American study published in 1938, in the year of 1936,
among all films shown in China, only 12 percent of them were local productions,
yet American films comprised more than 80 percent, and Soviet movies represented a mere 2.4 percent.[21] If this study was accurate, the left-wing cinema was
facing an extremely potent rivalry in spite of their remarkable efforts and accomplishments. Although ticket prices of most foreign films were usually higher
than Chinese films,[22] there were still more people attending Hollywood films
than the local productions, as many spectators still found the Hollywood productions to be of better quality and more entertaining. Language barriers were
usually not a determining factor for the spectators as many foreign film theaters
projected superimposed Chinese titles on or next to the screen. The Chinese
filmmakers and critics were obliged to persuade the moviegoers to stay away
from Hollywood films in order to improve attendance at the domestic films. But
in spite of the ear-splitting condemnation of the critics, many Chinese spectators,
particularly the ones from the middle-higher class, continued to favor Hollywood cinema.

Ironically and inevitably, Chinese filmmakers were also largely influenced
by the Hollywood mode of practice. While their spectators were habituated to
the American form of filmmaking, the Chinese filmmakers themselves also considered Hollywood productions as their greatest source of inspiration. Cheng
Bugao recounted that he was impressed by the ending of D. W. Griffith's *Way
Down East* (1920), where Lilian Gish's safety on the melting ice was heightened
by Hollywood editing techniques.[23] The flood sequence at the end of *Torrent*
was likely Cheng Bugao's rerendering of the ending sequence of *Way Down
East*.[24] The director also admitted that he modeled his productions after some
Chaplin films.[25] Cai Chusheng was another director heavily influenced by the
Hollywood practice. He mentioned that a filmmaker should concentrate on the
main themes of the film and avoid wasting time on other elements that might
distract spectators' attention. He also set up a rather rigid form, both in terms of
length and structure, for his films to follow so that their rhythm and pace could
be under his direct control.[26] This was certainly a narrative form closer to the
American practice than to both the montage cinema that devalues plot and the
traditional Chinese narrative that favors abundant details and branch developments.[27] Many films of Sun Yu, who studied photography and cinema in the
United States, were also influenced by the Hollywood cinematic practice. His

earlier films, like *Spring Dream in the Old Capital, Wild Flowers,* and *Loving Blood of the Volcano,* were clearly modeled after the Hollywood romance stories in theme and structure. Ideologically, Sun Yu was also honest in acknowledging his admiration of Western culture. As he admitted in an interview: "Presently what we need the most is the adoption of Euro-American civilizations in order to destroy all rotten traditional ethics."[28]

While we should remind ourselves that it is futile to argue how Hollywood influenced the Chinese cinema in exact details, as cinematic styles in the 1930s' were already largely global, the paramount impact of Hollywood to the development of Chinese cinema was beyond doubt. Particularly in the 1930s, when Chinese films were able to skillfully manipulate editing, shot angles, distance, and compositions, the Hollywood influence, conscious or unconscious to the Chinese filmmakers, were enormous. While there were a few left-wing filmmakers, like Sun Yu, who were more honest in admitting the influence from Hollywood, most others chose to keep silent in this aspect. As Bordwell argues, "to defend cinemas as an inherently popular art was inevitably to defend Hollywood."[29] This was a dilemma the Chinese leftist filmmakers also faced.

Since the 1920s, Hollywood cinema has successfully formulated a cinematic narrative which attracts spectators all over the world; film audiences can easily identify their beliefs, their concerns, their hopes, and their fears with the stories. In return, the films also change their value system and sense of identity. This mutually enhancing circulation allows the system to grow perpetually. As Bordwell, Staiger, and Thompson demonstrate, a classical Hollywood narrative politics, which emphasizes and combines harmony and order, unity of characters' identity, human psychological development, and standardized linear progression, produces a powerful form of cinematic experience. The Hollywood studio system, which emerged in the 1910s, also played a significant role in standardizing a cinematic form that habituated its global spectators to this cinematic experience. The industry's hierarchy of authority, division of labor, and assembly-line production process forced the film to become not the product of individual human expression, but a melding of institutional forces, which created a most effective narrative system that was able to take over the market.[30] The appeal of this system to most Chinese filmmakers, whose spectators favored stories to be told clearly and skillfully, was insurmountable. Miriam Hansen and others, on the other hand, argue that Hollywood's increasing power on a global scale has been constituted by a complex network of structural coercion, which Hansen terms as Americanism.[31]

To translate this Americanism for the specific case of Chinese markets in the 1930s, we discover that American studios devised many strategies to fit their productions into the specific Chinese environments. As Wang Chaoguang elucidates, Hollywood relied on innovative commercial practices to dominate Chinese markets in the beginning of the twentieth century. For example, Hollywood promoted the profit-sharing options and invited the distributors to publicize the films more aggressively. All the eight major Hollywood studios had specific representatives in China as early as the mid-1920s, and they promoted the films' media coverage by using novel advertising means, like not showing the ending of a film and inviting viewers to guess it for a prize. Another major strategy to gain the largest amount of profits is to keep a minimal number of copies of the film, say one to two, to be circulated in the market. Those one or two cinemas offering the highest bid could screen the films first, and others had to wait for second or third rounds. This line would extend to different cities in China, and usually Shanghai showed the film first, and then Tianjian, and then Beijing.[32]

As a whole, Hollywood gained so much weight in the left-wing cinema because it was really popular among Chinese viewers, who represented the categorical meaning of this nation-building project. Most of the major directors in the left-wing movement had expressed their loaded concerns on how the spectators would receive their films. Sun Yu in his autobiography writes that the ultimate indicator of a film's success resides in the spectators response in the theaters.[33] Both Xia Yan and Cheng Bugao have commented on the fact that their films were made to be watched by the mass public.[34] Cai Chusheng also wrote with an acute understanding of his films, his spectators, and himself:

> Let's assume there are two films here. One is simple and solemn and its ideology is 100 percent politically correct. However, there is only 20 percent of the audience who would watch it. The other film is entertaining and fun. Although its message is only 20 percent correct, it attracts 100 percent of the audience. The 20 percent of the audience in the former case usually are attentive and have a pertinent understanding of reality to start with; some of them may be superior to the filmmakers intellectually. There is nothing much you need to tell them. . . . Among the 100 percent audience in the latter case, at least 60 percent of them want or need to be educated by films. . . . To choose between the two, I would rather take the latter.[35]

The Petty Urbanites

However, although the left-wing cinema held the spectators so dear in its enterprise, it was by no means clear to the filmmakers and critics who their clients were. Identifying the spectatorship was of great importance to the filmmakers and critics involved in the movement, as they found themselves in incessant perplexity of spectators' reception. Some of the films, like *The Sisters* and *The Fishermen's Song,* were extremely popular, while many others were not. In fact, this awareness of spectatorship could be found in the film texts themselves. For example, in *Song at Midnight,* the Angel Drama Troupe is constantly struggling to attract more spectators. When their plays fail at the box office, the manager exclaims an intertextual remark: "it is really impossible to understand the audience." It is only until they perform the "progressive" play written by Song Dangping does the troupe become popular again, as Song promises the leading singer when handing him the script: "you shall have your audience back." This plot development is an interesting metanarrative commenting on the relationship between the recent success of Chinese cinema and the progressive ideology, although the cultural world was a bit more complicated. To investigate the cultural context at stake, let us use *The Sisters* as a point of departure.

The box office success of *The Sisters* marked a milestone of this cinema movement. It was written and directed by Zheng Zhengqiu, and the film was generally considered as his first attempt to change his filmmaking orientation from right to left. It was screened at the time when Zheng Zhengqiu published his article "How to enter the progressive path?" which I mentioned. The film was considered not only by others but also by the director himself as his first attempt in practicing the aesthetics and ideology of "The Three Anti-Principles" in filmmaking, which is evidenced in the film's strong reproach to the class division between the poor and the rich. The film was adapted from a popular "civilized play" in 1933: *The VIP and the Criminal*, which was also written and directed by him. To the surprise of many people, the film version was even more popular than the play. According to Tan Chunfa, Zheng Zhengqiu's biographer, "the film received a box office of two hundred thousand *yuan*. There were altogether 18 provinces, 53 cities, and 10 overseas cities which showed the film."[36] These were unprecedented records.

In spite of the director's moving statement and the film's strong dishonoring of class divisions, most of the left-wing film critics then did not embrace the film wholeheartedly. They claimed that the ending of the film did not criticize but promoted the reconciliation of the two classes.[37] Precisely because the film contained contradictory political messages, left-wing critics and filmmakers were eager to analyze the reasons behind the film's extreme popularity, who wanted to comprehend the mass' logic of thinking which could help them to devise more competent tactics in their movie making. Tang Na, the famous left-wing film critic, for example, ventured an explanation of the success of the film:

> The biggest lesson we can learn from [the success of] *The Sisters* is the strong resentment of the petty urbanites (xiao shimin) to society, which is channeled and released through the film's exposition of the repulsive reality. However, we must not encourage the illusive nature of the film. If we want to gain the support of the petty urbanites but not to follow them, we must get rid of the deceptive parts. We should instead educate them for new messages based on their dissatisfaction.[38]

Tang Na's statement summarized the general response of the left-wing film critics to this film. They considered the film as a reflection of the dissatisfaction, however unenlightened, of the mass toward society. It was so enthusiastically embraced by spectators because the film spoke to them and voiced their anger and despair. This was attested in the newspaper advertisement of the film which

stressed its reflection of people's real sufferings and praised the film according
to spectators' emotional response. It exclaimed, probably not too exaggeratingly,
that, "no female spectators of the film shed no tears; and 88 percent of the male
spectators did cry."[39] Critics acknowledged the power of such sentimental identification and maintained that the film's ability in evoking and manipulating
these emotions was key to its attraction to the mass.[40] In spite of the film's allegedly conservative ending which projected a false and "reactionary" solution
to society, most of the left-wing filmmakers and critics found the manipulative
power of cinema in this emotional purgation fascinating. Understanding and
analyzing the emotional structure of the spectators became the secret pathway
for them to use cinema politically. But who were these spectators? A contemporary commentator wrote about the success of *The Sisters*: "Attracting spectators
is in fact a question of attracting the petty urbanites."[41] The petty urbanites was a
key term in this "marketing" research.

The term "petty urbanites," according to Mau-Sang Ng, was a term coined
by film critics in the beginning of the 1930s to label the community of people to
whom Chinese films appealed.[42] Perry Link maintains that although this is a
term frequently referred to in modern Chinese literary histories, it has never
been adequately analyzed because statistics for the purpose are nowhere to be
found. "The most anyone says is that the term includes clerks, primary school
students, small merchants, and others of the so-called 'petty bourgeoisie.' "[43]
The petty urbanites were also referred to by the left-wing intellectuals then as a
new urban middle class active in consumption. Mau-Sang Ng further adds that
the term "quickly took on added meaning when critics saw this community of
people as unenlightened, conservative and with a taste for things popular (*su*)."[44]

A newspaper commentary that analyzed *The Sisters'* spectatorship revealed
blatantly how the left-wing ideology saw these "petty urbanites":

> The formation of Chinese capitalism is an extremely unnatural pro-
> cess because it is an embryo resulted from a rape. While international
> capitalism is on the decline because of malnutrition, the residue spirit
> of feudalism is able to continue to linger around China. The two op-
> posite forces [capitalism and feudalism] are embraced in one entity.
> The popularity of *The Sisters* demonstrates that the wishes and the
> needs of the petty urbanites have all been conditioned by this social
> structure.[45]

This piece of social criticism, however confusingly, reflected how the left-wing
intellectuals at that time understand the contemporary moviegoers. The spectators were seen as being caught between feudalism and capitalism, and as a result
they were doubly disenfranchised by the two social forces. Therefore, according
to the author, in order to understand these moviegoers, we only need to analyze
the two political-economic discourses by which they were conditioned. Although these petty urbanites were mostly discontented about current society, they
were entrapped by their socioeconomical conditions and could only wish an

elusive reconciliation within the corrupt structure. They were angry but were too unenlightened to fight back. The filmmakers and critics therefore occupied a crucial position to channel the emotions of the petty urbanites back to the right political track. In other words, the filmmakers saw cinematic experiences as a completely discursive event that could be calculated in ideological terms. Most assertively, by giving them a name—petty urbanites—they considered their attempt in identifying the spectators accomplished. However, other than an uncreative analysis of current social affairs, no critics then were able to reveal the identity and psychology of the petty urbanites in any satisfactory manner. In the new urban Chinese cities, the new movie spectators continued to escape the definition of the ideological structure of society and remain an anonymous mass.

Left-wing film criticisms of the time identified three subject positions in the cinematic discourse, namely, the filmmakers, the spectators, and the critics. The cinematic experience was composed by the participation and interactions of these agencies. It was under consensus that the filmmakers occupied the most important position in this pedagogical project—the filmmaker was the teacher while the spectators remained the students. But in the case of the less committed and enlightened filmmakers, Zheng Zhengqiu in *The Sisters* for example, the films they produced were usually more reflective than critical. As these filmmakers were not able to present the spectators the revolutionary ideology, critics assumed the role to elucidate the relations between the film and society, showing the spectators how to read the film against the grain. The spectators were seen in both cases as receptive and naïve, waiting to be taught and transformed. The ironic result was that, attempting to give a voice back to the mass, the left-wing critics in fact deprived them of any self-determined subject positions.

This inability to name the mass persists today. The contemporary historian Wen-Hsin Yeh tried to reconstruct Shanghai's petty urbanites by analyzing the published letters to and from the editor, Zou Taofen, of *Shenghuo zhoukan* (Life Weekly) in the 1920s and *Dazhong shenghuo* (Mass life) in the 1930s and 1940s, for the journals were highly popular among school teachers, clerks, apprentices—the younger members of the "old" as well as the "new" middle classes—in Shanghai during the Republican period. Yeh's thorough study remains one of the most careful readings of the city's emerging readership of the time, but these Shanghai petty urbanites in Yeh's analysis were more or less a group of blind followers of Zou Taofen's personal editorial stance than individuals possessing their own subject positions. That is to say, in identifying Shanghai's petty urbanites, Yeh recognizes only the individual history and struggles of Zou Taofen—the mass still remains undetermined.[46]

This result is not surprising. As demonstrated by Hanchao Lu, it was their diversification that characterized the petty urbanites in Shanghai at that time. "[The petty urbanites] came from all walks of life and had widely different backgrounds. Sociologists may have some difficulty in trying to classify them according to conventional sociological criteria."[47] In fact, in the practice of everyday life, people can never be measured and predicted perfectly. As Michel de Certeau argues, many everyday practices are "tactical," instead of "strategic," because most of the time we consume our lives in nondiscursive ways. "Strategy" is devised basically on rational terms, which can be executed and analyzed intelligently. But "tactics" is a calculus that cannot count on a "proper." Therefore, no matter how insightful and pertinent the "strategies" employed by the filmmakers in this cinema movement were, the spectators would conceive the films according to their own "tactics," in their own logic and habits which could not be completely justified intellectually.[48] There were different and even contradictory impulses comprising the experience and pleasure in movie-attending in the 1930s' left-wing Chinese cinema. The filmmakers as well as later scholars had worked so hard to identify the spectators, as the filmmakers wanted to devise more effective strategies for their pedagogical projects. However, the spectators eluded most of these "naming" attempts as they were ultimately unnameable, and this "petty urbanites" category continued to stay as an imaginary entity.

The Spectatorship in 1930s' Chinese Cinema

In spite of the impossibilities in defining the spectators and their receptions in exact terms, we could still provide a general cultural landscape in which these spectators are located. We can be sure that there is no research material available to us documenting scientifically the spectatorship in 1930s' Chinese cinema. The reconstruction of this film culture is bound to be incomplete. However, with the little information available, we can still build ourselves a window to study, if only partly, the demography of this cinema's participants. According to a crude estimation of the time, spectators in 1928 were basically categorized by the films they attended: whether the films were Western or Chinese. Zhou Jianyun, who was one of the three managing directors of Mingxing, classified the contemporary film-goers into four groups: one that watched Western films most of the time, one that watched Chinese films most of the time, the third one that never watched any Western films, and the last one that never watched any Chinese films. He further illustrated that the spectators who never watched Chinese films were a smaller group of intellectuals while those who never watched Western films belonged to a bigger group of the lower-middle class.[49]

In spite of the impressionistic nature of this account of Zhou Jianyun, it points out an issue of interest about the cinema spectatorship of the time. In 1928, the time before the left-wing cinema movement took root, Shanghai moviegoers attending Chinese films and the ones attending foreign films were clearly split along the line of class and educational background. The tickets of Western cinema were priced double or triple that of the Chinese films—the ticket price alone was enough to be a symbol of class status. Shanghai's intellectuals were attracted to Western cinema, also because of its allegedly higher artistic achievements. For example, Lu Xun's diary showed that he was a frequent cinema-goer, but among the 149 movies he attended between 1916 to 1936, only four of them were Chinese productions, and they were all produced between 1925-1927.[50] According to his wife, Xu Guangping, Lu Xun was so disappointed about the Chinese films he watched in the 1920s that he decided not to attend any Chinese productions any more, even in the 1930s when the left-wing cinema movement was at its height.[51]

The privileging of Western movies was evidenced not only among the Chinese intellectuals but also in the middle class. Beginning in the 1920s, many magazines devoted to cinema news appeared in the market, and they witnessed the increasing share of cinema in the general public culture. However, most of their articles and pictures were Hollywood's or European; scarcely any features were devoted to the local movie industry. This situation was substantially altered by the arrival of the left-wing cinema. Judging from the increasing numbers of articles about Chinese films and pictures of local movie stars in movie magazines, there was surging attention from the general public to Chinese cinema entering the new decade. Motion picture companies, like Mingxing, Lianhua, and Diantong, also published their own magazines that featured the news of their films and their performers.[52] The high profiled left-wing cinema began to attract the attention of spectators with stronger intellectual and economic backgrounds. According to the recounts of Tong Yuejuan, the wife of Xinhua's boss Zhang Shankan and herself a famous Peking Opera singer and movie star in the 1930s, high school and college students of both genders were particularly enthusiastic about the local cinema, and they comprised the most fervent part of the emerging fan culture.[53]

In his study of Chinese popular fiction in the beginning of the century, Perry Link argues that a "mass" readership was not yet developed in Shanghai during the teens because the bulk of Shanghai's population were illiterate migrant peasants turned urban laborers. It was not until the 1920s and the 1930s that their second generation become involved in the culture of modern popular fiction.[54] In the case of cinema, illiteracy seemed to not be a great barrier for lower-class people, as many theaters employed "interpreters" to speak out the titles. But the low educational background of the spectators discouraged sophisticated filmmaking, and the rising educational status of Shanghai's population was one of the basic conditions that caused this left-wing cinema to sprout.

The rising number and social status of spectators attending Chinese movies was related to the elevating popularity of Chinese movie stars among the middle class. As I illustrated in the last chapter, a powerful "star" culture began to grow in the 1930s. Not only were their news becoming major topics of the daily conversations of the urban population, but there were also more and more consumer products using the images of local film stars to promote their products, a phenomenon not seen in the 1920s. The image of Hu Die, generally known as the most popular Chinese movie actress of the time, was surely the adored one: her face, more than anyone's, was printed on numerous billboards, calendars, postcards, and other advertising materials for different commodities. The Chinese Fuchang Tobacco Company went so far as to use her name to brand their new product: Hudie cigarettes. Some of the other consumer products which employed the images of movie stars to promote their sales included Hu Die's Lux soap, the comedians Yin Xiucen and Han Lan'gen's stomach medicines *Weihuo*, Yuan Meiyun's Guansheng Garden Mid-Autumn Festival Cakes, Wang Renmei's Guangdong Brothers' Tennis Shoes, etc.[55] However, famous opera singers were seldom patronized by the commercial sectors although traditional operas were as popular as cinema then in many Chinese cities. The intimate relationship between cinema and the emerging consumer culture/middle class was clear.

Judging from the newspaper and magazine advertisements of the time, two types of products were most prominently associated with the movie industry: cigarettes and cosmetics, appealing to spectators of both genders.[56] They were also the two most representative commodities associated with modernity and the West. Not only did the commercial sectors contract movie stars to appear in their advertisements, but they also sponsored other activities in film circles so that their products were made to represent these events. For example, the 1934 Queen of Chinese Cinema and Ten Best Movie Actresses Awards was organized by *Jiabao* (Garbo) Cigarettes. The *Sanhua* (Three Flowers) Cosmetics went directly to the theaters and distributed their skin care products to the moviegoers. As a movie advertisement indicated, the cosmetic company was so attentive that they even distributed two different sets of products to male and female spectators.[57] While the films helped the promotion of the consumer products, these new cultural symbols also assisted the elevation of the Chinese cinema from a lowbrow mass amusement activity to a modern urban pastime with a sense of taste and class. It is obvious that the movie industry was already well integrated to a highly developed form of consumer society that bracketed different commodities into its profile to reinforce each other's appealing force to the consumers, and the local movie stars became the mirror reflecting the new economic structure.

But the spectators could not be comprised of only one social sector. In comparing the Chinese moviegoers with the Soviet's new proletariat spectatorship, the contemporary critic Bate argued that, "our cinema spectators are almost all "aristocrats," the rich or members of the idle class."[58] However, such political outcries were usually invested with exaggerations. There were 106 film theaters in China in 1927; but the figure rose to 239 three years later. The total number of seats in 1930 also doubled that in 1927.[59] Such rapid growth could not be brought about by one class alone but by a swift expansion of attendance across society. In fact, the lower-middle class was not particularly denied access to this form of entertainment because the cinema ticket price was low enough to attract their participation. Its price in 1935 was between 0.1 *yuan* in a dilapidated screening house to 2 *yuan* for the best first-run movie theaters, a range wide enough to suit spectators from different classes.[60] (For reference, the retail price of fresh pork was about 0.18 *yuan* per pound, and a dozen eggs cost 0.24 *yuan* at that time.[61]) Compared to Peking Opera, which usually asked for several *yuan* per ticket, a movie ticket, particularly the cheaper ones, was generally affordable by most. Except for the real poor, most of the urban population had the chance, however rarely, to attend movies, particularly the Chinese movies.

In a short newspaper article published in 1932, the reporter listed five groups of frequent moviegoers in Shanghai.[62] They included modern youngsters who went to movies with their dates, ladies of the leisured class who were tired of Peking Opera and other stage performances, rich businessmen who were bored by their lives, poor people who needed escapist entertainment, and the critics who came to evaluate the films with their social political agenda. Judging from this imprecise categorization, the current cinema spectatorship was comprised of a wide spectrum of city dwellers with different class and gender backgrounds, even including members of the lower class who were probably not able to afford paid entertainment of any other kind. We can safely conclude that the spectatorship of this cinema spanned a large spectrum of population in Shanghai. And these spectators might be attracted to cinema due to some simple pragmatic reasons like, for example, the enjoyment of air conditioning. As I mentioned earlier, Cai Chusheng's *The Fishermen's Song* set the record of an eighty-four-day screening period. The film was shown in one of the hottest summers in the history of Shanghai with the temperature exceeding 100°F. Xinguang, the only theater showing Chinese films equipped with air conditioning, used its new air conditioning for the first time in showing *The Fisherman's Song.*[63] This simple reason might contribute significantly to the high attendance at the film.[64]

The prosperity of cinema as a whole in the 1930s was also evidenced in the blossoming of publications that published news of all aspects of local and foreign filmmaking. As a magazine writer exclaimed in 1935, "no periodicals could afford to ignore news or pictures about cinema. The recent popularity of film publications have become such a powerful trend that obliges all people in the field of journalism to follow."[65] In this flourishing film culture, newspapers and magazines published opinions of critics, filmmakers, and spectators, indirectly encouraging this cinema movement to embrace multiple voices. There were also a number of film clubs set up in Shanghai inviting filmmakers, critics, and the general public to discuss issues related to the local and international cinema. For example, Shanghai's YMCA organized a series of film seminars in the summer of 1934 inviting famous filmmakers to give talks on different aspects of film productions and cinema studies. Those speakers on the list were all actively participating in the left-wing cinema movement, including Hong Shen, Xu Xingzhi, Zheng Zhengqiu, Shen Xiling, Shitu Huimin, and Cheng Bugao.[66] Beginning from the 1920s, cinema was becoming one of the most popular pastimes in the Chinese urban consumer society. Entering the 1930s, Chinese cinema had already earned enough support from its patrons to transform itself into a mature

and powerful medium, capable of combining the discourses of not only entertainment but also art and politics together.

The Cinematic Experience

A spectator of *The Sisters* wrote about his or her feelings about the film in a
newspaper: he or she had never watched Chinese movies in the last two years
but was persuaded by a friend to watch this film. The spectator was deeply
moved by the film and saw that the story about the warlords oppressing the people, which took place in 1924 mirrored the social reality of the day. He or she
saw the film as an honest representation that hinted at the dark side of contemporary society. However, in the last paragraph of this article, the author wrote:

> I was walking away from Xinguang Theater and pondering on the
> lives of ordinary people after watching the film. The sobbing of Hu
> Die [the actress who played the roles of both sisters] was still heard
> in my ears. The suffering of the family also remained in my eyes.
> When I walked across the road thinking about it, I saw a shop that
> sells lottery tickets. Then I suddenly asked myself, "isn't this the so-
> lution of life?" This might answer the questions raised by *The Sisters*.
> But unfortunately this lottery is only played once in several months.
> How wonderful it is if we can have the hope of winning the first prize
> everyday.[67]

The last thought of this spectator was completely out of the film's concerns.[68]
Drifting from the theater to a lottery-ticket sales station, the city-stroller connected his cinematic experience with the real happenings he encountered.
Counting on the lottery to save the lives of the sisters, i.e., attacking the capitalist social structure through a conspiracy with it, had probably never been entertained by Zheng Zhengqiu nor the left-wing film critics. But it was this digestion
process of the spectators that stamped the success of this film. In the cinema,
this spectator was told a narrative and explained the reasons behind this social
misery. He or she was offered a pedagogy that illustrated a lucid form of social
order in which the power relationships were clearly delineated. It was a linear
depiction of the causes and results, rendering the plot as reasoned and intelligi-
ble. However, the actual "walking" of this spectator created a spatial pattern
shattering the linear relationship into an ensemble of possibilities. As Michel de
Certeau argues, while the walker makes possibilities exist as well as emerge,
"[the walker] also moves them about and he [sic] invents others, since the
crossing, drifting away, or improvisation of walking privilege, transform or
abandon spatial elements."[69]

   The cinema experience is, always, a result of the fusion of not only historical horizons but also spatial encountering. Movie-attending, including these left-
wing films with such manipulative power, is not a passive activity to spectators.

Instead, spectators accept, experiment, suspect, or even denounce the trajectories of the film projected according to their own experience as well as knowledge. In the case of *The Sisters*, although the film was comprised of only a single narrative which documented and explained the sufferings of the entire family, spectators often found fissures and joints in the narrative which could be supported, contradicted, or complicated by their own daily encounters and imaginations, because the representations connected so intimately to social reality. It was the previous and later "walking" of the spectators in and around the films that empowered the films as a political tool, although many times the messages they received or elaborated might not be the ones intended by the filmmakers.

Theodor Adorno has argued that the ultimate aim of art is to overcome empirical time, as the best art is the most profound expression of the relations of domination within the field of consciousness. However, mass culture, as he exclaims, is able to attain a superficial ahistoricity not by challenging the temporal relationships of the empirical time but by an escape to confront conflicts. As a result, mass culture more fatally falls victim to its time.[70] The Chinese left-wing films under discussion might not be able to attain a historical transcendence as urged by Adorno; but, as a form of mass culture, the films portrayed not ahistoricity but stayed committed to social reality. In the 1920s, film-goers attending Chinese movies were mostly attracted either to Mandarin Ducks and Butterflies stories or swordsman movies, revealing a common fascination of the people to the depiction of the past and the fantasy.[71] In addition to the Chinese past, the contemporary West also appealed to the Chinese urban popular culture in the first two decades of the century. As Lee and Nathan delineate, Chinese popular fiction in the beginning of the century was usually a Chinese translation of Western fiction.[72] As I illustrated in chapter 1, in 1932, when Lianhua was beginning to make films, they attempted to attract higher class spectators by producing films with a Western outlook and having them titled bilingually. Contemporary Chinese social issues were never confronted or discussed in cinema.

However, the left-wing cinema disturbed this fantasy with the past and with the West. The progressive intellectuals in the 1930s were able to bring the mass culture to confront contemporary social conflicts. All the leftist films were set in contemporary China, presenting their stories squarely in "here" and "now." It compelled the mass culture to a commitment to the empirical present. Because of the proximity between the film's reality and their own, the spectators were able to walk in and around the space which overlapped the films with their own lives. In spite of the left-wing films' relatively rigid and uncreative understanding of the world, the cinematic representations often echoed themselves with the actual thoughts and experience of the people, rendering the "walking" space roomy enough for spectators to explore and provide their own response. If Adorno is right in his criticism of the mass culture, that "the lack of conflict within the work of art ensures that it can no longer endure any conflict with the life outside itself,"[73] the Chinese left-wing films seem to have enough capacity to embrace and tolerate conflicts both within and outside the works because of their proximity to the spectators' own horizons.

I am not here to suggest an innocent reflectionist claim that the works mirroring real lives are necessarily politically engaging or effective. In fact, the reliance of the spectators' own experience and imaginations could undermine the political projects of the filmmakers most severely. However, one of the secrets behind the success and merits of any popular culture is precisely this complexity woven by the text's space and the readers' reality and fantasy. This popular cinema revealed the contradictions and indeterminacy in the relationship between filmmakers and spectators, which complicates the system of control and manipulation on the one hand and the participants' individual subversion and emotions on the other hand. Most of the time, the oppositions or agreements made between the filmmakers and the spectators cannot be neatly described but rather constantly enmeshed with each other. The Chinese left-wing cinema movement under discussion is a particularly prominent example in this regard because, structurally, it was so deeply intertwined with the multiple social and personal concerns of the filmmakers and the spectators. As a result, the film movement was able to develop itself into an encompassing and dynamic culture that grew on its own ground.

In this cinema movement, which was as commercial as it was political, the distance between the filmmakers and the spectators, between film as a political tool and film as a consumer product, did not prevent but indeed encouraged the development of this cinema movement, both in terms of ideology and popularity. Although the welded ideological and commercial interests were so intertwined that we could hardly distinguish if the films' political impact or financial success came prior, we can be certain that Shanghai in the 1930s engendered a cultural environment that brought capital and alternative politics together, allowing the commercial sectors to exploit and be fortified by subversion, and vice versa. So it is difficult to conclude between the two poles where this left-wing cinema and the individual filmmakers were located. But this difficulty prevents us from assuming a simple identity or antagonism between the filmmakers and the spectators between the cinema as political and as commercial. Instead, it was the cinematic space shared by the filmmakers and the spectators, which they could run into, negotiate with, or ignore, each other, that determined the cinema's success. I would characterize Shanghai's film circles in the 1930s as a relatively dynamic and egalitarian one, which, along with other areas of the popular culture, was coherent and robust enough to embrace diverse sights and voices. We will keep this commercial/political dilemma in mind, and in the following two chapters we will revisit this tension from other perspectives.

Notes

1. Judith Mayne, *Cinema and Spectatorship* (New York: Routledge, 1993), 93.
2. *Mingxing yuekan* (Mingxing monthly) 1, no. 1 (May 1933). Rpt., *SNZDPW*, 614-17. Please note the pun with *Sanmin zhuyi* (Three Principles of the People) advocated by Sun Yat-sen.
3. Chen Wu, "Zhongguo dianying zhi lu" (The road of Chinese cinema) *Mingxing yuekan* (Mingxing monthly) 1, nos. 1 and 2 (May, June 1933). Rpt., *SNZDPW*, 601-13.
4. Chen Wu, "Zhongguo dianying zhi lu," 606.
5. According to Shanti Swarup, during the early 1930s Mao was also trying hard to persuade the Party leadership to follow a more liberal policy toward the rich peasants and the capitalists, for these classes were potentially useful to the cause of national revolution, a task most urgent to the Chinese under the immediate threat of Japanese invasion. See *A Study of the Chinese Communist Movement* (Oxford: Clarendon Press, 1966), 169-201.
6. For a complete list of the sixty most popular films in Shanghai during 1932 to 1937, see appendix 2.
7. Shen Xiling, "Zennyang zhizuo *Shizi jietou*" (How to make *Crossroads*) *Mingxing banyuekan* (Mingxing half-monthly) 8, no.3 (1937). Rpt., *ZZDY*, 397.
8. *SB*, Oct. 13, 1933.
9. *ZDFS*, vol. 1, 195.
10. *ZDFS*, vol. 1, 139.
11. Xia Yan, *Dianying lunwen ji* (Film writings) (Beijing: Zhongguo dianying, 1985), 84.
12. "Mitu de gaoyang zuotanhua" (A panel discussion on *Lost Lambs*) *Dawanbao* (The Great Evening News) Aug. 21, 1936. Rpt., *ZZDY*, 593-596. The influence of Chaplin's *The Kid* in the Chinese film was also obvious.
13. For Eisenstein's related discussion, see Richard Taylor and Ian Christie, eds., *The Film Factory: Russian and Soviet Cinema in Documents 1896-1939* (London: Routledge, 1994), 126; for Vertov's, see *Kino Eye: The Writing of Dziga Vertov* (Berkeley: University of California Press, 1984), 63-64.
14. Pudovkin, "On Editing" in *Film Theory and Criticism*, ed. Gerald Mast and Marshall Cohen (New York: Oxford University Press, 1985), 83-89.
15. For a history of the Soviet cinema in the 1930s, see Peter Kenez, *Cinema and Soviety Cinema, 1917-1953* (Cambridge: Press Syndicate of the University of Cambridge, 1992).
16. On the Russian influence in the May Fourth literature, see Mau-sang Ng, *The Russian Hero in Modern Chinese Fiction* (Hong Kong: The Chinese University Press, 1988).
17. Ma Ning, "The Textual and Critical Difference of Being Radical: Reconstructing Chinese Leftist Films of the 1930s" *Wide Angle* 11, no. 1 (1989): 24.
18. Lin Niantong, *Zhongguo dianying meixue* (Chinese film aesthetics) (Taipei: Yunshen, 1991), 11.
19. I will further discuss the melodramatic inclination of this left-wing cinema in chapter 8.
20. Liu Na'ou, "Efa de yingxi lilun" (Russian and French film theories) *Dianying zazhi* (Movie monthly) 1 (May 1, 1930): 74-78.
21. Rudolf Löwenthal, "Public Communications in China before July 1937," *Chinese*

Social and Political Science Review 22 (1938-39): 49.

22. *Diantong banyuekan* (Denton gazette) 1 (May 1935), n. p.

23. Cheng Bugao, *Yingtan yijiu* (Old memories of the film industry) (Beijing: Zhongguo dianying, 1983), 154-156.

24. Since *Torrent* is no longer available, this is only a speculation I reached after reading the script and the director's writings about the scene. Cheng, *Yingtan yijiu*, 5-13.

25. Cheng, *Yingtan yijiu*, 149.

26. Cai Chusheng, *Cai Chusheng xuanji* (Selected writings of Cai Chusheng), ed. Mu Yi and Fang Sheng (Beijing: Zhongguo Dianying, 1988), 418-428.

27. See Andrew H. Plaks, "Towards a Critical Theory of Chinese Narrative," in *Chinese Narrative: Critical and Theoretical Essays,* ed. Andrew H. Plaks (Princeton: Princeton University Press, 1977), 309-352; see particularly section 4.

28. *SB*, Oct. 20, 1933.

29. David Bordwell, *On the History of Film Style* (Cambridge, Mass.: Harvard University Press, 1997), 55.

30. David Bordwell, Janet Staiger, and Kristin Thompson, *The Classical Hollywood Cinema: From Style and Mode of Production to 1960* (New York: Columbia University Press, 1985).

31. Miriam Hansen, "The Mass Production of Senses: Classical Cinema as Vernacular Modernism" in *Reinventing Film Studies*, eds. Christine Gledhill and Linda Williams (London: Arnold, 2000), 339-42.

32. Wang Chaoguang, "Minguo nianjian Meiguo dianying zai hua shichang yanjiu" (The marketing research of American cinema in Republican China), *Dianying yishu* (Film art) no. 258 (Jan 1998): 57-64.

33. Sun Yu, *Dalu zhi ge* (The song of the big road) (Taipei: Yuanliu, 1990), 100-101.

34. Xia Yan, *Dianying lunwen ji* (Film writings), 97; Cheng, *Yingtan yijiu*, 79.

35. Cai Chusheng, "Huike shi zhong" (In the meeting room) *Dianying, xiju* (Film, drama) 1, nos. 2 and 3. Rpt., *ZZDY*, 139.

36. Tan Chunfa, *Kai yidai xianhe—Zhongguo dianying zhi fu Zheng Zhengqiu* (Breaking a new path—The father of Chinese Cinema Zheng Zhengqiu) (Beijing: Guoji wenhua, 1992), 439.

37. For the film's synopsis, see chapter 8.

38. *SB*, May 27-28, 1934.

39. *SB*, April 24, 1934.

40. See, for example, Xuxu's article in *Dawan bao* (The Great Evening News), Feb 28, 1934.

41. *SB*, May 27, 1934.

42. Mau-Sang Ng, "Popular Fiction and the Culture of Everyday Life: A Cultural Analysis of Qin Shouou's *Qinhaitang*" *Modern China* 20, no. 2 (April 1994): 154.

43. Perry Link, *Mandarin Ducks and Butterflies: Popular Fiction in Early Twentieth-century Chinese Cities* (Berkeley: University of California Press, 1981), 189.

44. Link, *Mandarin Ducks and Butterflies.*

45. Italics mine. *SB*, April 15, 1934.

46. Wen-Hsin Yeh, "Progressive Journalism and Shanghai's Petty Urbanites: Zou Taofen and the Shenghuo Enterprise, 1926-1945" in *Shanghai Sojourners*, ed. Frederic Wakeman Jr. and Wen-hsin Yeh (Berkeley: The Regents of the University of California, 1992), 186-238.

47. Hanchao Lu, *Beyond the Neon Lights: Everyday Shanghai in the Early Twentieth Century* (Berkeley: University of California Press, 1999), 167.

48. Michel de Certeau, *The Practice of Everyday Life* (Berkeley: University of California Press, 1984).

49. Zhou Jianyun, "Zhongguo dianying zhi qiantu" (The future of Chinese cinema) *Dianying yuebao* (Cinema Monthly) nos. 1, 2, 4, 8 (1928). Rpt., *ZWD*, 720-31.

50. Liu Siping and Xing Zuwen, eds., *Lu Xun yu dianying* (Lu Xun and Cinema) (Beijing: Zhongguo dianying, 1981), 221-30.

51. Liu and Xing, *Lu Xun yu dianying*, 170.

52. Mingxing Film Company incorporated the existing *Yingxi zazhi* (Film magazine) in 1922 and became the first film company to publish its own magazine in China. Lianhau established *Lianhua huabao* (Lianhua pictorials) in 1933, and Diantong first published their magazine *Diantong banyuekan* (Denton gazettes) in 1935.

53. Interview with Tong Yuejuan, Hong Kong, July 11, 2000.

54. Link, *Manderin Ducks and Butterflies*, 191-92.

55. Some of these advertisements are reprinted in *Lao Shanghai guangao* (Advertisements of the old time of Shanghai), ed. Yi Bin (Shanghai: Shanghai huabao, 1996). The pictorial also anthologizes two articles, written by Xu Baiyi and Ding Hao, which describe the general situation of Shanghai's advertising scene during the Republic period. See also Sherman Cochran, "Marketing Medicine and Advertising Dreams in China 1900-1950." In *Becoming Chinese: Passages to Modernity and Beyond* ed. Wen-Hsin Yeh (Berkeley: University of California Press, 2000), 62-97.

56. While cosmetics were largely female products, cigarettes were consumed by both genders. But one can easily determine the gender disposition of different brands of cigarettes by their names, and both types of cigarettes sponsored film activities.

57. See the newspaper advertisement of *The Future, SB*, May 20, 1932.

58. *SB*, Aug. 31, 1933.

59. *SB*, Dec. 9, 1932.

60. *Diantong banyuekan* (Denton gazette) 1 (May 1935), n. p.

61. Xin Ping, *Cong Shanghai faxian lishi* (Discovering history from Shanghai) (Shanghai: Shanghai renmin, 1996), 340.

62. *SB*, Nov. 29, 1932.

63. *SB*, June 11, 1934. Jay Leyda was wrong in writing that the theater was not air conditioned. *Dianying: Electric Shadows* (Cambridge, Mass., MIT Press, 1972), 93.

64. See, for example, how the contemporary writer Shi Zhecun described the uncomfortable feelings of attending movies in the hot and humid Shanghai summer at a theater without air conditioning. Shi Zhecun, "Zai Bali daxiyuan" (At the Paris Cinema), in *Shanghai de hubuwu* (Shanghai's Fox-trot), ed. Leo Ou-fan Lee (Taipei: Yunchen, 2000), 122-33.

65. *Diansheng* (Cinema voice) 4, no. 5 (Feb 1935): 104.

66. *SB*, July 16, 1934.

67. *SB*, March 5, 1934. Rpt., *ZZDY*, 471.

68. One can explain this lottery-winning dream as a sarcastic comment of the writer on society. I read it as the writer's spontaneous thought because it accords with the capricious tone of the rest of the article.

69. Michel de Certeau, *The Practice of Everyday Life*, 99.

70. Theodor W. Adorno, *The Culture Industry* (New York: Routledge, 1991), 63-65.

71. See Leo Ou-fan Lee and Andrew J. Nathan, "The Beginnings of Mass Culture: Journalism and Fiction in the Late Ch'ing and Beyond," in *Popular Culture in Late Imperial China*, ed., David Johnson, Andrew J. Nathan, and Evelyn S. Rawski (Berkeley:

University of California Press, 1982), 381.
  72. Lee and Nathan, "The Beginnings of Mass Culture," 386.
  73. Theodor W. Adorno, *The Culture Industry*, 67.

7

A Shanghai Cinema or a Chinese Cinema?

There has been a torrent of scholarship in recent years devoted to the study of the prewar Shanghai culture stressing the cultural pluralism of the city and its response to Westernization and modernity. Some of the English books published just in the last four years include Yingjin Zhang's anthology *Cinema and Urban Culture in Shanghai, 1922-1943*,[1] Leo Ou-fan Lee's *Shanghai Modern: The Flowering of a New Urban Culture in China, 1930-1945*,[2] Sherman Cochran's anthology, *Inventing Nanjing Road: Commercial Culture in Shanghai, 1900-1945*,[3] Hanchao Lu's *Beyond the Neon Lights: Everyday Shanghai in the Early Twentieth Century*,[4] Shu-mei Shih's *The Lure of the Modern, Writing Modernism in Semicolonial China 1917-1932*,[5] and Andrew F. Jones' *Media Culture and Colonial Modernity in the Chinese Jazz Age*.[6] These surging interests in Shanghai culture observed in American academia, interestingly, parallels the recent popular discourse developing on the Chinese mainland, which reconnects Shanghai before the Liberation with Shanghai in the "Open-Door Policy" period, bypassing the ultra leftist days to establish a running tradition of the city in materialism, diversity, sexual indulgence, and decadence.[7] The Republican Shanghai re-sketched in both of these discursive systems are similar in their Western outlook, nihilist essence, everyday life (non)politics, and romanticized aura, which stood apart from the Nanjing regime and developed its own cultural aloofness.

Shanghai in the first half of the twentieth century was, beyond doubt, one of the most exciting cities in the world. It hosted a large number of immigrants from all over the world and encouraged different lifestyles, particularly the Western ones, to flourish in the capitalist culture. I do not need to reproduce here the aforementioned extensive and rich body of scholarship accrued around the modernization and cultural diversity of the city. To situate the left-wing cinema in the specific discursive environment of Shanghai, my questions and interest in the city are, however, located on a slightly different ground, and the analyses I come up with may not conform with the aforementioned studies. My answer to the question I pose in the title of this chapter cannot be as direct and confident as the one I gave in the last chapter. This left-wing cinema might have succeeded in being both commercial and political, but it found itself much more uneasy and ungraceful in reconciling the city's and the nation's identities. Ultimately, I want to demonstrate that the equation between cultural diversity and political opposition should not be taken for granted; hegemonic seeds could in fact be germinated in the name of subversion. Neither a simple romanticization of the alternative Shanghai nor a blatant criticism of the dictating China could present the complicated network of discourse woven by conspiring and conflicting interests in the cultural scene.

The main focus of this chapter is to analyze Shanghai in this cinema as a cultural space as well as a symbol, a symbol that reveals the many ideological assumptions of this "national" cinema movement and their contradictions. On the one hand, the cinema was, to a large extent, shaped by the city's cultural-political landscape in the 1930s, and the films were specific products of the city rather than of the nation. However, its self-avowed national profile was obvious; its claim and conviction in representing China was attested not only in its political outlook but also in the later development of the (trans)national Chinese cinema indebted to these Shanghai films. Between the city and the nation, there were clearly conflicts, which can be most interestingly revealed when sound was first introduced into Chinese cinema. I will demonstrate how the representation of dialects crystallized the convoluted relationship between the Shanghai identity and the national identity that this left-wing cinema simultaneously represented, showing how cinema, as a new form of mass media, marked the introduction of China to a new mode of social and cultural economy.

Shanghai: The Chinese Hollywood

One can argue that Shanghai represented the struggling China in its quintessence in the 1930s; it was the Chinese city where Western influences were most prominent but Nationalism also thrived. It was the city where many intellectuals resided, and they were surrounded with the richest and poorest people in the nation. The new Shanghai urban culture required the city dwellers to establish new perspectives to look at their lives, urging them to explore new language and vocabulary that could describe their fresh experience of each day. However, an obsessive fascination with the city also blinded the filmmakers from comprehending issues that belonged outside Shanghai.

As argued by Heinrich Fruehauf, Chinese intellectuals, beginning in the 1920s, held the assumption that: " 'City' becomes a synonym for Shanghai, the only urban center in China that offered the necessary appearance of 'civiliza-tion.' "[8] The left-wing cinema in the 1930s obviously inherited this conviction and embraced the city as representing all honors and vices of the country's ur-banization and modernization. This Shanghai cinema and the city were organi-cally linked together. The young filmmakers belonged to this city; their love and hatred for it were recorded in the films they made. The left-wing movies in the 1930s never seriously dealt with the social situation of other major Chinese citi-es like Nanjing, Beiping (Beijing), Guangzhou, or Chongqing, where these movies were also screened.[9] There was no doubt that the cinema was intrinsi-cally linked with the city.

Among the seventy-four films listed in *The Chinese Left-wing Cinema Movement*, only one of them, *Wuxian shengya* (Career Without Limits), was produced outside Shanghai. Almost all filmmakers resided in Shanghai, and a large portion of the spectators attending these films also came from this metro-politan area. There were altogether 233 theaters with a seating capacity of 140,000 in the entire country in 1930. The city of Shanghai alone owned 53 theaters and 37,000 seats, taking up more than a quarter of the country's exhibi-tion capacity and looming large over all other cities in China.[10] According to the classification of moviegoers, as I delineated in an earlier chapter, they were squarely cosmopolitan in composition: rich businessmen, idle, "liberated," high-class ladies, young professionals, poor bohemians, film journalists, etc. The new urban spectatorship inevitably fashioned a new urban cinema.

Apart from many other historical contingencies, the development of this film movement took advantage of the city's prosperity that fueled the develop-ment of both Shanghai's entertainment industry and its intellectual culture since the 1920s. The two foreign concessions, French and International, attracted not only capital but also people from other parts of China and from countries all over the world. The city's population increased from 2.26 million in 1920 to 3.14 million in 1930, close to a 40 percent expansion in a decade.[11] The devel-opment of the city's infrastructure during this decade was also impressive. For example, between 1927 to 1936, the total length of the city's roads increased more than 100 percent, from 174,000 meters to 359,000 meters.[12] Public trans-portation, electricity supply, sanitary conditions, and other living conditions were also improved in the 1920s and 1930s.

The average income of the city members grew with the prosperity of this city, and it, as I have illustrated, provided a large population of "petty urbanites" who could not only afford but were also fond of movie-going. Recognized as one of the most affluent cities in the world at that time, Shanghai was the city with the highest cost of living in China. Research indicates that, in the 1920s, a Beiping (Beijing) working-class family spent only 203 *yuan* per year on average, while the average annual expenditure of a working-class family in Shanghai was around 454 *yuan*, twice as much as the former.[13] While some families were striving to make ends meet in this metropolis with such high living standards, many others were earning enough to look for new ways to improve and enrich life. Cinema became a fashionable leisure activity for this new group of city middle class.

Regarding the other three-quarters of the nation's spectators who resided outside Shanghai, the special status of the city also helped the promotion of a cinema that could help them to visualize, and therefore participate in, the new urban lifestyle. Fashions, casinos, cafes, stage performances, and dance halls, these were all symbols of a new, modern, and Western cosmopolitanism, and film-goers outside Shanghai could most directly participate in this new culture of taste and novelty through attending cinema right in their hometown theaters. Thanks to the city's control of the national information distribution network during the Republican period, the image of the city was transmitted to areas all over the country, promoting the city as the national capital of the new urban culture. For example, the Shanghai Commercial Press was the biggest publishing house in China then and owned branch bookstores in dozens of other major Chinese cities. Many books published there were written by Shanghai writers on Shanghai stories or information that pertained to the city. The newspapers published in Shanghai, instead of the ones printed in the capital, Nanjing, were also read all over the country, particularly the two major Shanghai newspapers, *Shanghai Daily* and *News Daily*, not to mention the large number of smaller newspapers and leisure readings published in the city.[14] Cinema and other mass media might have been the most powerful forces in this discursive formation, enticing the curiosity and desires of the other nationals to the new urban culture who would, in return, further intensify and perfect this Shanghai myth.

On the other hand, a large number of intellectuals and artists also began to gather in Shanghai in the late 1920s. While Beiping (Beijing) was losing its cultural momentum after 1927 and the political freedom of the new capital Nanjing was highly limited by government's intervention, Shanghai became the haven for dissidents and radical intellectuals. The city was soon seen as the new national center of elite culture and popular culture, a cozy home for both intellectuals and businessmen. In a developing country like China in the 1930s, where the national communication infrastructure was not perfected, the proximity of film production to the sites of major current events sharpened the sensitivity of filmmakers as well as of spectators to the latest national and international issues. Also, Shanghai had the largest number of major colleges and universities in China during the 1920s and 1930s.[15] It provided a large base for the targeted film spectators and an open-mindedness to things new.

Most significantly, the Nationalist government's control over the city was minimal. In the Nanjing decade of Nationalist rule (i.e., 1927 to 1937), various political powers were battling for control of the city, and the political machinery of the city was only a little better than simple chaos. As documented by Christian Henriot, the Nanjing leadership, the local municipal government, the interests of the foreign settlements, the Japanese invasion, the anti-Japanese movement, local merchants, and the CCP were all fighting for domination in the city from 1931 to 1932; martial law was declared twice during that time.[16] The efficiency of the GMD's policing on Shanghai's cultural activities as a result fell to a low level. This confusion allowed and urged the filmmakers to break new ground and the city members to accept novel means to express their anger and insecurity.

While Shanghai provided all these advantages to the development of China's film industry, there were still fierce criticisms to the location of Shanghai as the base of the national cinema, as both the city and the medium were condemned as sources of contamination. As early as 1928, there were suggestions to move the Chinese film industry away from Shanghai. "Shanghai is such a corrupt place: how dare we consider it the Hollywood of our grand Republic of China."[17] The author explained that earlier filmmakers had stayed in Shanghai, because during the chaotic warlord period, this city had been the only place where filmmakers were allowed creative freedom under colonial protection. But since the GMD government had already united the nation, and the country was now at peace, he recommended moving the country's movie base either to Beijing in the North or Hangzhou in the South, because these two places were still uncorrupted by the West and retained traditional culture and beautiful scenery. The angry author even concluded that: "As a whole, anywhere in our country can be the Hollywood of our Republic of China, but only the foreign settlements of Shanghai are unqualified, greatly unsuited. To be honest, if we cannot move China's film capital out of Shanghai, Chinese cinema can never be revived."[18]

Although this extreme statement represented only a conservative viewpoint, similar antagonism toward the city can indeed be observed in many left-wing movies produced there. For example, the tragic experience of the prostitute and her son represented in *The Goddess* was clearly connected to the city space. After an exhausting night of work, the prostitute goes home at daybreak and embraces her sleeping son. The close-up of her rising head looking out of the window is cut to a night scene of the city suggesting that her imaginative space is trapped within the dark and evil city (figures 7.1-7.2). This coincides with another imagination scene in the film when the "bad guy" gazes at the same city night scene after gambling, but this time the city is superimposed upon the smiling face of the prostitute (figures 7.3-7.4). And in the next scene, we see him and his followers going to her home, assaulting her, and taking control of her life. This superimposition of the city night with the villain's fantasy of the prostitute suggests that the space incorporates and encourages his evil thoughts. While the kind prostitute can see nothing in the Shanghai night scene, this very space belongs, rather, to the depraved rascal whose evil thoughts are reflected there; the affinity between the city and vice is obvious. Escaping from this space becomes the prostitute's wish. Although she fails to run away from Shanghai at the end, in the prison we are shown a different imaginative space for her. This time we no longer see a Shanghai night scene in her imagination but an empty darkness superimposed with her son's cheerful face (figure 7.5). The title states that "the prison is the only place in her life which gives her peace and comfort." She can now spend all her time hoping for a bright future for her son. The film

bitterly suggests that the prostitute finally succeeds in escaping the city by capturing herself in the cell, by sacrificing herself to give a new life to her son. As a
young, progressive, and cosmopolitan director like Wu Yonggang, how could he
cast such a cynical note about Shanghai while asking his spectators to accept his
film which was squarely a product of the city?

The Evil House versus the Embracing Shelter

The cinema's attitude to Shanghai was conflicting. On the one hand, as *Goddess*
shows us, Shanghai was tokenized as most fervently witnessing the negative
impact of Western cultural imperialism to China—this was a city polluted by
sex, violence, alienation, materialism, and human selfishness. On the other hand,
Shanghai offered the largest potential to save China from the above-mentioned
vices because of its proximity to the margin, to the aperture. Among the recent
Chinese critical voices to this left-wing film movement, the mainland critic Sun
Shaoyi argues that the left-wing filmmakers displayed the city of Shanghai as a
"non-Chinese" place for the sake of establishing a Nationalist discourse.[19] She
uses the examples of *Street Angel, Crossroads, Pink Dream, Sons and Daughter
of the Storm, Queen of Sport*, and *Song of China* to illustrate how Shanghai was
depicted in these films as the most corrupt city in the country. By ascribing the
root of all evil to Shanghai, i.e., a "foreign" place, China becomes the pure and
innocent land in which a new beginning can be imagined. Although the left-
wing cinema did show much antipathy to the Shanghai culture, this commonly
held criticism to these films was not unmarred by disparities.

First of all, Sun Shaoyi fails to mention that Shanghai was also seen as the
source of Western evils from the perspective of rightist cinema. While nationalist sentiments were prevalent in almost all left-wing movies, government films
like *The Iron Bird* and *National Style* were also presented in a self-avowedly
disdainful tone to the Shanghai culture. For example, *National Style*, a product
of the GMD New Life Movement that promoted a return to traditional culture
and ethics, overtly condemned the putrescent impact of Shanghai's culture on
the innocent Chinese youth.[20] It tells how a young country female student de-
generates in Shanghai. She even brings back these "non-Chinese" evils to her
hometown and corrupts the community's pure and simple ethics. Thanks to her
resolute sister who represents righteous traditional Chinese morality, the contaminated woman is saved from self-destruction and at the end of the film decides to dedicate her life to the education of village people.

Although anti-Western ideology was preached in films of the two political
camps, the representation of Shanghai in the left-wing cinema was characterized
by some intricacy that was lacking in the other. One important issue not developed in Sun's criticism of the left-wing cinema is the intimate relationship
shared between the city and these filmmakers. Shanghai was, beyond doubt, a

convenient scapegoat for the prevalent anti-imperialist sentiment in the Republic period because the city, as the country's first foreign settlement, embodied the negative Western influences on China to the largest extent. The allegedly widespread crimes, prostitution, suicides, and even mental disorders in the city were intolerable in the eyes of many Chinese.[21] However, this exciting city also represented the creativity and redemption many young progressive filmmakers aspired to obtain. The left-wing intellectuals could not just portray Shanghai as hopeless as *National Style* did because this city was one of the very few places in China in which they could still remain as dissidents and be allowed to have their voices heard. The city of Shanghai provided the young intellectuals access to absorb and cultivate new ideas, a place where they could organize and execute their political ideals. "The city space of Shanghai represents a 'necessary evil' for the cultural political struggles of the left-wing cultural workers."[22] We could not deny the validity of Sun's observation, but neither should we ignore the fact that Shanghai was also the filmmakers' base to revolt against the established hegemony. The representation of this city in these films was certainly more complex and ambiguous than many have claimed.

For example, Sun is right to point out that the opening montage sequence in *Street Angel*, which juxtaposes buildings tilted in different positions, depicts the city with "an alienated, unfamiliar, estranged, and brutal overall tone."[23] But this film, to read it more closely, described the city's space from dual perspectives, showing that the modern city was both an alienating cosmopolitan center and a warm local community, which was hinted at in the depiction of skyscrapers in the film. In the opening shot, the camera pans down a skyscraper to below ground level, bringing the spectators away from the elevated, Westernized location to the lowest level of the city. In a later scene, when Xiao Chen and Lao Wang visit a law firm located at the top of a skyscraper, they are ridiculed for their ignorance and stupidity in the high-tech office. In the original version, there was a scene before this office encounter showing the two entering the building from the street to the lobby suggesting a movement of the two rising up the building in contrast to the camera panning down the skyscraper in the opening shot.[24] In the later scene, the two are ultimately expelled from the office because they do not have enough money to hire a lawyer. These two scenes, similar to Fritz Lang's *Metropolis*, suggest the separation of two spaces in the city: the one on top oppressing and estranging the one down below. But unlike the lower ground world of *Metropolis,* whose space is defined and modeled after the one on top, *Street Angel* depicts the space of the lower city with its own complexity and integrity surpassing the flatness of the upper one.

As compared to the rigid and spiritless office of the law firm at the top of the skyscraper, the lower class people in *Street Angel* occupy a lively and stimulating environment. Xiao Chen and Lao Wang live in a room on the second floor of a two-story building opposite to the one occupied by Xiao Hong's family. This is a neighborhood for poor people, where worn buildings are jammed together, and the depth of this studio setting is rendered through the carefully orchestrated spots of light and the diagonal visual composition (figure 7.6 and plate 25). Similar to other national cinemas' experience, China's early sound films usually look "flatter" when compared to the silent films. Entering the talkie era, studio shooting was favored to location shooting to record synchronized sound. The abundant light available outdoors was now sacrificed, drastically reducing the level of illumination and, therefore, depth of field. And the limited studio space could not afford a spacious setting either. But Yuan Muzhi set up this elaborated scene here, rendering the depth of the scene by careful lighting and set design. In contrast, the law office scene is characterized by the dominating flat of whiteness in the lifeless office and is shot mostly in tight medium close-ups.

   Although there is an alley separating the rooms of Xiao Chen and Xiao Hong, they are able to communicate with each other through the open windows. While Xiao Chen performs tricks and mime shows to amuse Xiao Hong, she sings her favorite songs to express her love in return. The alley is too narrow to be an obstacle to their romance; and the intimate human relationship is symbolized by the cozy architecture. The fluid camera movement meandering around the space further brings the separated lovers together in their hearts.[25] The short physical distance between the two is ultimately bridged in a later scene when Xiao Chen and his friends connect the two windows with a plank on which Xiao Hong is able to walk from her apartment to Xiao Chen's (figure 7.7). Thus, in the film, the congested and bustling environment of this lower class section of the city does not suggest alienation but rather closeness and attachment among the people.

   In the scene when Xiao Chen performs the mime show for Xiao Hong, we are shown two layers of flat space represented by the two windows. Xiao Chen's curtain transforms his window frame into a stage, and Xiao Hong's window becomes an audience hall (figures 7.8-7.9). The director created a space which reminds us of the alleged root of Chinese cinema in "civilized play"; many Chinese at that time continued to perceive cinema as a branch of stage performance. However, Yuan Muzhi deliberately destroyed this two-dimensional space by having Xiao Chen throw an apple to Xiao Hong. When she fails to catch it, it flies into the inner room of Xiao Yun, who has secretly fallen for Xiao Chen but will later give up her unrequited love and help her sister escape with him (figures 7.10-7.12). Through this apple, the established flat space is broken, and it renders depth to the real environment of the lower class people. On the one hand, it calls attention to the editing possibilities unique to cinema: the two-dimensional space of the performance hall composed by Xiao Hong's and Xiao Chen's window frames is rendered three-dimensional through the editing of the flying apple. On the other hand, this apple establishes the depth of the space thematically. Spectators are not watching a two-dimensional tale created by the flat imagination of the filmmakers. Instead, we are witnessing a realistic, intimate, and humanistic environment in which the three characters develop their relationship. The private connections and the interdependence among the characters are contained in this small yet rich environment; it is this space which the film celebrated.

The Shanghai Diversity

Chinese filmmakers in the 1930s were not well paid. For example, Sun Yu recounted that he received one hundred *yuan* per month when he was working for the Minxin Film Company in 1929, a salary he claimed to be too small to support his parents back in Qingdao.[26] The economic situation of the Chinese film industry in the mid-1930s was much worse because of the financial difficulties experienced by the film companies. For example, according to a report published in a magazine then, in the toughest time in 1935, Mingxing laid off sixty-six people which saved only 1500 *yuan* per month.[27] That is to say, the average salary of these employees was only 22.7 *yuan*, a meager income that was hardly enough to pay the rent.[28] Living quarters were constantly in short supply in Shanghai, and rents became particularly burdensome to many people. According to the newspaper classified advertisement of the time, the monthly rent of a three- to four-bedroom, Western style, apartment cost more than 100 *yuan*. Most film personnel could only afford to live in their film studios or lower-class ghettos similar to the neighborhood portrayed in *Street Angel*. For example, recounting the struggles of his youth, the director of *The Goddess*, Wu Yonggang, wrote, "the social reality of Old Shanghai was brutal. Living in *tingzijian* or little attics, eating the cheap and cold meals prepared by the boarders, pawning some clothing when necessary: these were the lives of [mine and] many other intellectual youths."[29]

The adverse living conditions of Shanghai were part of the cosmopolitan life. Like most of the big cities around the world, the rapid growth of population and limited land supply gave no choice to the poor but to demand them to endure the worsening environment. According to the impression of Zheng Zhenduo, about 30 percent of the entire Shanghai population had no private space for themselves at all. They were either laborers living in their workplace or newcomers to the city staying with relatives and friends. Their beds were folded up in the mornings and not put back together until very late at night. 40 percent of the population was fortunate enough to be able to keep their beds in one place; but they had to share the room with many others. Usually more than six families occupied one standard apartment.[30] Most of the young filmmakers belonged to the second category, and many of them lived in little garrets named *tingzijian* (pavilion room) a side chamber located several steps lower than the top floor, with the balcony on top and the kitchen below.[31] In spite of its inadequate illumination and circulation, many young people chose to reside there because of their cheaper rents. A unique *tingzijian* culture was established in Shanghai among the youths: it represented a quasi-Bohemian life in which the youths shared a poor but inspiring collective life. As Sun Yu recounts:

> Before writing *Wild Rose*, I moved from the single dormitory in Lianhua Studio 1 on Avenue Joffre to the Dapeng neighborhood on Hart Road. I was living in a *tingzijian* with the young advertising artist Zong Weigeng who had just joined the Editorial Department of Lianhua. . . . This little *tingzijian* very soon became the meeting "salon" of Wang Renmei, Li Lili, Hu Jia, Nie Er, Jin Yan, and the younger members of the dance group like Bai Hong and Chen Qing. Although this group of ignorant young kids (I was the oldest, aged 31 at that time and could be considered as a "big kid") could not be compared with the famous salons in Europe where masters exchanged lofty artistic ideas, we honestly and bravely discussed our future grand projects and cultivated our creativity.[32]

Although this might be a romanticized recollection of a director famous for his idealism, the intimate and energetic environment was certainly significant to the creative process of the filmmakers.[33] In this open and bustling setting, the young filmmakers were more attentive to the lives of the people around them. The story of *Street Angel*, for example, was conceived in a similar environment.[34] Most importantly, the congested surroundings of the filmmakers allowed them to be more sensitive about the use of space, and many of their films displayed a unique sensitivity to the spatial relationships among characters. In *Street Angel*, the lawyer working on the top floor of a modern skyscraper is shown to have an aloof and apathetic, "flat" personality. However, the lower-class people residing in slums are rounded characters with individual personalities, ranging from amiable and passionate youths to the selfish parents of the sisters. The space of the lower class, both architecturally and culturally, is more complex and intimate when compared to that of the upper class. Unlike the complete rejection of Shanghai culture shown in the right-wing movies like *National Style*, *Street Angel* was critical only of the Shanghai upper class; it wholeheartedly celebrated the folk kinship of the city's lower class.

Sons and Daughters of the Storm, *Street Angel*, and *Crossroads* are all splendid examples of how the left-wing cinema represented characters with the high awareness of the space the characters occupied. In the case of *Crossroads*, for example, it showed another superb exercise of organically integrating the unique Shanghai lower-class space into the story. The romance between Lao Zhao and Zhiying develops around a thin wooden wall separating two rooms. By throwing trash and other objects into the adjacent rooms, their relationship is built by their increasing intrusion into each other's space. This wooden wall represents an obstacle to the lovers, and its final break-down becomes a metaphor for the unification of the two. Most importantly, the destruction of this wall signifies the union of the many isolated souls in the city. Despite being critical of the modern metropolitan culture, *Crossroads* did not choose to reject Shanghai completely. Instead, the film suggests an acceptance of the city, which is hinted at the end when the four decide to walk back to the city instead of boarding the departing ships. The four major characters have been disillusioned by their Shanghai lives and decide to take leave of the city. But after seeing each other at the ferry station, they resolve to head the opposite direction and walk back to the city. At this crossroads, the youths embrace instead of renounce the allegedly evil Shanghai.

The congested space also inevitably gave rise to an enormous amount of noise, which was heard in most parts of the city any hour of the day: radio programs, mahjong, chanting of hawkers, yelling of children, etc. The bustling polyphony of sound in the city also sharpened the audio sensitivities of these early sound filmmakers. *Plunder of Peach and Plum*, for example, was conscious in incorporating the "Shanghai" sound into the film. The first view of the film is an establishing shot of a busy Shanghai street where a school is located, and it features an audio track with clamorous city noise. This opening, unruly noise prepared the audience for the disheartening story, in which two pure and innocent young students will be corrupted by this evil city, succumbing to depravity and death. This sound track was the first ambient sound produced in China's film history, which symbolically established Shanghai as the unseen but loudly heard backdrop of this film.

However, this cinematic sensitivity to the truncated space and obstreperous timbre of the city was not translated ideologically according to a critique of "sameness" or an assertion of plurality, theories we might use for contemporary artworks. As seen in these films, the linear "National History" was not transgressed and disseminated; instead, the criticism itself was just another form of hegemony that, after all, still asserted unity and solidarity in the name of nation. Like other urban narratives, many of these left-wing films set in Shanghai, like *Twenty-four Hours in Shanghai, Old and New Shanghai,* and *Lianhua Symphony,* did not stay with one perspective but were constantly moving from person to person, bringing the viewer along to experience the different facets of Shanghai society. However, the ultimate aim of these tours was not to exemplify multiple voices embodied in the city but to stress the unified social circumstances, which could explain all these seemingly diverse and independent happenings.

The New Year's Gift, for example, was devoted to the representation of diversity: it displayed different facets and lifestyles of the city, juxtaposing the disenfranchised with the rich, comparing the greedy and the generous. But the film ultimately told only one message: individuals were all subject to the same corrupt and unjust social political environment. This message was most evidenced in *Scenes of City Life,* which did not show sympathy or preference to any particular characters. Instead, they were all victims of the alienating capitalist culture. *Twenty-four Hours in Shanghai* also employed similar representation tactics that privileged the city more than individuals. In order to help liberate the people from suffering in the urban culture, the filmmakers suggested changing the institutional structures top-down instead of encouraging individuals to assert their different individual needs bottom-up. Although the Shanghai stories in this cinema, unlike those taking place in rural areas, were often narrated from multiple points of view, individual characters were not necessarily privileged over the collective; human emancipation was not an issue of interest in most of these city films. In the remaining parts of this chapter, I will focus on the hegemonic aspect of this left-wing cinema, which reflected the centered geo-cultural position of Shanghai as compared to other parts of China. These Shanghai stories were often delimited by a narrow city mentality that further restrained the already monophonic left-wing ideology.

"Non-Shanghai"

The Shanghai factor made itself most prominent in this cinema not in its representation but its "non-representation," i.e., the representation of "non-Shanghai." As cosmopolitan Shanghai was easily targeted as the embodiment of Western evils, the countryside became its antithesis and was cast as utopia in the eyes of many Chinese filmmakers. Among the initial efforts made by the Party members in Mingxing Film Company, bringing villages to the screen was one of the most important. Three of the earliest films written by the members were related to peasantry. *Iron Plate and Red Tears*, the first film written by Yang Hansheng, told about how a Sichuan warlord oppressed the peasants. Zheng Boqi's *Salt Tide* portrayed the class struggle between salt workers and the capitalists. Together with Xia Yan's *Spring Silkworms*, the Party writers introduced to the city spectators the hardships suffered by Chinese peasantry. As most of the rural areas in China at that time were not equipped with cinema facilities, the target spectators for these films were clearly those in the cities than the peasantry themselves.

Unfortunately, none of the three films were box office hits. The failure of *Salt Tide* was inevitable because of the unmerciful editing carried out by the GMD censors. The spectators did not find the other two films attractive mostly because of the unexciting plots. As Hong Shen, the director of *Iron Plate and Red Tears*, admitted: "Most critics complain that the two films [*Iron Plate and Red Tears* and *Spring Silkworms*] are boring and lack exciting plot developments. But I don't agree with them. The films are not farce or commercial products; they are sincere and honest as attempts to present serious national social problems."[35] This statement of Hong Shen revealed the general attitude of left-wing filmmakers toward their village films. They saw the realistic portrayal of social problems in the rural area a serious political commitment. Since most of the filmmakers had been living in cities and did not have much real-life experience with peasantry, they had to be particularly cautious in preventing any distortions of the representation of village life. As a result, they chose a style with fewer dramatic interventions and a stronger documentary disposition.

In spite of the box office failure of the three Mingxing peasant films, movies set in villages were popular in the 1930s. In contrast to the Party filmmakers who were concerned with the political effects of the films' depiction of rural life, many of their successors simply portrayed villages as the exotic "other" and the ideal site to portray simplified human relationships and emotions. Even Tianyi, the overtly commercial film company, produced many movies with stories related to peasants' sufferings. Although films with rural settings, including the famous 1913 *Suffering Husband and Wife*, were frequently seen in the 1910s and 1920s, this subgenre had never been as popular as it became in the 1930s.

Among the left-wing village films produced in this movement, the exact geographical locations of the villages were seldom identified; these villages were usually portrayed as generic and deprived of all cultural specificity. A rural area in Sichuan differed little from a Guangdong farmland, both of which were created under the imagination of the filmmakers who had never visited these places before. These representations were, simply, "non-Shanghai." Compared to the Shanghai city represented in the left-wing cinema, which displayed more depth and vigor, the village usually appeared undistinguished and attested to its shallow and unimmaginative meanings in the film. As an apparent example, the city Shanghai in *The Goddess* was definitely a space more profound than the imagined Taiping zhuang village in *Soaring Aspirations*, although both films were directed by Wu Yonggang.

The rural areas of the Republic of China experienced a social and cultural transformation as rapid and as complicated as the cities did. But instead of analyzing the social environment of the villages in depth, the left-wing filmmakers chose to equate the countryside with natural beauty. In the beginning of *Spring Silkworms*, for example, via an opening montage of natural images, spectators are brought to a village where Lao Tongbao's family lives. After the title "An afternoon with a gentle breeze of spring," the film cuts to a montage of different natural images of catkins, rice fields, trees, and flowers; it ends in a village where a little bridge on top of a running stream is at the center. Only after this little prelude are the spectators introduced to the major characters and the plot of the film. The above montage sequence was structured as if it were a continuous journey, as the individual shots all slowly pan to the left, coinciding with the direction of the lightly blowing wind in some of the images, a representation echoing the previous title. This opening sequence seems to function as a vehicle to bring the audience away from their bustling cities to this remote yet tranquil village by "this gentle breeze of spring." The little bridge over a running stream (*xiaoqiao liushui*) is a common poetic trope in traditional Chinese literature and painting which represents idealized village life. Establishing the poetic gracefulness of this village in the beginning of the film through this montage series, the later human sufferings brought by Western imperialism can be contrasted and intensified. This Chinese village was portrayed as the site of natural beauty that was, therefore, easily contaminated by foreign defilement.

Similar tactics were employed in *The Boatman's Daughter*. This film tells how a boatman's daughter, A Ling, is taken captive by a group of Shanghai, good-for-nothing artists to become a prostitute to pay off her father's medical bills. The story takes place in the scenic *Xi hu* (West Lake*)*; its breathtaking natural scenery has been considered by many as among the most beautiful in China. An allegorical network is set up among A Ling, the West Lake, and China in the film. In the initial establishing shot of the lake, we see painters, dressed in Western, long, white gowns, painting the West Lake landscape on their canvases. This common enough scene become highly symbolic when linked to the later experience of A Ling, who is forced to serve as a model for three young painters and photographers from Shanghai. They ask her to pose in different "artistic" postures embarrassing to A Ling in order to satisfy their "Western" aesthetics without taking her feelings into consideration (figure 7.13). Although A Ling is dressed, the requests of these well-off Westernized Chinese artists are portrayed in the film as sexual assaults, and their so-called art is only an excuse to gratify their voyeuristic desires and power of control. The film further connects this sexual aggression to a nationalist discourse by having A Ling's lover Tie Er arrested during a strike. The aggravated Tie Er and his fellow workers are arrested during their protest against the increasing foreign imperialist economic activities jeopardizing their livelihoods. In this film, the West Lake, A Ling, and Tie Er are integrated into a unified symbol of victimized China being trampled by foreign forces, both politically and ideologically.

Like Lao Tongbao's village in *Spring Silkworms*, the ignorant poetic beauty of the West Lake is essential to the film's anti-imperialist discourse because it is established as the symbolic site where abstract political forces can be visualized. The German colony Qingdao in *Plundered Peach Blossom*, Anle village in *To the Northwest*, and the unnamed small town in *Bloodbath on Wolf Mountain* all served similar functions in the films' nationalistic discourse. The filmmakers' sentiments towards the countryside can be illustrated in an interview with Cheng Bugao in 1934. He revealed:

> I just went to Sahailu for the location shooting of *To the Northwest*. The further I was away from Shanghai, the further I took leave of material civilization. I felt like I was finally able to go to the real China. What I saw was real Chinese people, and I seemed to become a foreigner. . . . From then on I assumed a heavier responsibility: How should we improve their livelihoods and education? This is our greatest mission.[36]

Shanghai and the countryside were mutually antagonistic in the eyes of this famous left-wing filmmaker, and the authentic China resided in the latter. But the greatest irony was his conviction of his responsibility: a non-Chinese saving the future of the real Chinese. He seemed to be, on the one hand, proud of his Shanghai, therefore, he maintained a Westernized identity in calling himself the foreigner and was endowed the job to save China. But on the other hand, he knew so well of his nationalist responsibility precisely because he is a Chinese. The opposition between city and village surrounding around nationalist identity seems to be an everlasting dilemma for Chinese intellectuals. The countryside had been, on the one hand, the creative source of so many wonderful artistic works, like the poems of Tao Yuanming. But, on the other, it also challenges the city intellectuals' self-identity, particularly evident in the self-tortures we witnessed in the Cultural Revolution when the intellectuals were trying so hard but futilely to cast off their urban identity.

The Introduction of Sound: The Dialect-cinema Debate

This distinct Shanghai identity, interestingly, fostered, instead of discouraged, the national identity shared among Shanghai's intellectuals who more often saw themselves as the representatives of the national culture rather than the provincial culture. This was most intricately revealed in the debate on the use of dialect in cinema. Years before sound was successfully incorporated in Chinese cinema, intellectuals already entertained the idea of using sound films to teach the mass how to speak a unified national language in this country where thousands of dialects were spoken.[37] When sound finally arrived in Chinese cinema, this issue became urgent. Whether Chinese films should speak Mandarin alone was not only a debate among the intellectuals but also a real policy issue of the government who needed a unified national language to facilitate its ruling. There had been a vague policy since 1935 prohibiting all non-Mandarin films from screening in the nation. However, it took effect only in those areas where the central government had direct control; the peripheral provinces, particularly Guangdong, continued to screen the films they made in their own dialects. According to Hu Peng's account, the 1935 Cantonese movie *Modeng xinniang* (Modern Bride) produced in Hong Kong was allowed by the government to be shown, but it was restricted to the two provinces of Guangdong and Guangxi.[38] The confusion was to last until 1937 when the Sino-Japanese war brought the policy to a halt,[39] and Cantonese and other dialect movies continued to be produced during and after the war period.

Parallel to this government policy, Shanghai's left-wing film circles also wallowed in the issue. An article written by Ni Lu promoting the use of drama and film to teach the masses the proper use of Mandarin first started the dialect-cinema debate.[40] Xu Xingzhi, later the director of *Sons and Daughters of the Storm*, published an article in *Shanghai Daily* right after Li Nu's call to solicit film critics' and filmmakers' opinions on this issue. Many critics immediately submitted their views, and a heated debate was generated.[41] Diverging ideas were heard even within left-wing film circles, to which most of the participants of the debate belonged. Although it was a discussion about cinema, this debate can be seen as a textual site reflecting the opinions of Shanghai's left-wing intellectuals about the unification process of China under the common Nationalist concern.

In the midst of the relatively congenial discussion, Tang Na's voice was an alternative one. He argued that local cinemas with local dialects should be tolerated because these dialect films honestly reflected the current audience's linguistic diversity. Facilitating the communication among different dialect groups was important, but a unified national language should be formed by a natural synthesizing process instead of being forced by any hegemonic intellectual coercion. Recognizing the existence of the many diverging subcultures in China, Tang Na argued that the most urgent task was to refine the many local dialects so that, in the future, the individual dialects would be organically integrated to form a truly functional mass language.[42] However, Xu Xingzhi and many other left-wing critics disagreed and argued that the many dialect cinemas would only encourage sectarianism in the already disunited Chinese nation. Their common rhetoric was that "a mass language could not be formed without a revolutionary act,"[43] and the revolutionary act referred precisely to the left-wing cinema.

Obviously, individual critics had their own understandings of national cinema, but almost all who participated in this debate agreed that movies' dialogues either reflected or would pose direct impacts on the audience's linguistic practices. Therefore, the language used in cinema was linked to the national agenda in consolidating the many regional dialects, which was essential to the national unification process. These opinions diverged only around the means to obtain this goal. But even within the discussion about how to achieve this end, most critics agreed that allowing the use of local dialects in cinema hampered the formation of a unified national language; the voice of Tang Na remained a feeble one.[44] The collective well-being of the nation was certainly the most urgent concern of most intellectuals, left or right, in China at that time. They were ready to sacrifice almost everything to achieve this goal. The debate on the use of dialects in cinema was easily converted from a specific technical topic within given professional circles to a weighty national issue, through which film critics could elevate cinema from a form of entertainment to a medium loaded with political significance. The introduction of the Mass Language debate from the literary circles made this connection possible.

The idea of reforming the official written language, which distanced tremendously from everyday language, to a vernacular one has a long history in China, with a beginning which might be traced all the way back to the Buddhist prose (bianwen) in the Southern and Northern Dynasties (317-589 AD). But the events most crucial to the development of modern Chinese in the first half of the twentieth century are definitely the Vernacular Language (*baihua wen*) Movement in the May Fourth period and its immediate predecessor, the left-wing Mass Language (*dazhong yu*) Movement in the 1930s.[45] To briefly summarize the connections between the two: both advocated a new, modern Chinese written language developed according to people's spoken vernacular. The Mass Language Movement, however, was a left-wing reaction to Vernacular Language Movement criticizing May Fourth's indebtedness to the West and Japan as well as its traits of class stratification. The Mass Language movement can be seen as more the left-wing intellectuals' political gesture to their forebears than a purely scholarly endeavor.

The ideological positions of the left-wing filmmakers and critics in this debate were clearly observed in their wholesale adoption of the Mass Language terminology and rhetoric. However, the Mass Language discussed hitherto in literary circles concerned mostly the written language. When this debate was transferred to the cinema, the issues of the spoken language were necessarily obfuscated. With a unified writing system, China, however, is a country where thousands of dialects are spoken. The reformation of China's written language is always a more agreeable project than any attempt to unify the country's verbal diversity.

Such difficulties notwithstanding, along with the Vernacular Movement and the Mass Language Movement, whose targets were both the written language, there developed a relatively low-profile, verbally oriented National Language (*guoyu*) Movement, which unfolded in a longer span and with broader practical resonance.[46] This movement was a combined effort of the government and some scholars in developing and endorsing a set of standardized pronunciations of a spoken language for the entire nation, which was predominately based on the Beijing dialect. In fact, the accomplishments of the modest National Language Movement can be seen as the prerequisites of the two "written" language movements, instead of vice versa, because both the May Fourth scholars and the leftists in the 1930s advocated a written language built on the spoken, which had to be already unified to start with. Obviously, this National Language Movement was in closer consonance with the concerned filmmakers and critics then. The unified national language promoted in the dialect-cinema debate, although never spoken, was clearly *guoyu*, the official national language promoted by the government. However, the name and ideas developed in the National Language Movement were rarely mentioned in the dialect-cinema debate. Leftist film circles instead borrowed the ideological arguments mostly from the more politically charged and written language based Mass Language Movement.

In fact, the academic National Language Movement also had political undertone: a unifying national communication tool would facilitate GMD's administration more effectively. This should explain the leftist filmmakers' and critics' obvious neglect of the event. However, the core problem of the dialect-cinema debate was the common unspoken assumption shared by most participants that *guoyu* should be the language used in all sound films, while left-wing intellectuals were always urging to look for a new voice, in both its literary and symbolic meanings, to legitimate their dissident position. The claimed pedagogical concerns advocated in this cinema debate were clearly a pretext for the renegade filmmakers and critics to define themselves against the official voice. But they ended up choosing the language they rebelled against.

As a result, we see the irony in the fact that the left-wing filmmakers and critics were not able to elucidate their new language in specific terms. For example, among all articles contributed to this debate, Dan Feng's "Dazhong yu zai dianying zhong zhi yunyong" (The utilization of mass language in cinema) was the only one which cited concrete examples to illustrate the suggested cinematic mass language.[47] However, in illustrating the idea of "What shall we do if there is no rain?" what he came up with was only *"tian bu xiayu, zenmo ban?"* This sentence reveals nothing revolutionary linguistically but clearly obeys the established *guoyu* in structure and grammar. More disturbingly, this model was only cited as an example of the inter-titles in silent cinema. The author discussed little about the pronunciation of the mass language in sound films, which was supposed to be the core issue of the debate. The hidden problem for these dissident intellectuals, then, was their approval of the GMD official language, against which they should fight. As Zhiwei Xiao mentions, between the Nanking Government and the Cantonese filmmaking community, Shanghai's left-wing filmmakers completely sided with the former.[48] Obviously, the actual language being promoted was less significant than the left-wing intellectuals' fetishization of an intellectual discussion of their own. This dialect cinema debate had little real political meaning other than to reveal their own ideological and commercial interest.

The National Market

In spite of the demand of Shanghai's leftist circles for a new ideological position, their commercial concerns also inevitably preconditioned their common disapproval of dialect cinemas in China. Although Mandarin had long been widely accepted as the national language by the mid-1930s, cinema-goers still preferred those movies spoken in their own daily-used dialects when sound was successfully incorporated in cinema. There were fifty-five film companies in China in 1934. Among them, most were Shanghai-based; only a few were scattered around the country, with one in Nanjing, one in Chongqing, five in Guangzhou, and one in Taishan, Guangdong.[49] Some of them were also attempting to make their own talkies. However, they had posed little threat to Shanghai's establishment because the sizes and financial situations of these scattered studios were of no comparison to those in the famous cosmopolitan city. As the city where the films produced excelled the others in terms of both quality and quantity, Shanghai's position as China's film capital was never questioned.

However, the relatively more mature film industry in the British Colony of Hong Kong was always Shanghai's major rivalry because of its early development and large market. Hong Kong started its first cinema productions in 1909, even earlier than those in Shanghai; and these Hong Kong films were watched among a large Cantonese-speaking population in China and South East Asia.[50] Beginning in 1933, film companies in Hong Kong also started to produce sound films with its local dialect. The first Cantonese film introduced to the Shanghai market, a city with a large Cantonese-speaking population, was *Baijinlong* (The white golden dragon) in 1934. This Cantonese Opera film received such a high box office receipt in both domestic and foreign markets that Shanghai's Tianyi Film Company decided to establish a new studio in Hong Kong in order to produce Cantonese films alone.[51]

I would argue that it was the increasing popularity of Cantonese movies, more than any other ideological reasons, which most directly triggered the dialect-cinema debate. The Cantonese dialect is China's second largest linguistic group, spoken mainly by the wealthiest population in the country. Together with the thirty to forty million Cantonese-speaking populations in the southern provinces, there is also a Cantonese-based global Chinese Diaspora. This relatively affluent and extensive dialect group became a strong cultural ground to nourish and support the development of Hong Kong cinema. As recounted by I. C. Jarvie:

> By the late thirties Hong Kong was the established centre of Cantonese film production, and the films went to Macau, Kwangtung [Guangdong], Kiangsi [Jiangxi], and parts of Fukien [Fujian]. Overseas, the films played in Malaya, Singapore, Siam, the East Indies, Burma, and the Philippines, not to mention Chinatowns in Australia, America, Canada, etc.[52]

The Tianyi Film Company started to establish its distribution line in Southeast Asia as early as 1928. According to Law Kar, in 1934 there were fifteen cinemas in Southeast Asia that were owned by the Shaw brothers, who also owned Tianyi, and many of these theaters started to screen the movies made in Tianyi's Hong Kong studios.[53] While those smaller regional studios in the other Chinese cities were hardly competitors to the Shanghai film mecca, an extensive Cantonese market provided the financial security to the development of the industry in Hong Kong. More importantly, Hong Kong cinema more unabashedly tailored itself for the taste of the mass audience. The commercial success of the film industry of the southern periphery posed double threats to the centered position of the Shanghai productions: not only was their share of the market jeopardized but cinema's claimed ideological and pedagogical nature was also under threat. From Shanghai's perspective, Hong Kong's Cantonese cinema must be exterminated from the new Chinese cinema in order to maintain Shanghai cinema's commercial and ideological dominance.

The resolute efforts of the Shanghai film industry in the 1930s to prohibit Cantonese films from screening in the nation testified to Shanghai's anxiety over the immense market potential of the evolving Hong Kong film industry.

The rapid development of Hong Kong cinema after Shanghai's swift deteriora-
tion in the 1950s also revealed the once fierce competition between Hong Kong
and Shanghai.[54] The Shanghai filmmakers' and critics' ideological concerns in
national unification as proclaimed in the dialect-cinema debate were conflated
with the market and political anxiety of their own. Therefore, this relatively
unilateral conclusion of the debate in excluding dialect films in Chinese cinema
might be more a defense mechanism than a pure political aspiration.

This debate in many respects reveals the underlining assumptions of the
current left-wing cinema, in which the nationalist discourse at stake was ultimately hegemonic in nature. Reflected in these films, we saw that problems of
Shanghai were prototypes of all the national problems that the entire Chinese
population was facing. Contrary to some critics' arguments that Shanghai considers herself as marginal to the nation, in the 1930s, these left-wing intellectuals
were self-avowed representatives of all Chinese and saw themselves squarely at
the heart of the nation. Dialects other than *guoyu* were not heard, social issues of
other local areas were not seen. In fact, not only the dialect-cinema debate but
also the entire Mass Language Movement was initiated and dominated by the
Shanghai-based intellectuals, and the Shanghai environment largely conditioned
and empowered their positions and arguments. For example, when discussing
his understanding of the new Chinese mass language, Qu Qiubai argued:

> A new Chinese common language is evolving among the proletariat
> class in the hybridized cosmopolitan environment and modern facto-
> ries. This common language is not the bureaucratic Mandarin. But it
> is a form of language that assimilates new foreign vocabulary and lo-
> cal dialects, embracing modern concepts of politics, technologies,
> science, and the arts. People from different provinces can use this
> new language to communicate and exchange ideas in the new cosmo-
> politan. This is the real modern Chinese language.[55]

Obviously, Qu Qiubai's new cosmopolitan was Shanghai, the city where he was
residing. According to him, the new Chinese Mass Language could only be
formed in this city that represented the hope for a new China. Lu Xun also raised
a similar point: "A new language is evolving in those areas where transportation
is prosperous and diverse languages are spoken, because these are the places
where you can find new vocabularies and experience of everyday. I think this is
the embryo of the new 'mass language.'[56] Once again, it was the Shanghai metropolitan environment that shaped this argument of Lu Xun. The identity between modernization and Shanghai was clearly hinted at in both the statements
of the two famous leftist intellectuals. And Shanghai's ability to lead the nation
in historical progression justified the intellectuals' residence in this semi-colony.

It was Shanghai, the modern cosmopolitan city, that brought people with different dialects together. It was also this Shanghai that legitimated the political positions these dissident intellectuals occupied.

This domination of the Shanghai theme in the left-wing movies paralleled the filmmakers' and critics' repudiation of dialect cinema. Even though most people in Shanghai spoke Shanghainese, it was not the local dialect being promoted. On the one hand, it was the Shanghai context being reified as archetypal to the current national experience. On the other hand, however, it was not the city's local dialect but the official state spoken language, *guoyu*, which enjoyed the exclusive right in Chinese cinema. Obviously, Shanghai's overriding position in this cinema was not a reflection of localism, which celebrates not one local but many, but a nationalism centered in Shanghai. The political and geographical periphery of Shanghai was the only means for the intellectuals to claim their pivotal position in national issues.

Under the consensus that dialect cinema inevitably promoted sectarianism in a country that was urgently in need of unification, there was a subtle mechanism at work in the left-wing cinema to maintain its supremacy in the nationalist enterprise. Conflicts abound when commercial cinema, which demands market monopolization, and voice, which materializes in diversification, hit one another. The spoken is always less easily tamed than the written. Both the Vernacular and the Mass Language Movements were more keen on defining a new written Chinese language than a spoken one, suggesting less the intellectuals' contentment with the nation's chaotic verbal diversity than the difficulties in any attempts at unifying it. The written words are always more politically malleable and manageable than the verbal ones, because the more transient, volatile, and immediate spoken language always escapes discursive definitions. When such verbal disarray, however, confronted the development of the commercial moviemaking business, the discord seen in this debate could be seen as unavoidable. The survival of cinema, as a quintessential form of modern entertainment that lives off a mass consumption market, is subject to the development of an extensive yet unified audience. This homogenizing effect is unavoidable in the capital-intensive nature of the process of filmmaking, which requires a large market to support the huge investments in the various aspects of production and distribution. As revealed in this debate, it was the standardization of commodity that reigned over the originality of art. The confrontation between dialect cinema and Shanghai cinema can be seen as an inevitable conflict aroused between China's handed-down cultural diversity on the one hand and the evolution of a new modernist economy on the other. This debate thus revealed an early form of capitalist desire to break down subregional frontiers in tastes and values. Therefore, not surprisingly, so many left-wing filmmakers and critics, who were supposedly stern believers in choice and freedom, doggedly insisted that Chinese cinema be unified in its verbal presentation. At the same time, the dominant Nationalist discourse also empowered, both in its positive and negative sense, the intellectuals to subdue alternative voices. As a result, the hegemonic nature of cinema both as a political tool and a mass commodity reinforced one another's legitimacy, echoing the issues we discussed in the previous chapter.

The left-wing filmmakers' and critics' repudiation of dialect cinemas can be seen as an effort to "write down," and therefore to tame, the diversification of the vast Chinese population represented in the disorder of their spoken words.[57] By defining their words as the only legitimate spoken language in Chinese cinema, Shanghai film circles continued to own the ultimate sovereignty of the national market, allowing only their "voices" to be heard, also revealing a key stage in the development of Chinese modernism/capitalism. As Scott Eyman comments on the arrival of sound in Hollywood: "Talkies were not an evolution, but a mutation, a different art form entirely; as a result, an art form [of the silent cinema] was eliminated and hundreds of careers were extinguished."[58] The new talkies offered cinema a completely new structure and aesthetic, and also provided the space for a new set of politics to be developed and the old set to be replaced. In the case of China, the Nationalist discourse and the economy of the capitalist market seized this rare opportunity in the national cinema and filled up the historical gap with their own interests.

Interestingly, the alleged plurality embodied in Shanghai cinema also contained the seeds of hegemony in regard to both the filmmakers' ideological and commercial concerns. Those aspiring young intellectuals, fighting against a totalitarian government, struggled hard to hold onto the inherent power of multiplicity embodied in cinema and the urban Shanghai culture, where possibilities in gaining alternative ideological power can be realized. However, the inherent subversive ideological power contained in this plurality could easily be corrupted; in this case, the commercial interests offered by capitalism and their own wish to stay ideologically dominant debauched it.

Paul Willeman has argued that:

> A cinema addressing national specificity will be anti- or at least non-nationalist, since the more it is complicit with nationalism's homogenizing project, the less it will be able to engage critically with the complex, multidimensional and multidirectional tensions that characterize and shape a social formation's cultural configurations.[59]

If we follow Willeman's logic, the position of this left-wing cinema was clearly ambiguous in relation to the notion of national cinema. On the one hand, this cinema was anti-nationalist in its opposition to the Nationalist Government's policy and ruling; but on the other hand, it also clearly provoked nationalist sentiments on a populist level. The films were devoted to the address of national specificity, but they also sacrificed social complexity to the homogenizing project. I hope that, by now, this study has demonstrated that this Chinese nationalist cinema was subversive yet hegemonic at the same time, which is certainly not the only example among other nationalist discourses. As we can criticize this left-wing cinema for too easily letting go of its marginal and critical position and turn it into a site to germinate ideas of domination, has it not been the case in so many other alternative cultures claiming power?

Notes

1. Yingjin Zhang, ed., *Cinema and Urban Culture in Shanghai, 1922-1943* (Stanford, Calif.: Stanford University Press, 1999).
2. Leo Ou-fan Lee, *Shanghai Modern: The Flowering of a New Urban Culture in China, 1930-1945* (Cambridge, Mass.: Harvard University Press, 1999).
3. Sherman Cochran, ed., *Inventing Nanjing Road: Commercial Culture in Shanghai, 1900-1945* (Ithaca, NY: East Asia Program, Cornell University, 1999).
4. Hanchao Lu, *Beyond the Neon Lights: Everyday Shanghai in the Early Twentieth Century* (Berkeley: University of California Press, 1999).
5. Shu-mei Shih, *The Lure of the Modern, Writing Modernism in Semicolonial China 1917-1932* (Berkeley: University of California Press, 2001).
6. Andrew F. Jones, *Media Culture and Colonial Modernity in the Chinese Jazz Age* (Durham, N.C.: Duke University Press, 2001)
7. There are many popular guidebooks, picture books, collections of anecdotes, and serious academic writings published in the mainland in these several years depicting the lives of old Shanghai. The connection between prewar Shanghai and contemporary Shanghai is also directly and indirectly alluded to in many recent literary writings, including Wang Anyi's *Changhen ge* (Song of everlasting regrets) (Hong Kong: Tiandi, 1996), Wei Wei's *Shanghai Baobei* (Shanghai's baby) (Shanghai: Chunfen wenxue, 1999), and Chen Danyan's *Shanghai de fenghua xueyue* (Shanghai memorabilia) (Beijing: Zuojia, 1999).
8. Heinrich Fruehauf, "Urban Exoticism in Modern and Contemporary Chinese Literature," in *From May Fourth to June Fourth*, ed. Ellen Widmer and David Der-wei Wang (Cambridge, Mass.: Harvard University Press, 1993), 141.
9. There were seventy-one cities in China that had cinemas in 1934. See "Zhongguo dianying shangye gaikuang" (The general overview of Chinese cinema industry), in *Chinese Cinematographic Yearbook of China*, n. p.
10. Eugene Irving Way, *Motion Pictures in China* (Washington, D.C., Bureau of Foreign and Domestic Commerce, U.S. Department of Commerce, 1930), 4-5.
11. Xin Ping, *Cong Shanghai faxian lishi* (Discovering history from Shanghai) (Shanghai: Shanghai renmin, 1996), 40.
12. Xin Ping, *Cong Shanghai faxian lishi*, 377.
13. Xin Ping, *Cong Shanghai faxian lishi*, 338.
14. According to Löwenthal's finding, between 1934-36, there were more newspapers published in Beijing than in Shanghai. But the average circulation per issue was over 1 million for the Shanghai newspapers, while the figures for Nanjing's and Beijing's newspaper is 60,000 and 100,000 respectively. Obviously, the entire country, instead of the city alone, is reading these newspapers. Rudolf Löwenthal, "Public Communications in China before July 1937" *Chinese Social and Political Science Review* 22 (1938-39): 46.
15. E-Tu Zen Sun, "The Growth of the Academic Community," in *The Cambridge History of China vol. 13, Republic China 1912-1949, Part 2*, ed. John K. Fairbank and

Albert Feuerwerker (Cambridge: Cambridge University Press, 1986), 378-79, 394.

16. Christian Henriot, *Shanghai 1927-1937*, trans., Noël Castelino (Berkeley: University of California Press, 1993), 65-102.

17. Chen Dabei, "Zhongguo dianying zhi jianglai" (The future of Chinese cinema) *Dianying yuebao* (Cinema Monthly) 7 (Oct. 28, 1928). Rpt., *ZWD*, 732.

18. Chen Dabei, "Zhongguo dianying zhi jianglai," 734.

19. Sun Shaoyi, "Dushi konjian yu Zhongguo minzu zhuyi: jiedu sanshi niandai Zhongguo zuoyi dianying" (City space and Chinese nationalism: Reading Chinese left-wing films in the thirties) *Shanghai wenhua* (Shanghai culture) 16 (May 1996): 37-44.

20. Regarding the New Life Movement, see Lloyd Eastman, *The Abortive Revolution: China Under Nationalist Rule, 1927-1937* (Cambridge, Mass.: Harvard University Press, 1974), 66-79; James E. Sheridan, *China in Disintegration: The Republican Era in Chinese History, 1912-1949* (New York: The Free Press, 1975), 218-19; and Jonathan D. Spence, *The Search for Modern China* (New York: W.W. Norton and Company, 1990), 414-16.

21. For a detailed analysis of the social problems brought by the rapid Westernization in Shanghai in the Republic time, see chapter 7 of Xin Ping's *Cong Shanghai faxian lishi*, which shows that all these negative social indicators were extremely high in Shanghai when compared to those in other major cities of both the country and the world.

22. Sun Shaoyi, "Dushi konjian yu Zhongguo minzu zhuyi," 43.

23. Sun Shaoyi, "Dushi konjian yu Zhongguo minzu zhuyi," 38.

24. Zhao Dan explained that this scene is no longer present in the current version of the film because the original print had been so badly handled that this part of the film was ruined. See Zhao Dan's *Diyu zhi men* (The gateway to the hell) (Shanghai: Shanghai wenyi, 1980), 69.

25. Joris Ivens, after making movies in China for several years, commented about the Chinese cinema in an interview in Paris in 1978: "It's just that Chinese movies are different from ours, they're more contemplative, more static. The camera is not part of the action, but records, observes it. According to the old Chinese philosophy: 'Man stands between heaven and earth and looks at the thousand things of the universe.' The result is that the camera does not move." (Unpublished materials from MoMA New York). It is, of course, impossible to confirm whether the static Chinese camera was due to this "old Chinese philosophy," but it is true that, at least until the Fourth Generation, there was a general lack of experimentation in camera movement. The Shanghai cinema in the 1930s might be a contributive factor in this stylistic habit. However, there were many individual efforts to experiment with camera movements during that period, and they were particularly evidenced in some of the films of Fei Mu, Yuan Muzhi, and Ying Yunwei. Yuan Muzhi's superb use of camera movement in *Street Angel* is clearly an example that surpassed Ivens' generalized comment.

26. Sun Yu, *Dalu zhi ge* (The song of the big road) (Taipei: Yualiu, 1990), 110.

27. *Dianying xinwen* (Film news) 1, no. 6 (Aug. 11, 1935): 5.

28. The monthly rent of Lu Xun's apartment was 60 *yuan*. *Lu Xun yu dianying* (Lu Xun and cinema), ed. Liu Siping and Xing Zuwen (Beijing: Zhongguo dianying, 1981), 323.

29. Wu Yonggang, *Wo de tansuo he zhuiqiu* (My search and pursuit) (Beijing: Zhongguo dianying, 1986), 182.

30. Zheng Zhenduo, "Shanghai de juzhu wenti" (The living problems in Shanghai),

in *Langtaosha: Mingren bixia de lao Shanghai* (Langtaosha: The old Shanghai under the writings of celebrities), ed. Ni Moyan (Beijing: Beijing chubanshe, 1998), 121-22.

31. For an elaborate discussion of Shanghai's living environment at that time, see Hanchao Lu, *Beyond the Neon Lights: Everyday Shanghai in the Early Twentieth Century*, 138-85.

32. Sun Yu, *Dalu zhi ge*, 113. Quotes and parentheses original.

33. The average living area per person in Shanghai in the 1930s was 3.9 square meters, equivalent to 40 square feet approximately. In some of the lower class neighborhoods, like Lao Zha or Yi Zhuang, the figure dropped down to 15 square feet per head. See Xin Ping, *Cong Shanghai faxian lishi*, 427.

34. Zhao Dan recounted that he and Yuan Muzhi and a group of their friends frequented a run-down bar where they observed the lives of different types of people. The story of *Street Angel* was conceived in this bar collectively in these drinking meetings. See Zhao Dan, 65-67.

35. *SB*, Dec. 15, 1933.

36. *SB*, Oct. 15, 1933.

37. *ZWD*, 102.

38. Hu Peng, *Wo yu Huang Feihong* (Me and Huang Feihong) (Hong Kong: Sanhe, 1995), 71-72.

39. For the reactions of Hong Kong's film circles to this policy, see the many related articles published in *Yilin* (The Forest of Art), nos. 1-7 (March to June 1937).

40. *Dawan bao* (The Great Evening News), July 6, 1934. The dialect-cinema debate is a name I coined. I have not come across any scholarship, in any languages or any periods, which have discussed this event.

41. Many articles related to this issue were published in the "Film Page" in *SB* and "Films of Everyday" in *CB* in the months of July and August in 1934.

42. *SB*, July 24, 25, 1934.

43. *SB*, July 28, 1934.

44. There was a "Dialect Literature" movement in the 1920s, which would be out of fashion the next decade, led by notable May Fourth figures like Hu Shi, Zhou Zuoren, and Gu Jiegang. Hu Shi argued that in order to create a new national language literature, one had to seek material from every possible source, which certainly included dialect literature. This view was similar to Tang Na's idea about dialect cinema. But judging from the rapid changes in the intellectual milieu between the 1920s and the 1930s, the overwhelming number of oppositions to Tang Na's arguments were not surprising. For a brief discussion of the "Dialect Literature" movement in the 1920s, see Chang-tai Hung, *Going to the People: Chinese Intellectuals and Folk Literature, 1918-1937* (Cambridge, Mass.: Harvard University Press, 1985), 62-65.

45. There are many studies devoted to the analysis of the two movements' positions in relation to language use and its pedagogy; I do not need to reiterate them here. For a succinct discussion, see Amitendranath Tagore, *Literary Debates in Modern China, 1919-1937* (Tokyo: The Centre for East Asian Cultural Studies, 1967), 156-160. For a detailed study, see Lydia H. Liu, *Translingual Practice: Literature, National Culture, and Translated Modernity China, 1900-1937* (Stanford, Calif.: Stanford University Press, 1995). A very good Chinese source is Gao Tianru, *Zhongguo xiandai yuyan jihua de lilun he shijian* (Theory and practice of modern Chinese language) (Shanghai: Fudan University Press, 1993).

46. For an introduction to this National Language Movement, see chapter 4 of Gao Tianru's *Zhongguo xiandai yuyan jihua de lilun he shiqian.*

47. *SB*, July 22, 1934.

48. Zhiwei Xiao, "Constructing a New National Culture: Film Censorship and the Issues of Cantonese Dialect, Superstition, and Sex in the Nanjing Decade," in *Cinema and Urban Culture in Shanghai, 1922-1943*, ed. Yingjin Zhang (Stanford, Calif.: Stanford University Press, 1999), 185.

49. See "Zhongguo dianying shangye gaikuang" (The general overview of Chinese cinema industry), in Zhongguo jiaoyu dianying xiehui ed., *Chinese Cinematographic Yearbook of China* (Nanjing: Zhongguo jiaoyu dianying xiehui, 1934), n. p.

50. See Stephen Teo, *Hong Kong Cinema: The Extra Dimensions* (London: BFI, 1997), 3-8. For a more detailed study of the early Hong Kong cinema, see, in spite of its sometimes impressionistic documentation, Yu Muyun's *Xiangang dianying shihua* (The Cronicle of Hong Kong Cinema), vols. 1-3 (Hong Kong: Ciwenhua tang, 1996-97).

51. Yu Muyun, *Xiangang dianying shihua*, vol. 3, 72. This Tianyi Hong Kong Branch Studio was the embryonic form of the later Shaw Brothers Studio.

52. I. C. Jarvie, *Window on Hong Kong: A Sociological Study of the Hong Kong Film Industry and Its Audience* (Hong Kong: Centre of Asian Studies, University of Hong Kong, 1977), 9.

53. Law Kar, "Xianggang dianying de haiwai jingyan" (Foreign experience of Hong Kong cinema) in *Overseas Chinese Figures in Cinema* (The 16th Hong Kong International Film Festival Special Publication), ed. Law Kar (Hong Kong: The Urban Council, 1992), 15-21.

50. For a detailed study of the development of Hong Kong cinema in the 1950s and 1960s, see Stephen Teo, *Hong Kong Cinema*, chapters 3-5.

54. Qu Qiubai, "Dazhong wenyi de wenti" (Questions regarding mass culture) *Qu Qiubai xuanji* (Selected writings of Qu Qiubai) (Beijing: Renmin, 1985), 493.

55. Lu Xun, "Da Cao Juren xiansheng xin" (Letter replying Mr. Cao Juren), in *Lu Xun quanji* (Complete writings of Lu Xun) (Taipei: Gufeng, 1980), 75.

56. The National Language Movement can also be understood along the same lines.

57. Scott Eyman, *The Speed of Sound: Hollywood and the Talkie Revolution, 1926-1930* (New York: Simon & Schuster, 1997), 22.

58. Paul Willemen, *Look and Frictions: Essays in Cultural Studies and Film Theory* (London: BFI, 1994), 212.

Figure 7.1.
The Goddess. The prostitute (played by Ruan Lingyu) looking out of the window.

Figure 7.2.
Cut to her subjective view, seeing an empty sky of the Shanghai night scene.

Figure 7.3.
Later, when the rascal looks out the window of his own room . . .

Figure 7.4. . . . what he sees is the same Shanghai night view, but now superimposed with the prostitute's smiling face.

Figure 7.5. The ending scene of *The Goddess*, depicting the prostitute in the prison thinking of her son.

Figure 7.6. *Street Angel*. The elaborate street setting in a studio. The background is particularly lit in order to stress the depth of the scene.

Figure 7.7.
Xiao Hong on a plank
assisted by Xiao Chen
walking to the opposite
building where Xiao
Chen lives.

Figure 7.8.
Xiao Chen's apartment
as seen from Xiao
Hong's perspective.
The window curtain
serves as a stage drapery.

Figure 7.9.
Cut to Xiao Hong sitting
on the window frame in
her apartment, clapping
her hands waiting to
enjoy Xiao Chen's
magic show.

Figure 7.10. Cut back to Xiao Chen's apartment. He now appears on the stage and performs his show. He has just created an apple out of nothing.

Figure 7.11. Xiao Chen throws the apple to Xiao Hong. She fails to catch it.

Figure 7.12. The apple flies to the inner room where Xiao Yun is applying her makeup. It breaks the two planes of representation and introduces the depth of the space.

Figure 7.13. A Ling reluctantly poses for the painters.

8

Engaging Realism

Being the last chapter of this book, the following discussion is conclusive yet open-ended, and I will close my investigation of this cinema by offering a discussion of the cinema's form, which encompasses not only the visual stylistics but also its narrative structure, audio arrangement, and viewer's identification. Although issues related to representations have been central to many of my earlier discussions in this book, this chapter specifically focuses on analyzing if there was a specific and coherent cinematic aesthetic developed in this cinema. I place this part of the study at the end of the book for two reasons. This so-called aesthetic was less artistic achievements than products shaped by the cultural, social, and political events at stake, and the specific stylistic renderings of these films were results of the complex interactions among the many related discourses and parties I have mentioned in the earlier chapters. This chapter will provide a more precise discussion of how these many interests were translated into cinematic practices. Therefore, this "poetics" I am going to explore is not definitive, as it is interpretation and reconstruction instead of matters of fact. On the other hand, being one of the first attempts to provide a systematic analysis of the aesthetics of early Chinese cinema, this chapter is far from comprehensive and inevitably suffers from my own blind spots. I hope that the following pages can serve as an invitation for further dialogues that can open up a new field of study. Being the last chapter of this book, I hope that it will find new beginnings somewhere else.

In fact, there have been sporadic efforts attempting to build up a theory of Chinese cinema aesthetics. Lin Niantong has analyzed how the traditional hand-scroll painting and the complementary interdependence between the pictorial and the poetic in traditional art influence Chinese cinema.[1] He also argued that the aesthetics of early Chinese filmmaking was a unique combination of the two Western cinematographic systems: montage and single shot.[2] Catherine Yi-Yu

Cho Woo also illustrates a particular Chinese montage and composition that was developed from traditional Chinese poetry and painting.[3] Along a different scholarly and ideological trajectory, a group of young mainland film scholars in the 1980s developed an "Image Play" theory, arguing that Chinese cinema is often less willing to experiment with new cinematic techniques than to enrich the narrative details of the plot. It was the result, as they argue, of the early Chinese cinema conceptualizing itself as a branch of traditional drama instead of a new and independent art form.[4] These analyses are path breaking and influential in their own right, but they all fall short of a broader understanding of "aesthetics." Chinese cinema as a cultural form could not be established solely through the filmmakers' direct borrowing of some classical artistic theories or adoption of certain foreign practices and traditional habits. Instead, at stake was the structure and reasoning of the medium within the specific cultural environment, which revealed itself more than the apparent styles seen on screen. The interactions between representation and ideology must be addressed through the contractual relationship developed among the filmmakers, the films, and the viewers, which involved the mechanisms of identification, appropriation, emotional recognition, ethical approval, etc.

I will use the term "engaging realism" to describe the stylistic practice of this left-wing cinema and discuss how the realist projects closely conjoined with, or were constantly contaminated by, its sentimentalism and fictional aspects. This engaging realism was characterized by its melodramatic slant, and one can argue that the intensity of emotions portrayed or even celebrated in most of the films ultimately refuted any connections of this cinema movement to realism in its aesthetic and political objectives. However, the high level of emotional engagement facilitates spectators' participation in the films effectively, rendering the cinema politically committed yet not at the expense of the spectators' enjoyment of this popular cultural form.

Fiction and Emotion: Realism in the Chinese Context

Realism is definitely as slippery a style as an ideology, which has been used in many different texts and contexts throughout the last two centuries. As Julia Hallam and Margaret Marshment have demonstrated, realism in cinema could be manifested in drastically different forms and cultures, and it was used in the names of diverging agendas.[5] It is the specific manifestations of realism in this left-wing cinema, instead of what realism exactly means, which anchors the following discussion. While we have the right to argue whether this left-wing cinema was realist or not, we cannot doubt the convictions of these filmmakers in their realist approaches, as they all called their films so on many different occasions. In this section, I will first provide a theoretical framework to illustrate how this realist cinema defined itself and how it can be compared to other realist cinemas. With these general descriptions in mind, we can go to the texts and analyze in what specific ways the cinema developed its unique form within its own cultural political context.

The celebration of realism in 1920s' Chinese literary circles was largely based on its philosophical principles. On the one hand, realism, which celebrates objectivity and therefore connotes a certain scientific attitude, empowered the May Fourth challenge to the subjective and impressionistic components in the intellectual tradition of China. On the other hand, as a Western literary style, realism was seen as an imported weapon to legitimate the Chinese scholars in the combat against the status quo. The left-wing progressive movements in the next decade felt no hesitation to appropriate it with their own political concerns, although realism as a literary technique in the 1920s was linked more to liberalism than to socialism.[6] Realism was always more a political/philosophical notion than a set of stylistic renderings in Chinese art/literary circles, and the realism in this left-wing cinema should also be studied along this tradition.

Ling He provided us with a comprehensive theoretical illustration of how realism was understood in this cinema. As I illustrated in chapter 2, one of the most crucial theoretical debates defining this movement was the "Soft-cinema versus Hard-cinema" discussion leveled by the left-wing progressive theorists who represented the "Hard-cinema" on the one hand and the bourgeois modernist critics who represented the "Soft-cinema" on the other. Regarding the Soft-cinema critics' charge that the left-wing filmmakers were ignorant of the cinematic form, Ling He, the famous left-wing critic, argued that it was realism the leading theoretical principle that reconciled form and content in the left-wing cinema.[7] He proclaimed that the objective of film criticism was to determine whether a film was able to represent reality successfully through film art, in which form (film art) and content (the concerned social reality) reinforced and complemented one another. He argued that the two must not be dichotomized, as done by the Soft-cinema critics. On the one hand, only through a realist depiction of the world could the artistic function of the medium be fulfilled. On the other hand, the effectiveness of this realist portrayal was dependent upon the filmmakers' creativity and ability to command the art form. That is to say, according to the Chinese critic, realism was able to unite aesthetics and politics because it fulfilled the socialist ideological goal of social criticism and was also the highest standard by which to measure artistic achievement. Only those works that represented reality successfully could be considered artistically triumphant.

However, neither did Ling He nor any other critics/filmmakers illustrate clearly how this realism should be translated into cinematic representations. The way realism was understood theoretically could differ a great deal when used in practice, particularly with the fact that realism was an encompassing term that could easily be appropriated by a different ideology. After all, "reality" might be one of the most abstract and slippery notions to be defined. But it does not mean that realism in this cinema movement remained an abstract concept that could never be put into practice. In fact, I insist that there was a specific realist approach, although the critics/filmmakers failed to define it themselves, that was adopted and evolved in this cinema, most significantly marking the uniqueness and achievement of this cinema in aesthetic terms.

In relation to Hollywood, what this Chinese left-wing cinema practiced was hardly identical to the illusionary realism perfected by the American studios. Although, as I argued in chapter 6, this Chinese cinema was very indebted to the Hollywood practice, they took different platforms in approaching the "real." As Bordwell, Staiger, and Thompson demonstrated, the classical Hollywood cinema "created" realism by supplying causal motivation, turning verisimilitude into the real. "Classical Hollywood narrative thus often uses realism as an alibi, a supplementary justification for material already motivated causally."[8] While the American practice privileged the reality created on screen in order to allow audiences to escape from their own daily reality, the Chinese left-wing cinema, like all other politically committed cultural practices, could not afford valorizing the authenticity of the medium at the expense of their political objectives. Ma Ning has made a point of the "radicalness" of this Chinese left-wing cinema that its films invited the viewers to form critical judgment by a combination of prior actual social experience and their reception of the films.[9] He argues that the realist film brought its viewers to confront the "off-screen reality" in their everyday lives instead of lulling them to believe in the "on-screen reality" created by the filmmakers.

While I agree with Ma Ning on the intimate relationship between the two realms, I would argue that this Chinese left-wing cinema was politically radical not in terms of its engagement with audiences intellectually, which supposedly should provide the viewers critical distance from the depicted reality. Quite the contrary, this cinema often risks reason to celebrate and exploit emotions. While the classical Hollywood cinema "created" realism by supplying causal motivation that addresses the viewer's psychology, this Chinese left-wing cinema made its own by soliciting its spectators' identification emotionally. What Ma Ning has ignored is that this cinema was as much politically committed as commercially successful.

This Chinese left-wing cinematic realism was far from identical to the similar film theories developed in Europe right after the Second World War. Sigfried Kracauer compared cinema with photography, which are both capable of reproducing material reality precisely. "Film, in other words, is uniquely equipped to record and reveal physical reality and, hence, gravitates toward it."[10] André Bazin was more interested in the interaction between cinema and reality, in the sense that cinema's realistic basis derives from the possibility of not only documentation but also participation.[11] Together with a number of other theorists interested in the political responsibilities and effects of films, this European realist school advocated a cinema that was intimately engaging with social reality, that its inherent photographic nature could represent the complex reality not only on the level of reproducing the surface but its internal structure and meanings.

Although most of these realist theorists, particularly Bazin, emphasized cinema's ability to penetrate reality as more than mere scientific reproduction of objectivity, both the documentary values and the interpretive values of cinema, according to them, were based on spectators' detached and apathetic positions in observing and pondering on the representations. Therefore, the relationship between the films and the viewers was cognitive instead of affective. But the realism represented and advocated in this Chinese left-wing cinema was emotionally charged; the spectators participated in the cinematic world less through an intellectual process than a psychological one. This emotional identification is not equivalent to the spectators' unconditional submission to the cinematic apparatus and therefore their vulnerability to the ideology pertained. The cinema's success as both an entertainment industry and a pedagogical means resulted in, and were results of, a specific cinematic relationship built up between the viewers and the film texts.

In fact, one of the key underlying threads weaving the stylistic and ideological co-web of this engaging realism was the films' ability to reconcile the imported ideological goal of socialist realism and the specific cultural context of China, in which a millennium-long narrative tradition was deeply implanted. If the filmmakers concerned about socialist ideology seriously, the traditional viewing and reading habits of Chinese theater-goers and novel-readers should exert a greater influence on the filmmakers who had to seek the endorsements of their spectators. As a result, what we saw was a set of cultural products trying to reconcile both the imported socialist ideology, that valued objectivity and political actions, and the inherited narrative tradition, that was characterized by a heavy sentimentalism. In fact, the emotional components of this realist cinema were so apparent and dominating that many of these films could pass more as melodramas than realist works, which was a major feature defining this cinema. While the filmmakers were eager to advocate a realist cinema theoretically and practically, many viewers and scholars considered melodrama the dominant mode of filmmaking in this left-wing cinema. Paul Pickowicz, for example, proclaims that the progressive filmmakers in the 1930s failed to introduce May Fourth revolutionary thought into Chinese films and became "captives of melodrama."[12] He argues that the "Mandarin Duck and Butterflies" writers of the late Qing and early Republican times were influenced by the serialized newspaper fiction popular in late-nineteenth-century Europe, and this melodramatic structure influenced the Chinese film practices beginning in the 1920s.[13] Pickowicz also explains that "melodrama was appealing to [the left-wing filmmakers in the 1930s] because it used clear language to identify and combat evil. . . . Xia Yan wanted to force the genre to serve revolutionary political ends. He liked the fact that melodrama was an inherently manipulative form of art."[14]

I have no difficulties calling these left-wing films melodrama, as there are a number of similarities between that genre and these Chinese films. But a simple equation between the two is misleading. The term melodrama, or any concept similar to it, in fact never appeared in the writings of the filmmakers or of the film critics in the 1930s.[15] As Wimal Dissanayake has pointed out, none of the Asian languages has a synonym for the word melodrama, and "we need to constantly keep in mind that melodrama in Asia connotes different sets of associations from those obtained in the West."[16] In fact, many scripts of Xia Yan, like *Spring Silkworms*, *New Year's Gift*, and *Spirit of Freedom*, were emotionally and structurally some of the calmest works among other contemporary Chinese films, left-wing or not. We must be careful in specifying in exact terms why and how we call this left-wing cinema melodramatic.

Melodrama is known to intensify the fictional aspect of representation, privileging the personal and the subjective, which is clearly observed in this cinema. But the ultimate object of study in realism is social rather than psychological, collective rather than individual. Could these left-wing films entertain and achieve both missions? The answer is positive. In fact, the personal and the social are intimately linked with each other in many politically engaged cultural products. For example, in appraising those realist historical novels he exalted, Georg Lukács states that personal and sociohistorical fates can be closely connected in this literature, yet the individuals lose neither their personality, nor the immediacy of their experience.[17] On the other hand, a good melodrama, as considered by many critics, links the personal subjective with the sociocultural subjective in a similar way: the individual struggle is symbolic to the individual's cultural experience. As a result, melodramas are often evaluated in terms of their degree of subversion or servitude to authority, instead of on the mere level of characterization. In fact, a politically engaging work should reconcile the personal and the social by elucidating the intimate and inevitable links between them, which is, as I will discuss in detail, admirably achieved in this left-wing cinema.

These Chinese films could also be called melodramatic because of their strong moral dimensions. In his seminal discussion of melodrama, Peter Brooks argues that the "classical" melodrama, which developed at the dawn of the nineteenth century in France, was a historical response of the people to the loss of the divine. They needed to construct a new "moral occult" in order to fulfill their religious needs. Brooks argues that the melodramatists employed "the things and gestures of the real world, of social life, as kinds of metaphors that refer us to the realm of spiritual reality and latent moral meanings."[18] He also claims that melodrama represents a response to the destruction of the tragic vision both in the Greek perspective and in Christian doctrine. "It comes into being in a world where the traditional imperatives of truth and ethics have been violently thrown into question, yet where the promulgation of truth and ethics, their instauration as a way of life, is of immediate, daily, political concern."[19] According to Brooks, the popularity of melodrama in Europe beginning in the nineteenth century was a culturally specific incident and should be read within that historical context.

A similar "moral occult" also dominated the traditional Chinese narratives, although the Western melodrama was a negative reaction attempting to replace the lost Christian faith and Greek metaphysics, while the Chinese narratives' ethical concerns are generally a positive acknowledgment of the moral power already intrinsic in the cultural realm. The traditional Chinese narratives were always assigned a pedagogical role; so was the case of these left-wing films in the twentieth century. In fact, most of the realist theories, literary and cinematic, are ultimately ethically bound. But to this self-avowed realist cinema, the moral dimension was so strong that detached scientific observation of reality is simply impossible. It presupposed that orders and values were inevitably intrinsic in reality, and the restoration of these intrinsic orders and values was the ultimate goal of their realist undertaking.

In addition to the personal-subjective and moral dimensions, the level of fantasy observed in these films also characterized the intensity of emotions, instead of the degree of reality, represented in this cinema. As I demonstrated in chapter 4, we often observe a romantic and youthful spirit in these films, which was particularly reflected in an innocence and desire of war. Yet it was the war that taught the European realists in the 1950s the impact and brutality of reality, that people had confronted and should continue to investigate reality in its most naked form, stripping it of all its humanistic sugar coating. But this Chinese cinema in the 1930s could still afford the idea of wars or revolutions as hopes for China's future, meaning that the representations of violence did not necessarily require a confrontation of reality but illusion. Political engagement in these films, therefore, was always presented in a fantastic call for battles, battles against the Japanese invasion, on the international level, or within the nation, fighting against the class enemies and the corrupt government.

As a whole, the concept of realism used and postulated in this cinema was closer to the European realist literature in the nineteenth century and the theories of socialist realism that Lukács developed on literature than Bazin's cinematic celebration of the complexity and ambiguity of reality. If the realist film theories developed in Europe in the 1950s emphasized reality as elaborate and irreducible to simple categorization, the Chinese theories saw reality as basically innocent and lucid, in which its temporary disorder can be redeemed. In turn, these films were more in stride with the classic realist text, which does not and cannot deal with the real as contradictory.[20] But a simple equation between the two sets of text cannot be drawn, as Colin MacCabe illustrates that the narrative discourse in a classical realist text "is not present as discourse—as articulation. . . . The real is not articulated—it is."[21] But the narrative presented in this left-wing cinema was highly maneuvered, involving the dramatic and fictional orchestration on a high level. We start this investigation by first examining the cinema's relations with China's own narrative tradition.

Narrative Structure

In delineating the interrelationship between history and fiction in Chinese classical narratives, Andrew Plaks argues that: "In contrast to [the Western] general
reification of the event as a narrative unit, the Chinese tradition has tended to
place nearly equal emphasis on the overlapping of events, the interstitial spaces
between events, in effect on non-events alongside of events in conceiving of
human experience in time."[22] David Roston also raises a similar assertion by
suggesting an evolution from "plot-centered" to "character-centered" narratives
in Ming and Qing literatures. Authors and readers were interested in how a large
number of individual characters were depicted in details rather than in the continuous flow of the story line.[23] Under this tradition, for centuries Chinese novel
readers have cultivated a literary taste for lengthy plots rich in detail with episodic structure, emphasizing an elaborate depiction of the discrete characters
and events in the "fictive reality" rather than the fiction itself.

This preference for narrating relatively fragmented units of details continu-
ously might not be evident in Chinese cinema, as most films could only afford
one coherent dramatic unit within the standard two-hour span. But movies with
multiple episodes and lengthy dramatic development, parallel to the structure of
traditional novels and dramas, were in fact common in the 1920s. The stories of
swordsman movies, like the eighteen parts of *Huoshao hongliansi* (Burning the
Red Lotus Temple), can be prolonged infinitely by adding numerous sequels one
after another, a practice which was also common in popular novels at that time,
for many of them were serialized in newspapers. However, the box office failure
of Mingxing's 6-part *Marriage in Tears and Laughter* in 1932 indicated not
only the ending of a "period film" genre but also spectators' growing distaste for
films with multiple sequels. The rapid Westernization in the major Chinese cities also forced people to adopt a lifestyle much faster than the ones of their
predecessors. Unlike the traditional novel readers and opera spectators, many
contemporary movie-goers could no longer afford the time and patience to experience the slow unraveling of a story. In fact, a consumerist society would not
allow the mass to exhaust a product over too long a period. New products must
be perpetually shoved into the market in order to arouse the consuming urge of
the mass. After *Marriage in Tears and Laughter*, films with multiple parts simply disappeared from the market altogether in the 1930s.[24]

However, this cinematic standard and change of lifestyle did not immediately alter the traditional structure of narrative that was deeply rooted in the
collective memory. Giving up the "character-centered" narrative structure, Chinese films continued to tell a single story spanning a long period of time. As
Tony Rayns observes: "it is common for the action in a Chinese film to span
months or years, sometimes even decades."[25] Despite the fact that the two-hour
format of standard narrative film is not particularly appropriate for telling a long
story with such a wide temporal range, filmmakers in the 1930s continued to

make films with plots developing along decades, and spectators also continued to embrace these films wholeheartedly as standard of storytelling. The episodic structure was therefore retained. In analyzing the structure of a film script, Xia Yan repeatedly stressed the need to divide the story into sections. He emphasized that "chaptering" was a crucial concept in Chinese traditional novels and dramas, and so it was in films. He also used the analogy of Chinese architecture to illustrate the significance of clear divisions in a narrative.[26]

Many of the Chinese left-wing films in the 1930s adopted this narrative structure, which clearly set them apart from most other self-proclaimed realist films. This episodic structure did not only jam numerous plot details into a two-hour temporal nutshell, but it also encouraged the films' emotional compactness. And the competing emotions were usually framed in the notion of "balance"— an important concept in Chinese traditional philosophy stating that an overpowering of any components would lead to a collapse. In traditional narratives, contrasting elements, like comic and tragic, were often found together. In terms of characters, major figures were to be balanced either by themselves, like the five wives in *Jin ping mei* (Plum in the Golden Vase), or by minor figures, like the mistresses and the maids in *Honglou meng* (Dream of the Red Chamber, or Story of the Stone). In terms of the dramatic elements, sadness was to be balanced by gaiety, excitement by tranquillity, and action by dialogue. A traditional Chinese play always employed a fixed set of character types, and these characters would provide and balance different dramatic elements in the story.

In spite of the clear links between these left-wing films and the traditional narratives, the old practices and styles were not embraced unreflectively in the new medium. *Crossroads*, for example, combined the comedy-tragedy narrative structure as a result of not only a concern and a respect for balance but also of its particular ideological needs. It is a story about the fates of four young male adults, Lao Zhao, A Tang, Liu Dage, and Xiao Xu, after graduating from school, and its plot unfolds mainly around the romantic affair between Lao Zhao and Yang Zhiying, who live next to each other. The two rooms are separated by a section of wooden wall that does not even reach to the ceiling and has holes in it; they develop an aversion to each other because of their mutual intrusion into each other's space through the thin wall, either by driving nails through it or by throwing trash over the other side. Because Lao Zhao reports on duty at night and Zhiying goes to work during the day, they meet only at the tram stop in a crossroad everyday. They are attracted to each other and secretly fall in love in these daily ephemeral encounters. After knowing their neighboring relationship and their struggles between romance and careers, at the end of the film the two finally tear down the wall between the two rooms and devote themselves to confronting the challenges together with their two other friends, A Tang and Yao Dajie, who have been laid off from their jobs recently.

The film is a light-hearted romance comedy, but the comic portion is sandwiched by two tragic sections. It is preceded by a tragic part showing the male protagonist and his friends facing joblessness after graduation, and it is followed

by another tragic part which depicts the two lovers losing their jobs and pro-
posing to end their relationship. The tragic and comic sections are juxtaposed to
each other without any transition. In the first section, for example, when the four
graduates are desperate over their failure to find jobs, a gloomy setting is established by low-key lighting as well as a guitar solo and cello solo as background
music, although it is interrupted by a brief sporadic comic performance by A
Tang. The tragic section suddenly shifts to its emotional opposite right after Lao
Zhao receives his job offer. Without allowing the spectators any psychological
preparation, the lighting is abruptly shifted to high key, and the cello solo is replaced by cheerful orchestral music; even Lao Zhao's entire appearance is transformed from a dispirited tramp to a lively and handsome young man. Such sudden emotional shifts are constantly seen in early Chinese films, a "jumpy"
structure that characterizes traditional plays and novels.

This fragmented structure, however, should not be seen as reflecting only a
traditional practice. In the case of *Crossroads*, the episodic arrangement is also
connected to the ideological message of the film. There are two narrative levels
progressing at the same time: the happy-go-lucky psychology of youths and the
cruel reality. Liu Dage, the revolutionary and the most respected figure among
the four graduates, says: "Optimism is a virtue, but we also need to understand
reality clearly." The gaiety of Lao Zhao, Zhiying, and A Tang we see in the
middle part of the story can be seen as representing the optimism of Chinese
youths; but the suicide of Xiao Xu, Liu Dage's return to his hometown, the lay-
offs of the four main characters, and other tragic elements depicted in the beginning and the ending reveal the harsh reality that concerns Liu Dage.

This dual narrative structure is also evident in the recurring insertion of the
characters' subjective views of and comments on newspaper articles. These articles include news of young people committing suicide, factories closing down
because of competition from contraband, the Japanese invasions, and the miserable lives of female factory workers. These "nondiegetic" views of reality,
which can also be considered as diegetic for they correspond to Lao Zhao's reporter career, could all find their echoes in the story. Xiao Xu is too timid to face
his dismal future and commits suicide. The factory in which Zhiying and Yao
Dajie work is closed down due to the widespread smuggling of foreign goods
into the Chinese market. That Liu Dage is likely to participate in the anti-
Japanese war is hinted at by his returning home. Zhiying and Yao Dajie are female workers themselves who might also have miserable stories to tell. Ma Ning
argues that the juxtaposition of the newspaper articles about the suffering of
female workers and the romance between Lao Zhao and Zhiying prove that leftist filmmakers did not regard newspaper headlines as a reliable source of information because the film mocked the hypocrisy of Lao Zhao using newspaper
writing as a means to chase women.[27] However, I would argue the opposite:
Shen Xiling, the director and the scriptwriter of the film, took these newspaper
articles seriously because they represent one narrative level of the bipolar structure of the story: reality (as opposed to fiction) and tragedy (as opposed to com-

edy). Although the primary story line is a light-hearted romance, the reality is not. The film's tragic-comic structure is parallel with the underlying message of the film: the enchanting illusion in the minds of the ignorant youths, most evident in the dream sequence of Zhiying (figure 8.1), marks a stark contrast to the gloomy reality the country is facing. At the end of the film when the four characters join together shoulder to shoulder and walk toward the city, a synthesis of the two narrative levels is achieved: the youths confront the reality with confidence and collective dedication. Therefore, the juxtaposition between the comic and the tragic parts is not only a continuation of a traditional aesthetic practice but also a manifestation of the film's underlying leftist ideology. Most impressively, style and content do correspond in this film, proving that some of these early Chinese filmmakers, not to their full awareness probably, had already attained a high level of artistic control of the medium. And they were also starting to reflect on their romanticism more intriguingly.

The frequent juxtaposition of different dramatic forms in Chinese cinema also fostered a unique but seemingly flimsy technique—*guangming de weiba* (the bright tail). One of the common features found among all the left-wing movies is the aura of catastrophe—something disastrous is going to happen if no remedy is found. However, most Chinese spectators then cherished happy endings for tragic stories, as they preferred a balanced resolution for their earlier emotional catharsis.[28] A major problem the left-wing filmmakers had to face was that happy endings would curtail the demonstrative power of their story and contradict the reasons for revolutionary changes. The censor also prevented them from a clear elucidation of the political messages. Therefore, one strategy they frequently employed was the "Bright Tail" technique, a term widely used at that time. The "Bright Tail" simply meant a subtle hint of revolution at the end of the usually tragic story, promising a bright future if further action is taken. With the "Bright Tail," spectators can walk out of the theaters experiencing a sense of relief after watching the pain and suffering engendered by the national crisis, but at the same time the film could still harbor political idealism without directly confronting the censors.

The "Bright Tail" is extremely common in left-wing movies. The resurrection of the dead figures at the end of *The Highway* is one of the most straightforward "Bright Tails." Other important left-wing movies like *Three Modern Women, Cosmetics Market, Women's Outcry, New Women, Crossroads,* and *March of Youth* also employed similar promising and provocative endings as the concluding comment of the films. Interestingly, almost all of these films describe social darkness, but their "Bright Tail" endings are always blissful rather than dismal, and these happy endings do not fail to facilitate the filmmakers' ideological commitment to social change because they provide new beginnings to the stories rather than complete them. This commonly practiced technique, although simple and banal, offers us a way to unsettle the allegedly organic structure of Western classical narrative, which is supposed to be autonomous yet microscopic of the empirical world, and a final consummation of the narrative promises the spectators a resolve of conflicts and all other social disputes in reality. This "Bright Tail" technique is an alternative to this unity, always bringing a new beginning to the supposedly confined narrative. It is also a pertinent tool to close the gap between the Chinese spectators' desire of happy endings, which has been encouraged by the ones in power, for it celebrates the status quo instead of promoting changes, and the ideological needs of the cinema to challenge precisely these "reactionary" mentalities without alienating the spectators. The strategic use of this apparently melodramatic element in fact demonstrates the complexity of this cinema whose survival was subject to its ability to combine innovations with tradition.

New Year's Gift, a film inspired by the Hollywood film *If I Had a Million*, a 1933 Paramount film co-directed by Ernst Lubitsch and six other filmmakers, clearly manifests an episodic structure, and it also brings in a "Bright Tail" that successfully concludes the seemingly open-ended structure. *New Year's Gift* begins at a family's New Year's Eve dinner and shows the grandfather giving a silver coin to his granddaughter as the new year's gift. The film continues to trace the journey of this coin among people of different ages, genders, and classes. The coin is finally taken back by the government under the policy of currency consolidation, a real issue causing much social dispute at the time. At the end of the film we are shown the same family dining at the following New Year's Eve. This time the gift the grandfather gives his granddaughter is no longer a silver coin but a government issued paper bill.

In this episodic film, miseries and sufferings of different sections of society are revealed. And the fragmented structure is pieced together thematically into a coherent whole not only through the journey of the coin but also through the use of the "Bright Tail." The film opens and ends with two consecutive New Year's Eve dinners of the same family. But the major difference between the two dinners is the presence of the father in the second dinner; he was away from home in the first year. Although the father carries no meaning in the plot, his symbolic absence and re-presence serves as a subtle but important indicator for hope when the film ends and the future begins. Spectators witness the many human misfortunes and evil acts through the itinerary of the coin, but the two family dinners offer an optimistic echo of familial bonding that transcends grief. The final presence of the father, the leader of the household, brings the domestic metaphor back to a social level: he is the one who will bring improvements to the family, which can be seen as an allegory of social betterment or even political revolution.

With this subtle "Bright Tail" technique, spectators could walk away from the theater feeling satisfied after seeing the blissful reunion of a loving family. The tears they might have shed for the misfortunes they witnessed in the middle of the film were compensated by this happy ending, and they could go back to their own households to celebrate their own New Year Festivals—the film was first shown in the Chinese New Year period of 1937. On the other hand, this traditional happy ending does not present itself as reactionary to the original leftist messages because it provides hope and determination for social reforms, if not revolutions. The father is the symbolic force who would rectify the grievances we have just seen. Most importantly, the implicit message in the ending, i.e., the presence of the father, is too subtle for the censoring authority to detect, although it might also be too obscure for most spectators to understand.

There were other narrative and cinematic devices being developed in this cinema to use episodic structure to tell political messages, particularly those related to the visual representation of temporal passages. *The Sisters* broke all box office records when it was shown; and since Zheng Zhengqiu, the director and the writer, clearly presented the film as a leftist progressive one, it added much glamour to this cinema movement. However, the underlying reasons for the popularity of the films were definitely more than their left-wing elements; apparently spectators also found appealing the film's traditional narrative structure with a rich plot spanning a long time and congested with all kinds of emotion. It recounts the growth of the protagonists from childhood and narrates a story with a time-span of two decades.

Given this lengthy story to tell, one of the major technical problems the filmmaker had to solve and explore was the use of structural devices that could link episodic elements together. As shown in many of these films, the filmmakers most frequently employed cut away memory to serve this purpose, and it had become a narrative convention much practiced and perfected. At first sight, *The Sisters* might be considered, as a popular melodrama, too theatrical (the film was an adaptation of a play), lacking values both in content and form. But reading the film more carefully, we discover that Zheng Zhengqiu proved himself to be an eloquent master of filmmaking, whose distinct cinematic sensibilities were particularly shown in his interesting use of memory. Flashback became not only an economical means to connect fragmented episodes, but it was also used expressively to structure the narrative and to produce new meanings.

The Sisters is about a pair of twin sisters: the older one, Dabao, grew up with her mother in the village leading a harsh life, while the younger sister, Erbao, was taken away by her father to the city and later married a warlord under the arrangement of the father. Dabao assumes the virtues of traditional Chinese women by taking care of her mother, father-in-law, husband, and her children selflessly, but Erbao inherited the bad city habits and leads an extravagant and lustful life. When her husband, Taoge, falls sick after over-exhausting himself, Dabao decides to leave her family to become the wet nurse of Erbao's newborn. Without knowing their biological relationship, the sisters become master and servant. In the rich household, Dabao accidentally kills the sister of the warlord, and after many tears shed and misunderstandings resolved, in a family reunion Erbao finally decides to help her sister flee.

The film is set in the present where the two sisters are already grown-up, but their childhood is important to the plot, as it explains the current circumstances of the twins, and not surprisingly, Zheng Zhengqiu chose to show the past through flashbacks. In the beginning of the film, the mother is watching the grown-up Dabao playing with her lover, later husband, Taoge in the front yard of their house; it is followed by a dissolve showing two children, a boy and a girl, standing in the same place (figures 8.2-8.6). The spectators immediately understand that the two figures are Dabao and Taoge as children in the memory of the mother because of her earlier subjective shot looking at the two. In this memory, the girl is taller than the boy, and she is holding a book. Such a simple three-second flashback serves a succinct introduction to these two characters and efficiently provides the spectators crucial information about the relationship of this couple. First, the spectators are told that the bonding between Dabao and Taoge is strong because they have known each other since childhood, and this puppy love has been witnessed and approved by her mother. This shot also shows the intimate relationship between the mother and Dabao because of her constant attentiveness to the daughter. Most importantly, in this relation, Dabao is shown to be the stronger and more intelligent one; she seems to assume a position towering over her little boyfriend. This short flashback skillfully establishes the assertive personality of Dabao since childhood and prepares the spectators to accept her later decision to sacrifice her well-being to become the maid of the warlord in order to support the family. Although *The Sisters* was clearly a woman's story, it does not rely on heterosexual romance to anchor female viewers' identification. One of the few hints at romance in this film is this three-second flashback, which however suggests a reverse power relation between the two. What more can be said in three seconds?

Very soon after this flashback, we are shown another memory of the mother explaining the reasons of Erbao being taken away by the father. In this flashback, we see the husband about to leave the family. He tells his wife that he does not want to suffer from poverty by staying in the village; he wants to go to the city to start a new life by doing weapon business in the black market. Failing to persuade her husband to stay, the wife asks him to take the twin daughters with him because she has no hope of raising them by herself. The husband casts an unwilling look at the sisters. Finding the younger one more attractive, he thinks that she might bring him a fortune in the city later, therefore, he decides to take Erbao with him and leave Dabao behind with his wife.

This section is crucial to the entire story because it explains the separation of the sisters, and the film illustrates this past history by reproducing the quarrel between the couple. But the most important component of this flashback is not the history being replayed but the threshold between the past and the present. We are first shown the mother leaning on a table looking out (figure 8.7). This subjective shot is cut to a superimposition combining both the closed front door (demonstrating the vision of the mother in the present) with a younger her and a man walking out from the house and beginning to quarrel at the doorway (demonstrating the projected memory of the mother for the past) (figures 8.8-8.10). But this recalled past, unlike the one showing the childhood relation between Dabao and Taoge, is not projected from the exact same position of the recalling present: in the present the camera is positioned inside the house, but in the past it is reversed. In this dissolve from the present to the past, the door acts as the an-choring object holding the two periods together. As a metaphor for a temporal threshold, the door is the same door, but the camera's position is shifted from inside the house to outside the house; the door is also transformed from a closed one to an opened one. Here we are shown the direction of the wife's memory first projecting out but then returning back. She is first shown looking out of the house trying to escape the closed door and arriving at the distant past. But her memory is directed from outside back to the house through the open door in the subsequent shot. Her thoughts thus never escape her domestic place, and her concerns seem never able to transcend her family. This intimate relationship between a woman's subjectivity and her family is crucial to the film's ideologi-cal framework, in which, at the end of the film, the sisters reconcile with each other and thereby reestablish the destroyed order of the family caused by their irresponsible father.

Through this tactful representation of the mother's subjectivity, the film in-vites spectators' identifications by condensing her life-long sufferings into sev-eral pieces of memory, allowing them to experience the mother's history in first person, and therefore, it asks the spectator him/herself to provide the links be-tween the temporal segments. Interestingly, using its own specific cinematic devices, *The Sisters* connected itself to two essential features of traditional Chi-nese narratives: structurally, spectators experience a coherent life story, and emotionally, the mother's passions and struggles are also felt. One of the major accomplishments of these left-wing films was their ability to address the public through a maneuvering of the private, allowing an individual to penetrate into an intimate and deep section of the collective which cannot be deciphered but by his/her own private subjectivity. In the case of *The Sisters*, the several subjective shots of the mother thinking of her past allow us to see most intimately how she experiences the events, and, most importantly, how she feels about the events, instead of what the "real" really is. It fosters a bonding between the character and the spectators through a fictional and emotional engagement instead of a common, objective comprehension of the world. Like most other films of this movement, the political messages of *The Sisters* were conveyed through such emotional identification rather than in any specific rational enlightenment.

Diegesis and Identification

The narrative structure I have just illustrated was based on the strong emotional engagement of the viewers with the fictional world. Although I have illustrated several sets of subjective shots found in these left-wing films, the specific emo-tional identification was fostered less by directly suturing the viewer into speci-fic characters' experiential points of view than by inviting their passions felt through the characters. Therefore, when shot/reverse shots or subjective shots are seen in these left-wing films, it is the emotion, rather than the knowledge, that is emphasized, like Xin Baihua's gaze at his lovers in *Sons and Daughters of the Storm* and Wei Ming's daughter looking at her mother's picture in *New Woman*. The integrity of the real, therefore, is contingent not on a common experience of reality. Instead, it is the emotional coherence of the fictional world that anchors the spectators, which in turn is supported and fostered by the coherence of diegesis.

Almost as an unpronounced rule, with the exception of singing, all of the images shown and sounds heard in these Chinese films are diegetic. This emphasis on diegesis is evidenced in the apparent differences between the images shown in the "gods" sequence in *October* and the ones in the "Temple scene" in *Unchanged Heart in Life and Death*: the latter was an unmistakable imitation of the former. Many scholars consider the "gods" sequence as the most sophisticated representation of Eisenstein's "intellectual montage," the most advanced stage of montage theory. It signals an absolute liberation of the action from its determination by time and space. The cinematic progression is "intellectual," for it is a metaphorical operation that governs the leap from image to image.[29] The juxtaposed images of the various spirits in *October* are all extra-diegetic: they are not parts of the narrative and are included in the films only to heighten the psychological tension and to suggest religion's overwhelming control of people in different times and places. However, when Ying Yunwei transplanted this Soviet sequence to Chinese cinema in order to provoke a similar cinematic effect, he had to provide these images with a defined space within the diegesis. The montage sequence of the close-ups of the gods becomes the subjective view of the heroine when she wakes up in the temple. The chosen spiritual images in *Unchanged Heart in Life and Death*, therefore, are the ones normally seen in a Chinese temple, unlike those in *October* that are brought from different traditions.

Ying Yunwei relied on the heroine's subjective view to inscribe the intellectual montage within the diegesis. This sequence in the Chinese film evokes a rather different set of effects when compared to the Soviet original. For the sake of the diegetic realism, the latitude, both temporally and spatially, of Ying's sequence must be sacrificed to allow spectators' identification with the images in a realist setting. However, the emotional impact of the "Temple scene" is not necessarily leveled. Because the images are inscribed within not only the narrative space of the film but also the psychological space of the heroine, identification of the audience with this montage sequence is encouraged and heightened.

This resolute concern with diegesis also forced the filmmakers to pay close attention to the use of motif, referring usually to an object repeatedly seen in association with a character or situation. A sophisticated use of these objects placed in certain syntagmatic positions within the film would allow them to take on a value greater than their own, which would compensate the narrow signifying scope of the confined diagetic narrative reality. This fascination with objects was not similar to the way symbols are used in, for example, expressionist films which are paradoxical to the alleged realist project; instead, in the Chinese films, they are all objects present in the film's "fictitious reality," and they all have diegetic significance in the story. For examples, the *qipao* (the Manchurian-style female long gown) in *The Goddess* is a symbol of oppressed womanhood; the round-bottomed roly-poly figurine in *New Woman* represents the unyielding attitude of the new revolutionary females; Lao Zhao's Mickey Mouse and Zhi-ying's little doll in *Crossroads* combine to symbolize the naiveté and purity of the youngsters. Other motifs used might be less tangible than the above men-tioned, yet they are still concretely seen, touched, and spoken of by characters in the film. The road under construction in *The Highway* symbolizes the collective efforts of national defense in the face of the Japanese invasion. But it is also on this road where characters meet and the story develops; it is this road which pieces the narrative together. The family estate in *Plundered Peach Blossom* is also a metaphor for the Chinese land under the threat of colonialism. All these metaphors were carefully chosen for their relevance to the filmmakers' particu-lar ideological concerns, but at the same time they were also deeply rooted in the films' narrative. The employment of these motifs became particularly important at a time when political censorship was tight and the left-wing filmmakers had to rely on subterfuge to convey their political criticism. One can call these styles a specific left-wing aesthetics; but they might simply be the direct result of pragmatism.

In order to encourage spectators' identification with these specific objects within the diegesis, the filmmakers usually took extra efforts to introduce and locate these motifs at the beginning of the films. For example, before spectators are introduced to the characters in *The Goddess*, the camera has already shown us a close-up pan shot of the prostitute's home that locates the exact positions of her two *qipaos* and the other daily objects she uses within the room. Her status as a prostitute would be represented skillfully by these two *qipaos* in this exact location several times later in the film. Similar techniques are also utilized in *Crossroads*, where a slow pan shot of the two rooms is introduced in the earlier part of the film in order to situate the dolls of the two protagonists within their daily lives. Other than the use of motifs, diegetic writing is another commonly used narrative device in the sound films of this cinema. These films often relied on the close-ups on newspapers, notice boards, letters, and other printed materi-als to provide extra-narrative information to the story.[30]

In this cinema, spectators are encouraged to identify with the represented reality when the narrative structure is coherent and the diegesis is not challenged. In other words, the identity between the represented reality and the empirical reality is not pertinent to the spectators' identification with this cinema; instead, it is the internal logic of the representation itself that matters. The Chinese cine-matic realism, along the same line as traditional Chinese operas, presupposes a distance between the narrative reality and the empirical reality. It is not the con-flation between the representation and the reality that determines the degree of spectators' identification of cinema. Instead, it is the coherence and the solidarity of its narrativity and its emotion that authenticates the film as a realistic representation of the human's world. The use of film songs is most exemplary in demonstrating the cinema's presentation and manipulation of this cinematic order.

Film Songs

This left-wing cinema's emotional identification engenders a network of cinematic language, in which the use of film songs in the specific cultural context in 1930s' Shanghai illustrates most pertinently the particularity of this Chinese realism. As a major element to mark the transition from silent to sound cinema, song was extremely common and important in many early sound films across the world. It was also the first sound element introduced in Chinese cinema.[31] Many of the films of the Lianhua Film Company in the first half of the 1930s were silent movies with synchronized singing and sound effects.[32] And the discourse of music represented in these left-wing films was intimately connected to the contemporary music culture. But before we go on analyzing the relationship between songs and diegesis, let us first analyze this music culture and its relationship with the left-wing cinema.

The popular music in 1920s' Shanghai was still dominated by traditional operas, particularly the Peking Opera, which were performed live in theaters around the city. Western songs were restricted to the expatriate and elite culture, and almost all other popular Chinese ditties, like *Shiba mo* (Eighteen Caresses) and *Hong xiuxie* (Red Embroidered Shoes), belonged to the vulgar side filled with pornographic lyrics. However, entering the 1930s, the "sound" of Shanghai was changing rapidly, and popular songs in Western format and traditional folk songs with new styles of lyrics were taking up the major share of the new music culture. The popularity of radio gave rise to the rapid increase of the number of radio stations, which demanded a wider variety of music. Other performance industries also relied heavily on music. Hollywood's musicals were extremely popular and helped familiarize Chinese ears to Broadway music. The Westernized musical theater, particularly the troupes lead by Li Jinhui, was also gaining its momentum and threatened the domination of Peking Opera in the performance entertainment among the city dwellers.[33]

The new popular music also attracted the attentions of the new leftist intellectuals, who wrote progressive and patriotic lyrics to the popular tunes, developing a new genre of patriotic music in the 1930s. In fact, the left-wing cinema contributed substantially to the development of this new music culture. On the one hand, this new commodity form was clearly an accomplice of cinema in its commercial logic. The films and the film songs in partnership reinforced one another's rising symbolic positions in the new cosmopolitan culture, generating a new sensibility and logic of desire in this emerging urban identity. Combining the efforts of the film companies, the record companies (particularly Pathé Records), the radio stations, and the publication houses that anthologized the lyrics into film song collections, these film songs became the quintessential form of the new musical commodity. On the other hand, the left-wing filmmakers also relied heavily on the same form of Westernized songs to convey their patriotic messages, and most of these film songs spoke for and even embodied the propaganda apparatus. This dynamic was itself represented in many left-wing films, which condemned the new music culture associated with corruption and imperialism yet also relied on their own songs to criticize this music culture, attempting to develop a new sound, in addition to a new sight, to challenge the old order.

This musical tension is clearly observed in *New Year's Gift*. As I illustrated, the film is extremely episodic, in which the different unrelated stories are connected by the coin traveling around the different segments of society. However, the coherency of the film is also formally maintained by the interesting music discourse represented. As one of the earliest sound films in China, the film is rich in its aural display. There are different kinds of music and sounds featured, including Western music, popular tunes, traditional songs, and many other forms of sound. These sounds are all presented within their own specific social context, being fastened to the contemporary social reality. We hear the songs broadcasted from radio stations, the licentious music heard in dancing halls, laborers' working chants, hawkers' shouting one's wares, and even the bangs of firecrackers are clearly marked, producing a symphony of Shanghai's sound in addition to the different stories and characters featured. And this variety of sound is connected by three major women characters, who are all singers.

The granddaughter Rong'rong is a Chinese version of Shirley Temple, whose singing, dancing, and appearance are clear imitations of the Hollywood star. Rong'rong is the major anchor of the film, as the film begins with her and ends with her, and it also highlights her singing and dancing several times. In the first New Year's Eve dinner portrayed in the film, Rong'rong's cousin Jiang Xiuxia, who is an emerging star in Shanghai's entertainment circles, persuaded Rong'rong's grandfather to let her join their performance troupe. Under much reluctance, the grandfather finally accepts Jiang's and her boyfriend's proposal by allowing Rong'rong to sing on stage just once. Later in the film we see Rong'rong performing with Jiang, attracting tremendous admiration from the audience. While the story goes on depicting how Jiang's boyfriend betrays Jiang and her final deprivation as a prostitute, the film also introduces another singer Yang Lijuan, whose song "Wuxie zhige" (Song of the dance hall) is so famous that everyone in the city knows it by heart. The song is also featured several times in the film, each located in a different context: one time aired through the radio, another time sung by her with piano accompaniment, and another time she sings the song in a dance hall after being deserted by her banker lover. At the end of the film, when the song is once again heard in the second new year's eve dinner, the song is rewritten with patriotic lyrics and sung by a chorus of schoolchildren. As pointed out by Sue Tuohy: "This transformation of the lyrics and

the performance style of one song . . . creates a musical metaphor of the transformation of the characters' lives, the consciousness of the people, and the
country."[34] While Tuohy argues that the changes in the music refer to the transforming social conditions, something, however, stays unchanged, which is the
naivete and idealism represented by Rong'rong. Interestingly, like the coin,
Rong'rong also travels through the wide-spectrum of society. While the coin is
transformed into paper money at the end, Rong'rong just resists all contamination. Similarly, both embodying the contemporary popular musical discourse,
Cousin Jiang becomes depraved but Rong'rong stays pure. This parallelism represented the two opposite ways of the left-wing culture to understand popular
music. The modern entertainment culture was evil, but it was also justifying for
the left-wing cultural workers to use popular songs for the exalted political projects because there was something pure enough to resist corruption. When
Rong'rong at the end of the film sings this new "Jiuwang zhige" (Save the nation song) along with the radio program, our earlier anxiety of the girl being
contaminated by the new music culture is released, and her father coming back
to the second dinner is connected to the new future that has been projected.
Similar criticism and representation can be seen in many other left-wing films,
in which patriotic songs and corrupt Westernized music were dichotomized,
although both sets of music belonged to the same new city music culture.

Film songs are important to these left-wing films on several grounds.
Commercially, they help attract the attention of the viewers who were still fascinated by the media speaking for the first time and by the new Western sensibility incarnated in the new form of music. Yet politically, the films' social criticism and wish for change were also effectively put forward through the
manipulation of these songs, as the new music culture, like cinema itself, embodied both the manifestations of corruption and its rupture. In fact, music itself
is a great propaganda tool in terms of its direct emotional impact and availability.
But as I will illustrate below, film songs also served crucial structural functions
in this cinema that was greatly hindered by its loyalty to realism and diegesis.
The Chinese audience has long been accustomed to the free assertion of arias
breaking the continuity of a narrative in traditional Chinese operas, and film
songs also provide a space in the cinematic narrative that can be manipulated in
and out of the confinement of the diegesis.[35]

Voice was considered the element to attest the "presence-to-itself" of
cinema when sound was first introduced. According to Mary Ann Doane, the
unification of sound and image, particularly in the form of sync-sound, was essential in early talkies. "The addition of sound to the cinema introduces the possibility of representing a fuller (and organically unified) body, and of confirming
the status of speech as an individual property right. The potential number and
kinds of articulations between sound and image are reduced by the very name
attached to the new heterogeneous medium—the talkie."[36] The introduction of
sound in cinema, therefore, restricted the representation of human beings to the
rule of "presence-to-itself," as voice gives a more organically unified body to a

human being, and it discouraged other forms of less "full" representations. However, in the early sound stage of Chinese cinema, song, also in the form of human voice, is the only element that can elude not only the presence of the subject but also the entire umbrella of diegesis, which violates, as I argued in an earlier section, a rule of thumb in the cinema's granted narrative logic.

David Bordwell demonstrates that when historians come to the time when sound was introduced, either they consider it a regression to theater or they argue that sound moved cinema one more step closer to fulfilling the realistic nature of the medium.[37] However, few mention is made of how sound can interpret and expand the representation of the real. Although the dialectic montage theory impacted little on the visual of this Chinese left-wing cinema, these filmmakers tried out a different version of montage that combined different visual and audio elements together.[38] Different meanings can be generated by juxtaposing various sound tracks with the same image, or vice versa. Singing in the sound track, therefore, does not need to correspond to the actual performance in the image track. While most of the Hollywood musicals "ornamented" their singing sections simply by enriching the visual effects of its performance, e.g., displaying sexy girls and beautiful choreography, Chinese filmmakers in the 1930s freely inserted different visual elements to the singing so that new meanings were created through a marriage of the two originally unrelated texts. Not only are subjective feelings of the characters expressed, comments from the filmmakers are also presented.

For example, in *The Highway*, when Moli is singing the song *New Song of Fengyang* in the restaurant to the construction workers, documentary images showing battle scenes as well as the sufferings of the people are inserted into the film. Although untold by the film directly, these human sufferings are the underlying reasons that unite the workers to construct the roads. The singing of this song, therefore, creates a nondiegetic narrative space to introduce political messages, which are otherwise difficult to convey because of the censorship. *Street Angel* also uses similar tactics. When Xiao Hong is singing the *Siji ge* (Song of Four Seasons) to Xiao Chen, documentary images of war scenes are inserted in the singing. But unlike the earlier example, these images do not correspond to the lyrics: this *Song of Four Seasons* is about the yearning of a girl for her separated lover. Written by Tian Han, the famous left-wing playwright and screenwriter, the song tells a story about a girl leaving her family and looking for her lover. Although, superficially, the lyrics and the images are disconnected, reading them together creates a new hermeneutic space. Through the lyrics, the singer/narrator of the song only expresses her tormented feelings but does not explain the cause behind the sufferings; however, the accompaning images of war scenes suggest the connection between the girl's tragedy and the Japanese invasions. Most importantly, not only can this association be applied to the song's narrative, but it can also be connected to the life of Xiao Hong, who is singing the song now in the restaurant and is also featured in the images accompanying the song as the protagonist of the story. Xiao Hong and Xiao Yun are two sisters living with an older couple who forces the younger sister to be a singing girl and the older one a prostitute. But the film provides no explanation for why the two sisters (they might not even be biologically related) are being controlled by this couple. The images inserted in the singing implicitly connect the misfortunes of the two sisters to the Japanese invasions. Although the film does not offer any direct criticism of this foreign power, through subtle techniques, like the images of war scenes accompanying the song, the film conveys strong anti-Japanese statements, which were censored by the Chinese government then.[39]

According to Claudia Gorbman, nondiegetic inserts were more frequently employed in silent cinema than in sound films because the new talkies, which were considered as more "realist," saw these inserts as interrupting the flow of the diegesis.[40] However, the situation was different in China. Nondiegetic inserts were not commonly found in Chinese silent movies, as the function of the cinematic narrative was to present a plot clearly and logically, instead of to confuse the spectators about the linear development of the story. The famous writer and "Soft-cinema" critic Liu Na'ou complained in 1932 that most of the Chinese silent movies remained "photographic" instead of "filmic" because the function of camera was only to recapture actions and dialogues (through titles); cinematic language like editing, superimposition, and dissolves were seldom used in any sophisticated way.[41] But when song was introduced in cinema entering the sound age, Chinese cinema became more "cinematic." Extra-narrative elements finally found a way to break the domination of the diegesis. It is well understood in the culture that songs in its dramatic art serve as a springboard for the narrative to jump to a different horizon. The arrival of songs in this "photographic" cinema encouraged more expressive elements to be inserted in the Chinese cinema as the songs provide bridges to connect the diegesis and the nondiegesis, allowing pauses in the narration without alienating the audience's identification with the story.

In fact, before the shooting of *Street Angel*, the director Yuan Muzhi had been boldly experimenting with the use of music in cinema in *Scenes of City Life*. As a Chinese musical within the Chinese reality, *Scenes of City Life* is surprisingly unusual because its overtly unrealistic style is clearly Yuan Muzhi's attempt to parody the Hollywood musicals so popular among Chinese audiences in the 1930s. Instead of presenting robot-like beautiful blondes in sexy outfits dancing and singing in glamorous settings, the musical scenes in *Scenes of City Life* are performed by ordinary Shanghai people in ordinary Shanghai settings. For example, for the bird's-eye-view shots of geometric dancing so common in Hollywood musicals in the 1930s, this Chinese film replaces the angelic dancing boys and girls and the fantastic settings with some busy salesmen running on a stock exchange floor or a group of rickshaw boys fighting over a customer. The choreography in the Chinese film is also more mechanical and rigid, suggesting a capitalist way of estranged city life (figure 8.11). Lighting is harsh, and the accompanying music is usually more comical than euphonious. There are no lyrics in some of the songs, and we only hear wordless and inarticulate mutter-ings, which once again suggest a meaningless and absurd way of living.[42] In watching *Scenes of City Life* the spectators witness a group of miserable people greedy for money living ridiculously in the capitalist city of Shanghai.

Jane Feuer argues that most of the Hollywood musicals valorize the myth of entertainment through a double gesture: to demystify the production of enter-tainment by going behind the scenes in the theater or Hollywood, in order only to remystify the film and its musical which they set out to expose.[43] In the case of *Scenes of City Life*, however, the film stays mostly on the first level of de-mystifying the production of musicals but refuses to reify the film itself as another form of entertainment. The music is not pleasurable to the ears, neither is the dancing appealing. While in most of the Hollywood musicals "the use of theatrical audiences in the films provides a point of identification for audiences of the film,"[44] those spectators watching the one performance featured in *Scenes of City Life* are the story's protagonists who are going to experience the alienat-ed life in Shanghai themselves. If the narrative encourages the film spectators to identify with the audience portrayed in this scene, it is the suffering of the pro-tagonists instead of the pleasurable voyeuristic consumption that is featured. This identification, therefore, encourages the film's spectators to question rather than to devour uncritically the representations.

Unfortunately yet understandably, *Scenes of City Life* was not too enthusi-astically embraced by spectators at that time, and Yuan Muzhi shifted the direc-tion of his experimentation and made the extremely popular semimusical *Street Angel*. And *Scenes of City Life* also failed to invite further attempts at experi-menting with music more radically in the later Chinese cinema.[45] Although by today's standards this film could be held as a masterpiece in terms of its creativ-ity and insight, a major reason for its failure might be explained by the rather uncanny alienating effect it produced. Chinese audiences might have had a lot of difficulties appreciating the exaggerations, and the failure of this musical may also be explained by the accustomed perception of songs in Chinese dramatic arts, which is mostly expressionistic. However, if the songs are so deliberately manipulated as another pedagogical tool, they would immediately lose their ap-peals for the audience.

In fact, some of the political messages of *Scenes of City Life* conveyed through the representation of songs are rechanneled in the songs of *Street Angel*, if only in a more subtle and congenial way. As Yeh Yueh-yu points out, in the "Song of Four Seasons" sequence in *Street Angel*, which I just analyzed, the singing girl Xiao Hong shows little respect to and never looks at the audience when singing the song in the teahouse; she gives all her attention to braiding her hair (figure 8.12).[46] The reluctance of Xiao Hong to address the audience di-rectly challenges the forms of entertainment both in the film and of the film, criticizing the teahouse audience listening to Xiao Hong's performance and the audience watching this film at the same time. These two scenes can be seen as the film's questioning of the performance of song-singing as a popular cultural

practice; implicitly it further challenges cinema as a form of entertainment instead of as a pedagogical tool. But this criticism was presented in a much more
astute and sophisticated fashion in *Street Angel* than in the blunt and direct
challenge featured in *Scenes of City Life*, documenting the maturing art and craft
of both Yuan Muzhi the director and the entire left-wing film movement as a
whole.

Type Figures

After these detailed analyses of the stylistic renderings of Chinese left-wing
films, many readers may still have their major question unanswered, which is
likely to be their key point of interest in these films: should we read these films
as alternative classics to the canonized ones? In the introduction, I made it clear
that I consider these films more as interesting cultural products than as cinematic
masterpieces. If *The Birth of a Nation, Battleship Potemkin,* and *Metropolis* are
considered as great art because they introduced ground-breaking ways of cinematic representation and exerted immense impact on the later development of
cinema, these Chinese left-wing films might not have achieved similar tasks. In
fact, the aesthetic achievements of these films were clearly curtailed as the films
were often used as cultural political tools rather than as art itself. The movement
did witness different efforts to introduce new cinematic styles and practices, but
they were usually sporadic attempts that were not enthusiastically followed up
on or developed afterward. For example, Fei Mu's short film "Broken Dream in
the Women's Apartment" was the first, and perhaps the only, surreal-
ist/expressionist film produced in the early Chinese cinema.[47] It depicts the
dreams of two women, in which soldiers are fighting in battles and the two
women are assaulted by a devil-like man. This was another effort of Fei Mu to
produce anti-Japanese National Defense Cinema under the surveillance of the
GMD government. In order to avoid censorship, Fei Mu chose to rely on heavy
symbolism. But this symbolism was clearly an exception to the accepted practice because a lot of the symbols employed were not diegetic. It was clearly an
effort on the part of the director to introduce European avant-garde filmmaking
to the local cinema.

Both "Broken Dream in the Women's Apartment" and *Scenes of City Life*
were uncommon attempts of the left-wing filmmakers to experiment with the
style of filmmaking. Unfortunately, the nationalist urgency, i.e., the Japanese
military threat and the increasingly corrupt society, at that time prevented the
cinema from exploring further other alternative cinematic approaches. Artistically, the overemphasis on the social relevance can be seen as the weakest dimension of this cinema movement. By focusing too much on the political dimensions, many of these films discouraged new creative styles that could enrich
the hermeneutic possibilities of the text. And the collective urge of any national

discourse also sacrificed the complex psychological makeup of individuals in their characters. There were only a few exceptions, like "Broken Dream in the Women's Apartment" and *Scenes of City Life*, which were able to show us new modes of characterization.

The American cinema has strong reservations about type figures and often reads them negatively as stereotypes or shallow depictions. Jim Cook and Mike Lewington explain the situation this way:

> In our society, it is the novelistic character that is privileged over the type, for the obvious reason that our society privileges—at any rate, at the level of social rhetoric—the individual over the collective or the mass. For this reason, the majority of fictions that address themselves to general social issues tend nevertheless to end up telling the story of a particular individual, hence returning social issues to purely personal and psychological ones.[48]

While Hollywood's identification is grounded on spectators' encountering of a new experience, the identification we observed in this Chinese cinema is basically sympathetic and shared. The American practice presumes that personal experiences are differed one from another, yet the Chinese left-wing cinema concerns the fates of the individuals only when they are subjected to a larger collective fate. Therefore, novelistic characters have little significance to the Chinese filmmakers as they represent the reality of themselves instead of that of society.

There are abundant examples in this cinema movement showing the intimate and nonseparable relationship between characters and society. Almost no leading figures of the films can escape the control of the political reality to which he or she is either subjugated or subversive, with the obvious example of *The Highway*, which I illustrated in chapter 4. But there were still exceptions: one rare example can be found in *Song at Midnight*, an adaptation of *Phantom of the Opera*.[49] In the film, Song Danping was once a hero in the Republic revolution and later established a theatrical career by continuing to write and perform progressive plays after the Republic's triumph. Disfigured by a fire set by his enemy, he hides himself away from people, including his lover. At the end of the film, when he finally revenges and kills his enemy, he is also burnt by a fearful mob who are scared of his hideous face. At the verge of being burnt to death, he jumps to the sea not allowing the spectators to know his final fate.

Song Danping is quite an exceptional character in this cinema movement who evinces contradictory character traits; he is both a hero and a loser—a hero when he devotes his life to revolution, a loser when he is timid to confront himself (figure 8.13). He claims that he would sacrifice everything for his lover, but with his deformed face, he refuses to see her, although knowing clearly his reappearance is the only way to cure her mental illness. He has been a committed revolutionary and was celebrated as a political hero, but he would not allow

himself to be seen by anybody at the expense of his self-esteem. And most interestingly, almost all revolutionary messages delivered in the film are conveyed
on stage during various theatrical performances, hinting at an unpolitically correct equation between politics and fiction. But the ultimate death/disappearance
of this novelistic figure can be read as symbolic to the general ideological disposition of this cinema. Characters who represent not the social reality but their
own individualistic strengths and weaknesses were not allowed to survive in this
cinema of socialist realism: society is so clearly divided and demarcated on materialist grounds that no human psychological/emotional idiosyncrasies are rele-
vant.[50]

As a result, most of the heroes and heroines represented were type figures
who were relatively shallow and bland. However, this cinema's strong commitment to its sociopolitical reality was precisely the feature that distinguished itself from many other great early cinemas, providing us with one of the first
models in non-documentary political filmmaking. In this early Chinese cinema,
we discover that revolutionary concerns could be readily introduced to popular
cinema without alienating spectators' taste and habits in attending movies, and
that filmmakers' political interests and the spectators' expectations of cinema
could be intricately linked. In fact, this cinema's high emotional involvement
challenged the assumed dichotomy between emotion and intellect in the Western
tradition, which associates emotion with femininity and the body, assuming that
emotional identification would necessarily induce a critical loss on the part of
the spectator. If there is anything intrinsically valuable in this engaging realist
cinematic model in the larger context of world cinema, it is not its aesthetic
achievements in any transcendental term but the "differences" they provide that
merit our attention and celebration. But if we are not interested in circumscrib-
ing these specific Chinese cultural products within the transhistorical, transcultural standards already dominated by Western values and experience, I think it is
clear that the cinema movement can stand for itself in its own right.

Notes

1. Lin Niantong, "A Study of the Theories of Chinese Cinema in Their Relationship
to Classical Aesthetics," *Modern Chinese Literature* 1, no. 2 (Spring 1985): 185-200.
2. Lin Niantong, *Zhongguo dianying meixue* (Chinese cinema aesthetics) (Taipei:
Yunchen, 1991), 7-38. But one may argue that no cinema practice is not composed of
montage and single shot.
3. Catherine Yi-Yu Cho Woo, "The Chinese Montage: From Poetry and Painting to
the Silver Screen," *Perspectives on Chinese Cinema*, ed. Chris Berry (London: BFI,
1991), 21-29.
4. See, for example, Chen Xihe, "Zhongguo dianying meixue de zai renshi: ping
'Yingxi juben zuofa' " (Reevaluating Chinese film aesthetics: a review of "Manual of
shadowplay writing") *Zhongguo dianying lilun wen xuan* (Chinese Film Theory: An An-

thology), vol. 2 (Beijing: Wenhua yishu, 1992), 296. The article has been translated by Hou Jianping, Li Xiaohong, and Fan Yuan into English: "Shadowplay: Chinese Film Aesthetics and Their Philosophical and Cultural Fundamentals," in *Chinese Film Theory: A Guide to the New Era*, ed. George S. Semsel, Xia Hong, and Hou Jianping, (New York: Praeger, 1990), 192-204.

5. Julia Hallam with Margaret Marshment, *Realism and Popular Cinema* (Manchester: Manchester University Press, 2000), 24-61.

6. For detailed analyses of how modern Chinese literature used realism, see Marston Anderson's *The Limits of Realism: Chinese Fiction in the Revolutionary Period* (Berkeley, Calif.: University of California Press, 1990) and David Der-wei Wang's *Fictional Realism in 20ᵗʰ Century China: Mao Dun, Lao She, Shen Congwen* (New York: Columbia University Press, 1993).

7. *SB*, April 17, 1934.

8. David Bordwell, Janet Staiger, and Kristin Thompson, *The Classical Hollywood Cinema* (New York: Columbia University Press, 1985), 19.

9. Ma Ning, "The Textual and Critical Difference of Being Radical: Reconstructing Chinese Leftist Films of the 1930s," *Wide Angle* 11, no. 2 (1989): 29.

10. Sigfried Kracauer, *Theory of Film* (New York: Oxford University Press, 1960), 28.

11. See Bazin's *What is Cinema?* (Berkeley: University of California Press, 1972).

12. Paul Pickowicz, "Melodramatic Representation and the 'May Fourth' Tradition of Chinese Cinema," in *From May Fourth to June Fourth: Fiction and Film in Twentieth-Century China*, ed. Wang David Derwei and Ellen Widmer (Cambridge, Mass.: Harvard University Press, 1993), 301.

13. Pickowicz, "Melodramatic Representation," 302.

14. Pickowicz, "Melodramatic Representation," 304.

15. The Chinese translation of melodrama is *tongsu ju*, a term meaning "popular play" literally.

16. Dissanayake, "Introduction," in *Melodrama and Asian Cinema*, ed. Wimal Dissanayake (Cambridge: Cambridge University Press, 1993), 3-4.

17. Georg Lukács, *The Historical Novel* (Lincoln: The University of Nebraska Press, 1983), 285.

18. Peter Brooks, *The Melodramatic Imagination: Balzac, Henry James, Melodrama and the Modes of Excess* (New Haven, Conn.: Yale University Press, 1995), 9.

19. Peter Brooks, *The Melodramatic Imagination*, 15.

20. Colin MacCabe, *Tracking the Signifier, Theoretical Essays: Film, Linguistics, Literature* (Minneapolis: University of Minnesota Press, 1985), 39.

21. MacCabe, *Tracking the Signifier*, 39.

22. Plaks, "Towards a Critical Theory of Chinese Narrative," *Chinese Narrative: Critical and Theoretical Essays*, ed. Andrew H. Plaks (Princeton: Princeton University Press, 1977), 315.

23. Rolston, *Traditional Chinese Fiction and Fiction Commentary: Reading and Writing between the Lines* (Stanford, Calif.: Stanford University Press, 1997), 191-208.

24. The only exception, to my knowledge, was the famous two parts of *The Metamorphosing Girl*.

25. Tony Rayns, "An Introduction to the Aesthetics and Politics of Chinese Cinema," *On Film* no. 14 (1985): 28.

26. Xia Yan, *Dianying lunwenji* (Film writings) (Beijing: Zhongguo dianying, 1985), 137.

27. Ma Ning, "The Textual and Critical Difference of Being Radical: Reconstructing Chinese Leftist Films of the 1930s," 28, 31.

28. One could also argue that this traditional practice of happy ending for a tragic story is a means for the authoritative power to persuade the masses to accept the status quo.

29. See Jacques Aumont, *Montage Eisenstein*, trans. Lee Hildreth, Constance Penley, and Andrew Ross (Bloomington: Indiana University Press, 1987), 156-79.

30. They could also be seen as residues of the silent film practices, which can be seen in many early sound cinemas.

31. The first sound film in China was Mingxing's *Genü hong mudan* (The Singing Girl, Red Peony), directed by Zhang Shichuan in 1931. As its name suggests, the songs of the singing girl are the selling point of the film. The first Hollywood sound film was *The Jazz Singer*, directed by Alan Crosland in 1927, in which the songs of the singer Al Jolson were also the center of attention.

32. The use of film songs was an innovative marketing strategy of Lianhua. Only after the success of these tactics clearly seen did other film companies join.

33. For a more elaborate description of Shanghai's popular music culture in the 1920s and 1930s, see Andrew Jones, *Media Culture and Colonial Modernity in the Chinese Jazz Age* (Durham, N.C.: Duke University Press, 2001).

34. Sue Tuohy, "Metropolitan Sounds: Music in Chinese Films of the 1930s," in *Cinema and Urban Culture in Shanghai, 1922-1943*, ed. Yingjin Zhang (Stanford, Calif.: Stanford University Press, 1999), 218.

35. For a detailed discussion of the structural and expressive significance of arias in Peking Opera, see Rulan Chao Pian, "Aria Structural Patterns in the Peking Opera," in *Chinese and Japanese Music-Dramas*, ed. J. I. Crump and William P. Malm, Michigan Papers in Chinese no. 19, 1975 (Ann Arbor: The University of Michigan, 1975), 65-97. See also Elizabeth Wichman, *Listening to Theater: The Aural Dimension of Beijing Opera* (Honolulu: University of Hawaii Press, 1991), for the aural dimenions in Chinese operas as the "total theater."

36. Mary Ann Doane, "The Voice in the Cinema: The Articulation of Body and Space," in *Film Theory and Criticism: Introductory Readings*, ed. Leo Braudy and Marshall Cohen (New York: Oxford University Press, 1999), 364.

37. David Bordwell, *On the History of Film Style* (Cambridge, Mass.: Harvard University Press, 1997), 35-61.

38. The montage of sound also generates an important debate in the Soviet cinema circles in the late 1920s and early 1930s. But the montage between sound and image, to my knowledge, was not much discussed. See *The Film Factory: Russian and Soviet Cinema in Documents 1896-1939*, ed. Richard Taylor and Ian Christie (London: Routledge, 1988).

39. Another famous technique the film employed to convey anti-Japanese messages was the wordplay of the Chinese character *nan*, meaning difficulties and catastrophe, when the friends were attempting to title their photo. See Ma Ning, "The Textual and Critical Difference of Being Radical: Reconstructing Chinese Leftist Films of the 1930s," 27-28; and *ZDFS*, 444.

40. Claudia Gorbman, *Unheard Melodies: Narrative Film Music* (Bloomington: Indiana University Press, 1987), 32.

41. Na Ou (Liu Na'ou), "Yingpian yishu lun" (The Discussion of Film Art), *Dianying zhoubao* (Cinema weekly), (July, August, 1932). Rpt., *ZWD*, 489-97.

42. Tuohy suggests that we hear humming instead of real words of the songs because some of the lyrics were banned by the censors. Tuohy, "Metropolitan Sounds," 213. If this was really the case, the censors had in fact encouraged a more abstract form of criticism: wordlessness is sometimes symbolically more powerful than words.

43. Jane Feuer, "The Self-Reflexive Musical and the Myth of Entertainment" in *Film Genre Reader II*, ed. Barry Keith Grant (Austin: University of Texas Press, 1995), 441-55.

44. Feuer, "The Self-Reflexive Musical," 451.

45. Before *Scenes of City Night*, there were a couple of Chinese musicals being produced, like *Qiangwei zhi ge* (Song of the rose) directed by Yin Yiqiu and produced by Meihua Film Company in 1934, but these films are no longer available for us to study. According to the newspaper descriptions at that time, *Song of the Rose* was a production trying to imitate the Hollywood models, but it failed. *SB*, March 18, 1935.

46. Yeh Yueh-yu, "Singing Women in Classical Chinese Films: A Discourse of Sinification" (paper presented at Hong Kong Baptist University for the "Asian Cultures at Crossroads" conference, Hong Kong, Nov. 1998).

47. The short film is included in *Lianhua jiaoxiangqu* (Lianhua Symphony), which is composed of eight short stories directed by eight Lianhua directors.

48. Jim Cook and Mike Lewington, "The Role of Stereotypes," in *The Matter of Images: Essays on Representation*, ed. Richard Dyer (London: Routledge, 1993), 13.

49. Although being considered as left-wing, the film has attracted criticisms about the correctness of its ideology. For example, Cheng Jihua, Li Shaobai, and Xing Zuwen considered Song Danping as a petit bourgeoisie rather than a revolutionary. See *ZDFS*, 490-91.

50. Ma Xu Weibang's position in the left-wing cinema movement is ambivalent. Compared to other left-wing filmmakers, Ma Xu was more an auteur director. Chen Huiyang even describes his works as narcissistic. See Chen's *Mengying ji* (Collection of dreams and shadows) (Taipei: Yunchen wenhua, 1990), 25-40. But *Song at Midnight* also shows strong patriotic sentiments. We should note that Tian Han supervised the film's scriptwriting, which might contribute to the film's strong left-wing ideological slant. See *ZDFS*, 490. See also Yomi Braster, "Revolution and Revulsion: Ideology, Monstrosity, and Phantasmagoria in Ma-Xu Weibang's Film Song at Midnight" *Modern Chinese Literature and Culture* 12, no. 1 (Spring 2000): 81-114.

Figure 8.1.
The dream sequence in *Crossroads* where Zhiying is dressed like a Barbie doll and engages in a love affair with the aristocrat-looking Lao Zhao in a Western fairy-tale setting.

Figure 8.2.
The Sisters. The mother looking at Dabao and Taoge.

Figure 8.3.
Cut to her subjective view.

Figure 8.4.
Slowly dissolves to the childhood of Dabao and Taoge on the same spot.

Figure 8.5.
Dissolves back to the current time.

Figure 8.6.
Cut back to the smiling mother.

Figure 8.7.
The mother sitting by herself looking out of the dark room recollecting her past memories.

Figure 8.8.
Her subjective view of her seeing the closed door, but it is superimposed with the same door opened, introducing us to her memory of twenty years ago.

Figure 8.9.
Slowly dissolving to the past. We see her husband sneaking out of the room. Notice that the position of the camera is now outside the room.

Figure 8.10. She begged her husband to stay, but he refused and finally agreed to bring one of their daughters away with him.

Figure 8.11. The carefully orchestrated mise-en-scène in Scenes of *City Life.*

Figure 8.12. *Street Angel*. Xiao Hong braids her hair refusing to look at her customers when singing. Superimposed is the song's script, with a function probably similar to today's Karaoke to encourage spectators to sing along.

Figure 8.13. Clear light and dark juxtaposed in *Song at Midnight*. The one on the left is the defaced Song Danping.

Epilogue

Although China's left-wing cinema halted shortly after the beginning of the Sino-Japanese War, the year 1937 was not the end of this movement, as the scattered filmmakers gathered back in Shanghai after the war and resumed the second phase of this left-wing cinema. And most importantly, the impact of this 1930s' cinema was immensely felt in the later development of Chinese cinema. In this epilogue, I will continue to trace the influence of this cinema to its progeny, demonstrating the significance of these films not only within its specific cultural-political context but also in a larger historical framework. But the following analysis is bound to be incomplete. The purpose of this epilogue is not to provide a thorough follow-up on all the manifestations and influences of this left-wing cinema in and on later Chinese films but simply to highlight some of the more consistent and powerful components of this cinema by tracing the historical development of Chinese cinema.

The commercial filmmaking industry continued to bloom in Shanghai during the Orphan Island period (1937-41) and the subsequent Pacific War period (1942-45), but patriotic films were no longer produced because of the immediacy of the Japanese regime.[1] Left-wing filmmakers had to leave the city for other areas to continue their nationalist propaganda, usually through participating in troupe performance. After the eight years of wartime, another new wave of left-wing cinema was to establish in Shanghai again. The dispersed filmmakers gradually gathered back in this Chinese Hollywood and made some of the best known movies in Chinese history. These films witnessed and participated in the historical 1949 Revolution; they also represented the height of Chinese cinema before 1949.

But the films produced in this second phase of China's left-wing cinema movement were not the same as those made in the 1930s. As I illustrated in chapter 4, the left-wing films in the 1930s manifested a youthful and romantic spirit that desired war and glorified death. The upcoming eight-year Sino-

231

Japanese military confrontation completely destroyed such enchantment, speeding up the maturing process of this cinema by bringing the object of desire (war) directly to confront the ideology (nationalism). In order to reenact the patriotic call for revolution after the devastation of war, revolution itself must be presented through a different tactic. Emphasis was no longer on an idealized and romanticized future toward which people must be working toward at all costs; instead, it was the brutal reality people were going through everyday that was highlighted and, to a certain extent, exploited for propaganda purposes.

There were other social factors that distinguished the second phase of this left-wing cinema from the first one. First of all, left-wing films were no longer just made in Shanghai in the postwar period. Besides the commercial market, leftist filmmakers found other channels to screen their films and, therefore, formulate and package cinema. Because of the redistribution of the geopolitical powers after the war, three different locations—Shanghai, Hong Kong, and the "liberated areas" in the northern parts of China—could now produce and show pro-communist films. In the "liberated areas" particularly, film studios were directly owned by the CCP, and they could make propaganda films without relying on the distribution network of the commercial market, so other formats of cinema, like animation, documentary, or education films, could also be produced.

For these Shanghai filmmakers who continued to produce left-wing films in the commercial market, they now had to face a much more unfriendly social environment. As the CCP expanded its production line, the GMD government also took over film studios owned by the Japanese right after the war and made their own pro-government propaganda films. The GMD-CCP cinema confrontation had now shifted to the foreground, and film censorship was much tighter when compared to the prewar period. The national economy was also severely damaged in the eight-year resistance, and it continued to deteriorate rapidly after the war. Life was much more difficult, and inflation was extreme. As Ding Yaping documents, a film ticket in Nanjing in 1948 priced 600,000 Chinese dollars, a 1.2 million times increase compared to the ticket price just before the war.[2]

Therefore, we can expect the left-wing films produced after the war to be quite different from those of the 1930s. The new films became more militant, more sober, and less merry; they embraced the notion of history in its more immediate and prominent presence. The youthful spirit that characterized the films in the 1930s disappeared; the left-wing films in the 1940s were more solemn and contemplative at heart. Film songs were not used as often in the left-wing films in the 1940s, as they were more directly associated with the consumer culture and with outwardly commercial films alone. Romance became nothing but national allegory, and the cinema market was now in favor of epic films. Spectators no longer saw the playfulness and lofty ideals of young people as observed in *Crossroads*, *The Highway*, or *March of the Youth*. The youthful enthusiasm and ambiguities were displaced with political urgency and graveness. Realist representations were also more developed and emphasized. Many who started their filmmaking in the 1930s' left-wing cinema continued to make films in the 1940s, and some of the films they made represent the highest achievement of Chinese cinema before the Fifth Generation. Examples include *Baqianli lu yun he yue* (Eight Thousand Miles of Cloud and Moon), directed by Shi Dongshang in 1947, the two-part *Yijiang chunshui xiang dong liu* (A Spring River Running to the East), directed by Cai Chushang in 1947, *Wuya yu maque* (Crows and Sparrows), directed by Zheng Junli, who was and actor in the 1930s, in 1949, and the famous *Xiaocheng zhi chun* (Spring of a Small Town), directed by Fei Mu in 1949, which, however, was not considered progressive at the time.[3]

After the establishment of the People's Republic of China (PRC), the left-wing films made in the 1930s and 1940s became the embryo of the dominant cinematic form of the new communist State.[4] But 1949 also brought an end to the left-wing cinema which had dominated China's film market in the last two decades. The new PRC argued that when the state was transformed into a Socialist structure, the specific political function of this cinema was no longer necessary. But at least the Soviet Union would disagree with it: the strong promotion of didactic cinema by Lenin after the Bolshevik revolution is a clear example of the need for propaganda even within a "liberated" state. The most crucial reason for the forced discontinuation of this cinematic tradition was, ironically, the potentially mutinous power the movement could hold over the newly established order. While Shanghai posed a strong threat to the previous Nationalist government, this marginal modern culture could also exert similar challenges to the new Communist government. While Shanghai had been a revolutionary mecca for the left-wing intellectuals due to the city's openness to the exciting but insecure future, the ex-colony was also easily scapegoated as the source of moral impurity and ideological danger in the eyes of the newly established power. The pluralistic political/ideological environment in Shanghai before the Liberation forced the filmmakers to reflect constantly on their ideological stance, but their successors were no longer allowed to engage in similar self-reflection under the communist regime.

However, the 1950s were still basically a period of promise in China. In order to strengthen its political power, the ruling CCP wholeheartedly encouraged those cultural activities that supported its sovereignty. The left-wing cultural movement of the earlier two decades was also documented by the new State in a heroic fashion. The writing of Cheng Jihua's *The Development of Chinese Cinema* was one of the resulting political products under the full support of the government. The left-wing cinema movement was depicted as a glamorous golden age of Chinese cinema; the converging of Party leadership and intellectual participation was held as an example for the new generation to follow. Because the writing of *The Development of Chinese Cinema* was fully supported by the government at that time, the three writers were allowed easy access to all available films and documents. Despite the obvious ideological distortion, this work is still considered as the best Chinese film history for the pre-1949 period.

Many Shanghai left-wing filmmakers, like Xia Yan, Yuan Muzhi, and Cai Chusheng, were assigned top official positions in the new state machinery after the revolution; but their loyalty to the Party was soon thrown into question. The first attack directed at this filmmaking tradition can be traced to the nationwide criticism of Sun Yu's *Wu Xun zhuan* (The Story of Wu Xun) in 1951. Shortly after a warm welcome from both audiences and critics, the film suddenly received a fierce critique from Chairman Mao who published an article "*Yingdang zhongshi dianying Wu Xun zhuan de taolun*" (We should pay attention to the discussion of *Wu Xin zhuang*) denouncing the film as "fervently promoting feudal culture" and "introducing capitalist reactionary ideology to the revolutionary Communist Party."[5] Abruptly, critics all over the nation reversed their earlier comments and criticized the film as reflecting the residual Shanghai petit-bourgeois attitude of Western-trained intellectuals.[6] Although after this surge of criticism the Party continued to allow Sun Yu to make films, the creative freedom granted to filmmaking shrank, and the Party's trust of the filmmakers also declined. The national film center was moved from Shanghai to Beijing, where the central government could police the industry more conveniently and efficiently. Furthermore, films made in the 1930s were collected and institutionalized in Beijing so that their screenings could be completely controlled by the State.

There were altogether seven political purges directed by the CCP toward the Shanghai intellectuals since the Yan'an period.[7] The last one, which was also the biggest one, took place during the Cultural Revolution in the mid-1960s. Most people involved were physically and psychologically tormented under the numerous political power struggles. A systematic reproach to the left-wing Shanghai cinema also climaxed then, and many related filmmakers and critics were tortured on various pretexts. Even the three writers of *The Development of Chinese Cinema* could not escape the fierce criticisms, owing to their high acclaim for the Shanghai left-wing cinema in the book. A number of major figures of the cinema died and left no "honest" words recounting their past histories; important documents were also destroyed indiscriminately. Many believe that the tortures experienced by these filmmakers were partly the result of the personal interests of the wife of Chairman Mao, Jiang Qing. Lan Pin, the name Jiang Qing used in the 1930s, was an actress who actively participated in left-wing cinema and drama circles at that time (see plate 20). As many argue, trying to conceal this part of her life, not only did Jiang Qing destroy or institutionalize all related filmic and written documents, but she also tortured many people who knew about her private life in the 1930s.[8] This political tragedy greatly hampered any further efforts to honestly document the history of this cinema movement.

The downfall of the Gang of Four completely reversed the fate of this cinema movement and made the voices of the pre-1949 left-wing figures stronger than ever. In the early 1980s, the old left-wing filmmakers, critics, and performers, like Sun Yu, Wu Yonggang, Ling He, and Zhao Dan, were rehabilitated. As the recognized leader of the cinema movement and one of the film figures who had suffered the most in the Cultural Revolution, Xia Yan gained a tremendous amount of respect from academic and political circles starting in the 1980s. The elder was tokenized not only as the spokesperson for the film movement of the 1930s but also as the ultimate adviser for the entire Chinese cinema. The publication of *The Chinese Left-wing Cinema Movement* in 1993 can be seen as the Party's official recognition and reinstatement of the ideological and historical significance of this movement.

Unfortunately, many other significant filmmakers were not physically strong enough to wait for their fame reclaimed. Shen Xiling and Fei Mu died young: Shen Xiling died in 1940, and Fei Mu died shortly after the Liberation. The sufferings they may have otherwise encountered would be unimaginable if they had lived longer and stayed in the mainland. Cai Chusheng and Tian Han died on account of extreme political torture in 1968; Qian Xingcun and Zheng Boqi passed away right after seeing the end of the Cultural Revolution in 1977 and 1978. One can only wonder whether we should congratulate the two old comrades for witnessing the restoration of their political reputations, or whether we should wish that they had died ten years earlier in order to avoid political suffering.

Although these left-wing filmmakers no longer produced any important works after the Liberation, the practice and style they set up continued to influence the later generations of Chinese filmmakers. For example, a published lecture given by of Xia Yan in the Beijing Film Academy in the 1950s was the only guidebook for film writing available to Chinese film students for more than two decades.[9] The major concepts of this lecture, including utilitarianism, realism, and comprehensibility, were all essential ideas governing the production of Shanghai left-wing cinema in the 1930s; by this means, the concepts were effortlessly transmitted to the Third and the Fourth Generations of Chinese filmmakers.[10] Although Hollywood films were banned completely from China after 1949, many basic editing techniques and structural concepts common in the American practice continued to influence Chinese filmmaking in the 1950s and 1960s, mostly through the agency of this pre-1949 left-wing cinema.

The relationship between the Fifth Generation and the Shanghai cinema, or the Second Generation, is more ambiguous. One feature of the Fifth Generation, particularly evident in its earlier movies, is the distrust of the cinematic assumptions of its predecessors, both in ideology and style. Strong doubts are cast not only on the filmmakers' supposed uncritical loyalty to the Party's ideology but also to the filmmaking style created by it, specifically the realist and didactic approaches. For example, as the first film disclosing the emergence of the Fifth Generation, *Yige he bage* (One and Eight), directed by Zhang Junzhao in 1984, challenged the political authority partly through its attempted destruction of many established cinematic conventions.[11] Lighting, color, composition, camera position, editing, narrative structure, and the use of symbolism are all conceptualized from a perspective unseen in earlier Chinese movies. The practices established in the Shanghai left-wing cinema were finally challenged systematically half a century later. Although it might be a revision too long in coming, the power this belated venture evoked is evident to us all.[12]

However, although the Fifth Generation emphasizes depiction (*miaoshe*) more than narration (*xushi*), which is the opposite of the left-wing filmmakers in the 1930s, the *tour de force* behind the ideology of the two generations are similar. Some intrinsic mental dispositions of the Fifth Generation filmmakers are closely connected to their Shanghai precursors. The overwhelming sense of belonging to and responsibility for the nation is still the major ideological engine of this new generation of cinema. The nationalism which had burdened so many left-wing filmmakers in the 1930s continued to exert its power in the 1980s. The courage and dedication to challenge the status quo are common to both generations; their distaste for tradition and their yearning for a new era also obviously govern both the content and styles of the films of the two separate eras. In spite of their many obvious shortcomings, these ideological preoccupations also provide to the young filmmakers, both in the 1930s and in the 1980s, strength and vigor, making their films really stimulating.

While the political situation of the mainland and Taiwan prevented this Shanghai cinema from taking root in the sovereign land of the CCP and the GMD after 1949, the Hong Kong movie industry indeed inherited the most, directly and indirectly, from it. The relation between the cinemas of Hong Kong and Shanghai had been intimate since the 1920s. Li Minwei established the Minxin Film Company in the British colony in 1922, and the company moved north to Shanghai four years later. With the later establishment of Lianhua, Li Minwei became the major figure connecting the two regional cinemas in the 1920s and early 1930s. The Shao (Shaw) brothers of Tianyi also established a sister company, Nanyang, in Hong Kong in the early 1930s making Cantonese films specifically geared for the Southeast Asian market. The left-wing scriptwriter Su Yi also came to Hong Kong from Shanghai and began to participate in the making of local films in 1935. But the first large-scale influx of Shanghai filmmakers to the colony took place after the beginning of the Sino-Japanese war. This became the first wave of a filmmaking personnel migration from Shanghai to Hong Kong: in addition to a large number of famous talents like Hu Die, Li Lili, and Li Zhuozhuo, some major filmmakers of the left-wing cinema like Xia Yan, Cai Chusheng, Situ Huimin, Ouyang Yuqian, and Shen Xiling all joined in the migration to Hong Kong to continue their filmmaking during the war. Some of them attempted to escape from the war; others received special political tasks. For example, Xia Yan was instructed by Zhou Enlai to join the Hong Kong branch of the Party to continue to produce political films.[13] Most of the films the leftist filmmakers made during this period had strong anti-Japanese components, like the Cantonese *Xuejian baoshan cheng* (The Blood Spilt in the Treasure Mountain City) directed by Situ Huimin and the Mandarin *Gudao tiantang* (Heaven of the Orphan Island) directed by Cai Chusheng. Because a very large percentage of the Shanghai filmmakers and performers were ethnic Cantonese, their filmmaking careers in this colony were mostly smooth. And the films they made became some of the best and most important Chinese movies produced during that period.[14]

As I have mentioned, many of these filmmakers came back to Shanghai immediately after the war starting the second phase of the left-wing cinema movement. However, many of these left-wing filmmakers and performers returned to Hong Kong on the eve of the outbreak of the civil war in 1948 in the event that the CCP failed and needed a new cinema base to be set up in the South.[15] Between 1945 and 1949, numerous other filmmakers and stars also arrived in this city for various reasons. Some came to escape the accusation of treason, like Zhang Shankun; others found the colony a better place to stay and to make films, like Bu Wancang. A large number of them, particularly the more ideologically committed ones like Xia Yan, Cai Chusheng, and Yang Hansheng, went back to the mainland after the CCP victory; others, like Bu Wancang and Zhu Shilin, stayed in the colony and contributed to the development of the local cinema.

Like the post-1949 mainland cinema, the development of Hong Kong cinema is so complicated that this brief account can by no means summarize it all. But to our interest it is important to point out some of the parallel strategies that were utilized by the left-wing filmmakers/critics in Shanghai in the early 1930s and in Hong Kong during the 1940s. After coming to Hong Kong, the left-wing critics first took up newspaper columns and, later, editorial positions to control information distribution of cinema.[16] A "Cleaning-up of the Cantonese Cinema Movement" was also launched by these Shanghai left-wing filmmakers two times; in 1938 and in 1949. They condemned the contemporary Cantonese cinema as commercial poison spreading evil messages to its audience. Headed by Cai Chusheng, the 1949 movement was so influential that it attracted the participation of more than one hundred film workers; and many of the best Cantonese films made in the 1950s can be seen as direct or indirect products of this movement. The Shanghai intellectual filmmaking of the early 1930s appeared to repeat itself in Hong Kong a decade and a half later.

The most prominent heritage the later Hong Kong Cantonese cinema received from the Shanghai predecessors was, interestingly, not their revolutionary ideology but their didactic collectivist ethics. Although there was a clear left-wing branch in Hong Kong cinema in the 1950s,[17] the socialist commitment shown in their left-wing films were certainly not as strong as that in the Shanghai cinema twenty years before. After all, the political and social environments in the two lands and periods were so different that an exact copy of the left-wing movement in Hong Kong was impossible. But a similar emphasis on realism and collectivism in the two cinemas is evident. As Stephen Teo comments, "the leftist line in Cantonese filmmaking was not a hard ideological one. While they were not neutral, many of its actors and directors could hardly be considered true communist believers. Their cinema was oriented more towards social themes and issues, veering away from ideology while remaining tainted by a didactic intent, which meant that the attempt to relate to common people usually came across as genuine and sincere."[18]

Yet many Shanghai leftist filmmakers who decided to stay in Hong Kong gave up their political enthusiasm altogether and started to make entertainment films only. These Shanghai filmmakers brought their Westernized lifestyles and ideas to Hong Kong cinema. Despite being a British colony, Hong Kong's modernization and Westernization were far behind what Shanghai had achieved at that time. Through their films, the Shanghai filmmakers presented to the Hong Kong audience a new way of living. This is most apparent in the comparison between the Mandarin films, which were mostly made by Shanghai immigrants, and the Cantonese films in the 1950s.[19] The Mandarin films were usually more open minded to new objects and ideas; their settings, costumes, and ideology were often more Westernized when compared to those presented in the Cantonese films.[20] In fact, both the two major groups were indebted to the pre-1949 Shanghai's left-wing cinema, but the Mandarin films inherited the cosmopolitan outlook while the Cantonese films remain socially committed. These two branches developed in Hong Kong cinema indirectly reveal the major conflicts of the Shanghai root, which is, as I have mentioned many times in the previous pages, as commercial as political, as cosmopolitan as parochial. The Cantonese didactic melodramatic tradition gradually died out in the late 1960s when the capitalist ways of living prevailed. The thereafter development of Hong Kong cinema inherited the most from the Shanghai filmmakers this general milieu of Westernization, which, probably, will define the future development of Chinese cinema as a whole.

Notes

1. For the cinema in these two periods, see Poshek Fu's *Passivity, Resistance, and Collaboration: Intellectual Choices in Occupied Shanghai, 1937-1945*, (Stanford, Calif.: Stanford University Press, 1993).

2. Ding Yaping, *Yingxiang Zhongguo, Zhongguo dianying yishu: 1945-1949* (Imaging China, Chinese film art: 1945-1949) (Beijing: Wenhua yishu, 1998), 45.

3. For more information and analysis of the second phase of this left-wing cinema movement, see Ding Yaping's *Xingxiang Zhongguo, Zhongguo dianying yishu*.

4. For a more detailed account of the history of Chinese cinema between 1949 and 1986, read Paul Clark's *Chinese Cinema: Culture and Politics since 1949* (Cambridge: Cambridge University Press, 1987).

5. *Renmin Ribao* (The people's daily), May 20, 1951.

6. See Sun Yu, *Dalu zhi ge* (Song of the big road) (Taipei: Yuanliu, 1990), 179-202.

7. Li Mu, *Sanshi niandai wenyi lun* (Arts and literature in the thirties) (Taipei: Limin Wenhua, 1977), 267-280.

8. These are all hearsay accounts that I have not substantiated. But Jiang Qing's personal involvement in the torture of the filmmakers and dramatists is a general belief shared by many. Being unable to provide supporting or disproving materials, I would

only like to stress here that it is almost too easy to find a scapegoat, particularly a wicked woman, to explain the many events in a large history which might bear no direct relation to each other.

9. It is anthologized in Xia Yan's *Dianying lunwen ji* (Film writings) (Beijing: Zhongguo dianying, 1995), 93-181.

10. Chinese filmmakers are generally classified into six generations. The First Generation refers to the early filmmakers who first started the Chinese film industry in the beginning of the twentieth century, like Zheng Zhengqiu and Zhang Shichuan, who learned the art through practicing. Most of the filmmakers we have discussed in this study are considered as the Second Generation. The filmmakers in the Third Generation, like Xie Jin, Shui Hua, and Ling Zhifeng, were trained and began their careers right after the Liberation and became particularly prominent in the Hundred Flowers period (1956-57). The Cultural Revolution separated these filmmakers from the following Fourth Generation filmmakers, who were trained in the 1960s and began their careers not until the early 1980s when the cinema industry began to resume normal functioning. Representatives include Wu Tianming, Wang Jiangzhong, and Wang Shuqin. The Fifth Generation, which is well-known to the world, are mostly 1982 graduates of the Beijing Film Institute, like Chen Kaige, Tian Zhuangzhuang, and Zhang Yimou, who started to gain international reputations in the late 1980s. The Sixth Generation refers to the young filmmakers in the 1990s who first attempted independent filmmaking autonomous from the Party's control.

11. For a general discussion of the film, see Ma Ning, "Notes on the New Filmmakers," *Chinese Film: The State of the Art in the People's Republic*, ed. George Stephen Semsel (New York: Praeger, 1987), 73-77.

12. There are a number of recent studies done in English about the Fifth Generation of Chinese filmmakers. Examples include Shelia Cornelius' *New Chinese Cinema: Challenging Representation* (London: Wallflower Press, 2002); Jerome Silbergeld's *China into Film: Frames of Reference in Contemporary Chinese Cinema* (London: Reaktion Books, 2000); Zhang Xudong's *Chinese Modernism in the Era of Reforms: Cultural Fever, Avant-garde Fiction, and the New Chinese Cinema* (Durham, N.C.: Duke University Press, 1997); Rey Chow's *Primitive Passions* (New York: Columbia University Press, 1995); Nick Browne, Paul Pickowicz, Vivian Sobchack, and Esther Yau, eds. *New Chinese Cinemas: Forms, Identities, Politics,* (Cambridge: Cambridge University Press, 1994); Chris Berry ed. *Perspectives on Chinese Cinema* (London: BFI, 1991); and George Stephen Semsel, *Chinese Film: The State of the Art in the People's Republic* (New York : Praeger, 1987).

13. Tan Chunfa, "The Influx of Shanghai Filmmakers into Hong Kong and Hong Kong Cinema," in *Cinema of Two Cities: Hong Kong—Shanghai*, ed. Law Kar (Hong Kong: Urban Council, 1994), 76.

14. For reference to the history of early Hong Kong cinema, see Yu Muyun, *Xianggong diaying shihua* (The chronicle of Hong Kong cinema), vols. 1-3. (Hong Kong: Ciwenhua tang, 1996) 1997.

15. Law Kar, "Introduction," in *Cinema of Two Cities: Hong Kong—Shanghai*, ed. Law Kar, 8.

16. For the specific writers and newspapers involved, read Tan Chunfa, "The Influx of Shanghai Filmmakers into Hong Kong Cinema," 79.

17. Law Kar, "The Shadow of Tradition and the Left-Right Struggle," in *The China Factor in Hong Kong Cinema*, ed. Law Kar (Hong Kong: Urban Council, 1990), 14.

18. Stephen Teo, *Hong Kong Cinema: The Extra Dimensions* (London: BFI, 1997), 45.

19. Luo Mingyou, however, is one of the few Shanghai filmmakers who produced Cantonese movies in Hong Kong after the war. He established a Minghua Film Company with Jin Qingyu in 1950.

20. For details, read *A Comparative Study of Post-War Mandarin and Cantonese Cinema: The Films of Zhu Shilin, Qin Jian and Other Directors*, ed. Shu Kei (Hong Kong: Urban Council, 1983).

Appendix I

Chinese Left-wing Movies of the 1930s

The following seventy-four films are included in the left-wing movies list in *The Chinese Left-wing Cinema Movement*. Films marked with "*" are the ones still available. All the others, according to China Film Archive, are either lost or waiting to be restored.

Mingxing Film Company

Kuangliu (Torrent), 1933. Dir: Cheng Bugao.
*Chuncan (Spring Silkworms), 1933. Dir: Cheng Bugao.
Nüxing de nahan (Women's Outcry), 1933. Dir: Shen Xiling.
**Shanghai ershisi xiaoshi* (Twenty-four Hours in Shanghai), 1933. Dir: Shen Xiling.
*Zhifen shichang (Cosmetics Market), 1933. Dir: Zhang Shichuan.
Qiancheng (The Future), 1933. Dir: Zhang Shichuan.
Tieban hong lei lu (Iron Plate and Red Tears), 1933. Dir: Hong Shen.
Yan chao (Salt Tide), 1933. Dir: Xu Xinfu.
Shidaide ernü (Sons and Daughters of the Times), 1933. Dir: Li Pingqian.
Fengnian (Good Harvest), 1933. Dir: Li Pianqian.
Xiangcao meiren (Sweetgrass Beauty), 1933. Dir: Chen Kengran.
Yabi (Oppression), 1933. Dir: Gao Lihen.
*Zimei hua (The Sisters), 1934. Dir: Zheng Zhengqiu.
Tong chou (Shared Hate), 1934. Dir: Cheng Bugao.
Dao xibei qu (To the Northwest), 1934. Dir: Cheng Bugao.
**Nü'er jing* (The Classic for Girls), 1934. Dir: Zhang Shichuan, Cheng Bugao, Shen Xiling, Yao Sufeng, Zheng Zhengqiu, Xu Xinfu, Li Pingqian, and Chen Kengran.
Xiang chou (Country Worries), 1934. Dir: Shen Xiling.

241

Huashan yanshi (Colorful Story of Huashan), 1934. Dir: Cheng Bugao.
Rexue zhonghun (Ardent, Loyal Souls), 1935. Dir: Zhang Shichuan, Xu Xinfu,
 Zheng Zhengqiu, Wu Cun, Cheng Bugao, Shen Xiling, and Li Pingqian.
Jiehou taohua (Plundered Peach Blossom), 1935. Dir: Zhang Shichuan.
*Chuanjia nü (The Boatman's Daughter), 1935. Dir: Shen Xiling.
*Xin jiu Shanghai (Old and New Shanghai), 1936. Dir: Cheng Bugao.
Haitang hong (The Crabapple is Red), 1936. Dir: Zhang Shichuan.
Xiao Lingzi (Little Lingzi), 1936. Dir: Cheng Bugao.
*Shengsi tongxin (Unchanged Heart in Life and Death), 1936. Dir: Ying Yunwei.
Qingming shijie (At the Qingming Festival), 1936. Dir: Ouyang Yuqian.
*Yasuiqian (The New Year's Gift), 1937. Dir: Zhang Shichuan.
*Shizi jietou (Crossroads), 1937. Dir: Shen Xiling.
*Shehuizhi hua (Flower of Society), 1937. Dir: Zhang Shichuan.
*Malu tianshi (Street Angel), 1937. Dir: Yuan Muzhi.
Yeben (Night Run), 1937. Dir: Cheng Bugao.

Lianhua Film Company

Sange modeng de nüxing (Three Modern Women), 1932. Dir: Bu Wancang.
Chengshi zhi ye (City Nights), 1932. Dir: Fei Mu.
Tianming (Daybreak), 1933. Dir: Sun Yu.
*Duhui de zaochen (Early Morning in the Metropolis), 1933. Dir: Cai Chusheng.
*Muxing zhi guang (Maternal Radiance), 1933. Dir: Bu Wancang.
Feng (The Wind), 1933. Dir: Wu Cun.
*Xiao wan'er (Little Toys), 1934. Dir: Sun Yu.
*Yuguang qu (The Fisherman's Song), 1934. Dir: Cai Chusheng.
*Shennü (The Goddess), 1934. Dir: Wu Yonggang.
*Xin nüxing (New Woman), 1934. Dir: Cai Chusheng.
*Dalu (The Highway), 1935. Dir: Sun Yu.
*Mitu de gaoyang (Lost Lambs), 1936. Dir: Cai Chusheng.
*Langshan diexue ji (Bloodbath on Wolf Mountain), 1936. Dir: Fei Mu.
*Lianhua jiaoxiangqu (Lianhua Symphony), 1937. Dir: Situ Huimin, Fei Mu,
 Tan Youliu, Shen Fu, He Mengfu, Sun Yu, and Cai Chusheng.
Tianzuo zhi he (Heaven-made Unity), 1937. Dir: Shen Fu.
*Yaoqianshu (The Money Tree), 1937. Dir: Tan Youliu.
*Wang laowu (Fifth Brother Wang), 1937. Dir: Cai Chusheng.
Dujinde cheng (Gilded City), 1937. Dir: Fei Mu.

Diantong Film Company

Taoli jie (Plunder of Peach and Plum), 1934. Dir: Ying Yunwei.
Fengyun ernü (Sons and Daughters of the Storm), 1935. Dir: Xu Xingzhi.
Ziyoushen (Spirit of Freedom), 1935. Dir: Situ Huimin.
Dushi fengguang (Scenes of City Life), 1935. Dir: Yuan Muzhi.

Xinhua Film Company

Taowang (Runaway), 1935. Dir: Yue Feng.
Xin taohua shan (The New Peach Blossom Fan), 1935. Dir: Ouyang Yuqian.
Kuanghuan zhi ye (Nights of Revelry), 1936. Dir: Shi Dongshan.
Zhuang zhi ling yun (Soaring Aspirations), 1936. Dir: Wu Yonggang.
Yeban gesheng (Song at Midnight), 1937. Dir: Ma Xu Weibang.
Qingnian jinxinqu (March of Youth), 1937. Dir: Shi Dongshang.

Yihua Film Company

Minzu shengcun (National Existence), 1933. Dir: Tian Han.
Zhongguohaide nuchao (Angry Tide in China's Seas), 1933. Dir: Yue Feng.
Roubo (Hand-to-hand Fighting), 1933. Dir: Hu Tu.
Lieyan (Raging Flames), 1933. Dir: Hu Rui.
Huangjin shidai (Golden Age), 1934. Dir: Bu Wancang.
Taowang (Runaway), 1935. Dir: Yue Feng.
Sheng zhi aige (Elegy of Life), 1935. Dir: Hu Rui.
Ren zhi chu (Men at Their Birth), 1935. Dir: Shi Dongshan.
Shishi yingxiong (Hero of the Times), 1935. Dir: Ying Yunwei.
Kaige (Song of Triumph), 1935. Dir: Bu Wancang.

Tianyi Film Company

Zhengzha (Struggling), 1933. Dir: Qiu Qixiang.
Feixu (Flying Catkins), 1933. Dir: Shao Zuiweng and Tang Xiaodan.
Piaoling (Wandering), 1933. Dir: Tang Xiaodan.
Haizang (Burial at Sea), 1935. Dir: Wang Bin.

Xibei Film Company of Taiyuan

Wuxian shengya (Career Without Limits), 1935. Dir: Shi Qipu.

Yiji Film Company

Chenxi (First Rays of the Morning Sun), 1933. Dir: Wu Wenchao.

Appendix II

Chinese Films with the Longest First-Run Screening Periods in Shanghai,

January 1932 to July 1937

English Name	Director	Company	Period	Theater[a]	Days	Total
*The Fishermen's Song	Cai Chusheng	Lianhua	6/14-9/5/34	Jincheng	84	84
*The Sisters	Zheng Zhengqiu	Mingxing	2/13-4/14/34	Xinguang	60	60
Orchid in the Empty Valley	Zhang Shichuan	Mingxing	2/2-3/15/35	Xinguang	42	42
Reborn Flower	Zheng Zhengqiu	Mingxing	12/15-2/2/35	Xinguang	38	38
*Song at Midnight	Ma Xu Weiban	Xinhua	2/19-3/25/37	Jincheng	35	35
Beheading in the Hall of Classics	Zhou Yihua, Fei Mu	Lianhua	6/11-7/15/37	Xinguang	35	35
The Metamorphosing Girl II	Feng Peilin	Yihua	1/1-1/14/37	Ka'erdeng	14	34
			1/22-2/10/37	Xinguang	20	
Song of China	Fei Mu	Lianhua	12/11-12/12/35	Daguangming	2	32
			12/13/35-1/11/36	Ka'erdeng	30	
Spring Dreams of the Land of Peach Blossoms	Yang Xiaozhong	Xinhua	7/11-8/11/36	Jincheng	32	32
The Guangling Tide	Chen Kengran	Yihua	12/3-12/18/36	Xinguang	16	31
			12/3-12/17/36	Ka'erdeng	15	
Back to Nature	Sun Yu	Lianhua	9/24-10/7/36	Xinguang	14	28
			9/24-10/7/36	Ka'erdeng	14	
*The Classic for Girls	Zhang Shichuan	Mingxing	10/9-11/3/34	Xinguang	26	26
*Bloodbath on Wolf Mountain	Fei Mu	Lianhua	11/20-12/2/36	Xinguang	13	26
			11/20-12/2/36	Ka'erdeng	13	
*City Nights	Fei Mu	Lianhua	3/8-3/21/33	Beijing	14	22
			3/8-3/15/33	Guanghua	8	
100 Treasures Picture	Yue Feng	Yihua	11/6-11/13/36	Xinguang	8	22
			11/6-11/19/36	Ka'erdeng	14	
*New Peach Blossom Fan	Ouyan Yuqian	Xinhua	9/12-10/2/35	Xinguang	21	21
*Lost Lambs	Cai Chusheng	Lianhua	8/15-9/4/36	Jincheng	21	21

Continued on next page

Appendix II—Continued

English Name	Director	Company	Period	Theater[a]	Days	Total
*Little Sisters	Xu Suling	Yihua	10/8-10/20/36	Ka'erdeng	13	21
			10/8-10/15/36	Xinguang	8	
Chaste Woman of the Lonely Town	Zhu Shilin	Lianhua	12/18/36-1/7/37	Xinguang	21	21
Song of a Loving Mother	Zhu Shilin	Lianhua	3/26-4/14/37	Jincheng	21	21
*Maternal Radiance	Bu Wancang	Lianhua	8/6-8/12/33	Nanjing	7	20
			9/1-9/13/33	Beijing	13	
*New Woman	Cai Chusheng	Lianhua	2/2-2/21/35	Jincheng	20	20
National Style	Fei Mu, Luo Mingyou	Lianhua	5/4-5/23/35	Jincheng	20	20
The Elastic Girl	Chen Kengran	Yihua	3/27-4/14/37	Xinguang	20	20
*Flower of Society	Zhang Shichuan	Mingxing	6/6-6/24/37	Jincheng	19	19
*Early Morning in the Metropolis	Cai Chusheng	Lianhua	3/22-4/18/33	Beijing	18	18
Song of Everlasting Sorrow	Shi Dongshan	Xinhua	2/8-2/25/36	Ka'erdeng	18	18
*The Highway	Sun Yu	Lianhua	1/1-1/17/35	Jincheng	17	17
The Wedding Night	Yue Feng	Yihua	1/23-2/1/36	Ka'erdeng	10	17
			2/28-3/6/36	Ka'erdeng	7	
Secret Code	Huang Tianzuo	Zhongyang	4/18-4/21/37	Daguangming	4	17
			5/1-5/13/37	Xinguang	13	
Night Fragrance	Cheng Bugao	Mingxing	10/3-10/18/35	Xinguang	16	16
*Scenes of City Life	Yuan Muzhi	Diantong	10/9-10/24/35	Jincheng	16	16
*Plundered Peach Blossom	Zhang Shichuan	Mingxing	1/22-2/6/36	Jincheng	16	16
Woman's Rights	Zhang Shichuan	Mingxing	9/23-10/8/36	Jincheng	16	16
Spring Comes to the World	Sun Yu	Lianhua	2/11-2/24/37	Ka'erdeng	14	16
			3/9-3/10/37	Ka'erdeng	2	
*Crossroads	Shen Xiling	Lianhua	4/15-4/30/37	Jincheng	16	16
Lost Pearl in the Crowd	Zhu Shilin	Lianhua	4/15-4/30/37	Xinguang	16	16
*Three Modern Women	Bu Wancang	Lianhua	12/29/32-1/7/33	Beijing	10	15
			12/29/32-1/7/33 #	Shanghai	5	
*Soaring Aspirations	Wu Yonggang	Lianhua	12/31/36-1/14/37	Jincheng	15	15
*Lianhua Symphony	various	Lianhua	1/7-1/21/37	Xinguang	15	15
Mysterious Flower	Yue Feng	Yihua	5/13-5/27/37	Xinguang	15	15
An Immortal in the World of Men	Dan Duyu	Yihua	10/13-10/26/34	Jincheng	14	14

Continued on next page

Appendix II—Continued

English Name	Director	Company	Period	Theater[a]	Days	Total
*Ardent, Loyal Souls	Zhang Shichuan	Mingxing	6/5-6/18/35	Xinguang	14	14
Beacon for the Autumn Fan	Tan Youliu	Lianhua	7/5-7/18/35	Jincheng	14	14
The Jadeite Horse	Xu Xinfu	Mingxing	11/8-11/21/35	Jincheng	14	14
*The Boatman's Daughter	Shen Xiling	Mingxing	11/29-12/11/35	Jincheng	14	14
The Metamorphosing Girl	Feng Peilin	Yihua	6/6-6/19/36	Jincheng	14	14
Lively as a Dragon and Tiger	Xu Xinfu	Mingxing	5/14-5/27/37	Jincheng	14	14
*March of Youth	Shi Dongshan	Xinhua	7/10-7/23/37	Jincheng	14	14
Goddess of Wealth	Wu Chuan	Yihua	7/16-7/29/37	Xinguang	14	14
A Sea of Fragrant Snow	Fei Mu	Lianhua	9/30-10/12/34	Jincheng	13	13
*Men at Their Birth	Shi Dongshan	Yihua	6/7-6/19/35	Jincheng	13	13
*Old and New Shanghai	Cheng Bugao	Mingxing	5/1-5/13/36	Jincheng	13	13
Happiness at the Threshold	Yue Feng	Yihua	10/24-11/5/36	Xinguang	13	13
*Heaven-Made Unity	Shen Fu	Lianhua	2/24-3/8/37	Xinguang	13	13
Life	Fei Mu	Lianhua	2/1-2/12/34	Jincheng	12	12
Lady Pear Blossom	Wang Junda	Yucheng	9/19-10/1/35	Jincheng	12	12
*The Crabapple is Red	Zhang Shichuan	Mingxing	9/5-9/16/35	Xinguang	12	12
*Nights of Revelry	Shi Dongshan	Xinhua	9/9-9/20/36	Jincheng	12	12
*Unchanged Heart in Life and Death	Ying Yunwei	Mingxing	11/29-12/10/36	Jincheng	12	12

Note: This list is compiled based on the film advertisements in *Shanghai Daily* during this period. This list should not be considered as a completely accurate reflection of the films' popularity because the attendance of each screening might vary from the others to a large extent. Also, I only count the first-run screening periods of the films, and the length of subsequent screenings might be disproportional, although rarely, to their first-run records. The films made in 1935 to 1936 tended to have longer screening periods; it might owe less to their high attendance than a shortage of film supplies. It was a period of recession in the film industry, and many film companies underwent reorganization and cut down productions; the theaters might have been forced to extend the screening periods of the films regardless of their popularity. Without any historical data of the real box office records, this list can only be used as a reference.

a   Each theater has a different capacity: Beijing, 800 seats; Daguangming, 1986 seats; Jincheng, 1786 seats; Nanjing, 1450 seats; Xinguang, 1186 seats. *Source (for theater capacity):* Hu Peng's *Wo yu Huang Feihong* (Me and Huang Feihong) (Hong Kong: Sanhe, 1995), 46; and *Diantong banyuekan* (Denton gazette) 1 (May 1935), n. p.

*   The films marked with this sign are among the seventy-four left-wing movies accredited in *The Chinese Left-wing Cinema Movement.*

I am not able to confirm the closing day of *Three Modern Women* at Shanghai Theater because of the New Year Holiday. It should be between January 2 to January 6.

Bibliography and Filmography

Note: Abbreviations used in the "Bibliography and Filmography" section appear on pages xiii and xiv of the "Translations and Abbreviations" section.

Books and Articles

Adorno, Theodor W. *The Culture Industry*. New York: Routledge, 1991.

Allen, Joseph. *In the Voice of Others: Chinese Music Bureau Poetry*. Ann Arbor: Center for Chinese Studies, University of Michigan, 1992.

Altman, Rick. "Semantic/Syntactic Approach to Film Genre." In *Film Genre Reader II*. Edited by Barry Keith Grant, 26-40. Austin: University of Texas Press, 1995.

Anderson, Marston. *The Limits of Realism: Chinese Fiction in the Revolutionary Period*. Berkeley, Calif.: University of California Press, 1990.

Aumont, Jacques. *Montage Eisenstein*. Translated by Lee Hildreth, Constance Penley, and Andrew Ross. Bloomington: Indiana University Press, 1987.

Barlow, Tani. "Theorizing Woman: Funü, Guojia, Jiating." In *Body, Subject and Power in China*. Edited by Angela Zito and Tani Barlow, 253-289. Chicago: The University of Chicago Press, 1994.

Bazin, André. *What is Cinema?* Translated by Hugh Gray. 2 vol. Berkeley: University of California Press, 1972.

Benjamin, Walter. "The Work of Art in the Age of Mechanical Reproduction." In *Illuminations*, 217-51. New York: Schocken Books, 1968.

Berry, Chris. "The Sublimative Text: Sex and Revolution in *Big Road*." *East West Film Journal* 2, no. 2 (June 1988): 66-85.

———. "Chinese Left Cinema in the 1930s: Poisonous Weeds or National Treasures." *Jump Cut* 34 (1989): 87-94.

———, ed. *Perspectives on Chinese Cinema*. London: BFI, 1991.

249

Bordwell, David. "Contemporary Film Studies and the Vicissitudes of Grand-Theory." In *Post-Theory: Reconstructing Film Studies*. Edited by David Bordwell and Noël Carroll, 3-36. Madison: The University of Wisconsin Press, 1996.

———. *On the History of Film Style*. Cambridge, Mass.: Harvard University Press, 1997.

———. "Transcultural Spaces: Toward a Poetics of Chinese Cinema." *Post Script* 20, nos. 2/3 (Winter/Summer 2001): 9-23.

Bordwell, David, Janet Staiger, and Kristin Thompson. *The Classical Hollywood Cinema*. New York: Columbia University Press, 1985.

Braster, Yomi. "Shanghai's Economy of the Spectacle: The Shanghai Race Club in Liu Na'ou's and Mu Shiying's Stories." *Modern Chinese Literature* 9 (1995): 39-57

———. "Revolution and Revulsion: Ideology, Monstrosity, and Phantasmagoria in Ma-Xu Weibang's Film *Song at Midnight*" *Modern Chinese Literature and Culture* 12, no. 1 (Spring 2000): 81-114.

Brooks, Barbara J. *Japan's Imperial Diplomacy: Consuls, Treaty Ports, and War in China, 1895-1938*. Honolulu: University of Hawaii Press, 2000.

Brooks, Peter. *The Melodramatic Imagination: Balzac, Henry James, Melodrama and the Modes of Excess*. New Haven, Conn.: Yale University Press, 1995.

Browne, Nick, Paul Pickowicz, Vivian Sobchack, and Esther Yau, eds. *New Chinese Cinemas: Forms, Identities, Politics*. Cambridge: Cambridge University Press, 1994.

Cai Chusheng 蔡楚生. *Cai Chusheng xuanji* 蔡楚生選集 (Selected writings of Cai Chusheng). Edited by Mu Yi 木藝 and Fang Sheng 方聲. Introduction by Ke Ling 柯靈. Beijing: Zhongguo Dianying, 1988.

Calinescu, Matei. *Five Faces of Modernity, Modernism, Avant-Garde, Decadence, Kitsch, Postmodernism*. Durham, N.C.: Duke University Press, 1987.

de Certeau, Michel. *The Practice of Everyday Life*. Berkeley: University of California Press, 1984.

Chang, Michael. "The Good, the Bad, and the Beautiful: Movie Actresses and Public Discourse in Shanghai: 1920s-1930s." In *Cinema and Urban Culture in Shanghai, 1922-1943*. Edited by Yingjin Zhang, 128-159. Stanford: Stanford University Press, 1999.

Chen Dieyi 陳蝶衣, Tong Yuejuan 童月娟, Yi Wen 易文, and Tan Zhongwen 譚仲文. *Zhang Shankun xiansheng chuan* 張善琨先生傳 (The biography of Mr. Zhang Shankun). Hong Kong: Dahua, 1958.

Chen Huiyang 陳輝揚. *Mengying ji* 夢影集 (Collection of dreams and shadows). Taipei: Yunchen wenhua, 1990.

Chen Ji 沉寂. *Yidai yingxing Ruan Lingyu* 一代影星阮玲玉 (The film star of a generation: Ruan Lingyu). Beijing: Zhongguo dianying, 1985.

Chen, Xiaomei. *Acting the Right Part: Political Theater and Popular Drama in Contemporary China, 1966-1996.* Honolulu: University of Hawaii Press, 2002.

Chen Xihe 陳犀和. "Zhongguo dianying meixue de zai renshi: ping 'Xingxi juben zuofa' " 中國電影美學的再認識：評《影戲劇本作法》(Reevaluating Chinese film aesthetics: a review of "Manual of shadowplay writing"). In *Zhongguo dianying lilun wenxuan* 中國電影理論文選 (Chinese film theory: an anthology) Volume Two. Edited by Luo Yijun 羅藝軍, 289-306. Beijing: Wenhua yishu, 1992. Translated into English by Hou Jianping, Li Xiaohong, and Fan Yuan. "Shadowplay: Chinese Film Aesthetics and Their Philosophical and Cultural Fundamentals." In *Chinese Film Theory: A Guide to the New Era.* Edited by George S. Semsel, Xia Hong, and Hou Jianping. New York: Praeger, 1990.

Cheng Bugao 程步高. *Yingtang yijiu* 影壇憶舊 (Old memories of the film industry). Beijing: Zhongguo dianying, 1983.

Cheng Jihua 程季華, ed. *Ruan Lingyu* 阮玲玉 (Ruan Lingyu). Beijing: Zhongguo dianying, 1985.

Cheng Jihua, Li Shaobai 李少白, and Xing Zuwen 刑祖文. *Zhongguo dianying fazhan shi* 中國電影發展史 (The development of Chinese cinema). 2 vol. Beijing: Zhongguo dianying, 1980.

Cho Woo, Catherine Yi-Yu. "The Chinese Montage: From Poetry and Painting to the Silver Screen." In *Perspectives on Chinese Cinema.* Edited by Chris Berry. London: BFI, 1991.

Chow, Rey. *Woman and Chinese Modernity: The Politics of Reading between West and East.* Minneapolis: University of Minnesota Press, 1991.

————. *Primitive Passions: Visuality, Sexuality, Ethnography, and Contemporary Chinese Cinema.* New York: Columbia Press, 1995.

Chung, Dooeum. *Elitist Fascism: Chiang Kaishek's Blueshirts in the 1930s China.* Aldershot: Ashgate, 2000.

Clark, Paul. *Chinese Cinema: Culture and Politics since 1949.* Cambridge: Cambridge University Press, 1987.

Cochran, Sherman, ed. *Inventing Nanjing Road: Commercial Culture in Shanghai, 1900-1945.* Ithaca, NY: East Asia Program, Cornell University Press, 1999.

————. "Marketing Medicine and Advertising Dreams in China 1900-1950." In *Becoming Chinese: Passages to Modernity and Beyond.* Edited by Wen-Hsin Yeh, 62-97. Berkeley: University of California Press, 2000.

Cook, Jim and Mike Lewington. "The Role of Stereotypes." In *The Matter of Images: Essays on Representation.* Edited by Richard Dyer, 11-18. London: Routledge, 1993.

Cornelius, Shelia. *New Chinese Cinema: Challenging Representations.* London: Wallflower Press, 2002.

Denton, Kirk. *The Problematic of Self in Modern Chinese Literature: Hu Feng and Lu Ling*. Stanford, Calif.: Stanford University Press, 1998.

Ding Ling 丁玲. "Shui" (Water). In *Ding Ling wenji* 丁玲文集 (The Writings of Ding Ling). 2 vol, 369-406. Changsha: Hunan Renmin, 1982.

————. *Miss Sophie's Diary and Other Stories*. Translated by W. J. F. Jenner. Beijing: Chinese Literature, 1985.

Ding Yaping 丁亞平. *Yingxiang Zhongguo, Zhongguo dianying yishu: 1945-1949* 影像中國, 中國電影藝術: 1945-1949 (Imaging China, Chinese film art: 1945-1949). Beijing: Wenhua yishu, 1998.

Dissanayake, Wimal. "Introduction." In *Melodrama and Asian Cinema*. Edited by Wimal Dissanayake, 1-8. Cambridge: Cambridge University Press, 1993.

Doane, Mary Ann. "The Voice in the Cinema: The Articulation of Body and Space." In *Film Theory and Criticism: Introductory Readings*. Edited by Leo Braudy and Marshall Cohen, 363-75. New York: Oxford University Press, 1999.

Dong Xinyu 董新宇. *Kan yu beikan zhijian: dui Zhongguo wusheng dianying de wenhua yanjiu* 看與被看之間: 對中國無聲電影的文化研究 (Between looking and being looked at: Cultural studies of Chinese silent cinema) Beijing: Shifan, 2000.

Dyer, Richard. *Stars*. London: British Film Institute, 1979.

Eastman, Lloyd. *The Abortive Revolution: China Under Nationalist Rule, 1927-1937*. Cambridge, Mass.: Harvard University Press, 1974.

————. "Nationalist China during the Nanking Decade 1927-1937." In *The Cambridge History of China, vol. 13, Republic China 1912-1949, Part 2*. Edited by John K. Fairbank and Albert Feuerwerker, 116-67. Cambridge: Cambridge University Press, 1986.

Eyman, Scott. *The Speed of Sound: Hollywood and the Talkie Revolution, 1926-1930*. New York: Simon & Schuster, 1997.

Feuer, Jane. "The Self-Reflexive Musical and the Myth of Entertainment." In *Film Genre Reader II*. Edited by Barry Keith Grant, 441-455. Austin: University of Texas Press, 1995.

Freud, Sigmund. *Civilization and Its Discontents*. New York: W.W. Norton & Company, 1961.

Fruehauf, Heinrich. "Urban Exoticism in Modern and Contemporary Chinese Literature." In *From May Fourth to June Fourth*. Edited by Ellen Widmer and David Der-wei Wang, 133-164. Cambridge, Mass.: Harvard University Press, 1993.

Fu, Poshek. *Passivity, Resistance, and Collaboration: Intellectual Choices in Occupied Shanghai, 1937-1945*. Stanford, Calif.: Stanford University Press, 1993.

Furuya, Kenji, ed. *Chiang Kaishek: His Life and Times*. Abridged and translated by Chun-ming Chang. New York: St. John's University Press, 1981.

Gao Tianru 高天如. *Zhongguo xiandai yuyan jihua de lilun he shijian* 中國現代語言計劃的理論和實踐 (Theory and practice of modern Chinese language). Shanghai: Fudan University Press, 1993.

Gilmartin, Christina Kelley. *Engendering the Chinese Revolution: Radical Women, Communist Politics, and Mass Movements in the 1920s.* Berkeley: University of California Press, 1995.

Gong Jia'nong 龔稼儂. *Gong Jia'nong congying huiyi lu* 龔稼儂從影回憶錄 (The memories of Gong Jia'nong regarding the film industry). Taipei: Chuanqi wenxue, 1980.

Gorbman, Claudia. *Unheard Melodies: Narrative Film Music.* Bloomington: Indiana University Press, 1987.

Gu Menghe 顧夢鶴. "Yi Tianhan tongzhi zai Nanguo she de dianying chuangzuo" 憶田漢同志在南國社的電影創作 (Memory of comrade Tian Han's film production in Nanguo Society). *Dianying yishu* 電影藝術 (Film art) 93 (April 1980): 56-57.

Guangbo dianying dianshi bu dianying ju dangshi ziliao zhengji gongzuo lingdao xiaozu, zhongguo dianying yishu yanjiu zhongxin 廣播電影電視部電影局黨史資料徵集工作領導小組，中國電影藝術研究中心 (Chinese Film Art Research Center, Leading Group of the Party's Historical Information Collection, Film Section, the Broadcast, Film and Television Department), ed. *Sanshi niandai zhongguo dianying pinglun wenxuan* 三十年代中國電影評論文選 (Anthology of Chinese film theories and criticism in the thirties). Beijing: Zhongguo dianying, 1993.

———, ed. *Zhongguo zuoyi dianying yundong* 中國左翼電影運動 (The Chinese left-wing cinema movement). Beijing: Zhongguo dianying, 1993.

Hallam, Julia, with Margaret Marshment. *Realism and Popular Cinema.* Manchester: Manchester University Press, 2000.

Han Suyin. *Eldest Son.* New York, Toyko and London: Kodansha International, 1995.

Hansen, Miriam. *Babel and Babylon: Spectatorship in American Silent Film.* Cambridge, Mass.: Harvard University Press, 1991.

———. "Early Cinema, Late Cinema: Transformations of the Public Sphere." In *Viewing Positions: Ways of Seeing Film.* Edited by Linda Williams, 134-52. New Brunswick, N.J.: Rutgers University Press, 1994.

———. "Fallen Women, Rising Stars, New Horizons: Shanghai Silent Film as Vernacular Modernism." *Film Quarterly* 54, no. 1 (2000): 10-22.

———. "The Mass Production of Senses: Classical Cinema as Vernacular Modernism." In *Reinventing Film Studies.* Edited by Christine Gledhill and Linda Williams, 332-50. London: Arnold, 2000.

Harris, Kristine. "The New Woman Incident: Cinema, Scandal, Spectacle in 1935 Shanghai." In *Transnational Chinese Cinemas: Identity, Nationhood,*

Gender. Edited by Sheldon Hsiao-Lu, 277-302. Honolulu: University of Hawaii Press, 1997.

Harrison, Henrietta. *China*. London: Arnold; New York: Oxford University Press, 2001.

Heath, Stephen. *Questions of Cinema*. Bloomington: Indiana University Press, 1981.

Henriot, Christian. *Shanghai 1927-1937*. Translated by Noel Castelino. Berkeley: University of California Press, 1993.

Holub, Renate. *Antonio Gramsci: Beyond Marxism and Postmodernism*. London: Routledge, 1992.

Hong Shen 洪深. *Hong Shen wenji* 洪深文集 (Writings of Hong Shen). 4 vols. Beijing: Zhongguo xiju, 1957.

Hsia, C. T. *A History of Modern Chinese Fiction*. New York: Columbia University Press, 1979.

Hu Die 胡蝶. *Hu Die huiyi lu* 胡蝶回憶錄 (The reminiscence of Hu Die). Edited by Liu Huiqin. Taipei: Lianhe baoshe, 1968.

Hu Peng 胡鵬. *Wo yu Huang Feihong* 我與黃飛鴻 (Me and Huang Feihong). Hong Kong: Sanhe amoyi, 1995.

Huang, Martin W. *Literati and Self-Representation: Autobiographical Sensibility in the Eighteenth-Century Chinese Novel*. Stanford, Calif.: Stanford University Press, 1995.

Hung, Chang-tai. *Going to the People: Chinese Intellectuals and Folk Literature, 1918-1937*. Cambridge, Mass.: Harvard University Press, 1985.

Iriye, Akira. "Japanese Aggression and China's International Position, 1931-1949." In *The Cambridge History of China, vol. 13, Republic China 1912-1949, Part 2*. Edited by John K. Fairbank and Albert Feuerwerker, 492-504. Cambridge: Cambridge University Press, 1986.

Jarvie, I. C. *Window on Hong Kong: A Sociological Study of the Hong Kong Film Industry and Its Audience*. Hong Kong: Centre of Asian Studies, University of Hong Kong, 1977.

Jones, Andrew F. *Media Culture and Colonial Modernity in the Chinese Jazz Age*. Durham, N.C.: Duke University Press, 2001.

Ke Ling 柯靈. *Ke Ling dianying wencun* 柯靈電影文存 (Ke Ling's writing of cinema). Edited by Chen Wei 陳緯. Beijing: Zhongguo dianying, 1992.

Kenez, Peter. *Cinema and Soviet Society, 1917-1953*. Cambridge: Cambridge University Press, 1992.

King, John. *Magical Reels: A History of Cinema in Latin America*. London: Verso, in association with the Latin American Bureau, 1990.

Kracauer, Siegfried. *Theory of Film: The Redemption of Physical Reality*. New York: Oxford University Press, 1972.

Law Kar 羅卡. "The Shadow of Tradition and the Left-Right Struggle." In *Xianggong dianying de Zhongguo mailuo* 香港電影的中國脈絡 (*The China Factor in Hong Kong Cinema*) (The 14th Hong Kong International Film

Festival). Edited by Law Kar 羅卡, 15-20. Hong Kong: The Urban Council, 1990.

————. "Xianggang dianying de haiwai jingyan" 香港電影的海外經驗 (Foreign Experience of Hong Kong Cinema). In *Dianying zhong de haiwai huaren xingxiang* 電影中的海外華人形象 (*Overseas Chinese Figures in Cinema*) (The 16th Hong Kong International Film Festival). Edited by Law Kar 羅卡, 15-21. Hong Kong: The Urban Council, 1992.

————. "Introduction." In *Xianggong—Shanghai: Dianying shuangcheng* 香港—上海電影雙城 (*Cinema of Two Cities: Hong Kong—Shanghai*) (The 18th Hong Kong International Film Festival Retrospective Section). Edited by Law Kar 羅卡, 10. Hong Kong: Urban Council, 1994.

Lee, Leo Ou-fan. *Voices from the Iron House: A Study of Lu Xun*. Bloomington: Indiana University Press, 1987.

————. *Shanghai Modern: The Flowering of A New Urban Culture in China, 1930-1935*. Cambridge, MA: Harvard University Press, 1999.

Lee, Leo Ou-fan and Andrew J. Nathan. "The Beginnings of Mass Culture: Journalism and Fiction in the Late Ch'ing and Beyond." In *Popular Culture in Late Imperial China*. Edited by David Johnson, Andrew J. Nathan, and Eveyln S, Rawski, 360-395. Berkeley: University of California Press, 1982.

Levenson, Joseph. *Confucian China and Its Modern Fate*. 2 vol. London: Routledge & Kegan Paul, 1965.

Leyda, Jey. *Dianying: An Account of Films and the Film Audience in China*. Cambridge, Mass.: The MIT Press, 1972.

Li Mu 李牧. *Sanshi niandai wenyi lun* 三十年代文藝論 (Arts and literature in the thirties). Taipei: Limin wenhua, 1977.

Li Shaobai 李少白. "Liangzhong yishi xingtai de duili" 兩種意識形態的對立 (The antagonism of two ideologies). *Dangdai dianying* 當代電影 (Contemporary cinema), no. 61 (April 1994): 35-40.

————. "Jianlun Zhongguo sanxi niandai 'dianying wenhua yundong' de xingqi" 簡論中國三十年代電影文化運動的興起 (A brief account of the rise of the film culture movement in the thirties). *Dangdai dianying* 當代電影 (Contemporary cinema), no. 60 (March 1994): 77-84.

Li Suyuan 酈蘇元, Hu Jubin 胡菊彬. *Zhongguo wusheng dianying shi* 中國無聲電影史 (The history of Chinese silent cinema). Beijing: Zhongguo dianying, 1996.

Li Zehou 李澤厚. *Zhongguo xiandai sixiang shi lun* 中國現代思想史論 (The discussion of modern Chinese intellectual history). Revised Edition. Taipei: Fengyun, 1990.

Li Zehou, Liu Zaifu 劉再復. *Gaobie geming: Huiwang ershi shiji Zhongguo* 告別革命：回望二十世紀中國 (Farewell revolution: Looking back at the 20th century China). Hong Kong: Tiandi, 1997.

Lieberman, Sally Taylor. *The Mother and Narrative Politics in Modern China.* Charlottesville: University Press of Virginia, 1998.

Lin Niantong. "A Study of the Theories of Chinese Cinema in Their Relationship to Classical Aesthetics." *Modern Chinese Literature* 1, no. 2 (spring 1985): 185-200.

——— 林年同. *Zhongguo dianying meixue* 中國電影美學 (Chinese cinema aesthetics). Taipei: Yunchen, 1991.

Lin Yu-sheng. *The Crisis of Chinese Consciousness: Radical Anti-Traditionalism in the May Fourth Era.* Madison: University of Wisconsin Press, 1979.

Link, E. Perry, Jr. *Mandarin Ducks and Butterflies: Popular Fiction in Early Twentieth Century Chinese Cities.* Berkeley: University of California Press, 1981.

Lipking, Lawrence. *Abandoned Women & Poetic Tradition.* Chicago: The University of Chicago Press, 1988.

Liu, Lydia H. "Narratives of Modern Selfhood: First-Person Fiction in May Fourth Literature." In *Politics, Ideology, and Literary Discourse in Modern China: Theoretical Interventions and Cultural Critique.* Edited by Liu Kang and Xiaobing Tang, 102-123. Durham, N.C.: Duke University Press, 1993.

———. *Translingual Practice: Literature, National Culture, and Translated Modernity—China, 1900-1937.* Stanford, Calif.: Stanford University Press, 1995.

Liu Siping 劉思平, Xing Zuwen 邢祖文, ed. *Lu Xun yu dianying* 魯迅與電影 (Lu Xun and cinema). Beijing: Zhongguo dianying, 1981.

Liu Ying 劉熒. "Lun Sun Yu dianying chuangzuo de yishu tezheng" 論孫瑜電影創作的藝術特徵 (A discussion of the artistic features of Sun Yu's films). *Dianying Yishu* 電影藝術 (Film art), no. 120 (Jan 1990): 80-107.

Löwenthal, Rudolf. "Public Communications in China before July 1937." *Chinese Social and Political Science Review* 22 (1938-39): 43-58.

Lu Xun 魯迅. *Lu Xun quanji* 魯迅全集 (Complete writings of Lu Xun). 16 vol. Beijing: Renmin wenxue, 1989.

———. *Diary of a Madman and Other Stories.* Translated by William Lyell. Honolulu: University of Hawaii Press, 1990.

Lu Hanchao. *Beyond the Neon Lights: Everyday Shanghai in the Early Twentieth Century.* Berkeley: University of California Press, 1999.

Lukács, Georg. *The Historical Novel.* Translated from German by Hannah and Stanley Mitchell. Introduction by Fredric Jameson. Lincoln: University of Nebraska Press, 1983.

Ma Liangchun 馬良春 and Zhang Daming 張大明, ed. *Sanshi niandai zuoyi wenyi ziliao xuanbian* 三十年代左翼文藝資料選編 (Selected collection of research materials about the left-wing literature in the 1930s). Chengdu: Sichuan renmin, 1980.

Ma Ning. "Notes on the New Filmmakers." In *Chinese Film: The State of the Art in the People's Republic.* Edited by George Stephen Semsel, 73-77. New York: Praeger, 1987.

————. "The Textual and Critical Difference of Being Radical: Reconstructing Chinese Leftist Films of the 1930s." *Wide Angle* 11, no. 2 (1989): 22-31.

MacCabe, Colin. *Tracking the Signifier, Theoretical Essays: Film, Linguistics, Literature.* Minneapolis: University of Minnesota Press, 1985.

Mayne, Judith. *Cinema and Spectatorship.* New York: Routledge, 1993.

Mulvey, Laura. "Visual Pleasure and Narrative Cinema." In Laura Mulvey, *Visual and Other Pleasures,* 14-26. Bloomington: Indiana University Press, 1989.

————. "It Will be a Magnificent Obsession: The Melodrama's Role in the Development of Contemporary Film Theory." In *Melodrama: Stage, Picture, Screen.* Edited by Jacky Bratton, Jim Cook, and Christine Gledhill, 121-133. London: British Film Institute, 1994.

Ng, Mau-Sang. *The Russian Hero in Modern Chinese Fiction.* Hong Kong: The Chinese University Press, 1988.

————. "Popular Fiction and the Culture of Everyday Life: A Cultural Analysis of Qin Shouou's *Qiuhaitang.*" *Modern China* 20, no. 2 (April 1994): 131-156.

The Party History Research Centre of the Central Committee of the Chinese Communist Party. *History of the Chinese Communist Party: A Chronology of Events (1919-1990).* Beijing Foreign Language Press, 1991.

Pian, Rulan Chao. "Aria Structural Patterns in the Peking Opera." In *Chinese and Japanese Music-Dramas.* Edited by J. I. Crump and William P. Malm, 65-97. Michigan Papers in Chinese no. 19, 1975. Ann Arbor: The University of Michigan, 1975.

Pickowicz, Paul. "Melodramatic Representation and the 'May Fourth' Tradition of Chinese Cinema." In *From May Fourth to June Fourth: Fiction and Film in Twentieth-Century China.* Edited by Wang David Derwei and Ellen Widmer, 195-326. Cambridge, Mass.: Harvard University Press, 1993.

Plaks, Andrew H. "Towards a Critical Theory of Chinese Narrative." In *Chinese Narrative: Critical and Theoretical Essays.* Edited by Andrew H. Plaks, 309-352. Princeton, N. J.: Princeton University Press.

Pudovkin, Vsvolod I. *Film Techniques and Film Acting/V. I. Pudovkin.* Translated by Ivor Montagn. New York: Grove Press, 1970.

Qu Qiubai 瞿秋白. "Dazhong wenyi de wenti" 大眾文藝的問題 (Questions regarding mass culture). In *Qu Qiubai xuanji* 瞿秋白選集 (Selected writings of Qu Qiubai), 488-498. Beijing: Renmin, 1985.

————. *Qu Qiubai wenji* 瞿秋白文集 (Writings of Qu Qiubai). 7 vols. Beijing: Renmin, 1991.

Rayns, Tony. "An Introduction to the Aesthetics and Politics of Chinese Cinema." *On Film* 14 (1985): 26-32.

Rui Heshi 芮和師 ed. *Yuanyang hudie pai wenxue ziliao* 鴛鴦蝴蝶派文學資料
(Information about "Mandarin Ducks and Butterflies" literature) Fuzhou:
Fuzhou renmin, 1984.

Sa Er'di 薩爾地 (Sardi). *Dianying yu Zhongguo* 電影與中國 (Film and China).
Translated by Peng Beichuan 彭百川 and Zhang Pairong 張培燦. Nanjing:
Zhongguo jiaoyu dianying xiehui, 1933.

Sarris, Andrew. "Notes on the Author Theory in 1962." In *Film Theory and
Criticism: Introductory Readings.* 5th ed. Edited by Leo Braudy and Marshall Cohen, 515-35. Oxford: Oxford University Press, 1999.

Schatz, Thomas. *The Genius of the System.* New York: Henry Holt and Company, 1996.

Semsel, George Stephen. *Chinese Film: The State of the Art in the People's Republic.* New York : Praeger, 1987

Sheridan, James E. *China in Disintegration: The Republican Era in Chinese
History, 1912-1949.* New York: The Free Press, 1975.

Shi Zhecun 施蟄存, "Zai Bali daxiyuan" 在巴黎大戲院 (At the Paris Cinema).
In *Shanghai de hubuwu* 上海的狐步舞 (Shanghai's Fox-trot). Edited by Li
Oufan (Leo Ou-fan Lee) 李歐梵, 122-33. Taipei: Yunchen, 2000.

Shih, Shu-mei. *The Lure of the Modern: Writing Modernism in Semi-colonial
China, 1917-1937.* Berkeley: University of California Press, 2001.

Shu Kei 舒琪, ed. *Zhanhou guo, yuyu pian bijiao yanjiu—Zhu Shilin, Qin Jain
dan zuopin huigu* 戰後國,粵語片比較研究—朱石麟,秦劍等作品回顧 (A
Comparative Study of Post-War Mandarin and Cantonese Cinema: The
Films of Zhu Shilin, Qin Jian and Other Directors). (The 7th Hong Kong
International Film Festival). Hong Kong: Urban Council, 1983.

Shu Yan 舒湮. "Yi jiu you" 憶舊游 (Memories of an old friend). In *Lun Xia
Yan* 論夏衍 (Discussion on Xia Yan). Edited by *Zhongguo dianying yishu
yanjiu zhongxin* 中國電影藝術研究中心 (Chinese film art research center),
378-384. Beijing: Zhongguo Dianying, 1989.

Shumway, David R. "Screwball Comedies: Constructing Romance, Mystifying
Marriage." In *Film Genre II.* Edited by Barry Keith Grant, 381-401. Austin:
University of Texas Press, 1995.

Silbergeld, Jerome. *China into Film: Frames of Reference in Contemporary
Chinese Cinema.* London: Reaktion Books, 2000.

Silverman, Kaja. *Male Subjectivity at the Margins.* New York: Routledge, 1992.

Snead, James. "European Pedigrees/African Contagions: Nationality, Narrativity,
and Communality in Tutuola, Achebe, and Reed." In *Nation and Narration.*
Edited by Homi K. Bhabha, 231-249. London: Routledge, 1990.

Spence, Jonathan D. *The Search for Modern China.* New York: W.W. Norton
and Company, 1990.

Stokes, Melvyn. "Female Audiences of the 1920s and early 1930s." In *Identifying Hollywood's Audiences: Cultural Identity and the Movies.* Edited by

Melvyn Stokes and Richard Maltby, 42-60. London: British Film Institute, 1999.

Sun, E-Tu Zen. "The Growth of the Academic Community." In *The Cambridge History of China vol. 13, Republic China 1912-1949, Part 2*. Edited by John K. Fairbank and Albert Feuerwerker. Cambridge: Cambridge University Press, 1986.

Sun Shaoyi 孫紹誼. "Dushi kongjian yu Zhongguo minzu zhuyi: jiedu sanshi niandai Zhongguo zuoyi dianying" 都市空間與中國民族主義：解讀三十年代中國左翼電影 (City space and Chinese nationalism: Reading Chinese left-wing films in the thirties). *Shanghai wenhua* 上海文化 (Shanghai culture), no. 16 (May 1996): 37-44.

Sun Yu 孫瑜. *Dalu zhi ge* 大路之歌 (Song of the big road). Edited by Shu Qi (Shu Kei) 舒琪 and Li Zhuotao (Li Chuek-to) 李焯桃. Taipei: Yuanliu, 1990.

Swarup. Shanti. *A Study of the Chinese Communist Movement*. Oxford: Clarendon Press, 1966.

Tagore, Amitendranath. *Literary Debates in Modern China, 1918-1937*. Tokyo: The Centre for East Asian Cultural Studies, 1967.

Tan Chunfa 譚春發. *Kai yidai xianhe—Zhongguo dianying zhi fu Zheng Zhengqiu* 開一代先河—中國電影之父鄭正秋 (Breaking a new path—The father of Chinese cinema: Zheng Zhengqiu). Beijing: Guoji wenhua, 1992.

———. "The Influx of Shanghai Filmmakers into Hong Kong and Hong Kong Cinema." Translated by Stephen Teo. In *Xianggong—Shanghai: Dianying shuangcheng* 香港—上海電影雙城 (*Cinema of Two Cities: Hong Kong—Shanghai*) (The 18th Hong Kong International Film Festival). Edited by Law Kar 羅卡, 74-82. Hong Kong: Urban Council, 1994.

Taylor, Richard and Ian Christie, eds. *The Film Factory: Russian and Soviet Cinema in Documents 1896-1939*. London: Routledge, 1994.

Teo, Stephen. *Hong Kong Cinema: The Extra Dimensions*. London: British Film Institute, 1997.

Tian Han 田漢. *Yingshi zhuihuai lu* 影事追懷錄 (Memories about the events in cinema). Beijing: Zhongguo dianying, 1981.

Truffaut, François. "On a Certain Tendency of the French Cinema." In *Movies and Methods I*. Edited by Bill Nichols, 224-237. Berkeley: University of California Press, 1976.

Tung, Constantine and Colin Mackerras, eds. *Drama in the People's Republic of China*. New York: SUNY Press, 1987.

Tuohy, Sue. "Metropolitan Sounds: Music in Chinese Films of the 1930s." In *Cinema and Urban Culture in Shanghai, 1922-1943*. Edited by Yingjin Zhang, 200-221. Stanford, Calif.: Stanford University Press, 1999.

Vertov, Dziga. *Kino Eye: The Writing of Dziga Vertov*. Translated by Kevin O'Brien. Edited by Annette Michelson. Berkeley, Calif.: University of California Press, 1984.

———. "Fiction Film Drama and the Cine-Eye. A Speech." In *The Film Factory*. Edited by Richard Taylor and Ian Christie, 115-16. London: Routledge, 1994.

Wang, Ban. *The Sublime Figure of History: Aesthetics and Politics in Twentieth-Century China*. Stanford, Calif.: Stanford University Press, 1997.

Wang Chaoguang 汪朝光. "Minguo nianjian Meiguo dianying zai hua shichang yanjiu" 民國年間美國電影在華市場研究 (The marketing research of American cinema in Republican China) *Dianying yishu* (Film art), no. 258 (Jan 1998): 57-64.

Wang Hongwei 王宏維. *Mingding yu kangzheng: Zhongguo gudian beiju ji beiju jingshen* 命定與抗爭：中國古典悲劇及悲劇精神 (Fate and struggle: Chinese classical tragedies and tragic spirit). Beijing: Sanlian, 1996.

Wang Xiangmin 王向民. "Shi Linghe" 石凌鶴 (Shi Linghe). In *Sanshi niandai zai Shanghai de "Zuolian" zuojia* 三十年代在上海的左聯作家 (The Shanghai "Left-league" writers in 1930s). Edited by Shanghai Academy of Social Science. Shanghai: Shanghai Academy of Social Science, 1988.

Way, Eugene Irving. *Motion Pictures in China*. Bureau of Foreign and Domestic Commerce, U.S. Department of Commerce, Trade Information Bulletin no. 722. Washington D.C. 1930.

Wenhua bu dangshi ziliao zhengji gongzuo weiyuan wui 文化部黨史資料徵集工作委員會 (Committee on recollecting Party's historical material, Culture Department), ed. *Zhongguo zuoyi xijujia lianmeng shiliao ji* 中國左翼戲劇家聯盟史料集 (Historical materials of the Chinese left-wing dramatist association). Beijing: Zhongguo xiju, 1991.

Wichman, Elizabeth. *Listening to Theatre: The Aural Dimension of Beijing Opera*. Honolulu: University of Hawaii Press, 1991.

Willemen, Paul. *Looks and Frictions: Essays in Cultural Studies and Film Theory*. London: BFI, 1994.

Wong, Wang-chi. *Politics and Literature in Shanghai: The Chinese League of Left-Wing Writers, 1930-36*. Manchester: Manchester University Press, 1991.

Wu Yonggang 吳永剛. *Wo de tansuo he zhuiqiu* 我的探索和追求 (My search and pursuit). Beijing: Zhongguo dianying, 1986.

Xia Yan 夏衍. *Dianying lunwen ji* 電影論文集 (Film writings). Beijing: Zhongguo dianying, 1985.

———. *Xia Yan dianying juzuo ji* 夏衍電影劇作集 (Film writings of Xia Yan). Beijing: Zhongguo dianying, 1985.

Xiao, Zhiwei. "Anti-Imperialism and Film Censorship During the Nanjing Decade, 1927-1937." In *Transnational Chinese Cinema: Identity, Nationhood, Gender*. Edited by Sheldon Lu. Honolulu: University of Hawaii Press, 1997.

————. "Wu Yonggang and the Ambivalence in the Chinese Experience of Modernity: A Study of His Three Films of the Mid-1930s." *Asian Cinema* 9, no. 2 (Spring 1998): 3-15.

————. "Constructing a New National Culture: Film Censorship and the Issues of Cantonese Dialect, Superstition, and Sex in the Nanjing Decade." In *Cinema and Urban Culture in Shanghai, 1922-1943*. Edited by Yingjin Zhang, 183-99. Stanford, Calif.: Stanford University Press, 1999.

Xin Ping 忻平. *Cong Shanghai faxian lishi* 從上海發現歷史 (Discovering history from Shanghai). Shanghai: Shanghai renmin, 1996.

Yao Guohua 姚國華 and Zhou Bin 周斌, "Wengu zhixin, jiwang kailai—jinian zuoyi dianying yundong liushi zhounian" 溫故知新,繼往開來—紀念左翼電影運動六十周年 (Revising the old and understanding the new; continuing the tradition and bringing it to the future—The sixtieth anniversary of the left-wing cinema movement). In *Dianying zongheng* 電影縱橫 (Cinema horizontal and vertical). Shanghai: Sanlian, 1993.

Yeh, Wen-Hsin. "Progressive Journalism and Shanghai's Petty Urbanites: Zou Taofen and the Shenghuo Enterprise, 1926-1945." In *Shanghai Sojourners*. Edited by Frederic Wakeman Jr. and Wen-hsin Yeh, 186-238. Berkeley, Calif.: The Regents of the University of California Press, 1992.

Yeh, Yueh-yu. "Singing Women in Classical Chinese Films: A Discourse of Sinification." Paper presented at Hong Kong Baptist University for the "Asian Cultures at Crossroads" Conference, Hong Kong, Nov. 1998.

Yi Bin 益斌, ed. *Lao Shanghai guangao* 老上海廣告 (Advertisements of the old time of Shanghai). Shanghai: Shanghai huabao, 1996.

Yu Muyun 余慕雲. *Xianggong dianying shihua* 香港電影史話 (The chronicle of Hong Kong cinema). 3 vols. Hong Kong: Ciwenhua tang, 1996, 1997.

Zhang Yingjin. "Engendering Chinese Filmic Discourse of the 1930s: Configurations of Modern Women in Shanghai in Three Silent Films." *positions* 2, no. 3 (winter 1994): 603-628.

————. "The Texture of the Metropolis: Modernist Inscriptions of Shanghai in the 1930s." *Modern Chinese Literature* 9 (1995): 11-30

————. *The City in Modern Chinese Literature & Film: Configurations of Space, Time, and Gender*. Stanford, Calif.: Stanford University Press, 1996.

————, ed. *Romance, Sexuality, Identity: Cinema and Urban Culture in Shanghai, 1910s-1940s*. Stanford, Calif.: Stanford University Press, 1999.

Zhang, Zhen. "Teahouse, Shadowplay, Bricolage: *Laborer's Love* and the Question of Early Chinese Cinema." In *Cinema and Urban Culture in Shanghai, 1922-1943*. Edited by Yingjin Zhang, 27-50. Stanford, Calif.: Stanford University Press, 1999.

————. "Bodies in the Air: Magic of Science and the Fate of the Early 'Martial Arts' Film in China." *Post Script* 20, no. 2/3 (Winter/Spring 2001): 43-60.

————. "An Amorous History of the Silver Screen: The Actress as Vernacular Embodiment in Early Chinese Film Culture" *Camera Obscura* 16, no. 3 (2001): 229-63.

Zhao Dan 趙丹. *Diyu zhi men* 地獄之門 (The gateway to hell). Shanghai: Shanghai wenyi, 1980.

Zheng Zhenduo 鄭振鐸. "Shanghai de juzhu wenti" 上海的居住問題 (The living problems in Shanghai). In *Langtaosha: Mingren bixia de lao Shanghai* 浪淘沙：名人筆下的老上海 (Langtaosha: The old Shanghai under the writings of celebrities). Edited by Ni Moyan 倪墨炎, 119-124. Beijing: Beijing chubanshe, 1998.

Zhong Dafeng, Zhen Zhang, and Yingjin Zhang. "From *Wenmingxi* (Civilized Play) to *Yingxi* (Shadowplay): The Foundation of Shanghai Film Industry in the 1920s. *Asian Cinema* 9, no. 1 (Fall 1997): 46-64.

Zhongguo dianying ziliao guan 中國電影資料館 (China Film Archive), ed. *Zhongguo wusheng dianying* 中國無聲電影 (Chinese silent cinema). Beijing: Zhongguo dianying, 1996.

Zhongguo jiaoyu dianying xiehui 中國教育電影協會 (Association of Chinese cinema for education) ed. *The Cinematographic Yearbook of China, Zhongguo dianying lianjian* 中國電影年鑑. Nanjing: Zhongguo jiaoyu dianying xiehui, 1934.

Zhu Jian 朱劍. *Dianying huanghou Hu Die* 電影皇后胡蝶 (The queen of cinema Hu Die). Lanzhou: Lanzhou Daxue, 1996.

Zhu Tianwei 朱天緯 and Wang Zhenzhen 王珍珍, eds. *Zhongguo yingpian dadian: gushi pian, xiqu pian, 1905-1930* 中國影片大典：故事片，戲曲片，1905-1930 (Encyclopaedia of Chinese Films, Narrative Films and Opera Films, 1905-1930). Beijing: Zhongguo dianying, 1996.

Zizek, Slavoj. *The Sublime Object of Ideology*. London: Verso, 1994.

Newspapers and Journals in the 1920s and 1930s

Chen bao 晨報 (Morning Daily)
Damei wanbao 大美晚報 (Damei Evening News)
Dawan bao 大晚報 (The Great Evening News)
Diansheng 電聲 (Cinema Voice)
Diansheng ribao 電聲日報 (Cinema Voice Daily)
Diansheng zhoukan 電聲周刊 (Cinema Voice Weekly)
Diantong banyuekan 電通半月刊 (Denton Gazette)
Dianying 電影 (Movie Monthly)
Dianying huabao 電影畫報 (Cinema Pictorial)
Dianying, xiju 電影戲劇 (Film, Drama)
Dianying xinwen 電影新聞 (News of Cinema)
Dianying yuebao 電影月報 (Cinema Monthly)
Dianying zazhi 電影雜誌 (Movie Monthly)
Dianying zhoubao 電影週報 (Cinema Weekly)
Jixing 畸形 (Odd Shape)
Lianhua huabao 聯華畫報 (Lianhua Pictorial)
Mengya 萌芽 (Sprouting)
Min bao 民報 (People's Daily)
Mingxing banyuekan 明星半月刊 (Mingxing Half-Monthly)
Mingxing ribao 明星日報 (Daily News of the Stars)
Mingxing yuekan 明星月報 (Mingxing Monthly)
Shalun 沙侖 (Siren)
Shen bao 申報 (Shanghai Daily)
Shen bao yuekan 申報月刊 (Shenbao Monthly)
Shi bao 時報 (Times)
Shishi xin bao 時事新報 (New News Daily)
Taibai 太白 (Taibai Monthly)
Wenxue congbao 文學叢報 (The Journal of Literature)
Wenxue daobao 文學導報 (Directed Readings of Literature)
Xiandai dianying 現代電影 (Modern Cinema)
Xiandai yanju 現代演劇 (Modern Drama)
Xinwen bao 新聞報 (News Daily)
Xinye bao 新夜報 (New Evening Daily)
Yilin 藝林 (The Forest of Art)
Yingxi shenghou 影戲生活 (Life in Cinema)
Yingxi zazhi 影戲雜誌 (Film Magazine)
Yinxing 銀星 (Silver Star)

Films

The Actress/The Centered Stage (*Ruan Lingyu* 阮玲玉), 1992, sound. Scr: Qiu-Dai Anping 邱戴安平. Dir: Stanley Kwan 關錦鵬. Golden Harvest.

Ailments within Heart and Stomach (*Xinfu zhi huan* 心腹之患), 1933, silent. Scr/Dir: Unknown. Central Film Studio.

All Quiet on the Western Front, 1930, sound. Scr: Lewis Milestone, Maxwell Anderson, Del Andrews, and George Abbott. Dir: Lewis Milestone. Universal.

Angry Tide in China's Seas (*Zhongguohai de nuchao* 中國海的怒潮), 1933, silent. Scr: Yang Hansheng 陽翰笙. Dir: Yue Feng 岳峰. Yihua Film Company.

Ardent, Loyal Souls (*Rexue zhonghun* 熱血忠魂), 1935, sound. Scr: The Mingxing Film Company's Script Department. Dir: Zhang Shichuan 張石川, Xu Xinfu 徐欣夫, Zheng Zhengqiu 鄭正秋, Wu Cun 吳村, Cheng Bugao 程步高, Shen Xiling 沈西苓, and Li Pingqian 李萍倩. Mingxing Film Company.

At the Qingming Festival (*Qingming shijie* 清明時節), 1936, sound. Scr/Dir: Ouyang Yuqian 歐陽予倩. Mingxing Film Company.

Back to Nature (*Dao ziren qu* 到自然去), 1936, sound. Scr/Dir: Sun Yu 孫瑜. Lianhua Film Company.

Ben-Hur, 1925, silent. Scr/Dir: Fred Niblo. MGM.

Battleship Potemkin, 1926, silent. Scr/Dir: Sergei Eisenstein. Goskino.

The Big Parade, 1925, silent. Scr: Harry Behn. Dir. King Vidor. MGM.

The Birth of a Nation, 1915, silent. Scr: Frank E. Woods and D. W. Griffith. Dir: D. W. Griffith. Epoch Producing Corporation.

The Blood Spilt in the Treasure Mountain City (*Xuejian baoshan cheng* 血濺寶山城), 1938, sound. Scr: Cai Chusheng 蔡楚生 and Situ Huimin 司徒慧敏. Dir: Situ Huimin. Xin Shidai Film Company.

Bloodbath on Wolf Mountain (*Langshan diexue ji* 狼山喋血記), 1936, sound. Scr: Shen Fu 沈浮 and Fei Mu 費穆. Dir: Fei Mu 費穆. Lianhua Film Company.

The Boatman's Daughter (*Chuanjia nü* 船家女), 1935, sound. Scr/Dir: Shen Xiling 沈西苓. Mingxing Film Company.

"Broken Dream in the Women's Apartment" (*Chungui mengduan* 春歸夢斷), in *Lianhua Symphony* (*Lianhua Jiaoxiang qu* 聯華交響曲), 1937, sound. Scr/Dir: Fei Mu 費穆. Lianhua Film Company.

Burial at Sea (*Haizang* 海葬), 1935, sound. Scr/Dir: Wang Bin 王斌. Tianyi Film Company.

Burning the Red Lotus Temple (*Huoshao hongliansi* 火燒紅蓮寺), 18 parts, 1928-1931, silent. Scr/Dir: Zhang Shichuan 張石川. Mingxing Film Company.

Career without Limits (*Wuxian shengya* 無限生涯), 1935, silent. Scr: Song Zhide 宋之的. Dir: Shi Jipu 石寄圃. Xibei Film Company.

Chapaev, 1934, sound. Dir: Georgii Vasilev. Leninfil.

City Nights (*Chengshi zhi ye* 城市之夜), 1933, silent. Scr: He Mengfu 賀孟斧. Dir: Fei Mu 費穆. Lianhua Film Company.

The Classics for Girls (*Nü'er jing* 女兒經), 1934, sound. Scr: Xia Yan 夏衍, Zheng Zhengqiu 鄭正秋, Qian Xingcun 錢幸村, Zheng Boqi 鄭伯奇, Shen Xiling 沈西苓, etc. Dir: Zhang Shichuan 張石川, Cheng Bugao 程步高, Shen Xiling 沈西苓, Yao Sufeng 姚蘇鳳, Zheng Zhengqiu 鄭正秋, Xu Xinfu 徐欣夫, Li Pingqian 李萍倩, and Chen Kengran 陳鏗然. Mingxing Film Company.

Colorful Story of Huashan (*Huashan yanshi* 華山艷史), 1934, sound. Scr/Dir: Cheng Bugao 程步高. Mingxing Film Company

Cosmetics Market (*Zhifen shichang* 脂粉市場), 1933, sound. Scr: Xia Yan 夏衍. Dir. Zhang Shichuan 張石川. Mingxing Film Company.

Country Worries (*Xiang chou* 鄉愁), 1934, sound. Scr/Dir: Shen Xiling 沈西苓. Mingxing Film Company.

The Crabapple is Red (*Haitang hong* 海棠紅), 1936, sound. Scr: Ouyang Yuqian 歐陽予倩. Dir: Zhang Shichuan 張石川. Mingxing Film Company

Crossroads (*Shizi jietou* 十字街頭), 1937, sound. Scr/Dir: Shen Xiling 沈西苓. Mingxing Film Company.

Crows and Sparrows (*Wuya yu maque* 烏鴉與麻雀), 1949, sound. Scr: Shen Fu 沈浮, Wang Lin'gu 王林谷, Xu Tao 徐韜, Zhao Dan 趙丹, Zheng Junli 鄭君里, and Chen Baichen 陳白塵. Dir: Zheng Junli 鄭君里. Kunlun Film Company.

The Cupid's Doll (*Aishen de wan'ou* 愛神的玩偶), 1925, silent. Scr: Pu Shunqing 濮舜卿. Dir: Hou Yao 侯曜. Chengchang Film Company.

Daybreak (*Tianming* 天明), 1933, silent. Scr/Dir: Sun Yu 孫瑜. Lianhua Film Company.

Early Morning in the Metropolis (*Duhui de zaochen* 都會的早晨), 1933, silent. Scr/Dir: Cai Chusheng 蔡楚生. Lianhua Film Company.

Eight Thousand Miles of Cloud and Moon (*Baqian li lu yun he yue* 八千里路雲和月), 1947, sound. Scr/Dir: Shi Dongshan 史東山. Kunlun Film Company.

Elegy of Life (*Sheng zhi aige* 生之哀歌), 1935. Scr: Yang Hansheng 陽翰笙. Dir: Hu Rui 胡銳. Yihua Film Company.

Evil Neighbor (*E lin* 惡鄰), 1933, silent. Scr: Li Faxi 李法西. Dir: Ren Pengnian 任彭年. Yueming Film Company.

Fifth Brother Wang (*Wang laowu* 王老五), 1937, sound. Scr/Dir: Cai Chusheng. 蔡楚生. Lianhua Film Company.

First Rays of the Morning Sun (*Chenxi* 晨曦), 1933, silent. Scr/Dir: Wu Wenchao 吳文超. Yiji Film Company.

The Fishermen's Song (*Yu guang qu* 漁光曲), 1934, sound. Scr/Dir: Cai Chusheng 蔡楚生. Lianhua Film Company.

Flying Catkins (*Feixu* 飛絮), 1933, sound. Scr/Dir: Shao Zuiweng 邵醉翁 and Tang Xiaodan 湯曉丹. Tianyi Film Company.

Flesh and Blood Kindness (*Gurou zhi en* 骨肉之恩), 1934, silent. Scr/Dir: Jiang Qifeng 姜起鳳. Lianhua Film Company.

Flower of Society (*Shehuizhi hua* 社會之花), 1937, sound. Dir: Zhang Shichuan 張石川. Scr: Hong Shen 洪深. Mingxing Film Company.

The Future (*Qiancheng* 前程), 1933, sound. Scr: Xia Yan 夏衍. Dir: Zhang Shichuan 張石川. Mingxing Film Company.

"Ghost" (*Gui* 鬼), in *Lianhua Symphony* (*Lianhua Jiaoxiang qu* 聯華交響曲), 1937, sound. Scr/Dir: Zhu Shilin 朱石麟. Lianhua Film Company.

Gilded City (*Dujinde cheng* 鍍金的城), 1937, sound. Dir: Fei Mu 費穆. Scr: Hong Shen 洪深. Lianhua Film Company.

The Goddess (*Shennü* 神女), 1934, silent. Scr/Dir: Wu Yonggang 吳永剛. Lianhua Film Company.

Going to the People (*Dao minjian qu* 到民間去), 1926, silent. Scr/Dir: Tian Han 田漢. Nanguo Cinema Society.

Golden Age (*Huangjin shidai* 黃金時代), 1934. Scr: Tian Han 田漢. Dir: Bu Wancang 卜萬蒼. Yihua Film Company.

Golden Mountains (*Zlatye glory*), 1931, sound. Dir: Sergei Yutkevich. Sovkino/Leningrad.

Good Harvest (*Fengnian* 豐年), 1933, sound. Scr: Qian Xingcun 錢幸村. Dir: Li Pianqian 李萍倩. Mingxing Film Company.

Hand-to-hand Fighting (*Roubo* 肉搏), 1933, silent. Scr: Tian Han 田漢. Dir: Hu Tu 胡涂. Yihua Film Company.

Heaven of the Orphan Island (*Gudao tiantang* 孤島天堂), 1939, sound. Scr/Dir: Cai Chusheng 蔡楚生. Dadi Film Company.

Heaven-made Unity (*Tianzuo zhi he* 天作之合), 1937, sound. Scr/Dir: Shen Fu 沈浮. Lianhua Film Company.

The Heir to Jenghis-Khan (a.k.a., *Storm over Asia*), 1928, silent. Dir: V.I. Pudovkin. Mezhrabpom.

Hero of the Times (*Shishi yingxiong* 時勢英雄), 1935. Scr: Hong Shen 洪深. Dir: Ying Yunwei 應雲衛. Yihua Film Company.

The Highway (*Dalu* 大路), 1935, sound. Scr/Dir: Sun Yu 孫瑜. Lianhua Film Company.

Humanity (*Rendao* 人道), 1932, silent. Scr: Jin Qingyu 金擎宇. Dir: Bu Wancang 卜萬蒼. Lianhua Film Company.

If I Had a Million, 1933, sound. Dir: Ernst Lubitsch et al. Paramount.

The Iron Bird (*Tie'niao* 鐵鳥), 1934, silent. Scr/Dir: Yuan Congmei 袁叢美. Lianhua Film Company.

Iron Plate and Red Tears (*Tieban honglei lu* 鐵板紅淚錄), 1933. Scr: Yang Hansheng 陽漢笙. Dir: Hong Shen 洪深. Mingxing Film Company.

Lianhua Symphony (*Lianhua jiaoxiangqu* 聯華交響曲), 1936, sound. Scr: Cai Chusheng 蔡楚生, Fei Mu 費穆, Tan Youliu 譚友六, Shen Fu 沈浮, He Mengfu 賀孟斧, Sun Yu 孫瑜. Dir: Situ Huimin 司徒慧敏, Fei Mu 費穆, Tan Youliu 譚友六, Shen Fu 沈浮, He Mengfu 賀孟斧, Sun Yu 孫瑜, Cai Chusheng 蔡楚生. Lianhua Film Company.

Little Angel (*Xiao tianshi* 小天使), 1935, silent. Scr: Jiang Xingde 蔣星德. Dir: Wu Yonggang 吳永剛. Lianhua Film Company.

Little Lingzi (*Xiao Lingzi* 小玲子), 1936, sound. Scr: Ouyang Yuqian 歐陽予倩. Dir: Cheng Bugao 程步高. Lianhua Film Company.

Little Toys (*Xiao wan'er* 小玩兒), 1933, silent. Scr/Dir: Sun Yu 孫瑜. Lianhua Film Company.

Lost Lambs (*Mitu de gaoyang* 迷途的羔羊), 1936, sound. Scr/Dir: Cai Chusheng 蔡楚生. Lianhua Film Company.

Lost Pearl in the Crowd (*Renhai yi zhu* 人海遺珠), 1937, sound. Scr/Dir: Zhu Shilin. Lianhua Film Company.

Love and Duty (*Lian'ai yu yiwu* 戀愛與義務), 1931, silent. Scr: Zhu Shilin 朱石麟. Dir: Bu Wancang 卜萬蒼. Lianhua Film Company.

Loving Blood of the Volcano (*Huoshan qingxue* 火山情血), 1932, silent. Scr/Dir: Sun Yu 孫瑜. Lianhua Film Company.

March of Youth (*Qingnian jinxinqu* 青年進行曲), 1937, sound. Scr: Tian Han 田漢. Dir: Shi Dongshan 史東山. Xinhua Film Company.

Marriage in Tears and Laughter (*Tixiao yinyuan* 啼笑姻緣), 6 parts, 1932, part sound. Scr: Yan Duhe 嚴獨鶴. Dir: Zhang Shichuan 張石川. Mingxing Film Company.

Maternal Radiance (Muxing zhiguang 母性之光), 1933, silent. Scr: Tian Han 田漢. Dir: Bu Wancang 卜萬蒼. Lianhua Film Company.

Men at their Birth (*Ren zhi chu* 人之初), 1935. Scr/Dir: Shi Dongshan 史東山. Yihua Film Company.

The Metamorphosing Girl (*Huashen guniang* 化身姑娘), 2 parts, 1936, sound. Scr: Huang Jiamo 黃嘉莫. Dir: Fang Peilin 方沛霖. Yihua Film Company.

Metropolis, 1926, silent. Scr/Dir: Friz Lang. UFA.

Modern Bride (*Modeng xinniang* 摩登新娘), 1935, sound. Scr/Dir: Guan Wenqing 關文清. Daguan Film Company.

The Money Tree (*Yaoqianshu* 搖錢樹), 1937, sound. Scr: Xia Yan 夏衍. Dir: Tan Youliu 譚友六. Lianhua Film Company.

Mother, 1926, silent. Dir: V. I. Pudovkin. Mezhrabpom-Rus'.

National Existence (*Minzu shengcun* 民族生存), 1933, silent. Scr/Dir: Tian Han 田漢. Yihua Film Company.

National Style (*Guofeng* 國風), 1935, silent. Scr: Luo Mingyou 羅明佑. Dir: Luo Mingyou 羅明佑, Zhu Shilin 朱石麟. Lianhua Film Company.

The New Peach Blossom Fan (*Xin taohua shan* 新桃花扇), 1935, sound. Scr/Dir: Ouyang Yuqian 歐陽予倩. Xinhua Film Company.

New Woman (*Xin nüxing* 新女性), 1934, silent. Scr/Dir: Cai Chusheng 蔡楚生. Lianhua Film Company.

The New Year's Gift (*Yasuiqian* 壓歲錢), 1937, sound. Scr: Xia Yan 夏衍. Dir: Zhang Shichuan 張石川. Mingxing Film Company.

Night Run (*Yeben* 夜奔), 1937, sound. Dir: Cheng Bugao 程步高. Scr: Yang Hansheng 陽翰笙. Mingxing Film Company.

Nights of Revelry (*Kuanghuan zhi ye* 狂歡之夜), 1936, sound. Scr/Dir: Shi Dongshan 史東山. Xinhua Film Company

Old and New Shanghai (*Xinjiu Shanghai* 新舊上海), 1936, sound. Scr: Hong Shen 洪深. Dir: Zhang Shichuan 張石川. Mingxing Film Company.

One and Eight (*Yige he bage* 一個和八個), 1984, sound. Scr: Zhang Ziliang 張子良, Wang Jicheng 王吉成. Dir: Zhang Junzhao 張軍釗. Guangxi Film Studio.

100 Treasures Picture (*Bai bao tu* 百寶圖), 1936, sound. Scr: Huang Jiamo 黃嘉莫. Dir: Yue Feng 岳楓. Yihua Film Company.

Oppression (*Yabi* 壓逼), 1933. Scr: Hong Shen 洪深. Dir. Gao Lihen 高梨痕. Mingxing Film Company.

Passion's Precious Mirror (*Qingyu baojian* 情欲寶鑑), 1929, silent. Scr: Zhu Shouju 朱瘦菊. Dir: Li Pingqian 李萍倩. Dazhonghua Baihe Film Company.

Peach Blossom Weeps Tears of Blood (*Taohua qi xue ji* 桃花泣血記), 1931, silent. Scr/Dir: Bu Wancang 卜萬蒼. Lianhua Film Company.

Pear Blossom in the Storm (*Baoyu lihua* 暴雨梨花), 1934, silent. Scr/Dir: Ma Xu Weibang 馬徐維邦. Lianhua Film Company.

Pink Dream (*Fenhongse de meng* 粉紅色的夢), 1932, silent. Scr/Dir: Cai Chusheng 蔡楚生. Lianhua Film Company.

Plunder of Peach and Plum (*Taoli jie* 桃李劫), 1934, sound. Scr: Yuan Muzhi 袁牧之. Dir: Ying Yunwei 應雲衛. Diantong Film Company.

Plundered Peach Blossom (*Jiehou taohua* 劫後桃花), 1935, sound. Dir: Zhang Shichuan 張石川. Scr: Hong Shen 洪深. Mingxing Film Company.

Queen of Sport (*Tiyu huanghou* 體育皇后), 1934, silent. Scr/Dir: Sun Yu 孫瑜. Lianhua Film Company.

Raging Flames (*Lieyan* 烈焰), 1933. Scr: Hu Rui 胡銳, Tian Han 田漢. Dir: Hu Rui 胡銳. Yihua Film Company

Return Our Mountains and Rivers (*Huan wo shanhe* 還我山河), 1934, silent. Scr/Dir: Wang Cilong 王次龍. Da Changcheng Film Company.

Road to Life (a.k.a. *The Path to Life*), 1931, sound. Scr/Dir: Nikolai Ekk. Mezhrabpomfilm.

Runaway (Taowang 逃亡), 1935, sound. Dir: Yue Feng 岳峰. Scr: Yang Hansheng 陽翰笙. Xinhua Film Company.

Salt Tide (*Yan Chao* 鹽潮), 1933, silent. Scr: Zheng Boqi 鄭伯奇 and Qian Xingcun 錢幸村. Dir: Xu Xinfu 徐欣夫. Mingxing Film Company.

Scenes of City Life (*Dushi fengguang* 都市風光), 1935, sound. Scr/Dir: Yuan Muzhi 袁牧之. Diantong Film Company.

A Sea of Fragrant Snow (*Xiangxue hai* 香雪海), 1934, silent. Scr/Dir: Fei Mu 費穆. Lianhua Film Company.

Secret Code (*Mi dianma* 密電碼), 1937, sound. Scr: Zhang Daofeng 張道烽. Dir: Huang Tianzuo 黃天佐. Zhongyang Film Studio.

Shared Hate (*Tongchou* 同仇), 1934. Scr: Xia Yan 夏衍. Dir: Cheng Bugao 程步高. Mingxing Film Company.

The Singing Girl, Red Peony (*Genü hong mudan* 歌女紅牡丹), 1931, sound. Scr: Hong Shen 洪深. Dir: Zhang Shichuan 張石川. Mingxing Film Company.

The Sisters (*Zimei hua* 姊妹花), 1934, sound. Scr/Dir: Zheng Zhengqiu 鄭正秋. Mingxing Film Company.

Soaring Aspirations (*Zhuangzhi lingyun* 壯志凌雲), 1936, sound. Scr/Dir: Wu Yonggang 吳永剛. Xinhua Film Company.

Soldier (*Zhanshi* 戰士), 1936, sound. Scr: Wu Youren 吳佑人. Dir: Yu Zhongying 余仲英. Central Films Studio.

Song at Midnight (*Yeban gesheng* 夜半歌聲), 1937, sound. Scr/Dir: Ma Xu Weibang 馬徐維邦. Xinhua Film Company.

Song of a Loving Mother (*Cimu qu* 慈母曲), 1937, sound. Scr/Dir: Zhu Shilin 朱石麟. Lianhua Film Company.

Song of China (*Tianlun* 天倫), 1935, sound. Scr: Zhong Shigen 鍾石根. Dir. Luo Mingyou 羅明佑 and Fei Mu 費穆. Lianhua Film Company.

Song of the Rose (*Qiangwei zhi ge* 薔薇之歌), 1934, sound. Scr/Dir: Yin Yiqiu 殷憶秋. Meihua Film Company.

Song of Triumph (*Kaige* 凱歌), 1935, sound. Scr: Tian Han 田漢. Dir: Bu Wancang 卜萬蒼. Yihua Film Company.

Sons and Daughters of the Storm (*Fengyun ernü* 風雲兒女), 1935, sound. Scr: Tian Han 田漢 and Xia Yan 夏衍. Dir: Xu Xingzhi 許幸之. Diantong Film Company.

Sons and Daughters of the Times (*Shidaide ernü* 時代的兒女), 1933, silent. Scr: Xia Yan 夏衍. Dir: Li Pingqian 李萍倩. Mingxing Film Company.

Spirit of Freedom (*Ziyoushen* 自由神), 1935, sound. Scr: Xia Yan 夏衍. Dir: Situ Huimin 司徒慧敏. Diantong Film Company.

A Spray of Plum Blossoms (*Yijian mei* 一剪梅), 1931, silent. Scr: Huang Yicuo 黃漪磋. Dir: Bu Wancang 卜萬蒼. Lianhua Film Company.

Spring Dream in the Old Capital (*Gudu chunmeng* 故都春夢), 1930, silent. Scr: Zhu Shilin 朱石麟. Dir: Sun Yu 孫瑜. Lianhua Film Company.

Spring Dreams of the Land of Peach Blossoms (*Taoyuan chunmeng* 桃源春夢), 1936, sound. Scr/Dir: Unknown. Xinhua Film Company.

Spring of a Small Town (*Xiaocheng zhi chun* 小城之春), 1947, sound. Scr/Dir: Fei Mu 費穆. Minhua Film Company.

A Spring River Running to the East (*Yijian chungshui xiang dong liu* 一江春水向東流), 2 parts, 1947, sound. Scr/Dir: Cai Chusheng 蔡楚生, Zheng Junli 鄭君里. Kunlun Film Company.

Spring Silkworms (*Chuncan* 春蠶), 1933, silent. Scr: Xia Yan 夏衍. Dir: Cheng Bugao 程步高. Mingxing Film Company.

The Story of Wu Xun (*Wu Xun zhuan* 武訓傳), 1951, sound. Scr/Dir: Sun Yu 孫瑜. Zhongzhi Studio.

Street Angel (*Malu tianshi* 馬路天使), 1937, sound. Scr/Dir: Yuan Muzhi 袁牧之. Mingxing Film Company.

The Struggle (*Fendou* 奮斗), 1932, silent. Scr/Dir: Shi Dongshan 史東山. Lianhua Film Company.

Struggling (*Zhengzha* 掙札), 1933, sound. Scr: Yu Dingxun 于定勛. Dir: Qiu Qixiang 裘杞蕃. Tianyi Film Company.

Suffering Husband and Wife (*Nanfu nanqi* 難夫難妻), 1913, silent. Scr: Zheng Zhengqiu 鄭正秋. Dir: Zhang Shichuan 張石川. Asia Film and Theatre Company.

Sweetgrass Beauty (*Xiangcao meiren* 香草美人), 1933. Scr: Ma Wenyuan 馬文源, Hong Shen 洪深. Dir: Chen Kengran 陳鏗然. Mingxing Film Company.

The Tale of the Gallant Hong Yang (*Hong yang haoxia zhuan* 紅羊豪俠傳), 1935, sound. Scr: Wang Zhongxian 汪仲賢. Dir: Yang Xiaozhong 楊小仲. Xinhua Film Company.

The Ten Commandments, 1923, silent. Scr: Jeanie Macpherson. Dir: Cecil B. Demille. Famous Players-Lasky Corporation.

Three Modern Women (*Sange modeng de nüxing* 三個摩登的女性), 1933, silent. Scr: Tian Han 田漢. Dir: Bu Wancang 卜萬蒼. Lianhua Film Company.

To the Northwest (*Dao Xibei qu* 到西北去), 1934, sound. Scr: Zheng Boqi 鄭伯奇. Dir. Cheng Bugao 程步高. Mingxing Film Company.

Torrent (*Kuangliu* 狂流), 1933, silent. Scr: Xia Yan 夏衍. Dir: Cheng Bugao 程步高. Mingxing Film Company.

Twenty-four Hours in Shanghai (*Shanghai ershisi xiaoshi* 上海二十四小時), 1933, silent. Scr: Xia Yan 夏衍. Dir: Shen Xiling 沈西苓. Mingxing Film Company.

Unchanged Heart in Life and Death (*Shengsi tongxin* 生死同心), 1936, sound. Scr: Yan Hansheng 陽翰笙. Dir: Ying Yunwei 應雲衛. Mingxing Film Company.

Wandering (*Piaoling* 飄零), 1933, sound. Dir: Tang Xiaodan 湯曉丹. Scr: Gao Tianqi 高天栖. Tianyi Film Company.

Waves Washing the Sand (*Lang tao sha* 浪濤沙), 1936, sound. Scr/Dir: Wu Yonggang 吳永剛. Lianhua Film Company.

Way Down East, 1920, silent. Dir: D. W. Griffith. United Artists.

We from Kronstadt (*My iz Kronshtadta*), 1936, sound. Scr: Vsevolod Vishnevsky. Dir: Efim Dzigan. Mosfilm.

The White Golden Dragon (*Baijinlong* 白金龍), 1933, sound. Scr/Dir: Xue Juexian 薛覺先. Tianyi Film Company.

Wild Flowers (*Yecao xianhua* 野草閑花), 1930, silent. Scr/Dir: Sun Yu 孫瑜. Lianhua Film Company.

Wild Rose (*Yemeigui* 野玫瑰), 1932, silent. Scr/Dir: Sun Yu 孫瑜. Lianhua Film Company.

The Wind (*Feng* 風), 1933, silent. Scr/Dir: Wu Cun 吳村. Lianhua Film Company.

A Woman of Today (*Xiandai yi nüxing* 現代一女性), 1933, silent. Scr: Ai Xia 艾霞. Dir: Li Pingqian 李萍倩. Mingxing Film Company.

Women's Outcry (*Nüxing de nahan* 女性的吶喊), 1933, silent. Scr/Dir: Shen Xiling 沈西苓. Mingxing Film Company.

Zhuangzi Tests His Wife (*Zhuangzi shi qi* 莊子試妻), 1913, silent. Scr/Dir: Li Minwei 黎民偉. Huamei Film Company.

Index

The Actress / The Centered Stage, 132n41
Adorno, Theodor, 13-14n7, 159-60
advertising, 150, 151-52, 155-56
Ailments within Heart and Stomach, 56
Akira, Iwasaki, 31
All Quiet on the Western Front, 103-6
Angry Tide in China's Seas, 53, 58, 75
Ardent, Loyal Souls, 61

Back to Nature, 63
Barlow, Tani, 116
Battleship Potemkin, 145, 146
Bazin, André, 200-201
Ben-Hur, 30
Benjamin, Walter, 6, 7
Berry Chris, 8, 99, 100-101
The Big Parade, 103-6
Bing Xin, 92
Bloodbath on Wolf Mountain, 61, 63, 178
The Blood Spilt in the Treasure Mountain City, 236
The Boatman's Daughter, 115, 178
Bordwell, David, 149, 200, 217
"Bright Tail," 207-8
"Broken Dream in the Women's Apartment" (in *Lianhua Symphony*) 61, 63, 220
Brooks, Peter, 202-203
Bu Wancang, 25-27, 44, 47-48, 53, 75, 237
Burning the Red Lotus Temple, 66n33, 206

Cai Chusheng, 27, 42, 43, 48, 49, 60, 62, 63, 64, 76, 86, 123, 145, 148, 150, 233, 234, 235, 236, 237
camera movements, 171, 172, 188n25
Career without Limits, 167
censorship, 10, 29-30, 57-58, 60-61, 207, 213, 217, 220
Central Film Studio, 56
Chapaev, 145
Chaplin, Charlie, 148, 161n12
Chen Bo'er, 54
Chen Duxiu, 21, 33n6, 92
Chen Wu, 27, 32, 39, 40, 51, 58, 143
Cheng Bugao, 42, 43, 44-45, 46, 62, 75, 144, 148, 150, 157, 178
Chinese Communist Party (CCP), 20-21, 39-41, 50, 52, 54, 56, 58, 232, 233-35, 237
Chinese film history, the writing of, 3-6, 15n20, 233
Chinese intellectuals 1-2, 6-8, 74-87, 233-35
Chinese League of Left-wing Writers, 20, 41
Chinese Left-wing Dramatists Association, 3, 37-38
Cho Woo Catherine Yi-Yu, 197-98
Chow, Rey, 126-28
City Nights, 45, 93, 115
civilized play, 34n14, 48, 151, 172
Classical Chinese novels, 204-05
The Classics for Girls, 115
close-up, 87, 97, 101, 127-28, 169, 172, 212, 213
Cochran, Sherman, 165
Cook, Jim, 221
Cosmetics Market, 57, 85, 93-94, 115, 116,

207
Country Worries, 115
The Crabapple is Red, 115
Crossroads, 63, 85, 103, 115, 170, 174-75,
    205-07, 123
Crows and Sparrows, 233
The Cupid's Doll, 121

Daybreak, 47, 115
death, representations of, 105-06, 120-29
de Certeau, Michel, 10, 154, 158
Denton, Kirk, 77
Dialect-cinema debate, 179-87
Diantong Film Company, 53-55, 155
Ding Ling, 27, 92
Dissanayake, Wimal, 202
Doane, Mary Ann, 216
documentary, 9, 39, 44, 56
Dovzhenko, Aleksandra, 145

Early Morning in the Metropolis, 86
Eight Thousand Miles of Cloud and Moon,
    233
Eisenstein, Sergei, 145, 146-47, 212
Evil Neighbor, 61
Eyman, Scott, 186

fan culture, 155
Fei Mu, 45-46, 49, 61, 63, 75, 76, 115, 124,
    220, 233, 235
Fifth Brother Wang, 61, 63, 115
Fifth Generation, 76, 235-36
film books, magazines, and journals, 31-32,
    41, 145, 147-48, 155. *See also* film
    criticism
film clubs, 157
film companies, 182, 183. *See also* names of
    specific film companies
film criticism, 27-28, 31-32, 49-52, 145-48.
    See also Dialect-cinema debate; film
    books, magazines, and journals; film
    critics; Soft-cinema versus Hard-cinema
    debate
film critics, 39-41, 49-52, 151-53. *See also*
    film criticism
film industry, in the 1930s, 41-64, 75-76; in
    the 1920s, 21-23, 47, 114; recessions, 42,
    58
film organizations: Association for the Anti-

Communist Comrades in the Film
    Industry, 53; Association of Chinese
    Cinema Culture, 43; Association of
    Chinese Educational Cinema, 56; Film
    Critics Group, 39-41; Film Group, 39-41;
    National Salvation Association of
    Shanghai Cinema, 60-61
film theaters, 29, 62, 157, 167; capacity, 167,
    247; ticket price, 156-57, 232
filmmakers, 5, 74-87, 153. *See also names of
    specific filmmakers*
The Fishermen's Song, 48, 49, 54, 157
flashback, 209-211
Flesh and Blood Kindness, 62
Flower of Society, 115
Flying Catkins, 115
Fruehauf, Heinrich, 166-67
The Future, 115

"Ghost" (in *Lianhua Symphony*), 75
Gilmartin, Christina Kelley, 91
The Goddess, 75, 79-80, 81, 115, 169-70,
    173, 177, 213
Going to the People, 23, 39
Golden Mountains, 145
Good Harvest, 45
Gorbman, Claudia, 218
Griffith, D. W., 148
Guo Moruo, 92
Guomindang (GMD), 10, 21, 25, 28, 32, 53,
    55-59, 63, 168-69, 181-82, 232, 236

Han Lan'gen, 156
Hand-to-hand Fighting, 53
Hansen, Miriam, 73, 114, 126, 149
Heaven of the Orphan Island, 236
The Heir to Jenghis-Khan, 145
Henriot, Christian, 168
The Highway, 49, 85, 98-106, 115, 207, 213,
    217, 221
Hollywood cinema: in China, 24, 25, 30,
    58-59, 214; criticism of, 31; comparison
    with Chinese cinema 73, 76, 78, 97-98,
    102-06, 116-117, 186, 200, 217, 221;
    influences on Chinese cinema, 26, 148-50,
    208, 214, 215; parody of, 218-19
Hong Kong cinema, 182-84, 232, 236-38
Hong Shen, 23, 42-43, 56, 76, 82, 157, 176
Hou Yao, 23

Hu Die, 114, 156, 236
Hu Feng, 59-60, 77
Hu Jia, 174
Hu Peng, 179
Huaying Film Company, 75
Humanity, 27, 47

If I had a Million, 208
"Image Play" theory, 198
initiation, theme of, 99-106
The Iron Bird, 56, 170
Iron Plate and Red Tears, 47, 57, 176

Japanese invasion, 28-29, 63-64, 231-32
Jarvie, I. C., 183
Jia Mo, 50-52
Jiang Qing (a.k.a. Lan Pin), 234
Jin Yan, 129n4, 174
Jones, Andrew F., 165

Ke Ling, 22, 47, 50, 61, 131n32
Kracauer, Sigfried, 200
Kuleshov, Lev V., 145

Law Kar, 183
Lee, Leo Ou-fan, 81, 165
Left-wing cinema movement: aesthetic
    rendering, 198-222; commercial nature,
    142-44; gender disposition of, 1-2, 114-17;
    history of, 37-64; naming of, 3;
    relationship with left-wing literature, 46-
    47; second phase, 231-33
Lewington, Mike, 221
Lieberman, Sally Taylor, 119-120
Li Dazhao, 21
Li Jinhui, 214
Li Lili, 99-100, 174, 236
Li Minwei, 24, 236
Li Pingqian, 45, 122
Li Shaobai, 4-5, 56, 57
Li Zhuozhuo, 236
Lianhua Film Company, 24-28, 44-49, 56,
    62-63, 117, 155, 214
Lianhua Symphony, 61, 63, 75, 175, 220
Lin Niantong, 147, 197
Ling He, 32, 40, 46, 51, 58, 199-200
Link, Perry, 152, 155
Little Angel, 56, 75
Little Lingzi, 115

Little Toys, 46, 47, 101-2, 115, 116, 118-19
Liu, Lydia, 77
Liu Na'ou, 50-51, 147-48, 218
Liu Zaifu, 6-7
Lost Lambs, 62, 145
Lost Pearl in the Crowd, 63
Love and Duty, 25-26
Loving Blood of the Volcano, 27, 149
Lu Hanchao, 165
Lu Si (a.k.a. Ke Ping), 32
Lu Xun, 20, 31, 59, 77, 81-82, 92, 120, 124,
    154-55, 184, 188n28
Lubitsch, Ernst, 208
Lukács, Georg, 202-03
Luo Mingyou, 24-25, 56, 62

Ma Ning, 200, 206
Ma Xu Weibang, 55, 61, 62, 63, 69n105
MacCabe, Colon, 203
"Mandarin Ducks and Butterflies" novels
    and films, 47, 159, 201
Mao Dun, 46, 92, 93
Mao Zedong, 21, 234
March of Youth, 55, 62, 84, 85, 103, 207
Marriage in Tears and Laughter, 42, 204
Marxism and socialism, 77, 144-48
Mass Language Movement, 184-85
Maternal Radiance, 47, 53, 115
May Fourth/New Culture Movement and its
    influences, 19-22, 77, 87, 92-93, 95, 102,
    121, 124, 147, 180-81, 199
Mayne Judith, 142
melodrama, 201-3
Meng Gongwei, 60
The Metamorphosing Girl, 52, 223n24
Metropolis, 171
Mingxing Film Company, 22, 23, 41-52, 57,
    58, 60-64, 155, 173, 176
Minxin Film Company, 24, 25, 62, 236
Modern Bride, 179
modernist literature, 50-52
modernity, 14n10, 19-23, 28-30, 154-60,
    185-87, 204, 214-20
Mother, 145
Motherhood, representations of, 117-20
music: background music, 206; film songs,
    81, 215-20, 232; National Anthem, 95;
    Shanghai's popular music, 214-215

National Defense Cinema, 59-62, 75, 220
National Defense Literature, 59-60
National Existence, 52, 53, 57
national language (*guoyu*), 184-86
National Style, 56, 170, 174
nationalism, 77, 178-79, 232; anti-Japanese sentiment, 21, 28; National Cinema, 10, 25; representation of, 79-87, 95-106; Year of Chinese Products (1933), 43
Nationalist Party. *See* Guomindang
newspaper, 32, 201, 206, 213. *See also* film criticism
The New Peach Blossom Fan, 55, 94
New Perceptionist School, 50-52
"New Song of Fengyang," 217
New Woman, 85, 98, 103, 115, 116-20, 123-26, 128, 213
The New Year's Gift, 63, 175, 202, 208-9, 215-26
Nie Er, 174
Night Run, 84

October, 212
Old and New Shanghai, 63, 175
One and Eight, 235
One Hundred Treasures Pictures, 53
Oppression, 57
Ouyang Yuqian, 23, 55, 56, 76, 236

Peach Blossom Weeps Tears of Blood, 26
Pear Blossom in the Storm, 62
petty urbanites, 150-54, 167
Phantom of the Opera, 221
Pickowicz, Paul, 22, 201
Pink Dream, 27
Plaks, Andrew, 204
Plunder of Peach and Plum, 54, 80-81, 83, 175
Plundered Peach Blossom, 213
public sphere, 126-27
Pudovkin, Vsevolod I., 145

Qian Xingcun (a.k.a. A Ying, Zhang Fengwu), 40, 41, 42, 58, 235
Qu Qiubai, 21, 31, 40, 42, 184
Queen of Sport, 170

radio, 214-15, 216

Raging Flames, 53
realism, 198-203
Return our Mountains and Rivers, 61
Road to Life, 145, 147
romance, representations of, 92-106, 232
Roston, David, 204
Ruan Lingyu, 117-20, 123-29
Runaway, 75

Salt Tide, 44, 176
Scenes of City Life, 54, 63, 83, 175, 218-20
scriptwriting, 42, 44-45. *See also* filmmakers
A Sea of Fragrant Snow, 49, 62
Secret Code, 56
Shanghai, 21-22, 165-87, 214-15, 218-19, 231-33, 238
Shared Hate, 45
Shen Xiling (a.k.a. Ye Chen), 38-39, 57, 59, 63, 115, 144, 157, 206-7, 235, 236
Shi Dongshan, 27, 42, 53, 55, 62, 76, 82, 233
Shih, Shu-mei, 165
Shu Yan, 32
Silverman, Kaja, 105
The Singing Girl, Red Peony, 224n31
The Sisters, 48-49, 54, 86, 115, 143, 151-53, 158-59, 209-11
Situ Huimin, 40, 42, 54-55, 76, 115, 157, 236
Soaring Aspirations, 55, 62, 75, 177
Soft-cinema versus Hard-cinema debate, 50-52, 199
Soldier, 56
Song at Midnight, 55, 62, 63, 221
Song of a Loving Mother, 63
Song of China, 170
"Song of Four Seasons," 217-18
Song of the Rose, 225n45
Song Zhide (a.k.a. Huai Zhao), 60
Sons and Daughters of the Storm, 54, 84, 85, 94-98, 174, 179, 212
Sons and Daughters of the Times, 45
sound cinema: audio representation of Shanghai, 175; delay of, 24; differences from silent cinema, 186, 216; equipment of, 54; use of dialects, 179-87
Soviet Cinema, 9, 145-47; influences on Chinese cinema, 41, 145-48, 190; Soviet films shown in China, 145
spectators, 25, 26, 28, 30, 128, 150-60
Spirit of Freedom, 54, 94, 115, 202

spoken drama, 23, 30, 34n14
A Spray of Plum Blossoms, 26
Spring Dream in the Old Capital, 24-25, 149
Spring Dreams of the Land of Peach Blossoms, 55
Spring of a Small Town, 233
A Spring River Running to the East, 48, 233
Spring Silkworms, 44, 46-47, 176, 177-78, 202
stardom, 114, 121-29, 155-56. *See also names of specific stars*
Stokes, Melvyn, 116
The Story of Wu Xun, 234
Street Angel, 63, 115, 147, 170, 171-73, 174, 127-18, 219-20
The Struggle, 27
Struggling, 46
Su Yi, 236
subjective shot, 97, 120, 210-22, 211-14
sublimation, 97-98
Suffering Husband and Wife, 23, 177
Sun Shaoyi, 170
Sun Yu, 24, 27, 42, 43, 47, 49, 56, 60, 62, 63, 75, 76, 99-100, 102, 105-06, 148-49, 150, 173, 174, 234
suture, 97, 120
swordsman films and novels, 29, 47, 52-53, 92, 114, 159, 204
Sweetgrass Beauty, 44, 57

The Tale of Gallant Hong Yang, 55
Tan Chunfa, 151
Tang Na, 32, 54, 151, 180
Temple, Shirley, 215
The Ten Commandments, 30
Teo, Stephen, 237
"Third" cinema, 8
Three Modern Women, 44, 47-48, 53, 57, 103, 115, 207
Tian Han (a.k.a. Chen Yu), 23, 40, 42, 44, 47-48, 52-53, 54, 56, 58, 60, 64, 75, 81, 145, 217, 235
Tianyi Film Studio, 22, 177, 183, 236
Tingzijian (pavilion room), 173-74
To the Northwest, 45, 178
Tong Yuejuan, 155
Torrent, 44-45, 93, 114, 115, 148
traditional Chinese opera, 155, 156, 157, 183, 213, 214, 216

Truffaut, François, 76
Twenty-four Hours in Shanghai, 47, 57

Unchanged Heart in Life and Death, 63, 82-85, 113, 212

Vernacular Language Movement, 180-81, 185
Vertov, Dziga, 145

Wang, Ban, 98
Wang Hanlun, 114
Wang Renmei, 156, 174
Wandering, 115
Waves Washing the Sand, 75
Way down East, 148
We are from Kronstadt, 145
The White Golden Dragon, 183
Wild Flowers, 24, 149
Wild Rose, 27, 99, 174
Willemen, Paul, 186
A Woman of Today, 121-22
Women's Outcry, 47, 57, 115, 207
Wu Yonggang, 49, 55, 62, 75, 79-80, 81-82, 115, 170, 173, 177 234
Wuxia. See swordsman films and novels

Xia Yan (a.k.a. Huang Zibu, Lo Fu), 38, 39-43, 44-45, 46-47, 50, 51, 53, 54, 58, 60, 64, 75, 75, 145, 146, 150, 176, 201, 202, 205, 234, 235, 236, 237
Xiao, Zhiwei, 182
Xinhua Film Company, 55, 62
Xu Xingzhi, 76, 95, 98, 157, 179-80

Yan Chuntang, 53
Yang Hansheng, 40, 53, 54, 58, 60, 84, 176, 237
Yeh, Wen-hsin, 153
Yeh, Yueh-yu, 219
Yihua Film Company, 52-54, 58
Yin Minzhu, 114
Yin Xiucen, 156
Ying Yunwei, 54, 63, 76, 80, 83, 212
Yu Dafu, 77, 92, 120
Yuan Meiyun, 156
Yuan Muzhi, 54, 63, 76, 83, 129n4, 172, 189n34, 218-20, 234
Yue Feng, 75

Zhang Junzhao, 235
Zhang Shankun, 55, 237
Zhang Shichuan, 43, 58, 62, 224n31
Zhang Zhiyun, 114
Zhang, Yingjin, 114-15, 165
Zhao Dan, 129n4, 189n34, 234
Zheng Boqi (a.k.a. He Dabai, Xi Naifang), 31, 41-42, 60, 146, 235
Zheng Junli, 233
Zheng Zhenduo, 173

Zheng Zhengqiu, 22, 23, 43, 48-49, 56, 75, 142-43, 151, 153, 157, 158, 209-11
Zhou Enlai, 21, 235
Zhou Jianyun, 41-42, 43, 60, 154
Zhou Yang (a.k.a. Qi), 59-60
Zhu Shilin, 63, 75, 237
Zhu Ziqing, 92
Zhuangzi Tests His Wife, 23
Žižek, Slavoj, 126-28
Zou Taofen, 153